Lenin's Government: Sovnarkom 1917–1922

D1032782

SOVIET AND EAST EUROPEAN STUDIES

Editorial Board

John Barber, Archie Brown, P. Hanson, M. Kaser,
David Lane, Mary McAuley, A. Nove, A. Pravda,
G. H. N. Seton-Watson

SOVIET AND EAST EUROPEAN STUDIES

Books in the series

Lenin's Government:
Sovnarkom
1917–1922

T. H. RIGBY

Professorial Fellow in Political Science
Research School of Social Sciences
Australian National University

CAMBRIDGE UNIVERSITY PRESS

CAMBRIDGE

LONDON · NEW YORK · MELBOURNE

Published by the Syndics of the Cambridge University Press
The Pitt Building, Trumpington Street, Cambridge CB2 1RP
Bentley House, 200 Euston Road, London NW1 2DB
32 East 57th Street, New York, NY 10022, USA
296 Beaconsfield Parade, Middle Park, Melbourne 3206, Australia

First published 1979

Printed in Great Britain by
Western Printing Services Ltd, Bristol

Library of Congress Cataloguing in Publication Data
Rigby, Thomas Henry Richard.
Lenin's government: Sovnarkom 1917–1922.
(Soviet and East European studies)
Bibliography: p.
Includes index.
1. Russia (1917– R.S.F.S.R.). Sovet
Narodnykh Komissarov–History. 2. Lenin,
Vladimir Il'ich, 1870–1924. I. Title. II. Series.
JN6515 1979. R54   354'.47'0009041   78–18754
ISBN 0 521 22281 8

TO IVAN IVANOVICH GAPANOVICH

Russian historian

Contents

Tables

PLATES

Between pages 112 *and* 113

Preface

The Constitution of the USSR describes the Communist Party as 'the leading and directing force of Soviet society and the nucleus of its political system, of all state organisations and all voluntary organisations'. In practical, institutional terms, this means the superordination of the executive bodies of the party over those of the state at the centre, in the constituent republics, and right down to the lowest level of local government. In official doctrine, this institutional embodiment of the party's leading and directing role is seen as essential to safeguarding the socialist order and ensuring its progressive transformation into the fully communist society envisaged by Marx and Lenin. It was above all the apprehension that the Czechoslovak Communist Party was abdicating this leading and directing role that motivated the Soviet Union and its Warsaw Pact allies to invoke the principle of 'proletarian internationalism' and intervene in Czechoslovakia in 1968 in order to overturn the Dubček regime and its reforms.

The best known and most important manifestation of the party's leading and directing role is that the effective government of the Soviet Union is not formally an organ if the state at all, but a party body, the Politburo of the Central Committee. It is the Politburo that takes the final and binding decisions at its weekly meetings on all significant questions of internal and foreign policy and whose members have final responsibility for the various bureaucracies through which these decisions are implemented. It is thus the functional equivalent of the Cabinet in countries like the United Kingdom. The Presidium of the Council of Ministers, which corresponds in a formal sense to the British Cabinet, plays a subordinate role as a committee on second-order business and an administrative workhorse for the Politburo.

The relationship of the party to the various governmental and

non-governmental organisations through which the Soviet Union
is run bears a striking resemblance to the relationship sketched out
by Lenin, long before the Revolution, of the party to the trade
unions and other organisations of the working class. The party
should seek to get its members into leading positions in these organisations, but at the same time should maintain a separate, tight-knit
and centralised organisation of its own, which would work out the
strategy and tactics for the working class as a whole and direct and
coordinate all working-class organisations in putting these into
practice. In both cases it was to be party discipline, the obligation of
party members to give priority to party directives over their commitment to the particular organisations in which they were working,
that was to ensure the party's leading and directing role.

Is, then, the present institutionalised role of the Communist Party
in the Soviet system of government merely a logical and inevitable
expression, once the party was in power, of the role Lenin sought
for the party before the Revolution as the 'vanguard of the proletariat'? This, certainly, is how it is seen in official Soviet political and
historical doctrine. But so, too, is it represented, explicitly or im-
plicitly, by many Western writers critical of the Soviet system, who
often trace the roots of the present one-party dictatorship in the
USSR back to the ideas Lenin expressed in such early articles as
'What is to be done?'

In the face of such unanimity of defenders and detractors of the
Soviet Union alike, the scholar hesitates to raise a dissenting voice.
And yet when one looks closely at how the infant Soviet Republic
was actually governed for the first three years or so, before the onset
of Lenin's illness, the conventional wisdom begins to look simplistic.
For neither the party's Central Committee, nor its Politburo once it
was established in 1919, functioned at this time as the 'government'
of the Republic in the sense we have indicated the Politburo as being
the effective government today. Instead it was the Council of
People's Commissars, chaired by Lenin and the constitutional
equivalent of the present Council of Ministers, that was government
in fact as well as name. Lenin certainly identified the 'dictatorship
of the proletariat' with rule by the Communist Party, but this did
not mean government by the party's executive machinery. Lenin's
'Cabinet' was not the Politburo, but Sovnarkom – the Council of
People's Commissars. Unlike the situation prevailing since Stalin
first established his dominance, neither Lenin himself nor the second

most prominent figure in his regime, Trotsky, occupied any post in the party machine.

Admittedly, well before the end of the Civil War the Politburo had begun to direct the implementation of certain important areas of policy, and in 1921–3 its sphere of action spread rapidly to embrace almost the whole range of government activity. Yet the long delay before the party's leading and directing role was institutionalised in this way raises serious doubts about its assumed inevitable logic. Moreover, while the prerevolutionary doctrine and traditions of the party clearly *facilitated* this process, there were other factors which had a large and perhaps a necessary part in bringing it about. What is more, by 1922 Lenin had become seriously concerned at the emergence of the Politburo as an organ of government super-ordinated over Sovnarkom, and in the final months of activity left to him made vain efforts to reverse the process.

In this book we try to show how Sovnarkom was organised and operated under Lenin. We trace the emergence of its internal machinery and procedures and seek to explain how and why these changed over time. We examine what kinds of Bolshevik leaders served in Sovnarkom under Lenin and how they were chosen. We consider Sovnarkom's relationships with the executive machinery of the soviets and the party, describing and suggesting reasons for the gradual eclipse of Sovnarkom by the Politburo and the failure of Lenin's counter-measures. In a final chapter we outline some parallels and continuities between the character and evolution of pre-revolutionary Russian institutions and those of Sovnarkom, and attempt to place these in the broader framework of Russian political development.

In the West the study of Soviet governmental institutions and their history has been rather neglected in favour of research on the party and the political struggles of the top leaders. The best available account of the early period is Walter Pietsch's *Revolution und Staat. Institutionen als Träger der Macht in Sowjetrussland 1917–1922.** Pietsch's analysis of the changing relationships among the chief decision-making bodies of party and state is largely confirmed by the evidence assembled in the present book, despite some differences on the level of explanation. Another path-breaking study is G.P. van den Berg's *De Regering van Rusland en de Sovjetunie*, which des-

* Details of publications mentioned here will be found in the Bibliography.

cribes the evolution of governmental structures in the Soviet
Union and its constituent republics from 1917 to the present. It is
a pity that neither of these works is available in English, in which
language the best account remains that given by E. H. Carr in the
first volume of his *The Bolshevik Revolution 1917–1923*. Though
much of Carr's analysis stands up remarkably well, it did not tackle
certain important issues and much new information has come to
hand since it was written.

During the Stalin era Soviet works dealing with the early years
of Sovnarkom were practically confined to general and formalistic
outlines by constitutional and administrative lawyers. With the post-
Stalin revival of historical scholarship, however, and particularly
from the mid 1960s, many valuable books and articles emerged from
the pens of such writers as E. B. Genkina, Ye. N. Gorodetsky, Ye. I.
Korenevskaya, and especially M. P. Iroshnikov. While much of
this work is heavily embellished by the official hagiology and
demonology, it also contains much interesting and important analysis
of primary research data. Meanwhile a great deal of relevant documentary material has been published over the same period, which
helps to make up for the inaccessibility of the relevant archival col-
lections to Western scholars.

In combination with contemporary publications and with memoirs
and scholarly articles published in the 1920s, this new material
provides opportunities for a far closer analysis of the origins of the
Soviet political system than was heretofore possible. The present
book is a pioneering attempt to exploit these opportunities, and as
such it takes a rather broad canvas. The topics of each of our chapters deserve, and are now susceptible to, separate book-length study,
and when this is done the description and judgments offered in this
book may call for reassessment. Meanwhile we must hope that one
day a Russian scholar will enjoy sufficient freedom from political
constraints to write an infinitely better book.

The system of transliteration followed in this book is a conventional
one. The forms 'yu' and 'ya' have been used rather than 'iu' and
'ia'. At the beginning of words and after vowels the Russian 'e' is
rendered as 'ye'. The traditional English '-sky' has been used in
names, and apostrophes as a rendering of the soft sign have been
avoided in the text. Dates are given in Old Style up to the introduction of the calendar reform on 1 (=14) February 1918.

Acknowledgements

Work on this book has proceeded intermittently over some ten years, during which the basic concept has twice changed. I should like to express my sincere thanks to the many persons and institutions who have helped me along the way – whatever reservations they might have about the results. My greatest debt is to the Australian National University for providing me with the conditions of work and opportunities for research abroad without which this book could scarcely have been written. I should like to record my thanks to the staff of the Lenin Library, Moscow, the British Library, the Library of the London School of Economics and Political Science, the Institut für Weltwirtschaft, Kiel, the Bodleian Library, Oxford, the Widener and Houghton Libraries of Harvard University, the Hoover Library, Stanford and the Australian National Library.

I am grateful to scholars in the Law Faculty of Moscow State University and of the Institutes of State and Law and of History of the Soviet Academy of Sciences for their useful suggestions at an early stage of my research, and to the many scholars who made valuable comments on drafts of various sections of the book, especially Peter Scheibert, John Keep, Stephen Sternheimer, Malvin Helgesen and Theodore Taranovski. Samuel Oppenheim generously made available to me a copy of his significant dissertation on Rykov.

A section of Chapter 1 and Chapters 2 and 4 are substantially based respectively on the following articles: 'The Birth of the Council of People's Commissars', *Australian Journal of Politics and History*, Vol xx (1974), No. 1, pp. 70–75; 'The First Proletarian Government', *British Journal of Political Science*, Vol. iv (1974), Part 1, pp. 37–51; and 'Birth of the Soviet Bureaucracy', *Politics*, Vol. vii (1972), No. 2, pp. 121–35. Appreciation is expressed to the editors of these journals for permission to reproduce this material here. I am also obliged to the Houghton Library for permission to cite documents from the Trotsky Archive.

Finally it is a pleasure to record my thanks to Natalie Staples for her assistance in collecting biographical data, to Olga Prokopovich for invaluable help with the index, to Celia Westwood for an impeccable typescript, and to those helpful and efficient persons at Cambridge University Press, especially Colin Day and Iain White, who ensured this book's speedy appearance.

THR

Abbreviations

CEC The Central Executive Committee (of the All-Russian Congress of Soviets) (*Vserossiiskii Tsentral'nyi Ispolnitel'nyi Komitet – VTsIK*).

CHREZKOMSNAB Extraordinary Commission on Supply of the Red Army (*Chrezvychainaya Komissiya po Snabzheniyu Krasnoi Armii*).

CHUSOSNABARM Extraordinary Plenipotentiary of the Defence Council for the Supply of the Red Army and Navy (*Chrezvychainyi Upolnomochennyi Soveta Oborony po Snabzheniyu Krasnoi Armii i Flota*).

GOSPLAN State General Planning Commission (*Gosudarstvennaya Obshcheplanovaya Komissiya*).

GUBKOM Regional (Party) Committee (*Gubernyi Komitet RKP (b)*).

MRC Military-Revolutionary Committee (*Voyenno-revolyutsionnyi Komitet*).

NEC (All-Russian) National Economic Council (*Vserossiiskii Sovet Narodnogo Khozyaistva – VSNKh*).

NEP New Economic Policy (*Novaya Ekonomicheskaya Politika*).

ORGBURO Organisational Bureau (of the Communist Party Central Committee) (*Organizatsionnyi Byuro TsK RKP(b)*).

POLITBURO Political Bureau (of the Communist Party Central Committee) (*Politicheskii Byuro TsK RKP(b)*).

RABKRIN Worker-Peasant Inspectorate (*Raboche-krestyanskaya Inspektsiya*).

SOVNARKOM Council of People's Commissars (*Sovet Narodnykh Komissarov*).

SRs	Socialist-Revolutionaries (*Sotsialisty-revolyutsionery*).

STO	Labour and Defence Council (*Sovet Truda i Oborony*).

TSEKOMPRODARM	Central Commission on Food Supplies for the Army (*Tsentral'naya Komissiya po uporyadocheniyu i pravil'noi postanovke dela snabzheniya armii prodovol'stviyem i produktami pervoi neobkhodimosti*).

TSENTROVOYENZAG	Central Department of Military Procurements (*Tsentral'nyi Otdel Voyennykh Zagotovok*).

TUC	(All-Russian Central) Trade Union Council (*Vserossiiskii Tsentral'nyi Sovet Professional'nykh Soyuzov – VTsSPS*).

VECHEKA	All-Russian Extraordinary Commission (for Combating Counter-Revolution, Speculation and Sabotage) (*Vserossiiskaya Chrezvychainaya Komissiya po Bor'be s Kontr-revolyutsiyei, Spekulyatsiyei i Sabotazhem*).

PART ONE

SMOLNY: SOVNARKOM TAKES SHAPE

I

The origins of Sovnarkom

Throughout the night of 24–5 October 1917, the Bolshevik Central Committee was gathered in a small room on the second floor of the elite girls' school in the Smolny district of Petrograd, which had been taken over by the parties represented in the soviets and in whose imposing assembly hall the Second Congress of Soviets was to convene the following day. A few hours earlier Lenin had arrived incognito from another area of the capital, where he had been in hiding. Anticipating a majority in the Congress, goaded for weeks by Lenin and at last provoked into action by the preemptive moves of the Provisional Government, the Central Committee was presiding over the forceful seizure of power in the Russian capital.

Meanwhile, actual operations were being directed from a room on the floor above by the Military Revolutionary Committee of the Bolshevik-dominated Petrograd Soviet, which had succeeded during the preceding fortnight in bringing under its effective control, through its corps of several hundred 'commissars', a motley conglomeration of military and naval units accepting Bolshevik leadership and of armed factory workers organised in 'Red Guard' detachments.

Starting with the Telephone Exchange, these forces occupied one after another the key government offices, culminating a few hours later in the Imperial Winter Palace, where the Provisional Government itself was gathered, the only point where significant resistance was encountered and a few lives were lost. Most of the ministers were taken into custody but Prime Minister Kerensky escaped and, after several days organising abortive military counter-moves, went into hiding until his departure from the country in mid-1918.[1]

It was not till late on the evening of 25 October, when the Winter Palace was already under attack, that the Second Congress of Soviets finally commenced, Lenin evidently having delayed the opening as long as possible with the object of presenting the delegates with a *fait accompli*. There was a substantial predominance of Bolsheviks and their Left Socialist-Revolutionary allies. After the election of a Bolshevik chairman and Bolshevik-dominated Presidium, the Congress exploded into violent recriminations between the Bolshevik leaders and Menshevik and Socialist-Revolutionary delegates, who bitterly opposed the Bolshevik assault on the Provisional Government, in which they were strongly represented. These exchanges led to the withdrawal of most of the moderate socialists from the Congress. Then, after a recess, the rump Congress reconvened at 3 a.m. to be told that the Winter Palace had fallen and the Provisional Government was under arrest, and they proceeded to formalise the situation by voting to approve a proclamation 'To workers, soldiers and peasants', drafted by Lenin.

Basing itself on the will of the vast majority of workers, soldiers and peasants, basing itself on the victorious rising of workers and of the garrison which has been achieved in Petrograd, the Congress takes power into its hands. . .All power in the localities passes to the soviets of workers', soldiers' and peasants' deputies, whose duty it is to establish genuine revolutionary order.[2]

The momentous first sitting of the Second Congress of Soviets closed at 5 a.m. on 26 October. The following evening it convened again for its second and final sitting, at which the basic planks of the Bolshevik platform found expression in decrees on peace (the warring nations were called upon to make peace without annexations or indemnities) and the land (private ownership of land was abolished without compensation and its use passed in effect to the peasants). The Congress went on to approve a resolution proposed by its Bolshevik chairman, Kamenev, on the formation of a Soviet government, called the 'Council of People's Commissars' (*Sovet Narodnykh Komissarov*) and headed by Lenin. Finally, it elected a Central Executive Committee of 101 members.

Apart from its outlandish and challenging name, there seemed on the face of it little to distinguish the new 'Soviet' Government from a modern 'bourgeois' ministry. It consisted of a Chairman (Lenin) and fourteen other members, all but three of whom were individually responsible for specific departments of government: A. I. Rykov (Internal Affairs), V. P. Milyutin (Agriculture), A. G. Shlyapnikov (Labour), V. P. Nogin (Trade and Industry), A. V. Lunacharsky

(Education), I. I. Skvortsov-Stepanov (Finance), L. D. Trotsky (Foreign Affairs), A. I. Lomov (Justice), I. A. Teodorovich (Food Supplies), N. P. Avilov (Posts and Telegraphs) and I. V. Stalin (Nationalities).[3] The remaining three, V. A. Antonov-Ovseyenko, N. V. Krylenko and P. E. Dybenko, constituted a Committee responsible for Military and Naval Affairs; this was indeed a departure from pre-revolutionary practice but it only lasted for a month or so, when separate Army and Navy portfolios were restored. The post of People's Commissar for Railways was temporarily unfilled. When the Council of People's Commissars (or Sovnarkom, to use its Russian acronym) is compared with the ministerial structure inherited by the Provisional Government from the Imperial regime, the conservative shape of the new government becomes even more apparent, for with minor exceptions the division of responsibilities among its members was identical.[4]

Was this, however, the whole story? Let us look at the preamble to the decree establishing Sovnarkom:

For the administration of the country up to the convening of the Constituent Assembly, a Temporary Worker and Peasant Government is to be formed, which will be named the Council of People's Commissars. Charge of particular branches of state life is entrusted to commissions, the composition of which should ensure the carrying into life of the programme proclaimed by the Congress in close unity with the mass organisations of working men and women, sailors, soldiers, peasants and office-workers. Governmental power belongs to the *collegium* of chairmen of these commissions, i.e. the Council of People's Commissars. Control over the activity of the people's commissars and the right of replacing them belongs to the All-Russian Congress of Soviets of Workers', Peasants' and Soldiers' Deputies and its Central Executive Committee.[5]

Here, intertwined with the conventional model of a government consisting of members each personally responsible for a particular branch of administration, there are suggestions of a different model, in which government would consist of a cluster of 'commissions' integrated through their members with the revolutionary organisations of the masses. That such an alternative model was ever canvassed, or even clearly conceived, is impossible on present evidence to establish, since there is no record of any discussions among leading Bolsheviks about the structure of the government they were establishing. Bonch-Bruyevich's oft-quoted recollections on this point are in fact not very helpful. He recalls how Lenin, in the course of the seizure of power and the Second Congress of Soviets, outlined the new government structure in a verbal aside between telephone calls. In language very close to that used in the Congress Decree itself, Bonch-Bruyevich quotes Lenin as saying:

It is necessary to set up commissions for the administration of the country, which will be commissariats. The chairmen of these commissions we will name People's Commissars. The *collegium* of chairmen will be the Council of People's Commissars, to which will belong full power. The Congress of Soviets and the Central Executive Committee are to control its activity, and to them belongs the right of replacing commissars.

Bonch-Bruyevich goes on to draw the conclusion that Lenin had evidently found time during his years of exile to work out a quite precise blueprint for the future revolutionary government.[6]

This account, written some fourteen years after the incident it purports to describe, appears to reflect Bonch-Bruyevich's vast admiration for Lenin and his sense of Lenin's mastery and farsightedness more than a concern to reconstruct sequentially the background to the foundation of the Sovnarkom. If we assume that Bonch-Bruyevich has recalled Lenin's words more or less accurately, they are unlikely to have been uttered before 26 October, i.e. between the two sittings of the Congress, for it would appear that as late as a day or two earlier Lenin had been thinking along substantially different lines. This is the conclusion we must draw from a page of notes evidently jotted down by him on the night of 24–5 October, probably in the course of a preliminary Central Committee discussion of the structure of government to be proposed at the Congress.[7] Fragmentary as it is, this document is of great interest since it provides the only existing evidence of the development of Lenin's thinking about these matters. It is therefore worth reproducing here in full.

Understandably enough, in view of the lack of other documentary evidence, some Soviet historians have tended to place more weight on these notes than they will really bear, and we should beware of making the same mistake. What we have here is obviously not a general plan of the future political structure, even a rough one, but rather a sheet of jottings on particular points, some of them related to the shape of the revolutionary government and some to various policy questions. Perhaps, therefore, we should hesitate to conclude from the fact that no mention is made here of a *Council* of People's Commissars that no such body was envisaged at this stage.[9] It is obviously significant, however, that the only collective policy body mentioned in this document, the Commission on Legislative Pro-

Lenin's Notes on the Structure of Government
24–5 (?) October, 1917[8]

Appointments	
Chairman of Commission of Revolutionary Order	[V. D.] Bonch-Bruyevich – Administrator of Affairs [*zaveduyushchii delami*] or 'People's Commissar for Revolutionary Order'

General [M. D.] Bonch-Bruyevich to check up and promote the principle of generally nominating commanders from below

---

Sokolnikov – Gazette of the Workers' and Peasants' Government
+?

Immediate setting up ... of Commissions of People's Commissars ... (ministers and deputy ministers)

Kamenev – Commission on Legislative Proposals

Chairman of 'Commission on Legislative Proposals'	(Under Minister-President)

Nadezhda Konstantinovna [Krupskaya – Lenin's wife] – Deputy Minister (under Lunacharsky)

organization of fraternization on all fronts ... immediate introduction of minimum programme (of Socialist Revolutionaries and Social Democrats) limitation of salaries to 500 roubles a month

---

2 stenographers for dictation and a *dictaphone*

---

bringing to light of stocks of raw materials and products in general

---

'Collection of Regulations and Enactments and *Acts* of the Government'

posals, was one that was *not* provided for in the decree setting up the Sovnarkom two days later. It is noteworthy that this potentially powerful body was not to be answerable to the People's Commissars collectively; it and its chairman were to come directly under the Minister-President' (*Ministr-predsedatel'*). The use of this traditional and prestigious title for the chairman of the government also arouses interest, though it would be risky to place much emphasis on points of nomenclature at this stage, when the concept of 'People's Commissar' had only just emerged. It is not clear from the references to 'Commissions of People's Commissars...(ministers and deputy ministers)' whether the title 'People's Commissar' was yet seen as limited to those performing the function of minister. The idea of a 'Commission on Revolutionary Order' was also one that was dropped by 26 October, and V. D. Bonch-Bruyevich, in whom Lenin appears to have reposed particular confidence at this time, did not gain a place in the Sovnarkom but instead became its chief administrative officer.[10]

It is evident, then, that Lenin's thinking about the shape of the revolutionary government altered in a number of respects, some very substantial, in the course of the seizure of power, and we must conclude either that his ideas were still rather tentative and fragmentary up to 24 October, or that over the next day or two he was brought by his colleagues or by circumstances to change his mind on the points mentioned – and perhaps on others for which we have no record of his thinking prior to 26 October.

These last-minute changes in the projected structure of government worked in the direction of simplification and closer approximation to pre-revolutionary patterns, and it would appear that suggestions for more radical structural change went by the board as the Bolshevik leadership sought to thrash out the practical implications of their assuming control over the administration. Two apparently important innovations were nevertheless incorporated into the new government. The first was the idea that, in the administration of his department, each member of the government (People's Commissar) should share authority with a 'Commission' of which he would be chairman. In the event these 'Commissions' rarely functioned as such, where they actually existed, although the subsequently established Boards (*kollegii*) introduced elements of collective decision-making into the leadership of the individual people's commissariats.[11]

The other innovation was in terminology. In calling their government the 'Council of People's Commissars', the Bolshevik leadership were seeking to de-emphasise formal and structural similarities to 'bourgeois' governments and to proclaim and dramatise the revolutionary role and class content they believed it to embody. As Krupskaya put it: 'These ministers would have to create completely new forms of work, forms qualitatively different from the work of the old ministers, and foreign to the old bureaucratic spirit. While it was not a matter of the name, nevertheless it was necessary to call the ministers by a new name...'[12]

Both Krupskaya and Bonch-Bruyevich gave Lenin the credit for inventing the title of the new government, a view unanimously endorsed by recent Soviet historians. There was an earlier tradition, however, which attributed it to Trotsky, and this continues to be accepted by most Western scholars. This is an intriguing but scarcely vital question, on which conclusive contemporary evidence is lacking. Perhaps the most persuasive witness is A. A. Yoffe, who touched on this question in an article written for the second anniversary of the Bolshevik Revolution.

> I remember that once in a gathering of those people who had headed the revolution right from the beginning, we were trying to recall, for instance, who first thought up the titles 'People's Commissar' and 'Council of People's Commissars', and it was only after prolonged arguments and swapping of reminiscences, that we managed to establish that these were proposed by L. D. Trotsky.[13]

Perhaps the most that can be said is that these terms emerged in the course of the phrenetic discussions within the Bolshevik leadership on 25 and 26 October, that Trotsky probably first hit on the actual formula, but that others (including Lenin) may have helped suggest the ideas to his mind, and the formula must have won Lenin's support to have been adopted.

That the title of the new government contained the word 'soviet' (*sovet*) some have seen as designed to identify it with the new revolutionary institutions of the masses, as the topmost soviet in a hierarchy of soviets.[14] This supposition seems highly dubious, since *sovet* is simply the usual Russian word for 'council', and the pre-revolutionary government executive had been called the *Sovet Ministrov* (Council of Ministers). There would in fact have been a sharper break with the old terminology if the new government had been called a Committee, Commission, or Board, rather than a Council. Admittedly, however, it might well have been so named had not the word 'soviet' meanwhile acquired revolutionary overtones.

No such doubt attaches to the deliberate choice of the term 'people's *commissar*' as a substitute for 'minister', in order to signal the new and revolutionary character of the office. The antecedents of this term may deserve a brief glance. The word 'commissar' (late Latin *commissarius*, French *commissaire*, English *commissary*, German *Kommissär*) has a long history in Europe in the meaning of an agent entrusted by higher authority with certain specific political or administrative tasks, frequently of an extraordinary or temporary nature. In this sense it passed into Russian in the early eighteenth century, and Peter the Great appointed *komissary* to run his re-organised *uyezd* administration in the provinces. While the term and its derivative 'commissariat' sometimes came to be employed for certain permanent jurisdictions, such as military provisions in England and police superintendents in continental Europe, other uses continued the earlier connotation of an *ad hoc* or plenipotentiary agent of some higher authority. For instance, a *commissaire des guerres* or *Kriegskommissär* was frequently attached to continental armies during the seventeenth and eighteenth centuries, linking the troops to the civilian inhabitants and placing them under semi-political control. The term was thus well established at the time of the French Revolution, and it was natural that the Convention should describe as *commissaires* its agents assigned to the various departments and troop formations. Though some of its modern uses in France are more equivalent to the English word 'commissioner', the term *commissaires régionaux de la République* was used by the Liberation regime in 1944–6 to denote its corps of plenipotentiaries charged with taking over the regional administration from the Vichy-appointed prefects.

Against this background, it is not surprising that the Russian Provisional Government in 1917 called its agents deputed to various jurisdictions *komissary*, and that the term was taken up by the Bolsheviks; it was constantly on their lips during the seizure of power, since, as we have seen, the agents assigned to the various Red Guard and troop units by the Military Revolutionary Committee were so called. Thus there was no more obvious term available to the Bolshevik leadership as it cast about on 25 and 26 October for a substitute for the obnoxious word 'minister'. Yet it is striking that they kept sight of the historical precedents, and the example of the French Convention evidently clinched the decision in favour of 'commissar'. To continue the quotation from Krupskaya's memoirs,

...it was necessary to call the ministers by a new name, the same way as they were called in the Great French Revolution, it was necessary that the name should bear witness to the fact that they were plenipotentiaries of the revolutionary people. It was necessary to call them 'people's commissars'. The Council would be called not a Council of Ministers, but a 'Council of People's Commissars'.[15]

Confirmation that the Convention afforded the Bolshevik leadership with its principal model in designing the new forms of government is provided by Sukhanov, who was told as much at the time by one of the Bolshevik Central Committee members.[16]

The resounding and challenging title chosen for the new 'workers' and peasants' government' was politically most apt and successful; in fact, we may note in passing that its very success was soon to lead to some embarrassment. For during the days and weeks that followed, as one after another the various provincial centres passed under the control of the local Bolshevik-led soviets, the latter in many cases hastened to set up their own 'Councils of People's Commissars', which in a number of instances proved most reluctant to accept the authority of the 'Petrograd' Sovnarkom. Moscow still had its own Sovnarkom when the Soviet Government moved there in March 1918, and it was only after delicate negotiations that it allowed itself to be absorbed by the latter and assimilated to the emergent Soviet administrative hierarchy.[17]

Yet there was no doubt what the Bolshevik leadership meant by the term 'people's commissar' – they meant 'minister'. The two terms were in fact used interchangeably in the initial period. 'We must have a Minister for Trade and Industry', wrote Trotsky to Shlyapnikov on 5 November[18] and about the same time Lenin wrote to A. G. Shlikhter, 'You are needed for Minister of Agriculture and must come immediately.'[19] The new title quickly established itself, but, as we shall see in Chapter 3, ambiguous use of the terms 'ministry' and 'people's commissariat' persisted for several more weeks. In fact, as late as March 1918, following the resignation of several people's commissars, Sverdlov introduced the issue of nominating replacements under the rubric 'the general ministerial crisis' (*ob obshcheministerskom krizise*).[20]

There remains one further formal aspect of the Council of People's Commissars as established by the Second All-Russian Congress of Soviets that requires comment: its provisional character. The Sovnarkom was described in the Congress decree, as we have noted, as a 'Temporary Worker and Peasant Government...up to the convening of the Constituent Assembly'. This at first sight curious concession to 'parliamentary cretinism' was tactically unavoidable, since the Bolsheviks had allowed themselves to become publicly committed, along with the other revolutionary parties, to the election of a Constituent Assembly and the entrusting to it of final responsibility for designing the future social and political order. Many of their own members and Left SR (Socialist-Revolutionary) allies accepted this commitment at face value, the machinery for holding the elections was already in existence, and flouting the prerogatives of the Assembly would therefore have introduced a further divisive factor into the situation which, on top of everything else, would perhaps have rendered the task of forming a Bolshevik government impossible.

Yet it is certain that Lenin had not the slightest intention of handing over power to the Assembly should the elections go against him, as indeed they did. His attitude is summed up by his comment shortly afterwards that it had helped '*prove* to the backward masses why such parliaments deserve to be broken up'.[21] In this case, as always, the question for Lenin was not the formal arrangements, but who would possess the organisational and coercive power to determine how these arrangements were to be implemented. His first task, therefore, was to win this power, even if one condition of this was that he should verbally qualify it by reference to the Constituent Assembly; it would later be a question of holding power and providing it with sufficient basis of support to enable him to deal with the Assembly as circumstances then required.[22]

2

'The first proletarian government'

A revolutionary movement which, like the Bolsheviks', aspired to the total transformation of society, might be expected to destroy and replace the whole institutional network of the existing state – not only its political nucleus, but also its central administrative machine and even its field units throughout the country. Such root-and-branch changes were, on the face of it, part of Lenin's vision. In his pamphlet *The State and Revolution*, written only a few weeks before the seizure of power, while arguing that the victorious proletariat would require a state of its own in order to prepare the conditions under which state power could ultimately 'wither away', Lenin nevertheless asserted that his would be an entirely new non-bureaucratic form of state after the style of the Paris Commune, erected on the ashes of the old state institutions which would have to be utterly shattered and swept away.

Marx teaches us to act with supreme boldness in destroying the entire old state machine, and at the same time he teaches us to put the question correctly: the Commune was able in the space of a few weeks to *start* building a *new*, proletarian state machine by introducing such-and-such measures to secure wider democracy and to uproot bureaucracy. Let us learn revolutionary boldness from the Communards; let us see in their practical measures the *outline* of urgently practical and immediately possible measures, and then, pursuing this road, we shall achieve the complete destruction of the bureaucracy. The possibility of this destruction is guaranteed by the fact that socialism will shorten the working day, will raise the *masses* to a new life, will create such conditions for the *majority* of the population as will enable *everybody*, without exception, to perform 'state functions', and this will lead to the *complete withering away* of every form of state in general. [Emphasis in original.][1]

We have seen how this vision found expression in the political nucleus of the state, with the establishment of a 'worker-peasant government' composed exclusively of members of the victorious revolutionary party and deriving its authority from institutions thrown up by the revolution and unknown under the previous political order – the soviets. Yet we have noted structural continuities with the old order even in this political nucleus, and, as we shall see in the next chapter, these continuities grew stronger as the new government began to operate.

At the basic level of the state, in its field units, continuity was widespread and obvious. Even in such institutions as the courts and the armed forces, where change predominated, there were significant continuities of structure, personnel and processes. In most spheres of state activity the field units underwent little change in the aftermath of the October Revolution. It might be objected here that in considering such institutions as post offices, schools or banks one must distinguish between their formal structure, which may be largely determined by technical considerations, and the content of their activities, which is the true measure of the system of state power of which they form a part. In his article 'Will the Bolsheviks Retain State Power', written less than a month before the insurrection, Lenin wrote: 'But the organisational form of the work we will not invent, but take it ready made from the capitalists – the banks, syndicates, best factories, experimental stations, academies and so on.'[2] Lenin's readiness to make use of such structures, based on the Marxist assumption that what matters socially is not the structure of institutions but who owns them, was obviously of vast importance in perpetuating elements of the old society in the new. Indeed one might argue that in terms of Lenin's pre-October vision such basic social activities as educating the young or the production and exchange of material values seemed to call as much for the creation of new, proletarian, non-bureaucratic structures as did, for example, military defence and justice. As against this, there is the practical consideration that radical change at the field unit level takes time, and in the interim the facilities concerned must be kept functioning. This is obviously true, but the point would carry more weight if one could argue that some effective general formula was devised for proletarianising and de-bureaucratising the field units of the Soviet state and consistently implemented in the post-revolutionary era. This whole aspect of the Bolshevik Revolution lies beyond the scope of this book, and still awaits systematic study. Yet it seems fair to assert, without minimising the vast outpouring of revolutionary zeal and energy which profoundly influenced all aspects of Russian life, that no such effective formula for proletarianising and de-bureaucratising the field units of the state was in fact devised and implemented.

If our evaluation of the impact of the Russian Revolution on the field units of the state in the light of Lenin's *State and Revolution* vision must remain somewhat tentative, the balance-sheet seems clear enough so far as the central administrative machine is concerned. A Russian revolutionary intent on 'destroying the entire old state machine' might reasonably be expected to move quickly to the abolition of the august ministries inherited from the Tsars. Of course new institutions would have to be substituted to link the political nucleus with the field units of the state. Lenin implied in much he wrote during 1917 that this was indeed what was intended – the old *chinovnik* apparatus would be destroyed and the soviets – non-bureaucratic, non-professional, with elective, changing membership – put in its place. ' "Take over" "the state apparatus" and "set it in motion" the proletariat *cannot* do. But it can *destroy* everything that is repressive, routine and incorrigibly bourgeois in the old state apparatus, putting in its place *its own*, new apparatus and this apparatus is the soviets of workers', soldiers' and peasants' deputies.'[3]

Still, there was a qualification to all this, and a most important one. For Lenin distinguished between the repressive, *chinovnik* aspects of the old state machine and its modern, regulative – especially economic-regulative aspects.

This apparatus we need not and must not destroy. It must be wrested from subjection to the capitalists, the capitalists and their lines of influence must be *cut* away, *sliced* away, *hacked* away from it, it must be subjected to the proletarian soviets, it must be made broader, more all-embracing, more part of the whole people.[4]

Moreover, in retaining this apparatus, it would also be necessary to retain – by compulsion, if necessary – the skills and experience of 'a certain upper stratum of the bourgeois intelligentsia, officials and so on', in order to keep it functioning.[5]

As we shall see in Chapters 4 and 5 it was the qualification, rather than the vision itself, which determined the impact of the Revolution on the central machinery of government. Indeed, by structuring their government to conform to the main divisions of the existing administrative machine the Bolshevik leaders clearly revealed their initial assumptions as to what form the principal link between the political nucleus and the field units of the state would take. Ironical though it may seem in the light of Lenin's constant stress on the *non-bureaucratic* character of the new proletarian state, equipping itself with an effective bureaucracy was in fact the main preoccupation of the Soviet state during its initial phase, and predominantly this expressed itself in efforts to 'take over' and 'set in motion' the old ministerial machine.

This, however, was not something that could be achieved with the stroke of a pen. It was to be several weeks before the Bolsheviks established control over the chief public offices in Petrograd and set them working for the 'worker–peasant government'. The process was hindered by the understandable failure of many civil servants to accept the legitimacy of the new regime and their consequent reluctance to serve it – a reluctance labelled as 'sabotage' by the Bolsheviks. Moreover the existing administrative machine was in any case ill-adapted to many of the immediate steps the revolutionary regime needed to take in establishing its authority. For these reasons, some *other* machinery was essential if the Bolsheviks were to successfully assert their rule. This machinery was found in the form of the Military-Revolutionary Committee (MRC), the same body that had organised and directed the seizure of power in the capital. Since neither the Council of People's Commissars, nor the Central Executive Committee (CEC) of the All-Russian Congress of Soviets, nor even the Central Committee of the Bolshevik Party, provided more than the most general guidelines within which the MRC operated, there is force in A. A. Yoffe's characterisation of this body, rather than Sovnarkom, as 'the first proletarian government' – provided we suspend any reservations we may have in identifying 'proletarian' with 'Bolshevik'.[6] For a student of Sovnarkom the MRC deserves attention not only because we need to understand what form the regime took while the proper 'worker–peasant government' geared up for action, and not only because of significant vestiges which the MRC left in the Bolshevik system of rule, but also because its structure and mode of operation provide points of contrast which can tell us much about the nature of Sovnarkom itself.

The MRC had its origin in an enabling decision taken by the Petrograd Soviet on 9 October,[7] which was to be implemented three days later at a closed meeting of the Soviet's Executive Committee.[8] At this stage the MRC was represented as an *ad hoc* multi-

party body set up to consider and act on the implications of a
Provisional Government move to transfer certain of the more revolutionary troop units out of Petrograd, but some at least of the
Bolshevik leaders probably intended it from the first as a cover for
the organisation of a 'general staff of the insurrection'.[9] The Committee, on which leading members of the Petrograd Soviet were
joined by representatives of soldiers' and sailors' organisations,
factory committees, trade unions, and the military organisations of
the revolutionary parties, was fluid and uncertain in membership
but in practice dominated by a Bolshevik core centred at first on the
Petrograd Soviet Chairman Trotsky, later augmented by a group
of five Bolshevik Central Committee members (Stalin, Sverdlov,
Bubnov, Dzerzhinsky and Uritsky) designated on 16 October as a
Military-Revolutionary Centre with instructions to join the MRC.[10]
It functioned through a hastily-formed corps of commissars posted
to units of the Petrograd Garrison and various institutions and
organisations and recruited largely from militant and resolute
members of the Bolshevik Military Organisation, many of whom
had suffered imprisonment by the Provisional Government following the 'July days'.[11] The first task of these commissars, to win
authority from the commissars of the Menshevik and SR-dominated
Central Executive Committee, thus ensuring that the troops would
act only on instructions from the MRC, was accomplished between
21 and 24 October. Then, on 24 and 25 October, as we have seen,
the MRC went into feverish action in its room on the third floor of
the Smolny Institute, deploying its forces and directing the actual
operations for the seizure of power.

The basic structure of the MRC was a very simple one. It consisted merely of the headquarters[12] and the commissars, in direct
communication (by telephone or through couriers), without any
intermediate echelons of command, or any subordinate structure
under the commissars, whose task it was to use the existing structures
and power-relationships in the military and other organisations to
which they were assigned to ensure that the commands of the MRC
were complied with. Having proved to the Bolshevik leaders its
effectiveness in winning power, this simple but flexible mechanism
was now employed to meet the immediate problems of exercising this
power. In part, and particularly at first, these were still problems of
a military order: suppressing pockets of resistance, taking charge of
and guarding vital facilities and institutions, preventing pogroms

and looting, and, most spectacularly, aborting a coup by military cadets in Petrograd and defeating Kerensky's attempt to retake the capital with the aid of General Krasnov and his Cossacks.[13] At the same time, however, the MRC began to assume tasks of civil administration, and within a week or so of the insurrection these had come to dominate its activities.[14]

Immediately after the insurrection the MRC began posting commissars to government institutions, and by 28 October there were already 185 of them in charge of various civil agencies.[15] MRC commissars were not supposed to be sent to the central offices of the ministries themselves, as these were in theory the exclusive preserve of the Council of People's Commissars,[16] but this restriction does not seem to have been seriously observed, and they too were frequently the object of MRC decisions, mainly related to the latter's role in countering civil service 'sabotage'[17] and recruiting new officials.[18] Initially, the MRC even played an important part in staffing and providing other services for the Council of People's Commissars itself.[19]

In the field of civil government, the most urgent task facing the MRC was the ensuring of food supplies to the capital. By the day after the insurrection stocks of grain in Petrograd had fallen far below the level required to supply the population for one day with the starvation ration of half a pound of bread. This desperate situation was further exacerbated by the blockade mounted by the Railwaymen's Union, whose leaders were trying to bring pressure on the Bolsheviks to agree to a multi-party government. The MRC met the immediate crisis by draconic measures of food requisitioning and control in Petrograd, and followed up by despatching 'flying food-supply squads' to the provinces, and by stern measures against speculation as new supplies began to flow into the capital.[20] As well as grain and other foodstuffs, the MRC became heavily involved in the requisitioning and distribution of other goods in short supply, such as fuel, winter footwear and clothing, especially for the army.[21]

A second urgent task was control of the press. It was the MRC that implemented Sovnarkom's Decree on the Press,[22] forcibly closing the more critically oriented newspapers, handing over their facilities to Bolshevik-controlled organisations, supervising the distribution of paper and suppressing clandestine publications.[23]

The wide-ranging activities of the MRC arising from its concern with the supply of goods soon extended to the control of foreign trade outlets. At the same time certain border points also attracted the attention of the MRC because of their importance in foreign political contacts.[24] It also took responsibility for the issue of exit visas,[25] and seems to have been a major channel for communication with V. V. Vorovsky in Stockholm, the new regime's first diplomatic representative abroad.[26]

At the other extreme the MRC became entrusted with a wide range of local administrative activities in Petrograd from the issuing of permits to live in the capital and to travel by train and the allocation of housing to the licensing of theatrical performances.[27]

The work of the MRC in maintaining order and combating attempts at counter-revolution quickly involved it in political police activities. As early as 29 October it created a 'special intelligence section' (Osobaya razvedka), disposing of squads of carefully chosen Red Guards, which rounded up and arrested large numbers of persons suspected of counter-revolutionary tendencies.[28] The Special Intelligence Section continued to be employed for carrying out searches and arrests[29] but another MRC department, the Military Investigation Commission (Voyennosledstvennaya komissiya), which was evidently set up at about the same time, quickly assumed the major role in security intelligence activities.[30]

On the model of the Petrograd MRC, in the weeks following the insurrection, military-revolutionary committees were set up in a large number of other towns and districts, and played an important part in establishing Bolshevik control in the provinces. While these were usually the product of local initiative – some of them had sprung up as early as September – and such guidance as emanated from Petrograd was exercised through several channels, nevertheless the Petrograd MRC played a major role, through the sending of agitators and other activists as well as by example, in inspiring, directing and coordinating these bodies.[31]

Writing in 1927, S. Piontkovsky attempted to summarise the manifold roles assumed by the MRC after the insurrection as follows: 'It was a curious mixture of protecting revolutionary order and combating counter-revolution, of measures of national political importance – virtually international importance – and of measures serving local interests and requirements.'[32] This remarkable combination of roles was reflected in the ambiguity of the MRC's formal status and title. While its origins as an organ of the Petrograd Soviet remained important throughout its existence, and the name

Petrograd Military-Revolutionary Committee never entirely disappeared from use, its national status was indicated by a decision of
the CEC on 29 October to post thirteen of its members to serve on
it,[33] and a further decision the following day stating that 'the
Military-Revolutionary Committee carries out all tasks assigned to
it by the Council of People's Commissars'.[34] Henceforth it became
in form a body attached to (*pri*) the CEC, yet it was scarcely ever
referred to in these terms, but simply as the Military-Revolutionary
Committee.

Throughout its existence, the membership and structure of the
MRC were in constant flux. Piontkovsky counted 66 persons identified in MRC documents as members, of whom 48 were Bolsheviks,
14 Left SRs and 4 Anarchists.[35] Subsequent research has increased
this number to 82.[36] What is clear is that in addition to the members
originally elected and others subsequently added by the Bolshevik
Central Committee and Petrograd Committee and the CEC, the
MRC itself engaged in large-scale coopting of members, while at
the same time other members were dropping out of MRC activities
as they became more involved in other work.[37] A recent study suggests that, in the period after the insurrection, the MRC had some
20–25 active members at any one time.[38] Members were assigned
to one or other of the Committee's departments, of which from time
to time new ones were formed or old ones merged.[39] Meetings of the
MRC were held at least daily, and usually twice a day. Details of
attendance are not available but it is likely that routine meetings
were attended simply by whoever was at hand and not too embroiled
in their departmental activities. From time to time meetings of the
full membership were convened to consider matters of particular
importance.[40] There was also a Bureau, originally of five members,
responsible for urgent decisions which could not await full meetings
of the MRC. However it is doubtful if this body played a major role
after the initial period, although it persisted at least until 23 November.[41]

The original Chairman of the MRC was the eighteen-year-old
Left SR P. E. Lazimir, whose chief function, it would seem, was to
serve as a 'front' for the Bolsheviks. Trotsky's supreme role at this
stage was legitimated not by any formal position in the MRC, but
by his Chairmanship of the Petrograd Soviet. Under his overall
guidance, the effective leader during the insurrection was Podvoisky,
with Antonov-Ovseyenko acting as Secretary, and Podvoisky claims

to have later taken over the Chairmanship.[42] In practice, the role of Chairman does not appear to have been firmly institutionalised or effectively appropriated by any individual. In the post-insurrection period, nearly two dozen MRC members signed documents as Chairman (apart from those who signed simply *for* the Chairman), sometimes several persons on the one day. Of these, some half a dozen signed at least as frequently as Podvoisky who, in fact, faded out of the MRC's activities completely in the last three weeks of its existence. Trotsky's influence over the MRC, previously decisive, seems to have come to an end after the defeat of Kerensky's attempted counter-blow.[43] Although the responsibilities of secretary were also widely shared in the post-insurrection period, the central role here was played by S. I. Gusev, an experienced party organiser who was entrusted by Sverdlov on 27 October with setting up the MRC Secretariat.[44] According to one MRC leader, office supporting staff were minimal, consisting of two or three persons performing secretarial duties and a handful of typists, so that the members themselves were engaged virtually full-time in receiving a constant stream of visitors bringing matters requiring decision, settling all but the most important of them on the spot, and themselves putting their decisions into writing.[45]

The MRC was not just a shapeless frenzied chaos, as some accounts of it would suggest. It had a certain structure and there were regularities and consistencies in its behaviour. It is nonetheless true that the hallmarks of this body were structural fluidity, improvisation and *ad hoc* adaptation. This was, indeed, what the situation required in the days of the insurrection and post-revolutionary paralysis of the normal machinery of government. As, however, the other instruments of the regime and especially the Council of People's Commissars began to operate, and the old ministerial apparatus was set in motion again, parallelism and duplication between the activities of these bodies and the MRC became more and more difficult to avoid, and in this situation the characteristic style of activity of the latter became a serious liability and attracted increasing criticism. 'There have been repeated discussions in the Military-Revolutionary Committee', wrote secretary Gusev himself towards the end of November,

of the arrangement of the MRC's work, and decisions have been taken on forming departments and commissions, members of the MRC being assigned to each department, and on a fixed roster of Bureau members, etc.

All these decisions have failed to be implemented, and the MRC's work has been carried on in the former disorderly chaotic way. There is no hope of giving order to the MRC's work, as members' attendance at meetings of the Committee is quite random and the meetings lack a properly drawn-up agenda, with minor matters not infrequently pushing out large and important issues.[46]

By this time the retention of the MRC was already in question. As early as 15 November the Council of People's Commissars had discussed inconclusively whether to abolish it or simply to prune it of some of its functions.[47] Ten days later the Sovnarkom returned to the issue, and after considering a proposal by Uritsky to gradually wind up the MRC, and one by Latsis to transform it into a department of the CEC for combating counter-revolution, adopted a motion by Lenin to divest it of a number of its functions, transferring these to the relevant people's commissariats. Thus the work of supplying food and clothing to the Army and of sending food procurement missions to the rural areas was transferred to the Commissariat of Food Supplies, the issue of passports to the Commissariat of Foreign Affairs, the control of military commissars to the War Commissariat, and so on.[48]

The abolition of the MRC was finally decreed on 5 December. A Liquidation Commission was appointed to wind up its affairs and to carry out *pro tem* urgent tasks of combating counter-revolution.[49] Meanwhile moves were in train for the creation of a new body to take over this last remaining function. On the initiative of Felix Dzerzhinsky, one of its senior members, the MRC had resolved on 21 November on the desirability of setting up a special commission for combating counter-revolution.[50] The issue was brought to a head immediately after the abolition of the MRC by a threatened strike of government officials, and the Sovnarkom resolved on 6 December to 'entrust cde. Dzerzhinsky with forming a special commission to clarify the possibility of combating such a strike by the most energetic revolutionary measures, and for clarifying the means of suppressing malicious sabotage'.[51] This gave Dzerzhinsky the opportunity to press on Sovnarkom the idea first aired in the MRC a fortnight earlier to create a special government organ to combat counter-revolution. He had his proposals ready the very next day, and these were duly endorsed by the Sovnarkom. Thus there came into existence the All-Russian Extraordinary Commission for Combating Counter-Revolution, Speculation and Sabotage (the

Vecheka), whose primary task was formulated as 'tracking down and liquidating all counter-revolutionary and sabotage attempts and actions throughout Russia, irrespective of from whom they stem'.[52] This organisation, perpetuated under various titles down to the present KGB, was the MRC's most fateful legacy to the infant Soviet state, though there can be little doubt that, even without the MRC's mediation, the new regime would have regarded a powerful political police as essential, as had their Tsarist predecessors.

Six weeks after the establishment of the new regime, the interim 'government' of the MRC was at an end, and its improvised, amateur administration was giving way to regular procedures of government, pursued by a new complex of full-time officials staffing the Sovnarkom and the inherited bureaucratic machine, in its new guise of 'people's commissariats'.

Many writers have observed what Leiden and Schmitt term the 'destruction–reconstruction dyad', the overlapping phases of a revolution.[53] While not originally designed as such, the MRC came through the logic of circumstances to be an institutional embodiment of this 'destruction–reconstruction dyad'. More broadly, one might view it as a structural coupling device linking two successive political systems.

And this, perhaps, is all that need be said. And yet this account of the origin, development and demise of the MRC leaves us with certain puzzles. To explore these thoroughly would take us too far from our central topic of Sovnarkom, but a brief consideration will help throw certain features of Sovnarkom itself into sharper relief.

History is replete with *ad hoc* bodies thrown up in the heat of revolution that subsequently evolve into permanent institutions of government. That the MRC failed to be so institutionalised is therefore scarcely explained by its intended roles as merely a temporary device for seizing power and placing it in the hands of other bodies, first and foremost the Sovnarkom.[54] Nor is it fully explained by reference to Sovnarkom's greater 'legitimacy', for both were creations of the same bid for power, both claimed their authority to derive from the soviets, and both needed to build up their legitimacy in the eyes of the public *after* the event. An opposite question also suggests itself: was the MRC really indispensable as a stop-gap organ of civil rule? The effectiveness of the MRC in large part rested, as we have seen, on its improvised, *ad hoc* style of operation.

But organisationally the MRC had only the shortest of starts on Sovnarkom, and if it could improvise, what was to stop Sovnarkom from improvising too?

An essential factor in approaching these questions is the organisational character envisaged from the outset for Sovnarkom. As we have noted, the resolution establishing Sovnarkom, while providing for elements of collective decision-making and for linkages with 'mass' organisations, also prescribed specific areas of responsibility for each member of the government and tied these into the existing structure of administration. This bureaucratic aspect of the concept of Sovnarkom could scarcely contrast more with the highly 'organic' character – to use the term suggested by Burns and Stalker – of the MRC. These authors, in their study of industrial firms in Britain, distinguished two management systems, which they termed 'mechanistic' and 'organic', the former associated with a predominance of routine, 'programmed' decisions, and the latter with a predominance of *ad hoc*, 'non-programmed' decisions.[55] In mechanistic systems there is a clear allocation of distinct roles and the methods, duties and powers attaching to them, and these are arranged in a command hierarchy, 'with information flowing up through a succession of filters, and decisions and instructions flowing downwards through a succession of amplifiers'.[56] In organic systems, by contrast,

individuals have to perform their special tasks in the light of their knowledge of the tasks of the firm as a whole. Jobs lose much of their formal definition in terms of methods, duties and powers, which have to be redefined continually by interaction with others participating in a task. Interaction runs laterally as much as vertically. Communication between people of different ranks tends to resemble lateral consultation rather than vertical command. Omniscience can no longer be imputed to the head of the concern.[57]

The two systems are not mutually exclusive, but constitute poles in a continuum. Burns and Stalker discovered that firms involved in major technical innovation, and constantly faced with unforeseen tasks which did not resolve themselves into a set of sub-tasks fitting the pre-existing pattern of roles, tended, often without anyone willing it, to transform their management system in the direction of the organic pole.

Although it may seem a far cry from contemporary British industrial firms to the government institutions of revolutionary Russia, the organic–mechanistic distinction is applicable to the analysis of most

administrative systems and can often reveal the logic of arrangements that seem inexplicable in terms of conventional administrative
theory.[58] It will be clear now from our account of the MRC that it
possessed an extreme form of the organic system, and the appropri-
ateness of this to the circumstances scarcely needs elaborating. As
Walter Pietsch puts it, 'the Committee was thus able to adapt itself
to every change in the mood of the revolutionary masses, to assume
the greatest variety of organisational forms, and to react to every
change of situation, since its own structure was supremely flexible'.[59]
In a revolution most tasks are by definition novel, and the context in
which the Bolshevik leaders operated was analogous to that facing
the management of an industrial organisation going over to a radically new technology. The MRC's organic system was not consciously contrived (remember those repeated attempts to make it
more mechanistic) nor, on the other hand, was it simply the consequence of the lack of administrative experience or organisational
discipline of those involved. The system emerged amongst men
dedicated to a common goal and seeking under enormous pressure
to cope with a constant stream of urgent and unfamiliar tasks, men
for whom 'coping' was essential and not to be frustrated by pre-
ordained relationships or role-distribution.

Meanwhile, however, the Soviet leadership was engaged not only
with the current crisis, but also with enacting the patterns of the
future society. From the first days of the new regime decrees initiating new norms and programmes in every field of social life issued
in rapid sequence from Sovnarkom and the CEC. To implement
and manage these, programmed action was clearly needed and, what
is more, was seen to be needed. This perception of the need for
programmed action and the structures to accommodate it may not
chime in with the more utopian passages in *The State and Revolution*, but it accords well with the organisational traditions of
Bolshevism, and reflects Lenin's overwhelming concern, once in
power, with precision, discipline and accountability in government.
In this context the old ministries and government departments were
perceived as a resource of crucial importance, since they offered
established channels of command and information, and patterns of
specialised roles. As we shall see in Chapter 4, within three weeks of
the overthrow of the Provisional Government, Lenin had set about
merging the new people's commissariats, heretofore operating
from the Smolny Institute, with the old administrative machine,

and establishing decision-making structures and procedures within Sovnarkom congruent with the structures and procedures of this machine.

Thus, alongside the organically operating MRC, which bore the brunt of day-to-day crises, new, more mechanistic systems were being created, and as these began to operate, crossed lines soon became frequent. Overlapping of jurisdictions and flux of roles, acceptable *within* the MRC, could not be tolerated *between* it and Sovnarkom without frustrating the latter's efforts to evolve effective mechanistic systems. What was involved here was not simply organisational rivalry (there was far less of this than might have been anticipated), but tension between the imperatives of ushering in the new and of making it work. Within the MRC itself this tension manifested itself in increasing exasperation at its own entrenched organic pattern, well illustrated by the *cri de coeur* of its secretary Gusev, quoted above. For Sovnarkom and its Chairman, nothing less than the dismantling of the MRC and the distribution of its functions among the 'regular', specialised agencies of government would suffice for, while Sovnarkom was still far from achieving a fully operative and effective mechanistic system, further progress in this direction was blocked as long as the MRC was in the field. The inevitability of dismantling, despite sharp disputes over timing and details, seems to have been accepted by all concerned.

3

Sovnarkom takes over

What distinguished the Council of People's Commissars from the other supreme bodies established by the Bolshevik regime was that it had direct responsibility for the inherited central machinery of government, which it was supposed to drastically purge and refashion for the purposes of the revolution, and through this machinery for the field administrative units of the State. In order to exercise this role, however, it had to accomplish two things: to develop effective internal procedures for taking decisions and controlling their implementation, and to establish its authority over the various ministries and other government agencies and get them working for the 'Workers' and Peasants' Government'. We shall be giving separate consideration to these two topics in this chapter and the next, but it must be borne in mind that the developments described occurred simultaneously and were mutually dependent. First of all, however, we must take note of the political circumstances amid which these developments took place.

The four months when the Council of People's Commissars and the other supreme organs of Soviet rule all continued to operate from the Smolny Institute in Petrograd were a period of continuous flux and uncertainty. There were early abortive attempts to overthrow the infant Soviet regime by force, and the possibility of more massive 'counter-revolutionary' blows was constantly present. It was long in doubt whether the writ of revolutionary Petrograd could be made to run effectively in the country at large, or whether the tragic experience of the Paris Commune would be repeated. There was the problem of relationships with the Left SR allies – and, indeed, with the other socialist parties as well. Behind all this, and growing constantly more pressing, was the problem of the War: it was one thing to decree peace, another to achieve it. And finally, there were the sharp differences which these problems, and particularly the last two, generated among the Bolshevik leaders themselves.

The Bolsheviks undertook the seizure of power divided not only over what kind of revolution they were making[1] but also over the place of their party in the revolutionary process. At one extreme Lenin, while accepting the expediency of including some Left SR representation in the Government, and of ruling through the soviets, was concerned above all to win power *for his party*, and was prepared, if necessary to seize power *against* the soviets. At the other extreme was the view, perhaps predominant in the party at large, that the essence of the Revolution was 'all power to the soviets', which meant the participation of all the socialist parties.[2] Two members of the Central Committee, Zinoviev and Kamenev, had voted against the armed rising, and later sought to postpone it till the Congress of Soviets convened. On 26 October, between the two sessions of the Congress, there were feverish negotiations with the Left SRs, which broke down on the insistence of the latter that they would enter the Government only as part of a grand socialist coalition. Though a large part of the Bolshevik leadership also favoured a broadly-based coalition, Lenin's view, as reported by Krupskaya, was that this would be tantamount to 'harnessing to the Soviet cart the swan, the pike and the crab, setting up a government incapable of working harmoniously, and of even moving from the spot'.[3] The two great questions of the composition of the 'Workers' and Peasants' Government' and of its structure were thus being argued out during the same hectic hours in the midst of the Congress, and the issues involved must often have become interwoven, but unfortunately no details of these discussions are available.[4] The upshot, as we have seen, was a Council of People's Commissars consisting solely of Bolsheviks, which the Left SRs agreed to support, while retaining their independence of action.

The coalition issue became critical again just four days later. A rising of military cadets in Petrograd had just been suppressed, Kerensky was advancing on the capital, and at this point the Central Executive Committee of the Railwaymen's Union threatened a strike if a coalition were not formed. Lenin agreed to enter into discussions in order to gain time, but some of his colleagues, who entertained theoretical or tactical misgivings about the one-party dictatorship, supported the coalition proposals and, when Lenin eventually won Central Committee support to break off the discussions, there were several resignations from leading bodies, including three (Rykov, Nogin and Milyutin) from Sovnarkom.

Meanwhile two of the People's Commissars appointed on 26 October (Skvortsov-Stepanov and Oppokov-Lomov) had failed to take up their duties, the former choosing to remain working in Moscow and the latter being sent there on a special assignment by the Central Committee. Hence within the very first days of the Council's existence it was necessary to find replacements for five of its fifteen original members.[5]

In the middle of November new political developments effected a sharp change in the relations between the Bolsheviks and the Left SRs. The results of the elections to the Constituent Assembly impressed on Lenin the precariousness of his popular support and the consequent need to broaden the base of his regime. Meanwhile the Left SRs, having failed to achieve a grand socialist coalition, and having definitely split with the rest of the Socialist-Revolutionary Party, perceived a danger of becoming isolated and ineffectual. Both parties also had an interest in discrediting and 'upstaging' the Constituent Assembly, with its majority of Right SRs and other opposition delegates. The Second All-Russian Congress of Peasants' Deputies, which convened at this time, and contained a majority of Left SRs, provided the opportunity they needed. It both gave substance to their claims that the Constituent Assembly was unrepresentative, and served as occasion for a Bolshevik–Left SR deal. To the 108 existing members of the CEC (the 101 originally elected plus seven since coopted) there were now added an equal number elected by the Congress of Peasants' Deputies, 100 delegates of military and naval units, and 50 trade union delegates – making over 350 in all. The Bolsheviks further agreed to a decree reaffirming the responsibility of Sovnarkom to the CEC (see Chapter 12), and to the inclusion of Left SR representatives in Sovnarkom.[6]

Initially, as decreed on 17 November, the Left SRs were given the Ministry (*sic*) of Agriculture, and the right of having representatives on the boards of all other commissariats, the Bolsheviks for their part nominating a representative to the Agriculture Board. Soon afterwards A. L. Kolegaev was appointed People's Commissar for Agriculture.[7] Meanwhile discussions continued, culminating in a further agreement on 10 December, which provided for the addition of six more Left SRs to Sovnarkom. Those appointed were I. Z. Shteinberg (Justice), V. Ye. Trutovsky (Local Government – a new commissariat), P. P. Proshyan (Posts and Telegraphs), V. A. Karelin (Properties of the Republic – also new, taking over the cultural and other facilities formerly belonging to the imperial court) and V. A. Algasov and...Mikhailov (People's Commissars without Portfolio and voting members of the Board of the Commissariat of Internal Affairs).[8]

Having broadened and strengthened his basis of support, Lenin went into attack on the Constituent Assembly. There was an intense campaign of propaganda and threats. The Cadet Party was declared illegal, and several Right SR leaders were arrested. By the time the Assembly convened on 5 January 1918, its political foundations had been undermined, and the Bolsheviks had no difficulty in dispersing it after the first day's sitting.[9] The word 'provisional' was now dropped from Sovnarkom's alternative title of 'Workers' and Peasants' Government', and the Third Congress of Soviets, timed to follow immediately after the Constituent Assembly, gave approval to its dispersal, and appropriated its prerogatives, authorising the preparation of a draft constitution of the Republic to be submitted to the next Congress.[10]

While the operation of the Soviet government during its brief two-party phase deserves much fuller study than it has yet received, it would take us too far from our main theme to attempt this here, especially as the coalition episode left little mark on the further evolution of Sovnarkom. Suffice it to mention that the initial spirit of cooperation was not unmarred by a considerable mutual wariness, which was soon to generate friction and conflicts, placing the coalition under severe strain well before the final break. For the student of political structures and processes, special interest attaches to the jurisdictional disputes which arose within the Council between Bolshevik and Left SR-controlled commissariats. For instance, there were repeated and unsuccessful efforts by the Left SRs to subject the Vecheka and the investigating commissions of the Revolutionary Tribunal to control by the Justice Commissariat. There were disputes over the structure and control of local government bodies between the Commissariat for Internal Affairs (Bolshevik), and the Commissariat for Local Government (Left SR). The Left SRs also attempted to increase their influence in provincial centres by setting up an Other Cities Department in the Commissariat for Posts and Telegraphs.[11]

The Brest-Litovsk Treaty, which provoked the final rupture with the Left SRs, also produced a new split among the Bolshevik leaders themselves. Since 1915, Lenin's oft-reaffirmed international strategy had linked peace with revolution, the role of the Russian Revolution being to spark off revolutionary uprisings in the imperialist and colonial countries, allowing the transformation of the imperialist war into a revolutionary war. However, the Bolsheviks won support in the soviets during 1917 largely through their promise of peace – in effect at any price. Meanwhile, the establishment of the Soviet regime generated in some of its supporters a militant desire to defend the revolutionary Fatherland against the imperialist aggressors. These diverse attitudes were found in the leadership as well as the rank-and-file and, as peace talks with the Germans got under way in December, the contradictions between them became obvious and gave rise to heated disputes. In practice, the option of revolutionary war was excluded by the demoralisation of the Russian army, which had been completed by Bolshevik propaganda advocating peace and fraternisation. This was clearly recognised by Lenin, but not by some of his colleagues. Throughout the winter the Bolshevik party was locked in bitter debate on this great issue, and when on 23 February the Central Committee finally voted on Lenin's proposal to accept the harsh German peace terms, the vote was seven in favour, four against, and four abstentions. Once again, a substantial minority of the Bolshevik leadership withdrew from their party and government positions, including People's Commissars Kollontai, Dybenko, Osinsky and V. M. Smirnov (who had been appointed Trade and Industry Commissar only three weeks earlier). Trotsky also resigned as Foreign Affairs Commissar, but was promptly given another portfolio. In March Lenin won a large majority for the Brest-Litovsk peace both in the Seventh Congress of the party and the Fourth Congress of Soviets. Thereupon the Left SRs, who were equally unable to accept Lenin's choice of a humiliating peace with the 'imperialists' rather than revolutionary war, finally withdrew from Sovnarkom, though for the time being they maintained a limited cooperation with the Bolsheviks, retaining positions on the boards of individual commissariats as well as their membership in the CEC and the local soviets. Single-party rule was restored, and was destined to remain a permanent feature of the Soviet political system.

The German advance in the period preceding Brest-Litovsk, followed by the cession of territory under the Treaty, brought home the danger of retaining the seat of the revolutionary government in

Petrograd, and it was decided to move the central organs of the party, the CEC, Sovnarkom and people's commissariats, to the ancient capital of Moscow, in the heart of European Russia. On 10 March 1918 the members of the Council of People's Commissars and their staff took train for Moscow, and so ended the Council's 'Smolny' period.

These, then, were the political circumstances in which the new government institutions of revolutionary Russia took their first steps. We must now consider where those steps led them.

Early on the morning of 27 October, at the close of the Second Congress of Soviets, the Council of People's Commissars convened for the first time.[12] All its members were present, with the exception of I. I. Skvortsov-Stepanov, appointed Finance Commissar but, as noted, still in Moscow and destined to remain there.[13] The first meeting seems to have confined itself to organisational matters and the Council was convened again on the afternoon of the same day, this time to contract some important political business, including approval of the Decree on the Press and agreement on the main lines of a regulation on 'workers' control'.[14]

Despite these auspicious beginnings, it was to be several weeks before Sovnarkom evolved into a regularly functioning body. The next two recorded meetings were held on 3 and 15 November, and while it may possibly have convened on other occasions in between, it is clear that no regular pattern of formal meetings emerged in the first three weeks of the Council's existence.[15]

This did not prevent Sovnarkom from asserting from the first its authority as the 'Government' of Soviet Russia, by virtue of the number and importance of the decrees issued in its name. At this stage, however, the majority of these decrees were not considered at Council meetings, but were apparently agreed on by the Commissars directly concerned, in consultation with officials of the Council. According to Yu. Larin, Head of the Council's Legislation Bureau, this procedure applied to thirteen of the fifteen decrees published in the first issue of the new Government gazette (the *Sobraniye uzakonenii i rasporyazhenii Raboche-Krest'yanskogo Pravitel'stva*).[16]

The failure of Sovnarkom to achieve instant institutionalisation is scarcely surprising, especially when one considers the conditions under which its members were operating. As we have seen, for some weeks after the seizure of power it was the Military Revolutionary Committee which had immediate control of the Bolshevik cadres in the capital and which was making – and carrying out – the most immediate decisions of the revolutionary regime. Meanwhile major policy issues were being thrashed out in the party Central Committee. The two supreme bodies of the Soviet state, the Central Executive Committee of the Congress of Soviets (the CEC) and the Council of People's Commissars, thus fell between two stools so far as the practical business of the new regime was concerned. Their chief role in this period was to give formal expression to the major decisions of the regime, especially those having a 'programmatic' character. Moreover, in their performance of this role, it was not clear at this stage – nor, as we shall see in Chapter 12, for some time to come – just where the responsibilities of the CEC ended and those of Sovnarkom began. Of all these bodies, Sovnarkom was the newest and the last to acquire the basic human and material requirements of a functioning institution.

Shortly after the seizure of power Lenin appointed V. D. Bonch-Bruyevich as Head of the Sovnarkom Chancellery (*Upravlyayushchii delami* – literally 'Administrator of Affairs'), with full powers to establish a 'powerful apparatus', and by 30 October the latter had recruited his first staff member, the 25-year-old N. P. Gorbunov, who was appointed Sovnarkom Secretary.[17] It was to be another four days before a typist was found, and meanwhile Gorbunov was obliged himself to type out Council documents with two fingers.[18] Meanwhile in the first week or so the entire Chancellery of the 'Workers' and Peasants' Government' consisted of a single desk and it was short of paper, pencils and other office requisites.[19] In the following fortnight the efforts to build up a working 'apparatus' accelerated, and by mid-November the staff had risen to 21, Sovnarkom had acquired its own letter-headed paper and official stamps, office space had been found, partioned up and furnished on the third floor of the Smolny Institute, and a telephone switchboard installed.[20]

Likewise, it was to take several weeks before Sovnarkom was provided with a 'cabinet room' for its meetings. The first meetings, on 27 October, were probably held in the Bolshevik caucus room on the second floor of the Smolny Institute.[21] Within a day or so, a small office was set up for Lenin on the third floor, and this is where Sovnarkom held its next meetings, in cramped and inconvenient conditions that have been described by Alexandra Kollontai:

The set-up for meetings of Sovnarkom was businesslike to a fault. Vladimir Ilyich's desk was shoved up against the wall and the lamp was hanging over it. We people's commissars sat around Vladimir Ilyich and partly behind his back. Nearer the window there was the desk of Sovnarkom secretary N. P. Gorbunov, who took the minutes. Whenever Lenin gave someone the floor or issued instructions to Gorbunov, he had to turn around, but no one at that time thought of moving the desk, we were busy with larger matters. It was no time to be thinking about one's own convenience![22]

When in mid-November the Sovnarkom Secretariat eventually acquired its office (also on the third floor), Sovnarkom meetings were transferred there. It was only in December that a special meeting room was provided, the so-called 'Smolny red room', close by the Secretariat office.[23]

A fact which greatly influenced the mode of operation of Sovnarkom in this initial period was that the 'people's commissariats' themselves, i.e. the commissars, board members and their immediate staff, were not yet established in the various departments of state they were set up to administer but, as we have seen, remained at Smolny. Here they spent their days and evenings in constant direct contact with each other and with the rest of the Bolshevik leadership. This helps to explain the apparent paucity of formal meetings. There was little need for regular meeting times, and the commissars could be brought together in smaller or larger groups as the need for particular decisions required.[24] Moreover, since several of the commissars were at the same time members of other revolutionary bodies also operating from Smolny, since no patterns had yet evolved for the channelling and processing of business, and there had been no time for these men to develop an identification with particular institutions rather than the revolutionary regime as a whole, it is not surprising that the boundaries of Sovnarkom as a decision-making body were extremely vague at this stage. Smolny is in fact best thought of as a single fluid complex of government, in which the point where a matter requiring decision was taken up, the various individuals who became involved, and the channels along which communications flowed till it was resolved, often bore little relation to the formal structure. Decision-making, in fact, took on that 'concentric' structure which Burns and Stalker have identified as being characteristic of 'organic' systems, and which we observed in the previous chapter was manifested in high degree by the Military Revolutionary Committee. The 'organic' character of the Smolny headquarters complex comes through in accounts by contemporary observers and partici-

pants, couched though these be in the revolutionary Marxist terminology of the time. 'Not only events themselves', wrote A. A. Yoffe
in 1919, 'but also particular proposals, decisions and so on, it seemed,
arose and were created not by individuals, but by the whole revolutionary mass, by the spontaneous development of the revolution.'[25]

It was only after the middle of November that Sovnarkom began
to disengage itself from the Smolny complex and to emerge as a
distinct institution. As we have seen, it took till then to acquire the
necessary human and material resources and to begin seriously the
task of taking over the central administrative apparatus of the state.
An important turning point was the decision, issued on 15 November,
that commissars should begin functioning from offices situated in
their various departments of government. 'The Council of People's
Commissars remains at Smolny. The People's Commissars are to
transfer their work to the appropriate ministries, nominating set
hours for their attendance there. Towards evening the commissars
will gather at Smolny for consultation and for achieving contact
with other democratic organisations.'[26] It is not clear how long it
took to wind up the separate apparatuses of the commissariats in
Smolny[27] and the ambiguities in the people's commissars' situation
– between Smolny and 'ministry' – was reflected in inconsistencies
in the titles by which they were referred to during this period –
sometimes the People's Commissar for such-and-such, and sometimes
the People's Commissar for the *Ministry* of such-and-such.[28] However, the fact that henceforth people's commissars were usually not
available in Smolny during the day tended to break down existing
patterns of deciding matters as they came up by informal consultation, and necessitated greater reliance on regular formal meetings.

It was in fact from mid-November that Sovnarkom began meeting
regularly once a day, and sometimes twice. As a rule meetings
commenced between 5 and 8 p.m. and usually continued till late in
the evening, sometimes into the early hours of the morning.[29]
The Council's minutes indicate that it met 77 times between 15
November and its final meeting before transferring to Moscow on
10 March 1918 – a period of 102 days.[30] Since 25 of these meetings
were held in December,[31] and the Council met almost daily in the
second half of November, there must have been some falling off in
the frequency of meetings after the New Year.

It was in this period that the basic procedures of Sovnarkom as
an executive body were worked out.[32] In addition to the Council

members, meetings were usually attended by the Head of Chancellery Bonch-Bruyevich and the Secretary Gorbunov, and also by Yakov Sverdlov in his capacity as Chairman of the CEC. In addition, officials and board members from various commissariats were brought in to meetings either to report to the Council or to represent the interests of their commissariats on particular questions. Given the frequency of meetings and the multifarious responsibilities of several commissars it is not surprising that absences were frequent. Only five of the members attended nineteen or more of the twenty-five meetings held in December.[33] There was a marked tendency for the number of persons present at meetings to grow as the practice of inviting extra representatives of the commissariats became entrenched. The 15 November meeting was attended by seven Council members, Bonch-Bruyevich and three members of the Military Revolutionary Committtee – eleven in all. The next day eighteen attended, and on 13 December (the first meeting attended by Left SR commissars) there were twenty-three. Later in the month attendances sometimes approached thirty.[34] Lenin was evidently concerned at this tendency and took a number of steps to define more strictly the conditions under which non-members might attend. As early as 30 November the Council resolved that 'representatives of those boards (people's commissariats) affected by the matter under consideration are to be present at meetings of the Council of People's Commissars'.[35] On 23 January he had Sovnarkom approve a further decision authorising deputies to attend with voting rights in the place of absent commissars only in cases specifically approved by the Council. Some weeks later he had occasion to rebuke Gorbunov for allowing officials to be present when matters not affecting their commissariats were under discussion.[36]

Lenin clearly devoted much thought and effort to establishing effective, businesslike processes in Sovnarkom, paying infinite attention to detail and behaving towards his colleagues rather like a firm but good-humoured if occasionally irascible schoolmaster. The easy-going, spontaneous style of the first two or three weeks was soon a thing of the past, as rules were evolved and enforced with increasing severity by the Chairman. There was to be no more drifting in and out, and Lenin's growing exasperation with latecomers prompted him to introduce from 29 December a system of fines – five roubles for a half-hour late, ten roubles for an hour – in the absence of advance written warning to the Secretary giving adequate reasons.[37]

Lenin insisted on notice of agenda items being submitted to the Secretary in writing, with a brief exposition of the matter at issue, outline of the proposed decision (including specification of any funds required), and a statement as to whether other interested commissariats had been consulted, with their comments attached where appropriate.[38] The prepared agenda was not, however, treated as sacrosanct. Meetings normally opened with a discussion of proposals for additional items, for transferring consideration of agenda items to other bodies, and for changing the order of business, and Lenin himself frequently introduced a number of new matters requiring in his view immediate decision.[39]

Following a discussion in the Council on 20 November, there was an interesting early attempt to work out an 'internal constitution' for Sovnarkom. The main lines were sketched out and the CEC was invited to consider the matter with a view to embodying the proposals in a statute. This was entrusted to Justice Commissar Stuchka, who presented a draft to the Council at its meeting on 30 November. The text of this proposed 'internal constitution' is unfortunately unavailable, but it evidently provided, *inter alia*, for two standing committees, one on estimates and one on 'implementation' (*ispolnitel'naya komissiya*). The Council, however, decided against adopting a 'written constitution' and agreed only to the resolution restricting attendance by non-members.[40]

Despite the almost daily meetings of the Council during this period, agendas tended to be heavy. At the eleven meetings held between 15 and 25 November, agenda items averaged fourteen, and sometimes exceeded twenty. This was another problem to which the Chairman addressed himself. Gorbunov was instructed to abstain from placing on the agenda certain categories of items which could be settled administratively.[41] Moreover, the Council adopted from the first the practice of appointing *ad hoc* commissions to work out resolutions on particular agenda items or to look further into the matters concerned. The questions entrusted to such commissions during the first few weeks of the Council's existence included a draft decision on *volost'* (rural district) committees, a decree on revolutionary courts, a draft ultimatum to the Ukrainian Rada, changes in the composition of the Government connected with the negotiations with the Left SRs, a manifesto on socialist war, the protection of Polish objects of historical and artistic value, and a decree on liability for work in the Posts and Telegraphs Department.[42]

In addition to these *ad hoc* commissions, the need was soon perceived for some kind of standing sub-committee to deal with matters
of relatively minor importance, particularly requests for financial
allocations, which because they involved more than one commissariat
or for some other reason required decision at the highest level – by
December at least the Soviet leadership had picked up the old slang
term applied by senior Tsarist officials to such matters – 'vermicelli'.
Such a body did in fact soon emerge, evolving out of the efforts we
have already referred to to restrict the agenda of Sovnarkom meetings and divest it of minor items. On 20 November the Council
resolved that 'all financial submissions are to be directed to the
appropriate Ministry [*sic*], then to the Treasury, then to the Ministry
of Finance and to State Control, and only after that to the Council
of People's Commissars'.[43] From this point it was only one step to
combining the preliminary stages in one by having senior representatives of the departments concerned consider these matters in committee. This step was taken on 4 December in the form of a further
Sovnarkom decision: 'Matters involving finance and not subject to
dispute are to be decided by the people's commissars of the department concerned, of Finance and of State Control and referred to
Sovnarkom for the appropriate signatures.'[44] The early history of
this 'vermicelli commission' has recently been reconstructed for the
first time by Soviet historians, and the best available account is that
by M. P. Iroshnikov. According to Iroshnikov, its composition and
procedures were further considered by the Council on 18, 23 and 30
December. On the 23 it was decided to constitute the 'vermicelli
commission' of representatives of the Commissariats of Labour, War
and Food Supplies. A week later, on account of the excessive workload of the War Commissar Podvoisky, he was replaced by the
Commissar for Local Government, the Left SR Trutovsky. On the
same day, 30 December, the commission was officially referred to for
the first time as the 'Little Council' (*Maly Sovet*). Gorbunov was
to be secretary of both bodies.[45]

Iroshnikov quotes extensively from the unpublished memoirs of
D. P. Bogolepov, who frequently attended the early meetings of the
Little Council in his capacity as Finance Commissariat member 'in
charge of money questions'. According to Bogolepov,

its actual establishment was evoked by the circumstance that the Full
Sovnarkom wished to rid itself of the 'vermicelli'. . .But it was quite clear
that such 'vermicelli' questions nevertheless needed to be considered some-

where or other and considered in such a way that they would not escape entirely from control by the Full Sovnarkom or at least by its Chairman. That is why it was decided in December 1917 to set up under the chairmanship of comrade Shlyapnikov [People's Commissar for Labour] a Little Council of People's Commissars for the consideration of minor questions.

There were further membership changes: Shlyapnikov remained a member but the chairmanship fluctuated; Trutovsky was often replaced by one of the other Left SR Commissars, and the Food Supplies Commissar by the Commissar for Finance or by one of his deputies. At first the Little Sovnarkom met only once a week, on Wednesdays, its agenda consisting mainly of items discarded as 'vermicelli' by the Full Sovnarkom. From the beginning it was Lenin who was the effective master of the Little Council, and who sanctioned most of its decisions. 'It is simply amazing', writes Bogolepov, 'that such minor matters, and it was specifically such matters and them alone that formed the chosen speciality of the Little Council, should have attracted so much attention and the most painstaking consideration by Lenin, who, one might have thought, had enough work and worries without that.'[46]

An intriguing aspect of the emergence of the Little Sovnarkom, first pointed out by the constitutional lawyer Durdenevsky in 1922 but subsequently overlooked by Soviet and foreign scholars, was that it paralleled developments in the Council of Ministers when this body was established following the 1905 Revolution. Within a few months the Council of Ministers spawned a Little Council, consisting of deputy ministers, to take care of the 'vermicelli' and prepare business for the full Council. The existence of this body remained a secret till 1909, when an order regularising its status and functions was published.[47] Was this simply a case of like needs giving rise to like solutions? The identity of nomenclature – in both cases the terms 'Big' (which we render as 'Full') and 'Little' Council (*Bol'shoi Sovet* and *Maly Sovet*) were used – immediately suggests there was more to it than this. Furthermore, by the time the Little Sovnarkom came into existence, the Bolshevik Government enjoyed the services of senior officials of the old Council of Ministers certain of whom must have been familiar with the role of the Little Council and were now well-placed to suggest adopting this example. The main link may have been Treasury Director Trokhimovsky, who worked directly under Deputy Finance Commissar Bogolepov. It was the latter who proposed the arrangements on 4 December which led to the institutionalisation of the Little Sovnarkom, and he evidently played a key organisational role in its earliest period.[48] The Little Sovnarkom, which became a major component of Lenin's government, was therefore almost certainly an institutional borrowing from the old regime.

The initial contribution of the Little Council to relieving Sovnarkom's load was disappointing, owing partly to the relative infrequency of its meetings, its shifting membership and also, in Iroshnikov's view, to the lack of confidence among its members in their authority to settle many questions. This gave rise to a further Sovnarkom decision on 7 January aimed at strengthening the Little Council's arm. The people's commissars constituting it were obliged to attend its meetings personally or at least have one of their deputies attend, and all other commissars were instructed to allocate board members to assist in its work. From the time of its next meeting, on 9 January, minutes of the Little Council's proceedings were recorded and procedural rules were adopted: at least two of the three commissars constituting its basic membership had to be present at each meeting. Meetings were supposed to be held three times a week (they were not), the agenda was closed two days in advance (though there was provision for adding particularly urgent matters), a detailed submission on each agenda item was required, the official responsible for the submission was obliged to attend as well as representatives of all departments affected, and if all necessary officials were not present or the submission contained insufficient information the matter was to go to the bottom of the agenda.[49] On 23 January 1918 the Little Sovnarkom was renamed the 'Commission of Sovnarkom'.[50] From about this time, however, it went into a period of relative quiescence which lasted till after the transfer of the Government to Moscow. The reason for this was probably the preoccupation of the leadership with the Brest-Litovsk talks, and the consequent difficulty of getting Little Sovnarkom decisions sanctioned by its parent body.[51]

The institutionalisation of Sovnarkom, the formalisation of its procedures, was a process essential to regular and effective government in the new Soviet state. This process, however, inevitably involved some loss of flexibility in responding to the still highly fluid and unpredictable circumstances in which the regime found itself. The need for a body like the Little Council was one reflection of this. Another was the decision on 20 February, when the renewed

German advance appeared to place the very existence of the Soviet regime in jeopardy, to set up a 'Temporary Executive Committee of Sovnarkom', responsible to the full Sovnarkom and entrusted with the conduct of all current state work in periods between the meetings of the Council of People's Commissars.[52] This body consisted of three Bolsheviks (Lenin, Trotsky and Stalin) and two Left SRs (Proshyan and Karelin), and evidently met at least once. With the signature of the Peace Treaty a few days later, however, the need for it disappeared, and nothing further was heard of it.[53]

Although the four and a half months in which Soviet Russia was ruled from the Smolny Institute were a time of constant alarms, flux, and improvisation, and to an informed contemporary observer the initial experience of Sovnarkom must have seemed an odd mixture of grand rhetoric and a pragmatism striving desperately to keep abreast of events, nevertheless certain structural and procedural patterns emerged from this experience, which, as we shall see in the ensuing chapters, remained basic features of the operation of the Soviet government throughout the Lenin period. Indeed, their influence on the operation of the Soviet political system remains important to the present day.

4

Acquiring a bureaucracy

No systematic account yet exists of the early history of the Soviet administrative machine. This book is concerned with the command centre of that machine, the Council of People's Commissars, and the internal structure and operation of the various commissariats and other agencies of government lie outside our field of investigation. Nevertheless the steps whereby Sovnarkom acquired a functioning bureaucracy, largely inherited *via* the Provisional Government from the Imperial regime, deserve our attention, since they tell us much about the emergent character of Sovnarkom itself.

The establishment of the central bureaucracy of the Soviet state passed through three stages. First each of the people's commissars set up an office in Smolny, from which he proceeded to establish contact with his 'ministry' elsewhere in Petrograd. These offices, consisting of a handful of assistants and office-workers, were the original people's commissariats. In the second stage the people's commissars moved into their 'ministries', sometimes with a considerable retinue, but leaving the commissariats themselves behind in Smolny, where they themselves spent part of their time. Finally one by one the commissariats were moved out to the 'ministries', and the two apparatuses began to coalesce. The whole sequence, seriously delayed by the hostility and passive resistance of the bulk of civil servants, and complicated by the confused political events outlined in the previous chapter, dragged on into the early weeks of 1918 and was still incomplete when the Soviet Government moved to Moscow.

In the days following the seizure of power the typical people's commissariat consisted of a table, a couple of chairs, and a piece of paper stuck on the wall behind, bearing the name of the commissariat. By the second half of November most of them were located in two groups – a military group with a chancellery located in a room next to the Military Revolutionary Committee as well as a separate staff of eleven serving the Committee of Commissars of Military and Naval Affairs, and a civil group, comprising the Commissariats of Agriculture, Posts and Telegraphs, Education, Finance, Railways and Nationalities, squeezed into a single suite of offices along with the apparatus of the Sovnarkom itself. The two officials of the Commissariat of Foreign Affairs had a separate room to themselves.[1] The people's commissars, faced with the task of building their commissariats, had no blueprint to work to and, in the majority of cases, little relevant experience to guide them. They felt their way and improvised, constantly in touch with each other and particularly with Lenin, whose detailed involvement in the formation of the commissariats was indicative of the extent to which he identified his own role in the new regime with the institutions of Sovnarkom. In getting their offices working, the people's commissars also depended heavily on the chief administrative officials of Sovnarkom, Bonch-Bruyevich and Gorbunov (see Chapter 9) and on practical help from the Military Revolutionary Committee.[2]

One consequence, and at the same time a contributing cause of the confused conditions of these early weeks, was the constant flux in the leadership of the commissariats. The task of establishing effectively working 'commissions' of leading officials as provided for in the Decree establishing Sovnarkom was complicated not only by changes resulting from the political struggles outlined in Chapter 3, but also by the multiple responsibilities of many of their members, their constant comings and goings on assignments from above or on their own initiative, and by the 'accidents' of personal relationships.

To illustrate the conditions prevailing in this earliest period, we shall take as an example the People's Commissariat for Food Supplies, excerpting at length from the recollections of one of its leaders, P. A. Kozmin, as reported by him in 1920. At the time of the seizure of power, Kozmin had been active in the Military Revolutionary Committee, first in organising motor transport in certain key districts, then in taking over the Petrograd Food Supplies Directorate and seizing the flour-mills.

Towards the end of October, I was put in the newly-formed Food Supplies Commission (the commissariats were then called commissions). We established ourselves on the third floor [of the Smolny Institute] and occupied two desks. Teodorovich [the People's Commissar] was supposed to set up the commissariat. First of all he invited me, then M. I. Kalinin, Yakubov and Manuilsky. We thus represented the first commissariat to be established in Smolny. We had with us in the room one typist, whom we shared with some other commission. [Kozmin then describes the inconclusive arguments within the Commission as to what to do about taking over the Food Supplies Ministry.] Our Commission was attended regularly by Yakubov and myself; Cde Manuilsky dashed in from time to time, as did Cde Kalinin.

It must be said that right off Teodorovich quarrelled with Yakubov. The latter refused to carry out some assignment or other, and Teodorovich complained to me, 'It's terrible with these Left SRs.' Yakubov had never been a Left SR, and was incensed with Teodorovich, shouting 'I will go and tell Ilyich that I can't work here any longer.' However, I persuaded him to stay.

The job was not jelling. Then Teodorovich gathered us all together and proposed that we should stay there while he would travel along the Samara–Zlatoust railway to Siberia, and organise the grain districts in that direction, after which, as he hoped, we would be able to take the Food Supplies Ministry with our bare hands. We had no other plan or solution, so we agreed.

Yakubov and I remained, Manuilsky at this time stopped coming altogether – he was in the Petersburg [*sic*] City Directorate [*uprava*], responsible for distributing consumer goods, I think, and he was also in charge of the Zabalkansky *raion* and certain other jobs. . .

At the same time Cde Podvoisky began involving himself in Food Supply matters. He was then a member of the Board of the People's Commissariat of Military Affairs and was concerned about the supply of foodstuffs to Red Guard units. Always one to take on a job with fiery enthusiasm, he energetically set about this one too. . .But Podvoisky had thousands of jobs, all the more so as he was then bearing the full weight of the Military Revolutionary Committee and the whole of the People's Commissariat for Military Affairs, where he worked from one morning through to the next. The [latter's] Board included Cdes Dybenko, Krylenko, Mekhonoshin and Sklyansky, but in fact Krylenko was at the front, Dybenko was busy with his sailors, and Mekhonoshin and Sklyansky getting the apparatus of the [People's Commissariat] organised.

At this period our work had completely ground to a halt, as we were left without a Food Supplies Commissar. We had had absolutely no word from Teodorovich.

It was about 13 or 14 November when Yakubov and I met Cde A. T. Shlikhter, who was Deputy Commissar for Agriculture, since [People's Commissar] V. P. Milyutin had gone off to Moscow. Shlikhter had set about things with despatch. He had turned up in the Agriculture Ministry with some Red Guards. But this produced no results and he was left a commissar without a commissariat. And since we at least had an apparatus of some sort he expressed the wish to stay with us and get on with some more definite job. Yakubov and I then went to Vladimir Ilyich and said 'There's no Teodorovich and no news from him, so give us a temporary commissar, because we do finally have to take over the ministry.' And

Shlikhter was appointed Deputy People's Commissar for Food Supplies. [An account then follows of the takeover of the ministry and the first efforts there to establish a working apparatus.]

Teodorovich arrived at the end of November...The question was raised in Sovnarkom whose work plan to adopt, Shlikhter's or Teodorovich's. It was decided to stick to Shlikhter's proposals...Cde Shlikhter was sent off to Siberia for grain. Manuilsky temporarily replaced him...Soon afterwards Cde A. D. Tsyurupa was appointed People's Commissar for Food Supplies, and he immediately introduced a businesslike atmosphere into the work of the commissariat.[3]

As this account indicates, one could hardly claim that either order, discipline and harmony or clarity and unity of purpose prevailed among the Bolsheviks as they set about the task of building an administrative apparatus. Yet one thing was clearly understood by all: the essential task was to get effective control over the ministries and set them to work. The relationship between commissariat and ministry envisaged by the Bolshevik leaders was unequivocally spelt out in a decree issued on 9 November on the Commission for Education, the first decree of its kind; 'The Ministry should play the role of an executive apparatus under [*pri*] the State Commission for Education.'[4]

With this concept in mind the majority of people's commissars visited 'their' ministries within a few days of the seizure of power, usually taking along a few Red Guards, sometimes accompanied by a handful of colleagues. Everywhere they were met with a wall of hostility and non-cooperation. The officials rejected the legitimacy of the 'Workers' and Peasants' Government' and refused to work for it.[5] That such attitudes should have been widely and deeply held inside the government apparatus is scarcely to be wondered at.[6] Yet the solidarity and discipline displayed by officials in carrying out their passive resistance suggests something more than a spontaneous reaction, and it is clear that a considerable measure of organisation and coordination was achieved through a number of channels. Probably the most important of these were the several unions of employees of various branches of the government, grouped for the purpose of opposing the authority of the Bolshevik regime into a 'Union of Unions of Officials of the State Institutions of Petrograd', numbering several thousand members.[7] An important rallying point was the Petrograd City Duma, which continued to exist alongside the Petrograd Soviet, dominated by the liberal and moderate-left parties, and especially the 'Committee of Public Safety' set up by the Duma on 24 October – the very eve of the Bolshevik seizure of power. Evidently some part was also played by two other bodies carried over from the previous regime: the old pre-Second Congress of Soviets CEC, and the Little Council of Ministers, which continued for a time to operate clandestinely in Petrograd, claiming the authority of the Provisional Government.[8] It is very difficult on the available evidence to evaluate the role and unravel the relationships of these various bodies, but it is clear that between them they provided adequate organisational resources to create something approaching consensus on passive resistance among Petrograd officialdom and to coordinate efforts among the many agencies involved. This consensus reinforced an atmosphere in which collaboration with the Bolsheviks carried an aura of betrayal, and collaborators could be subjected to ostracism, insult or intimidation.[9] One important factor was money. It was unanimously alleged by the Bolsheviks at the time[10] and repeated by later Soviet historians that the 'sabotage' by government officials was heavily financed, partly by funds diverted from official purposes, and partly by contributions supplied by Russian and foreign capitalists and channelled through the various bodies mentioned above. The existence and disbursement of such funds does not seem open to doubt, although their alleged sources have not been convincingly demonstrated. Their prime purpose was to enable officials to be paid a month or two in advance, so that their income for this period would not be jeopardised by threat of sacking by the Soviet regime.[11] The hope was that a few weeks of non-cooperation might be sufficient to bring the Bolsheviks down, since 'the brute force of bayonets' could bring them to power but could not enable them to govern.

While the pattern of non-cooperation varied considerably from one ministry to another, two main strategies were in evidence. The first, employed in the majority of offices, was simple refusal to work. Officials either stayed home, or demonstratively vacated the office when representatives of 'their' commissariat or of the Military Revolutionary Committee descended upon them with demands for compliance. At the same time files and funds were removed or locked away and the whereabouts of the keys concealed. In one instance the 'saboteurs' went so far as to remove the nibs from pens and pour away all the ink.[12]

The second strategy consisted of keeping the office functioning but failing to implement or frustrating Bolshevik decisions and preventing information from reaching the people's commissar. This was the usual pattern in agencies responsible for essential services, especially those serving the capital itself, such as the Ministries of Railways, Posts and Telegraphs, Finance, Food Supplies and Trade and Industry, the State Bank, the Special Supplies Committtee and the Special Office for Food and Fuel Supply. In some cases offices passed over from strategy two to strategy one when Bolshevik pressure reached a certain point. There were also those officials who signed on regularly but simply slacked, doing as little as possible and as inefficiently as possible short of inviting dismissal; these were the so-called 'heroes of the twentieth' – the twentieth day of the month being pay-day. Finally, there were bodies such as the Senate (the supreme judicial body) and the Spiritual Office (responsible for the Church) which continued to operate in the name of the Provisional Government.[13]

The first step in the Bolshevik campaign against this 'sabotage' was to establish control over government finances. The concealment of funds by ministerial officials and passive resistance by the staff of the State Bank left the Bolshevik leadership without money to cover the day-to-day activities of government; the situation was such that the Sovnarkom itself even lacked the funds to buy elementary office requisites. Evidently this was a problem that force alone could solve and in mid-November the Bolsheviks proceeded to arrest senior bank officials and to seize the vaults and safes. Many of the staff then agreed to work provided the Bolsheviks stationed armed guards to demonstrate that they were doing so under duress – thus protecting them from reprisals by their fellow-'saboteurs'. Meanwhile the Bolsheviks had made a major break-through in the Ministry of Finance. The officials of the Treasury Department, believing it their national duty to remain at their posts, refused to participate in the 'sabotage' and within a day of the first contact being made by representatives of the Finance Commissariat, the Director of the Treasury, P. M. Trokhimovsky, had worked out budgeting procedures with them and set in motion arrangements for financing the work of Sovnarkom and the commissariats against credits held in the State Bank for the Provisional Government and the various ministries.[14] The Soviet Government was now in a position both to finance its own activities and to prevent the further diversion of government funds to support the 'sabotage'.

Throughout the first weeks of power the Bolsheviks undertook a number of measures designed to appeal to the more sympathetically disposed officials. There was a constant barrage of exhortation at meetings organised in their offices, at public meetings, in the press and through street-posters, urging them to break with the 'saboteurs' and get to work.[15] The salary scales of top officials were drastically reduced and those of the humbler ranks raised. The salaries of the people's commissars themselves were fixed at 500 rs per month – not much higher than was earned by a skilled worker.[16] While these measures seem to have had little immediate effect, they probably made some contribution to the ultimate change of atmosphere.

More effective than the carrot, however, was the stick. The arrest of members of the Committee of Safety and the abolition of the Petrograd Duma deprived the passive resistance campaign of its most important organisational centre.[17] The sacking and arrest of the more intransigent senior officials decapitated the resistance movement in several ministries and had a markedly intimidating effect on their juniors.[18] Steps were taken to neutralise the effects of salary advances. On 19 November the Sovnarkom issued a decision recommending commissariats to study their ministry accounts to determine whether salaries had been paid to 1 January, and if so to employ whatever measures were necessary to recover them, not stopping at arrest and committal to a revolutionary court. Officials were to be told either to return the money or start work immediately otherwise they would be tried for misappropriating state property.[19]

It was in this context that the remaining leaders of the passive resistance movement resolved early in December on a last desperate measure – a nationwide strike of government officials. As we have seen, this threat was the immediate occasion for the establishment of the Vecheka. Within three weeks the back of the movement was broken. Arrests made on 22 and 30 December, including the Chairman of the Union of Unions, his chief lieutenants, the members and staff of the strike committee and their contacts in the various government offices, destroyed the communications network of the movement and left it leaderless.[20] Nevertheless, many civil servants still held out, believing it would be a cowardly betrayal of their trust to capitulate to the Bolsheviks' strongarm methods on the eve of the Constituent Assembly, which was expected to establish a legitimate government. Lenin's armed dispersal of the Constituent Assembly in early January, however, destroyed all hopes for a peaceful solution to the question of legitimacy, and most officials now accepted the inevitable.

The stepping-up from mid-November of repressive measures against the 'saboteurs' went hand-in-hand with decisive moves to 'occupy' the ministries. As we have seen, Sovnarkom resolved on 15 November that 'the people's commissars are to transfer their work to the corresponding ministries, nominating specific hours for their attendance there'.[21] Up to this point only two ministries – Labour and Foreign Affairs – had been effectively taken over by the Bolsheviks. Now, in the second half of November and early December most other people's commissars and their commissions (those for Finance, Internal Affairs, Education, Military and Naval Affairs, Posts and Telegraphs, Social Welfare, Food Supplies, Agriculture, Justice and State Control) established regularly functioning offices in their ministries, and set about the task of getting the machine to work for them.

In these efforts the Bolsheviks sought help from whoever would work with them. Although a few senior officials were ready to collaborate, and some former officials also came forward and offered their services, it was at first mainly the 'proletarian' employees – guards, cleaners, office messengers and so on – who remained at their posts. The latter were sometimes of considerable value to the Bolsheviks in orienting themselves in their new, thoroughly unfamiliar setting. M. Latsis, in his account of the origins of the People's Commissariat for Internal Affairs, writes:

We did not even know how to set about the job, and we had to resort to the help of the messengers – it was them we learned from at first. You would start by questioning them about the conduct of the bosses, and about their work...and before us there was sketched the outlines and content of the job. The messengers, who had worked in the department for two decades and seen dozens of bosses change, turned out to be quite well-informed...[22]

In addition to these 'proletarian' employees, many of the junior office staff stayed at their jobs in some departments. In the State Bank, for instance, these played a vital part in getting things running. In the course of November the unions representing junior office workers in government and private organisations came out in favour of collaboration with the Bolsheviks. Amongst the few senior officials who were willing to serve the Soviet Government from the first, in addition to the Director of the Treasury, P. M. Trokhimovsky, were N. Faldeyev, the Head of the Forestry Department and former Deputy Minister of the Ministry of Agriculture, M. K.

Lemke, who had been Head of the Provisional Government's office for the Collection of State Documents, and several generals and admirals. Collaborating middle-rank officials often found themselves thrust into high office. Thus it was, for instance, that F. N. Petrov, an official of the Fourth Political Department of the Ministry of Foreign Affairs, came to be appointed Head of the Personnel Department in the Commissariat.[23]

In the efforts of the Bolsheviks to win the cooperation of officialdom, each ministry was a different story. In the Foreign Affairs Ministry there had been moves for a temporary compromise under which the officials, while refusing to acknowledge the authority of the Soviet government and to carry out its political assignments, would continue to handle consular and other routine matters, transfers of funds, functions relating to prisoners of war, and so on. However, this broke down through the insistence of Trotsky and his assistants that keys, files and ciphers be immediately handed over. The officials then went on strike, and Trotsky's men carried on with a handful of collaborators (notably E. D. Polyanov, a university teacher who had formerly worked in the Asian Department of the Ministry), virtually confining their efforts, however, to locating and publishing the 'secret treaties'.[24]

In the Ministry for Food Supplies, whose early vicissitudes we have already noted, determined action was finally taken on 20 November to seize effective control after several previous false starts. At that point the bulk of the employees went on strike, and the Bolsheviks then sought to get things moving with the assistance of commissars who had been appointed to the various departments by the old CEC in May 1917 and who were supported by officials both in the central offices and in the field. The old commissars, after considerable hesitation and under some coercive pressure, agreed to collaborate and the machine began to operate, but not before the Bolsheviks had removed Acting People's Commissar Shlikhter, whose strongarm methods had incensed the officials, and replaced him by A. D. Tsyurupa. This instance illustrates how crucial the inherited structures and their staffs could sometimes be for the Bolsheviks in governing effectively.[25]

The task facing the people's commissars in staffing their offices was twofold – getting the old ministerial officials, or a section of them, back to work, and bringing in new people of their own. Some of their initial efforts in the latter direction verged on the farcical.

Again one of the best instances comes from the Ministry of Food Supplies and relates to the period preceding the compromise with the old CEC commissars.

At this time there appeared before Shlikhter, sent from the People's Commissariat of Labour by Cde Shlyapnikov, an agitated and hysterical youth, recommended by Cde Shlyapnikov as an extraordinarily able person, capable virtually within a few days of forming the apparatus of the Commissariat. . .The name of this young man was Frantsuzov. He received an authorisation from Cde Shlyapnikov. . .in which he was vested with dictatorial powers of appointment, dismissal, etc.

Frantsuzov began by publishing in all our newspapers an advertisement for officials of the Food Supplies Commissariat. The following day. . . a colossal number of people turned up. . .This Frantsuzov proceeded dictatorially. He took on an improbable number of Lord Knows Who, and the final result was an apparatus that simply prevented work. . .

With colossal effort we succeeded in getting work going with these illiterate 'officials' and the former CEC commissars, who stayed on as heads of departments, and, acquiring a taste for 'power' were not inclined to obey the people's commissar.[26]

As Shlyapnikov considered that his commissariat bore the chief responsibility for staffing the government apparatus,[27] it is to be hoped that all its officers were not equally amateurish in their methods. There were, however, several other important sources of staff. At first the Military Revolutionary Committee was probably the most important. Its agents sent on assignments to government offices were frequently taken into the retinue of the people's commissars and stayed on in regular jobs; later in November, as the MRC was wound up, a large proportion of its remaining personnel was then assigned to the commissariats. Somewhat later the structure and staff of the CEC were heavily pruned, to reduce parallelism with the Sovnarkom apparatus, and most of the officials so released were transferred to the commissariats.[28] The richest recruiting ground for officials to staff the government machine, however, after the first few weeks, was the Bolshevik party organisation in Petrograd. By early 1918 the Petrograd Committee and the various district (*raion*) committees of the party had been virtually denuded of Bolsheviks of party standing, superior education or administrative experience, and there was a similar syphoning off of the more able Bolsheviks working in the offices of the soviets in Petrograd. In addition several trade unions helped by recruiting factory employees for the commissariats, while Bolshevik-influenced youth and student organisations as well as military and naval units also played their part.[29]

Meanwhile, as the campaign against 'sabotage' began to take effect, more and more of the old officials drifted back to work.[30] Not all those called were chosen. Many senior officials and the more determined passive resisters were sacked without pension and deprived of their government flats.[31] But the general run of officials got their old jobs back,[32] and those with specialist qualifications were made particularly welcome.[33]

Between December 1917 and February 1918 the disparate groups now staffing the old ministries began to shake down into a functioning central apparatus serving the new Soviet State, with a handful of Bolsheviks – and some Left SRs – occupying most (but not all) of the top posts, a considerable leavening of other personnel recruited through various channels since the seizure of power, and the bulk of officials carried over from the Provisional Government, and beyond that from the Imperial Government.

The same period also saw a number of structural changes. The various departments of the People's Commissariats for Foreign Affairs and Justice were radically reorganised, and there were substantial reorganisations in certain other commissariats.[34] In addition, two new organs of government were created, which were destined before long to assume great importance. The first of these, the Vecheka, has already been mentioned. The second was the All-Russian National Economic Council (VSNKh), formally established on 2 December.[35] The initial impulse for the creation of this body came partly from Bolshevik concern over the 'anarcho-syndicalist' dangers in their own campaign of 'workers' control' in industry, the objects of which were to foster support among the workers and to tame management but not allow the workers a free hand in the running of their workplaces. The National Economic Council integrated the organising centres of the workers' control movement with the government apparatus, and thus helped to ensure that the participation of workers' organisations in the running of industry would be exercised along lines conforming with Sovnarkom policies. However, it also in part continued the functions of the existing Chief Economic Council in the Ministry of Trade and Industry, in whose offices in fact the National Economic Council established itself after the first few days, and it quickly incorporated several other sections of the Ministry as well as the apparatus of the State Conferences and Committees on various industries which had been established during the War. Soon it was to assume a new importance as the authority responsible for taking over and administering nationalised industry.[36] While completing the abolition of the monarchy, the October Revolution put an end to several other hallowed institutions of the Imperial era, as well as certain new bodies created in the wake of the 1905 and February 1917 revolutions. Thus by the end of December the Governing Senate (the apex of the Imperial court system – inactive since the February Revolution), the State Council and its Chancellery, and the Chancellery of the State Duma were all no more.[37] When it came to the apparatus of the executive arm of the government, however, destruction was far less apparent. Apart from the changes within particular ministries already referred to, the only major government bodies abolished were the Ministry of the Court, the Procuracy of the Holy Synod, the Chancellery and Office of Petitions of the Provisional Government, and certain policy-administrative committees attached to ministries.[38]

In 1923 Lenin was to write: 'Our State apparatus, with the exception of the People's Commissariat for Foreign Affairs, represents in the highest degree a hangover of the old one, subjected to only the slightest extent to any serious change.'[39] While there is more than a grain of Leninist hyperbole in this statement, it is difficult to disagree with the thrust of Lenin's evaluation. It is clear, moreover – and here both contemporary Bolshevik participants and subsequent Soviet historians are in agreement – that had it not been for the early non-cooperation of government officials, the changes would have been even less. As it was, the structural changes were scarcely greater than those sometimes accompanying changes of government in Western parliamentary systems. The personnel changes were greater, and could perhaps be compared with those occurring in Washington in the heyday of the 'spoils system'.[40]

This high level of continuity in the central administrative machine of the Russian state probably had little effect on the major policies pursued by the Soviet government. It did, however, greatly influence the way that government operated, for the procedures and internal machinery of the Sovnarkom, to be effective, had to conform to the rationale of the machinery which provided its information and implemented its decisions. This quickly led to the emergence of structural and operational characteristics similar to those existing in the pre-revolutionary government, with implications which we shall take up in a later chapter.

PART TWO

THE KREMLIN: SOVNARKOM IN ACTION

5

The move to Moscow

In the seventeen hectic weeks between the Bolshevik seizure of power and the transfer of the capital to Moscow, Sovnarkom had established itself as the chief decision-making body in the new Soviet state. True, there were other bodies with great power and authority. The Central Committee of the Bolshevik Party was the final arbiter of policy, and the Central Executive Committee of the All-Russian Congress of Soviets (the CEC) became the embodiment of the proclaimed sovereignty of the soviets. However, the party Central Committee had no effective executive machinery of its own and, while taking occasional decisions of key importance (like that on the Brest-Litovsk Treaty) it generally relied on its party comrades in Sovnarkom to translate the Bolshevik programme into concrete decisions and secure their implementation. As for the CEC, although it formally combined at the supreme level of authority both legislative and executive powers, as did the soviets at lower levels, it began very quickly to evolve into a quasi-parliamentary body. The CEC never became a true parliament, since paradoxically the very rejection of the 'bourgeois' doctrine of the division of powers, while giving it executive prerogatives which it was unable effectively to exercise, also allowed Sovnarkom to assert an independent legislative role which rendered ineffectual its formal responsibility to the CEC. Thus in the early period of the Soviet regime, Bolshevik rule meant, in institutional terms at least, Sovnarkom rule.

In Part Three, and especially in Chapters 12 and 14, we shall be looking more closely at the relationships between these bodies, and also considering how and why they changed, with Sovnarkom ultimately losing its institutional primacy. First, however, we must examine how Sovnarkom functioned during its heyday, in the period up to the beginning of the New Economic Policy, and this we shall do in the four chapters of Part Two.

The drama of these stirring and terrible years has been often recounted, and here we need only recall its main lines, so we may have in mind the conditions under which Sovnarkom operated during this period. It is useful to distinguish three phases. The first, and briefest, was the 'peaceful breathing-space', as Lenin called it, between Brest-Litovsk and the onset of the Civil War in mid-1918. This saw the establishment of Sovnarkom in eighteenth-century administrative offices within the walls of Moscow's ancient Kremlin or citadel, the relocation of the central government machine and other national institutions in Moscow, and the consolidation and extension of the regime's authority and policies in the provinces, partly through establishing control over the executive bodies of the local soviets and partly through the build-up and deployment of such centrally-directed organisations as the Cheka, the Red Army and the food-procurement apparatus.

The second, 'Civil War' phase, lasted some two and a half years. Hostilities against the 'White' forces, who were backed by the Western Allies, raged throughout the second half of 1918 and the whole of 1919, during much of which period the territory controlled by the Soviet regime contracted to the ancient central heartland of European Russia. The defeat of the 'White' armies brought only a short-lived peace, for in April 1920 hostilities broke out with newly-independent Poland and continued till early 1921. This was a time when military necessity was the overwhelming determinant of Sovnarkom's functioning as of everything else. The replacement of 'workers' control' and other experiments in direct democracy by hierarchical bureaucratic authority, the nationalisation and central direction of industry, the compulsory acquisition of peasant grain 'surpluses' – all of them begun in the preceding phase – now blossomed into the system of 'War Communism'. Compulsion and repression, relatively mild in the first months of the Revolution, became the dominant mark of Bolshevik rule. The soviets atrophied, and the local organs of Trotsky's Revolutionary Military Council, Dzerzhinsky's Vecheka, and other 'emergency' bodies ruled the roost in the provinces, unchallenged in the exercise of their arbitrary powers except by each other. The same period saw the emergence of a new full-time Communist Party officialdom, controlled by its hierarchy of secretaries and in turn controlling the party rank-and-

file, progressively establishing its authority over other agencies of
the regime in the provinces, and directed by an equally new well-
staffed Secretariat in Moscow, under the guidance of an Organisational Bureau and a Political Bureau which increasingly took over
the decision-making prerogatives of the Central Committee.

The transition to the third phase was marked by the Tenth Party
Congress in March 1921, which began to replace the system of War
Communism by a New Economic Policy (NEP), whose main features
were the partial revival of market forces, the restoration of private
enterprise in the lower reaches of the economy, and the replacement
of forced requisitions from the peasantry by a modest tax in kind,
thus beginning the long haul to rehabilitate the shattered economy
and to build bridges to the alienated *muzhik*. The accompanying
political changes were contradictory. On the one hand the arbitrary
powers of the 'emergency organs' were curbed, there was a turn to
greater legality, and there were efforts to revive the soviets, albeit
now under close party control. On the other hand the dictatorial
powers of the ruling party–government oligarchy were reinforced,
party discipline was strengthened, and internal party dissent, which
the 'Workers' Opposition' and 'Democratic Centralists' had given
quasi-organised form in 1920 and early 1921, thereby presenting the
oligarchy with the spectre of a split, were vigorously suppressed.
Meanwhile Soviet institutions were being implanted in the vast
territories reclaimed from the 'Whites' and from various nationalist
regimes in non-Russian areas, thus reincorporating most of the lands
of the old Russian Empire in the new Soviet state, and preparing the
way for the establishment of the Union of Socialist Soviet Republics
at the end of 1922.

Nothing could more graphically illustrate the extent to which
Lenin had come to identify his regime and his personal role in it
with Sovnarkom than the organisation of the government's shift to
Moscow and its installation in the Kremlin. The operation was
master-minded and directed by V. D. Bonch-Bruyevich, the Head of
the Sovnarkom Chancellery, and he was Lenin's right-hand man
throughout. Although the shift automatically involved also the
party Central Committee and its rudimentary apparatus, it was not
the Central Committee but the members and senior staff of the
Sovnarkom that travelled with Lenin in his special train. As for the
CEC, its members – including its Chairman, Sverdlov, who also
directed the party apparatus – were assigned two trains departing

from a different station with less stringent security precautions.[1] It was again Bonch-Bruyevich who allocated office-space and quarters in the Kremlin. The Sovnarkom Chancellery occupied several rooms immediately adjacent to Lenin's apartment, and was flanked on the other side by the Cabinet Room and Lenin's office. The long corridor linking Lenin's working and living quarters was thus entirely taken up by the Sovnarkom apparatus and it was the Sovnarkom's communication centre set up in this corridor that provided the leader with his direct telephonic and telegraphic links with other institutions and provincial centres. Moreover, the Sovnarkom Cabinet Room came to be used for their meetings by other executive bodies of which Lenin was a member, including the party's Central Committtee and Politburo. During the next four years, until he was incapacitated by illness, Lenin's whole personal and political life was to be set in the constant daily ambience of the Sovnarkom.[2]

Because of the great secrecy in which the transfer of Sovnarkom to Moscow was planned and carried out, little could be done by way of preparing accommodation and facilities in advance. On their arrival on the evening of 11 March, Lenin and most of the leading members of the government were provided rooms in the National Hotel, while the remaining members and officials were assigned to other hotels. After ten days or so in the National, Lenin shifted to other temporary quarters inside the Kremlin walls, till his apartment was finally ready for occupation in the second half of April. Meanwhile the Sovnarkom offices were set up within a few days of arrival, and by 18 March Bonch-Bruyevich had the Chancellery well enough organised for the first Moscow meeting of the Government to be convened. It took much longer to get the Sovnarkom machine functioning smoothly. Efficient communication arrangements and technical facilities had to be established, and considerable restaffing was necessary. Of the 43 Sovnarkom staff members who transferred from Moscow, only four or five were administrative officers, the remainder being typists, telephonists, messengers and even cleaners. New staff had to be recruited and inducted, a further 18 being added by the end of May.[3] The confusion during these early weeks in Moscow was exasperating to Lenin. In a note to the Sovnarkom Secretariat on 26 April he acidly enquired whether Gorbunov was or was not still Secretary (in fact he was), adding the comment, 'What a mess we're in!'[4]

Meanwhile, the individual People's Commissars and their staffs had the task of relocating the central administrative machines of their various branches of government. The original allocation of commissariat headquarters seems to have been on a catch-as-catch-can basis. The Commissariat for Foreign Affairs was installed in the Hotel Metropole and the Commissariat for Railways and the National Economic Council in the hotel *Delovoi dvor*.[5] The Education Commissariat took over a lycée,[6] while Dzerzhinsky commandeered for the Vecheka an imposing insurance office building on Lubyanka (now Dzerzhinsky) Square,[7] which has remained the headquarters and symbol of the Soviet political police ever since. On 19 March the Sovnarkom belatedly resolved to set up a special 'Evacuation Commission' to supervise the further transfer of governmental organisations and staff from Petrograd and to establish control over the allocation of office space. Commissariats were required to submit to this Commission details of each additional section to be transferred and the number of staff involved, and sections transferred without Commission approval were liable to be returned to Petrograd. Moreover commissariat staff were forbidden to occupy further buildings without a requisition order approved by the Commission.[8] Nonetheless, it is clear that much continued to depend on the energy and initiative of commissariat leaders. Trotsky reports a 'fierce struggle' for suitable accommodation among the various commissariats, the less successful finding themselves scattered among numerous commandeered merchants' houses and offices around the city.[9] Stalin's Commissariat for Nationalities was one of these, and his deputy Pestkovsky describes an unsuccessful attempt by Stalin to take over in dead of night a former hotel building claimed by another department.[10] Accommodation was an acute problem even for the best-organised commissariats. The Finance Commissariat, for instance, managed to make some preparations in advance of the Sovnarkom move, its board member Olminsky being sent to Moscow to look out for office space and quarters. As a result a substantial part of the commissariat staff were already installed in Moscow within a few days of Sovnarkom's arrival, but the search for further accommodation and facilities continued for some time to hamper the restoration of effective work-patterns.[11]

While sections of certain commissariats remained in Petrograd for a considerable time,[12] the transfer of most of the central government machine to Moscow was accomplished with remarkable speed. It is hard to estimate the numbers of personnel involved. Undoubtedly many individuals, particularly in the lower echelons, chose to remain in Petrograd, but on the whole departments seem to have arrived in the new capital with their staff substantially intact. The shared experience of moving to a new environment can exert a potent unifying influence on the members of an organisation. The staffs of the commissariats, in most cases a motley conglomeration of Bolsheviks, former Imperial officials, and newly recruited personnel, now found themselves cut off from their familiar patterns and local associations, and obliged to face together the problems of adapting their working and personal lives to their new setting, and of coping with all the practical difficulties of establishing an effective corporate effort and identity. Some have seen in the transfer of the Soviet government to Moscow, with its traditional atmosphere, symbols of Holy Russia, and alleged petit-bourgeois smallmindedness, a major factor in that recrudescence of traditional bureaucratic methods and attitudes which became all too obvious in the ensuing years. While the notion of such atmospheric influences is not entirely fanciful, a more direct and powerful factor promoting continuity with the Tsarist bureaucratic past was probably this welding together of old and new staffs, and old and new ideas, in the shared crisis and challenge of reestablishing themselves and their departments in an unfamiliar and difficult environment.

One of the most urgent tasks facing the regime after its transfer was to impose its control over the institutions and population of Moscow itself. As mentioned earlier, the extension of power from Petrograd to provincial centres in Russia was largely accomplished by local Bolsheviks and their allies, who often proceeded to set up organs of rule modelled on the new institutions in Petrograd, in many cases actually called *sovnarkoms*, and claiming virtually sovereign power in their regions. Efforts to incorporate these provincial 'republics' (in a couple of cases they actually styled themselves thus) into a national system of government made only slow headway until the Civil War forced the pace. Moscow, of course, had a national importance which from the first attracted special attention from the party and government leadership in Petrograd, several prominent Bolsheviks being sent there to help establish effective control. Nonetheless, autarkic tendencies and a distinctive local style of rule remained very strong, so much so that a Moscow Regional Sovnarkom was set up on the very eve of the central government's arrival, under the chairmanship of a veteran Bolshevik, the historian M. N. Pokrovsky, with a full set of People's Commissars including one for Foreign Affairs. When Lenin was informed of this development he is said to have been highly amused and to have jibed about a revival of the patchwork of Russian principalities of 500 years earlier. However, he had no intention of tolerating this autonomous centre of authority in his new capital, and he instructed Bonch-Bruyevich to investigate and report within a month on measures to absorb the 'tsardom of Muscovy' into the nationwide system of rule.[13] At a meeting of *the* Sovnarkom on 19 April, Pokrovsky presented his views on relations between the two sovnarkoms, and a commission was set up to look into disputed matters and recommend on the proper boundaries of responsibilities. However, the Moscow Sovnarkom managed to maintain itself for several more weeks and it was only on 9 June that Lenin and his colleagues felt strong enough to have a decision pushed through the Presidium of the CEC disbanding it. Part of its staff was absorbed by central government bodies and the remainder merged in the local soviet apparatus.[14]

Meanwhile, there was the problem of creating elementary order in the new capital. The local Bolsheviks had permitted a high level of 'revolutionary spontaneity', and armed parties of self-styled anarchists, to which many criminal elements quickly gravitated, meted out 'revolutionary justice' and performed 'confiscations', dominating and terrorising whole districts. The Cheka was not yet effectively operating in Moscow, and it fell to Dzerzhinsky himself to establish the Cheka presence. He began by issuing a proclamation at the end of March demanding the surrender of all unregistered weapons, urging the public to report cases of unlawful demands and violence, and warning that unauthorised acts carried out by persons claiming to be 'anarchists, Red Army men or members of other revolutionary organisations' would no longer be tolerated, cases of violence or robbery being punished by shooting on the spot. The operation against the Moscow 'anarchists' represented an important teeth-cutting exercise for the Cheka, providing their first major experience both in the carrying out of summary executions and in the deployment of their own military forces. On 31 March, the various groups of troops and armed workers previously assigned to work with the Cheka were unified into a single Vecheka Fighting Detachment (*Boevoi otryad VChK*) and almost immediately deployed against the Anarchist headquarters, which were bloodily

destroyed in a lightning night operation. The vigorous protests of
the local Soviet authorities against these arbitrary acts of violence
by 'outsiders' went unheeded, order was established and the Cheka
was armed with fateful precedents and experience.[15]

Thus it was that in the second quarter of 1918 the essential conditions were created for the Soviet government to operate effectively
in its new setting in the Moscow Kremlin. Meanwhile its new
membership was now strikingly different from what it had been at
the time of the seizure of power. The main reasons for this have
already been examined in Chapter 3: the failure of two initial
appointees to take up office, the resignations over the failure to form
a broad-based coalition government, the inclusion, and then withdrawal, of the Left SR members, and the 'Left Communist' resignations over Brest-Litovsk. But other factors contributed to the truly
kaleidoscopic changes in Sovnarkom membership during these early
months. People's commissars were sent on assignments outside
Petrograd, and either never exercised their Sovnarkom responsibilities or ceased doing so long before they were formally replaced.
In other cases acting people's commissars (*vremennye zamestiteli* –
literally 'temporary deputies') were appointed who might or might
not be formally confirmed in office – and sometimes came to be
accorded the status and title of people's commissar without such
confirmation. There were also structural changes. Apart from the
two ephemeral commissariats formed to accommodate the Left SRs,
there were new Commissariats of Welfare (30 October – renamed
Social Security in April 1918) and State Control (20 November), as
well as the VSNKh or National Economic Council (12 December).
The experiment with a Committee on Military and Naval Affairs
proved very short-lived. The original members, Antonov-Ovseyenko,
Krylenko and Dybenko, were quickly joined by N. I. Podvoisky, who
had been the dominant figure under Trotsky in the Petrograd
Military Revolutionary Committee. Then a few weeks later the
Committee was replaced by separate Commissariats for the Army
and the Navy, the former under Podvoisky and the latter under
Dybenko.[16] In March both were brought again under single leadership, now in the person of Trotsky, although distinct administrations
were retained.[17]

It would be tedious to chronicle all these changes in detail (more
information will be found in Chapter 10 and all incumbencies are
tabulated in Appendix A). It is their cumulative effect that interests

us here. Of the original fifteen members of Sovnarkom, only three, namely Lenin, Stalin and Lunacharsky, were unchanged by the autumn of 1918, while two others, namely Trotsky and Rykov, remained in the Sovnarkom with different portfolios. To put it another way, over two-thirds of the Sovnarkom members by this time had taken up office since the shift to Moscow in March. We see, then, that it was very largely a new team that Lenin gathered around him in the Cabinet Room next to his office in the Kremlin. In getting this team operating, however, the lessons learned in the Smolny period were of crucial importance. This meant, most obviously, the experience accumulated by Lenin personally, in months of day-to-day management of Sovnarkom; but it also meant the acquisition of rules and conventions of procedure, governing such matters as meetings, preparation of decisions, consultations and coordination, and it meant a chancellery staff experienced in channelling business in conformity with these rules and conventions. In the second half of 1918 Sovnarkom's membership began to stabilise, and there were relatively few changes during the Civil War. Having survived a perilous infancy, it was now to mature in a prolonged and all-absorbing struggle for survival. The features and behaviour patterns it assumed will command our attention in the chapters that follow.

It remains here to take a closer look at the character of the Sovnarkom's bureaucracy as it entered the Civil War. In the spring and summer of 1918 the extensive nationalisation of industry, creation of new economic coordinating agencies, intensified direction of local government bodies, and the great expansion of the exceptional organs, necessitated the recruitment of many thousands of new central government officials. While these included quite a few Moscow Bolsheviks and pro-Bolshevik ex-soldiers, the main stress in this period was on attracting 'bourgeois specialists' to the service of the Soviet state, a policy which Lenin and Trotsky implemented with great resolution against powerful opposition within the party. It was in these months, for instance, that the Army Commissariat took on strength over a third of the old General Staff,[18] and there was similar large-scale recruitment of civilian specialists. The rapid growth of government officialdom during this period diluted and further diversified the commissariat staffs transferred from Petrograd, but a substantial core of the old officials remained, especially in the higher echelons.

In August 1918 a questionnaire survey of central government

officials was conducted, and the schedules have recently been analysed for the first time by the Leningrad historian, M. P. Iroshnikov.[19]
The survey covered the Moscow central offices of most commissariats, although in half of them it was confined to senior officials
only (roughly the top fifteen per cent). The latter circumstance is not
entirely unfortunate, since it gives us an idea of differences between
the upper and lower echelons.

The most interesting data produced by the survey related to the
sources from which commissariat officials were recruited, and these
we have summarised in Table 1.

The first thing that strikes us here is the extremely varied proven-
ance of the early Soviet bureaucracy, and the large numbers who
had not been working in the corresponding government department
before the Revolution. Secondly, we note that the proportion of such
'carry-overs' was very much higher in the upper echelons than in the
central government bureaucracy as a whole (although the contrast
may have been somewhat less than the table suggests, owing to the
particular departments represented in Groups A and B). Thirdly,
there were many other commissariat officials who had previously
been working in other administrative positions. Iroshnikov classes all
the officials in categories 1–8 as 'former officials' (*sluzhashchie*),
although they include some former employees of non-government
institutions like banks, insurance companies and national bodies
representing the zemstva, municipalities, cooperatives, etc. On this
formula about forty-five per cent of all the government officials in
Group A in August 1918 had been officials of some kind before the
Revolution, compared with fully eighty per cent of the senior
officials in Group B.[20] It would be misleading, however, to assume
that the rest were all drawn from the masses. Category 9 includes
former management and technical staff as well as former workers.
A certain (unknown) proportion of government officials recruited
from the armed forces (Category 10) had been in administrative jobs
before their military service. Officials transferred from other Soviet
government agencies (Category 12) may have worked in administrative jobs before the Revolution. The indications, then, are that over
half the officials in the central offices of the commissariats, and
perhaps ninety per cent of upper-echelon officials, had worked in
some kind of administrative position before October 1917. Those who
had not were drawn mainly from the following sources: (1) Communist Party members, mainly recruited from the district organisa-

tions in Petrograd and to a lesser extent Moscow;[21] (2) literate and politically reliable soldiers, sailors and factory workers; (3) students, vigorously recruited during the Smolny period, especially through the medium of G. S. Kordovsky, who combined the jobs of Head of the Labour Bureau of the Organisation of Petrograd Students and Head of the Mobilisation Department of the Commissariat for Labour.[22] These generalisations of course conceal marked differences as between departments. For instance the Commissariats for Finance

TABLE I   *Prior employment of central government officials: August 1918*

	Group A 9 Commissariats All Officials		Group B 8 Commissariats Senior Officials	
	No.	per cent	No.	per cent
1. Corresponding ministry	743	17.0	401	53.3
2. Other former ministries	73	1.7	10	1.3
3. Other pre-revolutionary government agencies	59	1.3	103	13.7
4. Pre-revolutionary local government bodies	398	9.0	36	4.8
5. Private business institutions	387	8.9	21	2.8
6. Pre-revolutionary national voluntary bodies	187	4.3	24	3.2
7. Educational and scientific institutions	102	2.3	9	1.2
8. Press and publishing	37	0.9	4	0.5
9. Factories and other production establishments	324	7.4	9	1.2
10. Armed forces	906	20.7	56	7.4
11. Party/trade union/Red Guards	82	1.9	8	1.1
12. Other Soviet central or local government bodies	501	11.4	62	8.2
13. No previous job/students	353	8.1	5	0.7
14. No information	225	5.1	5	0.7
Total	4377	100.0	753	100.1

Note: Compiled from figures in Iroshnikov 1974, pp. 366–9, Tables 6 and 7. Group A comprised the Commissariats for Internal Affairs, Health, Agriculture, Foreign Affairs, Navy, Justice and Nationalities, the Vecheka and the National Economic Council. Group B comprised the Commissariats for State Control, Army, Food Supplies, Transport, Social Security, Trade and Industry, Labour, and Finance. The figures for the Posts and Telegraphs Commissariat were too incomplete for meaningful analysis, and no figures were available for the Education Commissariat.

and the Navy had extremely large numbers of 'carry-overs', while the Internal Affairs Commissariat had very few.

Predictably, the distribution of Communist Party members was particularly uneven. Communists made up 767 (eighteen per cent) of the 4377 officials in the nine commissariats of Group A, but fully 408 of these were in the Vecheka, where they comprised fifty-two per cent of all officials. Without the Vecheka only ten per cent of Group A officials were Communists. This is very close to the proportion of Communists among the senior officials in the commissariats of Group B, which averaged eight per cent. Other commissariats with large numbers of Bolsheviks were Foreign Affairs (forty-nine per cent) and Nationalities (thirty-nine per cent). At the other extreme only four of the 209 senior officials of the Finance Commissariat were Communists.[23] The overwhelming majority of party members serving in the central government departments at this time were 'Old Bolsheviks', who had joined before the seizure of power, but the three departments with the highest party membership levels were exceptions to this. In the Vecheka thirty-one per cent of the Communists had joined the party since it took power, in the Foreign Affairs Commissariat thirty-seven per cent, and in the Nationalities Commissariat forty-three per cent.[24] While there was an obvious need to staff these departments with politically reliable personnel, it is hard to escape the impression that they were also attracting more than their share of those who, in their tens of thousands, were now throwing in their lot with the party for the advantages it could bring.[25]

Only scattered data are available on the composition of central government officialdom during the Civil War era, but it appears that overall patterns changed little after 1918, despite further expansion and considerable personnel transfers, particularly of young men into and out of the army. These patterns tell us much about the human environment in which Sovnarkom operated. With the exception of certain highly politicised departments, people's commissars could count on only a very small leavening of fellow-Communists on their staffs, while officials experienced as administrators under the old regime were far more numerous, and predominated in the upper echelons. The conditions were thus propitious for the transfer not only of specialist knowledge and administrative techniques, but also of less tangible behaviour patterns and attitudes. As the example of the Little Sovnarkom indicates, this could have a major influence on the structure and mode of operation of Sovnarkom itself.

6

Sovnarkom in session

When Lenin moved his government from Petrograd to Moscow, he was evidently satisfied in broad terms with how it had been evolving, for he immediately set about re-establishing the Smolny patterns in the Kremlin. These patterns assigned supreme importance, in the whole hierarchy of government decision-making, to the formal meetings of Sovnarkom, and it is to the organisation and character of these meetings that the present chapter is devoted.

As we saw in Chapter 3, initially Sovnarkom was convened every evening, but there was some falling off in frequency of meetings even before the transfer to Moscow. As effective procedures for the organisation of business and the devolution of matters to subordinate bodies – especially the Little Sovnarkom and later the Defence Council – were evolved, the trend to less frequent meetings continued. Lidia Fotiyeva, who was then working in the Sovnarkom Secretariat, recalls that in the initial period of its operation in Moscow the Sovnarkom was meeting daily except for Sundays and sometimes Thursdays.[1] In the middle months of 1918 it settled down to a routine of meeting on Mondays, Wednesdays, Fridays and Saturdays.[2] Then on 12 August a decision was taken to stop meeting on Saturdays. Six weeks later, however, the evenings of meeting were changed to Tuesdays, Thursdays and Saturdays. The next formal decision on the frequency of meetings was adopted on 8 July 1919, when it was resolved to convene on Thursdays and Saturdays only, but it is clear that the fall-off to twice-weekly meetings had occurred well before this: altogether Sovnarkom convened 203 times in 1918 and only 97 times in 1919.[3] By the following year the pattern evidently changed to *Tuesdays* and Saturdays,[4] before suffering a further reduction. There were 69 meetings in 1920 and 51 in 1921.[5] So we see that over the three-year period from the beginning of 1918 the periodicity of Sovnarkom meetings gradually changed from daily to weekly.

Meanwhile the preference for evening meetings persisted, and Sovnarkom often worked on well into the night, but there was a tendency to earlier and evidently less lengthy meetings. In 1918 the Sovnarkom was usually convened at eight p.m. (though sometimes seven) and it was often one or two a.m. before the members dispersed. By 1921 meetings were being scheduled for six and were usually over by ten, though in odd cases they were still going at midnight.[6] The main reason for this big reduction in the time spent by the Sovnarkom in session was obviously the increased handling of business by its 'standing commissions', the Labour and Defence Council and the Little Sovnarkom, although the accumulation of procedural experience probably also played a part.

In no respect did the character of Sovnarkom meetings differ more sharply from those of a Whitehall-type cabinet than in the qualifications for attendance. The loose and flexible patterns that emerged in the first weeks in Smolny (see above, pp. 33–4) were progressively extended and entrenched. The practice of allowing voting proxies to attend in the place of absent people's commissars, which was authorised in January 1918 as an exception requiring a specific Sovnarkom resolution in each case,[7] soon became the rule, and many people's commissars, i.e. those who alone had the formal right of membership of Sovnarkom, rarely attended its meetings. Trotsky, for instance, recalls in his memoirs that once the Civil War got under way any hope of keeping track of the ongoing business of Sovnarkom was ruled out by his frequent and prolonged absences from Moscow, and he therefore left participation in Sovnarkom to a deputy.[8] Trotsky may have been one of the more extreme non-attenders, but others were not far behind. In the memoirs of a Sovnarkom official the *personal* attendance of both Stalin and Dzerzhinsky at a 1921 meeting of Sovnarkom at which a major dispute involving Vecheka and the Little Sovnarkom was being considered is treated as an exceptional event.[9] There are some indications that the likelihood of a member of the Government's taking a personal part in its meetings was in inverse proportion to his relative standing and importance in the regime. The wider political significance of this will be discussed in Chapter 12.

What the Sovnarkom meetings may have lost in the quality of their participants they certainly made up in quantity.[10] All members of the Board of each people's commissariat had the right to attend, although only the people's commissar or his proxy had a vote. In addition, meetings were regularly attended by a number of accredited representatives (*otvetsvennye dokladchiki*) of various other central agencies who, regardless of constitutional niceties, were invested by Sovnarkom with *voting* membership. Unfortunately, published information does not permit us to establish the number of these accredited representatives, let alone the identity of all of them. The Secretary of the Central Committee of the Trades Union Council (from 1920 A. A. Andreyev) is known to have been a regular voting attender, and a representative of the Vecheka was another. A. I. Khryashcheva, Deputy Director of the Central Statistical Directorate, was a regular attender at Sovnarkom meetings from 1918 on,[11] as was G. M. Krzhizhanovsky, Chairman of the State Planning Commission (Gosplan) from 1921,[12] but whether they had the right to vote is unclear. Yakov Sverdlov, as Chairman of the CEC, was a frequent attender, and even chaired meetings (alternately with Rykov) during Lenin's convalescence following the assassination attempt of August 1918.[13] His successor Mikhail Kalinin was evidently a less regular participant.[14] During the two years following Sverdlov's death in March 1919 a form of representation of the Party Secretariat continued to be provided at Sovnarkom meetings through the person of Krestinsky, who combined the posts of Finance Commissar and Central Committee Secretary. Interestingly, however, after Krestinsky's replacement in the latter job there were evidently no party officials at Sovnarkom meetings.

Then of course there were Sovnarkom staff members: the Head of Chancellery, the Secretary (who kept the minutes, assisted from mid-1919 by a stenographer to record the precise wording of decisions),[15] and later also a representative of the Justice Commissariat to check the legality and formulation of proposed decisions.[16] Finally, there were the *rapporteurs*. Despite efforts to provide adequate prior documentation on all agenda items, the Sovnarkom persisted in its reliance on verbal reports (*doklady*) to introduce each item, presented as a rule not by the people's commissar but by the official of his commissariat directly responsible for the business in question. Sometimes there were also counter-reports presented by representatives of other interested departments. The waiting-room next to the Cabinet room was often full of such *rapporteurs* waiting for their agenda items to come up.[17] On contentious questions, or ones on which

Lenin considered the Sovnarkom should have the benefit of local or specialised experience, other junior officials in addition to the formal *rapporteurs* were invited to attend as discussants. For instance, a Sovnarkom meeting in April 1918 to decide the future of the industrial cooperatives was attended, *inter alia*, by a representative of the Central Cooperative Union, two from the Union of Workers' Cooperatives, one from the Moscow Central Workers' Cooperative and one from the Moscow City Food Supplies Committee.[18] Representatives of local soviets, usually those of Moscow and Petrograd, were prominent among such specially-invited discussants.[19]

These generous and complex rules for attendance required careful policing to prevent the size of meetings getting out of hand. There are many references in contemporary accounts to Lenin's constant attention to this problem, in particular by restricting the attendance of non-voting members to those agenda items in which they had an immediate interest. A note has survived which Lenin handed to the secretary during one of the first meetings held in the Kremlin. It reads: 'There are evidently people sitting here who were invited to attend for *other* items. I don't want to chase them out. However I hereby reprimand you and the other secretaries: you have been told a hundred times that people are to be invited to attend *solely* for the item in question.'[20] Efforts were also made to limit the number of representatives of the same agency present, and a May 1918 decision stated that, while it was desirable that each point of view held on any issue within a commissariat be represented in Sovnarkom discussions, the number of representatives of any one commissariat should not normally exceed three.[21] There is said to have been an improvement over time, but reports of crowded meetings persist. There were fifty-four at the meeting of 3 October 1922, the first chaired by Lenin for nearly a year, when 'there turned up not only the People's Commissars and their Deputies, but everyone with the remotest right to attend Sovnarkom meetings'.[22] While numbers of this order were evidently exceptional, it is clear that the size of Sovnarkom meetings was often far in excess of the usually accepted limits (about twenty) for an effectively operating committee, and the exertions required to manage such a body and maintain it as a genuine transactor of important business were almost certainly a major factor in the deterioration of Lenin's health.

No less important than who attended Sovnarkom meetings was what matters were submitted to them for decision and how they were prepared for consideration. Shortly after the move to Moscow, Lenin found it necessary to reissue his instructions requiring Sovnarkom members to submit agenda items in advance, with a brief outline of the relevant facts and a draft decision.[23] The response tended to be excessive. The meeting of 14 May 1918 was a light one, having only five agenda items, but the supporting documentation totalled 120 pages.[24] It is doubtful if Lenin ever won the battle for concise, businesslike briefs; he was certainly still waging it in 1921.[25] The heavy agendas of the Smolny period persisted in Moscow. Lenin's secretary Fotiyeva recalls meetings in 1918 when up to sixty items were dealt with.[26] This is one respect, however, in which improvement undoubtedly occurred, thanks to the expanding role of the Little Sovnarkom and the Defence Council and to the growing effectiveness of the Sovnarkom Chancellery in warding off business that could be settled administratively. By 1920–1 the average number of agenda items per meeting had fallen to sixteen.[27]

In order to avoid unnecessary arguments at Sovnarkom meetings, particular stress was placed on giving all interested departments the opportunity to consider draft decisions in advance and obtaining their agreement wherever possible. The responsibility for this was placed on the initiating department, which also had to secure the approval of the Finance and State Control Commissariats if the measure required non-budgeted financial allocations. Heads of interested departments were expected to supply written comments on projected measures for inclusion in the agenda papers, though they might simply minute the draft decision 'no objection' or 'agreed' if they did not wish to oppose or amend it. Chancellery officials were instructed to refuse to include items in the Sovnarkom agenda unless there was evidence that the necessary inter-departmental consultations and approvals had been completed. These arrangements were initiated even before the transfer to Moscow, were reaffirmed immediately thereafter, and further elaborated in subsequent years.[28] In August 1918 it was decided to terminate acceptance of agenda items the day before the meeting to ensure that Sovnarkom members had time to acquaint themselves with the papers in advance.[29]

Such, briefly, were the rules. From time to time details were amended, but these need not detain us here. More important is the question whether the sensible and practical arrangements prescribed by these rules corresponded with what actually happened or merely expressed pious intentions. Official procedures are rarely an adequate guide to the way decision-making bodies operate, and the gap seems to have been a large one in this case. For instance, there was a way of getting around the rule which forbade the introduction of agenda items on the actual day of Sovnarkom meetings, namely by moving its inclusion as a matter of urgency. Lenin invariably opened meetings with a call for motions on removing items from the agenda or *adding supplementary items*. That this was not a mere formality is evidenced by Leplevsky's observation that latecomers could be disadvantaged by missing these discussions on the agenda, when 'certain questions would be discarded or postponed and new ones inserted which had not been included in the previously-distributed agenda-paper'.[30] As to the rules for prior documentation of items included in the printed agenda, one does indeed encounter reports of Lenin's refusing to allow matters to be discussed on the grounds of incomplete documentation. One such case involved Dzerzhinsky, who claimed that an inadequately-documented item he had brought forward should be discussed at a particular meeting because it was the Chancellery that was at fault for failing to distribute the documentation in time. He later apologised when the Sovnarkom Secretary demonstrated that Dzerzhinsky's own staff had failed to supply the necessary briefs.[31] But how rigorously were these standards enforced in general? Grigori Leplevsky, who regularly attended Sovnarkom meetings from 1921 on, declares that despite Lenin's constant efforts to have the preparatory procedures properly observed, 'the prior distribution of materials on the basis of the agenda prepared in advance occurred neither in the Sovnarkom, the Little Sovnarkom, nor the Presidium of the CEC. The reference material and advance documentation, without which the conduct of even a single sitting of the government would today be unthinkable, did not exist.'[32] This bald generalisation may exaggerate the neglect of elementary preparatory procedures, but the stress by later writers on Lenin's persistent and at times exasperated championing of such procedures suggests that the realities may have been closer to Leplevsky's account than to the formal rules.

The same problem of establishing how far official regulations can be taken as a guide to actual behaviour applies to the conduct of Sovnarkom meetings themselves. It was not till April 1919 that a set of standing orders was formally adopted, although in all probability these simply codified conventions and practices of the chairman that

had emerged much earlier. They allowed *rapporteurs* a maximum of
ten minutes to introduce each agenda item. On disputed matters ten
minutes were also allowed for a counter-report. Members could
speak no more than twice to each agenda item – five minutes the
first time and three the second – and were supposed to be given the
floor in strict order of signifying their wish to speak. All members
had the right at any time to move closure of the discussion on any
item, and such motions were decided by simple majority vote. Points
of order could be put at any time, the mover being allowed one
minute to state his point, and one person disagreeing with it could
also speak for a minute. These procedures could be varied with
respect to any item or speaker by decision of the meeting. The standing orders also specifically prescribed that the Chairman should open
the meeting with a call for motions on varying the order of the
agenda or adding new items of which no prior notice had been
given.[33] These rules were to remain in force virtually throughout
Lenin's chairmanship, an amended set only being adopted in 1922.
Lenin is said to have policed them very strictly, keeping a constant
eye on his watch and stopping speakers when their time was up.
'It was hard for people to confine themselves to this framework',
writes Fotiyeva, 'and it sometimes happened that a member, wishing
to continue speaking for even one more minute, would put a point
of order. But Vladimir Ilyich would stop him, saying that this was
not a point of order but of disorder.'[34] According to Ya. I. Gindin,
who frequently attended Sovnarkom meetings as a representative of
the Little Sovnarkom, Lenin,

kind, pleasant and always smiling in personal life, was very strict and
demanding when on the job, cutting short the slightest violation of proper
order with harshly shouted remarks. In this respect, Vladimir Ilyich
admitted no exceptions. I remember, for instance, that there once suddenly
turned up at a meeting of the Sovnarkom, L. B. Krasin, directly on his
return from London, whence the press of the whole world had been
reporting his first meeting with Lloyd George. Some of the People's Commissars rushed up to him with greetings and questions, but Vladimir
Ilyich sharply rebuked both them and Krasin from the chair for the
violation of order. When, however, the meeting closed, after midnight or
thereabouts, Vladimir Ilyich ran up to Krasin with a joyful expression,
started talking with him in the kindest tone, and led him off to his room.
But that was already after the meeting, towards one a.m., on the close of
official work.[35]

While departures from standing orders were undoubtedly permitted, and not only for senior members of the Government,[36] their

inadequacy as a guide to what actually happened is due more to what they left out. For instance, they did not stipulate a quorum of voting members, and Lenin, who was a stickler for punctuality, would invariably open meetings on the minute irrespective of the number present.[37] A register of latecomers was kept, and these were subject not only to acid comments from the chairman but sometimes to formal sanctions. We noted in Chapter 3 how Lenin introduced a system of fines in the very first weeks of Sovnarkom. This was later made more elaborate and embodied in a formal resolution of the CEC applicable to all central decision-making bodies. This provided for the following penalties: for a single case of latecoming of ten minutes or more, a reprimand written into the official minutes of the meeting; for a second instance, loss of a day's pay; and for a third, a reprimand to be published in the daily press.[38] These sanctions were also on occasion applied by his deputies. For instance the Sovnarkom at its meeting of 24 January 1922 resolved to report seven of its members to the CEC for latecoming.[39] Similar measures were sometimes taken against members missing meetings or commissariats failing to ensure the attendance of representatives.[40] Lenin was also intolerant of noise during meetings, especially talking, even in whispers. If members *had* to communicate, they were to do so by notes. He would not allow speakers to be interrupted, and himself avoided interrupting, except to call speakers to order.[41] He pushed business along briskly; protracted discussion of agenda items was rare, and as a rule Lenin would himself move closure of the discussion after three or four participants had spoken.[42] On the other hand, if he thought someone should speak he would call on them to do so, even if they had not requested the floor.[43] It was not unusual for the Chairman to join in discussion himself. Fotiyeva states that the records show Lenin to have spoken on average three to four times per meeting,[44] but only on matters of particular importance would he introduce agenda items as *rapporteur*.[45] As discussion on each item was completed, Lenin usually gave a quick summary of the discussion and dictated a resolution, which was then subject to a formal vote (though on occasion he would call on some other member, who had suggested an apposite formula, to dictate the resolution).[46]

According to A. A. Andreyev, 'where there was the slightest hint of disagreement in opinions or proposals voting was the rule' in all committee meetings chaired by Lenin.[47] Decisions required no more

than an absolute majority of voting members present and this sometimes had anomalous consequences. For instance one decision was
carried in November 1921 on the basis of seven votes for and six
against. The seven supporting the decision constituted at the most
one-third and probably more like a quarter of the voting members of
Sovnarkom at that time.[48] It was not exceptional for Lenin to find
himself outvoted; in such cases he was evidently ready to accept
defeat on lesser matters, but on issues of any importance he would
carry the fight with his usual doggedness to other and 'higher'
forums, namely the CEC, its Presidium, the Politburo or the Central
Committee.[49] It would be surprising if the taking of decisions by
majority vote rather than by consensus did not affect the character
of these decisions, and paradoxically the willingness to accept occasional defeat made it easier for the Chairman normally to overrule
opposition and insist on the decision he wanted. Lenin's Commissar
for Health, Nikolai Semashko, in the following characterisation of
the summaries of discussion on which Lenin based the decisions he
put to Sovnarkom, tends to confirm this analysis, even if one allows
for an element of hero-worshipping hyperbole.

In this summary there was also something characteristic and remarkable.
It is customary for many chairmen to take something from one person and
something else from another, coming up with a proposal calculated to
unite as many participants as possible. With Lenin it did not work that
way: what he came out with was not a compromise but a sharply defined
line. Even the addresses of the speakers merely gave him material and
arguments for better supporting his proposals. In such cases there were
usually not a few advocates of somehow or other 'blunting disagreements',
of finding some formula which would reconcile the adversaries and smooth
the sharp corners. Lenin always stood out in the most determined fashion
against the papering over of disagreements.[50]

Most efforts by eyewitnesses to characterise the style and atmosphere
of Sovnarkom meetings under Lenin are more hagiographical than
historiographical in intent. Take, for instance, this oft-quoted passage
from Lunacharsky's memoirs.

It was businesslike and lively in the Sovnarkom in Lenin's day. It was
already under him that the outward forms of considering items were
established; the exceptional strictness in determining the time given to
speakers, whether these were our own *rapporteurs,* or *rapporteurs* from
outside, or participants in the discussion. Everyone who spoke was required
to be extraordinarily concise and businesslike. A sort of compressed atmosphere prevailed in the Sovnarkom; it seemed that time itself had become

more dense, so many facts, thoughts and decisions were poured into every
single minute. But at the same time one could not detect the slightest
flavour of bureaucratism, of pulling of rank or even of tension amongst
these people who were performing this job beyond the normal strength of
man.

Under Lenin, more than at any other time, this work seemed 'easy',
despite all its responsibility...In the Sovnarkom we worked effectively,
briskly, and with jests.[51]

One suspects it cannot always have been quite like this. What such
accounts leave out is the interplay of different activity levels and the
alternation of the humdrum with the occasional drama. The complex and flexible rules on participation meant that the faces gathered
round the table changed kaleidoscopically not only from one meeting
to another but even from one agenda item to another, according to
the nature and importance of the issues involved – a fact, incidentally, which helped reinforce the dominance of the ever-present
Chairman. A great deal of side-business was contracted. Members
would leave the table and go off for a quiet talk over a cigarette.[52]
Participants were constantly exchanging notes on various matters
that came up, and there was an especially vigorous exchange of
notes with Lenin. According to Lenin's sister Anna, who frequently
attended Sovnarkom meetings as representative of the Commissariat
of Education,

Vladimir Ilyich was never satisfied just with the meeting alone: now he
would be turning to the secretary, while still listening to the report or
discussion, to ask for some information or documents, now he would be
sending notes to some comrade or other present in the room, on some
question having nothing to do with the matter under discussion, or replying
to such notes from others. Some people who had no business affecting
them on the agenda for a particular night's meeting, would nevertheless
come along solely for the opportunity of exchanging a word on some
matter or other with Ilyich.[53]

The same witness, though also displaying a reverent admiration
for Lenin, offers perhaps the most realistic account of what a
Sovnarkom meeting was like under his chairmanship.

Meetings often provoked much nervous excitement and agendas were
usually long. All comrades who had business on the agenda came along
with their papers and documents, bringing their experts with them. Until
the item affecting them came up, everyone would go out for a smoke and
a chat in the next room, or, if they stayed in the Cabinet Room, looked
through their papers, or often just sat without listening to the reports and
discussion of no direct interest to them. Ilyich alone, as chairman, was

obliged to listen to everything, to go into everything, to give speakers the floor or stop them, and to find the most appropriate decision in confused and often labyrinthine disputes, with passions running high. He was required to be an expert on all matters.

I remember an occasion when one of the items on the agenda was 'small pelts'. Both I and my husband, M. T. Yelizarov,[54] were at the meeting that day. Mark Timofeyevich [Yelizarov], who was always getting indignant at the overloading of Vladimir Ilyich, was particularly incensed on this occasion. 'Is it really unavoidable to pile even such an insignificant matter as small pelts on Ilyich? Couldn't even such a trifle as this be settled without him?' he said. But the matter was left on the agenda and in due course up rose a comrade and started his report on it. Choking with haste he rattled off something or other, anxious to get out all his ideas in time. As usual, complete silence reigned, but it was obvious that hardly anyone was listening. Ilyich, however, has to listen with the same attention even to this, thought I, looking around the hushed room with its already thick atmosphere, and the imprint of weariness on the faces of all.

At that moment in came comrade Sverdlov through the door from Vladimir Ilyich's office behind his chair, and stopped beside Vladimir Ilyich, showing him a telegram he was carrying, and the two of them conversed about some obviously important matter.

'Well, now no-one at all is listening to that report on small pelts', I thought. But meanwhile the *rapporteur* was rattling on. Then at that point Vladimir Ilyich, seemingly absorbed completely in his conversation with Sverdlov, suddenly turned around and, raising his finger, took the speaker up on some point, while the latter then started to explain and correct himself.

'So Vladimir Ilyich was listening after all despite the telegram, and keeping track of what the *rapporteur* was saying', I thought, glancing at his white, concentrated expression. Quite a few others were also startled: I detected the same amazement on several faces. The discussion on the report got under way, the matter was eventually wound up, and some decision or other taken. On to the next item.[55]

Three points stand out in this discussion of the formal sessions of Sovnarkom: the dominance of Lenin, his efforts to maximise the decision-making effectiveness of these sessions, and the persistence of several factors limiting their effectiveness. We shall return to these adverse factors and their implications in Part Three. But these plenary sessions were only one part of the decision-making complex of Sovnarkom. It is to the remaining parts of this complex that we shall now turn.

7

'The minute hand'

Much of the business transacted in the name of the Sovnarkom[1] was not decided, or even discussed, at its formal meetings and frequently did not even appear on their agenda. To fully comprehend the decision-making significance of Sovnarkom, therefore, we must also examine its auxiliary bodies and internal machinery.

The first of these auxiliary bodies was the Little Sovnarkom (*Maly Sovet Narodnykh Komissarov*) which, as we have seen, had already come into existence before the end of 1917, replicating a similar development in the Russian Council of Ministers following the 1905 Revolution. Two weeks after the transfer to Moscow a decision was taken to re-establish and reinvigorate this body, its purpose being defined as 'the consideration of minor matters, not raising issues of principle'. It was to consist of four members, who might be people's commissars or their assistants, and meetings were to be convened three times a week. Its decisions were subject to confirmation by the Full Sovnarkom, which was to deal with them as the first item on its agenda at its next meeting. Matters were to be decided by simple majority vote (no formula for settling deadlocked votes being prescribed), but any member could insist on a decision being 'starred' for separate discussion by the full Sovnarkom.[2]

Almost immediately the Little Sovnarkom began to deal with a great deal of government business, and was soon meeting almost every day (compared with its weekly meetings in Petrograd). With Lenin's encouragement, its members took to convening two or three hours before Full Sovnarkom meetings, scrutinising the latter's agendas, and transferring to their own agenda all items they thought could be dealt with by the Little Council. Although matters involving budgeted or non-budgeted financial allocations made up much of its business, all sorts of other questions came before it as well. In addition to specific matters initiated by various government departments, it also took up more general questions either by reference from the Full Sovnarkom or on its own initiative.[3] One important role was the settling of inter-departmental disputes.[4] Occasionally its members were carried away and took decisions of a clearly political character, as when they instructed the Vecheka in May 1918 to arrest the leaders of the Cadets, the Right SRs and the Mensheviks as 'enemies of the people', a decision that was watered down by the Full Sovnarkom.[5]

At the beginning of its Moscow period there was an attempt by the Little Sovnarkom to restrict its meetings to its formal membership, but Labour Commissar Shlyapnikov complained about this and the Full Sovnarkom reaffirmed that all people's commissars had a right to attend in a consultative capacity. In mid 1918 the official membership comprised second-echelon officials from the Commissariats of Internal Affairs, Justice, State Control and Labour, but the Finance Commissariat was regularly represented by Bogolepov and a second deputy commissar, and a number of other officials, including some people's commissars, were frequent attenders.[6] Later an official representative from the National Economic Council was appointed and eventually one from the All-Russian Central Trade Union Council (the 'TUC').[7] The effective membership seems to have been highly fluid, and complicated by the attendance of authorised spokesmen of various commissariats and other agencies who enjoyed a vote on matters concerning their departments.[8] There was at first no formal provision for the chairmanship, which rotated among the members, and was often assumed by a people's commissar who happened to attend, but by 1919 it had settled on M. Yu. Kozlovsky, a Board member of the Justice Commissariat;[9] and in 1921 the step was taken of appointing an independent chairman not attached to any particular commissariat. The choice for this position fell on A. S. Kiselev, who had previously held various jobs in the National Economic Council, the military, and trade unions, and was both a member of the Presidium of the CEC and a candidate member of the Party Central Committee.

An official handbook published at the beginning of 1920 characterised the Little Sovnarkom and its functions as follows:

The Little Sovnarkom is a commission under the Council of People's Commissars which considers all legislative proposals and questions of the state administration of the RSFSR requiring preliminary discussion, and makes final decision on behalf of the Sovnarkom on those of them on which there is attained unanimity of all members of the Little Council along with representatives of interested agencies and the Justice Commissariat.[10]

As this implies, the effective powers and scope of activity of the Little Sovnarkom had by this point increased considerably over the levels of 1918. This development had been greatly facilitated by a Sovnarkom resolution of 27 March 1919 exempting unanimous Little Sovnarkom decisions from the necessity of subsequent endorsement by the Full Sovnarkom. Upon signature by Lenin, they now passed directly into force as Sovnarkom enactments.[11] The Little Sovnarkom's importance received a further boost from a Sovnarkom regulation adopted on 1 June 1920, which was the first attempt to combine systematically the various rules and conventions governing the status and structure of this body. The regulation now assigned four functions to the Little Sovnarkom: the preliminary consideration of matters subject to decision by the Full Sovnarkom; the 'vetting' of proposals for the Sovnarkom agenda to determine what body should consider them; consideration of all budgetary matters; and consideration of matters referred to it by the Full Sovnarkom or its chairman. A most important passage in the regulation lists a whole range of matters on which the Little Sovnarkom could take the final decision without endorsement by the Full Sovnarkom.[12]

From mid-1920, when this regulation was adopted, till the early part of 1922, when a new phase of Sovnarkom reorganisation began, the role and influence of the Little Sovnarkom was greater than at any other period of its existence, a fact that was reflected in a number of organisational developments. In order to cope with the volume of business it began to hold 'administrative' (*rasporyaditel'nye*) meettings, in addition to its 'plenary' meetings. It is worth mentioning here (we shall return to it in Chapter 9) that the Little Sovnarkom was also at this time making extensive use of sub-commissions. Secondly, in 1921 there was a change in the rule under which the objection of any member of the Little Sovnarkom to one of its decisions had sufficed to prevent its being implemented without reference to the Full Sovnarkom. Henceforth the right to demand reference of Little Sovnarkom decisions to the Full Sovnarkom was limited to the Little Sovnarkom chairman and to members of Sovnarkom and the Labour and Defence Council. Although on the face of it this narrowed the rights of individual Little Sovnarkom members, it had the effect of enhancing the autonomy of this body as a whole, by reducing the probability of its decisions being further considered by the Full Sovnarkom. The initiator of this change was Little Sovnarkom chairman Kiselev, whose original proposal had been to limit to himself the right to refer decisions to the Full Sovnarkom. Lenin was not prepared to go this far, and the new arrangement as ultimately approved was a compromise arrived at after consultation with other Sovnarkom members. Prior to this change the rule that Little Sovnarkom decisions were taken by majority vote had very limited force, since the right of individual members to insist that disputed decisions be referred to the Full Sovnarkom gave each of them a virtual veto. The new arrangement now made majority decisions in the Little Sovnarkom a reality.[13] The third innovation was the addition of independent full-time members not representing any particular commissariat. The first such appointment, that of A. S. Kiselev as Chairman, has already been noted. Later in 1921 two additional independent members were added. Little Sovnarkom members were not obliged even before this to vote for the proposals of the commissariats they were representing, although they *were* obliged to present and explain them, but 'it goes without saying', as Leplevsky points out, 'that in the overwhelming majority of cases the members of the Little Sovnarkom defended the interests of the departments they represented. This could not guarantee', he concludes, 'correct and objective decisions by this important body. . .'[14] By diluting the departmental dependence of its membership, this change further reinforced the autonomy of the Little Sovnarkom.

These developments were consolidated in a new statute on the Little Sovnarkom adopted in October 1921.[15] With the exception of defence and foreign policy matters *all* government business was now to go in the first instance to the Little Sovnarkom, and its decisions, taken by simple majority vote, were final once countersigned by the Sovnarkom chairman, unless referred to the Full Sovnarkom by the latter, by the Little Sovnarkom's own chairman, or by virtue of a protest in writing submitted within two weeks by the head of a Sovnarkom agency. Agencies thus no longer had the option of by-passing the Little Sovnarkom and submitting issues direct to the Full Sovnarkom. The Little Sovnarkom was also now empowered to deal with such defence and foreign policy matters as were referred to it by the Full Sovnarkom or its chairman. The membership was to consist of the chairman and two other independent members appointed by the Sovnarkom, as well as representatives of the Commissariats of Finance, Justice, Food Supplies, Labour, Nationalities and Agriculture and of the TUC Central Committee – ten in all. The quorum was fixed at seven. Two members (not necessarily the independent ones) were to be appointed by Sovnarkom as deputy chairmen.[16] 'Administrative' meetings were legitimised, their decisions having the same status as 'plenary' meetings of the Little Sovnarkom. The statute also made the Little Sovnarkom responsible for supervising the implementation of government decisions by the people's commissariats and other agencies, and to this end it was empowered to require the latter to produce relevant documents and information. Finally, the statute invested considerable authority in the Little Sovnarkom chairman in the organisation of business and the exercise of supervisory powers. Two months later, the enhanced status of the Little Sovnarkom was reflected in a decree authorising it to impose disciplinary penalties on people's commissariats for tardiness in reacting to government requests and enquiries.[17]

The main reason for the Little Sovnarkom's salience during this period was evidently Lenin's close involvement in its work and his heavy reliance on it. As we have seen, the original rule that Little Sovnarkom decisions were to be submitted for approval to the next meeting of the Full Sovnarkom was soon replaced by a procedure whereby they were 'vetted' by Lenin as Sovnarkom chairman and once signed by him immediately went into force as government decisions legally indistinguishable from decisions taken by the Full Sovnarkom. Although Lenin is said to have been punctilious about referring all contested Little Sovnarkom decisions to the Full Sovnarkom, it is obvious that this arrangement placed in his hands a powerful lever for maximising his influence over government decision-making. The Little Sovnarkom, required under its 1918 charter to meet three times a week, was evidently being convened almost every evening by 1920,[18] and one of Lenin's first tasks when he went to his office next morning was to scrutinise its decisions and decide what action to take on them. Broadly speaking, he had three options. He could approve a decision as it stood (and this he did in the great majority of cases),[19] refer it to the Full Sovnarkom with or without a recommendation on its adoption or amendment, or return it to the Little Sovnarkom, again with or without a specific recommendation.[20]

But there were numerous subtle variations. Little Sovnarkom members were encouraged to attach their criticisms and counter-recommendations to the official minutes of the meeting, and Lenin sometimes supported these rather than the majority decision in referring such matters to the Full Sovnarkom. In returning a disputed decision to the Little Sovnarkom, he might likewise propose that they resubmit it along the lines of a minority opinion. Lenin also asked for specific amendments to Little Sovnarkom decisions, sending the drafts back with the slips of paper containing his proposals pinned to the appropriate section.[21] He himself initiated proposals for Little Sovnarkom decisions on matters on which he wanted quick action without having to argue them in the Full Sovnarkom.[22] In view of his authority and effective veto power, it is scarcely surprising that such proposals were nearly always accepted without demur. But evidently his painstaking scrutiny of the Little Sovnarkom's work and his constant readiness to intervene vigorously sufficed to ensure that its decisions as they came to him usually harmonised with his known thinking and policy preferences. As Little Sovnarkom member Gindin puts it:

It is essential to note that Vladimir Ilyich's intensely serious attitude to the work of law-making bodies demanded the same attitude from all others participating in this work. We all tried to pay close attention to the work and to subject questions to thorough consideration not only in the Full Sovnarkom, where he was present, but also in the Little Sovnarkom, where he was not, *since the thought was constantly before one's mind that our work would be subjected the following day to exhaustive checking by someone from whom nothing escaped and who had no mercy for errors.*[23] [Emphasis in original.]

A number of cases is on record illustrating how Lenin's dominance of the Little Sovnarkom permitted him to secure government decisions he favoured or frustrate others he disapproved of. For instance groups of people's commissars sometimes combined to push through the Full Sovnarkom budgetary allocations which Lenin considered excessive, and Lenin would counter by commissioning the chairman of the Little Sovnarkom to lodge a protest.[24] Another example relates to the implementation of official policies towards the Church, which in 1921–2 was the concern of separate departments in the Commissariats of Internal Affairs and Justice, giving rise to inconsistencies in administration and jurisdictional disputes. The Little Sovnarkom took this up and in December 1922 resolved to recommend to the Full Sovnarkom that it abolish the Justice Commissariat's euphemistically titled Department on the Separation of Church from State, on the grounds that it hindered exploitation of opportunities for a major attack on the Orthodox Church by capitalising on its internal divisions. Lenin considered this a dangerous example of 'revolutionary maximalism' and, having been briefed on the background to the dispute by the head of the threatened department, he called the Internal Affairs Commissariat's representative on the Little Sovnarkom to his office and talked to him to such good effect that the latter volunteered to move for the rejection of his own proposal (having first obtained the verbal agreement of the other Little Sovnarkom members) at that evening's meeting of the Full Sovnarkom, doing so during the discussion on the agenda at the beginning of the meeting. The result was that Lenin's objective of retaining the Justice Commissariat's department was achieved without any substantive discussion of the issue in the Full Sovnarkom.[25]

Our investigation of the Little Sovnarkom tells us much about the operation of the Sovnarkom itself and Lenin's role in it. Given its unwieldy membership and the constant difficulties of imposing businesslike procedures on it, it is hard to see how the Sovnarkom could have coped with its vast powers and responsibilities without the aid of some subordinate body, capable of relieving it of many minor issues and predigesting those that came before it. The Sovnarkom needed, in Durdenevsky's apt metaphor, a 'minute hand',[26] and that role fell to the Little Sovnarkom. However, while this allowed the Full Sovnarkom to concentrate more on contentious issues and larger matters of policy, it also meant that policy lines on many matters tended to emerge incrementally from a succession of 'minor' decisions by the Little Sovnarkom, and the Full Sovnarkom, by the time it realised what was happening, could rarely afford the time to 'unscramble' the issues. Many Soviet writers rightly stress the alertness of Lenin to the wider policy implications of many minor issues, and there are several cases on record where he brought such matters to the attention of the Full Sovnarkom. However, apart from Lenin's fallibility, he was, after all, the *only* Sovnarkom member with ready and constant access to information on the 'minute hand', and thus frequently the only one capable of 'telling the time' on many matters on the Sovnarkom agenda. This must have contributed to the sense of futility that some senior members of the government felt about Sovnarkom meetings. At the same time one can readily understand the personal value Lenin himself placed on the Little Sovnarkom. Symptomatic of this is the fact that even when Lenin was 'resting' at Gorki, and thus not directly participating in the work of Sovnarkom, he had the Little Sovnarkom minutes sent to him for checking and action almost daily.[27] According to N. A. Milyutin, one of its members, Lenin was wont to describe the Little Sovnarkom as his 'first assistant'.[28]

8

Sovnarkom's *alter ego*

The other main auxiliary organ of the Sovnarkom was the Defence Council. Established almost a year after the emergence of the Little Sovnarkom, it resembled it in several basic respects: it was a relatively small body of senior government officials, operating from the Sovnarkom offices in the Kremlin, and relieving the Full Sovnarkom of much of the detailed and urgent business of government. In one important respect, however, the two bodies differed. While Little Sovnarkom decisions required approval by the Sovnarkom chairman, and were subject to appeal to the Full Sovnarkom, Defence Council decisions had the immediate and unqualified force of law. In practice, since Lenin, the effective master of the Little Sovnarkom, was also chairman of the Defence Council from its inception, this difference was less than absolute. Nonetheless by and large the Little Sovnarkom is best regarded as a body *subordinate to* the Full Sovnarkom and the Defence Council as a body *coordinate with* it at least till 1920.

The Defence Council was set up to organise the economy for war. It was not responsible for the conduct of military operations as such, which were the province of the new Revolutionary Military Council of the Republic, chaired by Trotsky. While strategic issues could come before it if they had serious political implications,[1] such cases were more likely to go straight to the Party Central Committee. As the war came to a close, the Defence Council, having proved its value as an economic coordinator, was adapted to the purposes of reconstruction and, weathering the transition to the New Economic Policy, remained a major organ of government till well into the 1930s.

Two separate but interacting developments in the middle months of 1918 formed the immediate background to the creation of the

Defence Council: the slide into civil war and the catastrophic collapse of economic production. As the new Red Army grew and was deployed for action the difficulties of supplying it with uniforms, arms, munitions and food became acute, and threatened to immobilise it. The first efforts of the government to deal with this crisis through existing and *ad hoc* instrumentalities met with very limited success. The inefficient and amorphous National Economic Council (NEC) had already demonstrated its ineffectiveness as an economic coordinator and overlord, but still insisted on having a finger in every pie. The Revolutionary Military Council attempted to step into the breach but its instructions to officials responsible for production, transport and supply facilities were resisted by the commissariats administering these facilities, which saw the Revolutionary Military Council as in effect just another commissariat which should keep to its own sphere of jurisdiction.[2]

Accounts of the evolution of governmental machinery can be rather tedious, but if the reader will bear with us for a few pages a glance at some of the administrative reorganisations leading up to the creation of the Defence Council will help to put the matter in fuller perspective. The first stage was the emergence within the existing branches of government of special bodies to coordinate the military procurement activities of their own subordinate agencies. Thus on 1 July the Army Commissariat set up a Central Supplies Directorate (*Tsentral'noe upravleniye snabzhenii*),[3] and the NEC followed suit by establishing a Central Department of Military Procurements (*Tsentral'nyi otdel voyennykh zagotovok – Tsentrovoyenzag* for short).[4]

The second stage saw the creation of coordinating machinery transcending the individual branches of government. In August 1918 the Sovnarkom set up, on the basis of an existing Bureau that had been formed to deal with the critical supplies situation on the Eastern front, an Extraordinary Commission for the Production of Military Supplies for the Army (*Chrezvychainaya komissiya po izgotovleniyu predmetov voyennogo snaryazheniya*) under the general aegis of the NEC. It was very soon realised, however, that this body lacked the powers and the organisation to cope with the situation, and on 4 September a commission was established under M. K. Vladimirov as independent chairman and with a representative each from the NEC and the Commissariat of State Control, to take thorough stock of the whole existing machinery and make recommendations.[5] Its report resulted in a decree of 2 November converting the Extraordinary Commission for the Production of Military Supplies for the Army into an Extraordinary Commission on Supply of the Red Army (*Chrezvychainaya komissiya po snabzheniyu Krasnoi Armii* – *Chrezkomsnab* for short), giving it direct authority over all plants and organisations engaged in production and handling of military supplies (except those administered by the Army Commissariat itself), irrespective of their formal jurisdiction. *Chrezkomsnab* was run by a committee of representatives of the CEC, the NEC, the Army and Navy Commissariats, and the Central Committee of the Trades Union Council, was answerable directly to Sovnarkom, and had the power to hand over anyone disobeying its instructions to a revolutionary tribunal.[6] Despite these developments, the NEC continued its efforts to mark out an area of exclusive competence for itself, and shortly after the establishment of *Chrezkomsnab* issued a decree empowering its Central Department for Military Procurements to coordinate the production and supply of uniforms, footwear and certain categories of engineering equipment to the armed forces.[7]

Organising food supplies for the army was another story again. With the great expansion of the Red Army in the middle months of 1918, neither the Commissariat for Food Supplies nor the existing interdepartmental Committee on Organising the Provisioning and Outfitting of the Army could keep the troops fed, and military units began to resort to direct requisitioning of food. The resulting conflict between the Army and the Food Supplies Commissariats was patched up by a decree approved by the Sovnarkom on 14 September, which created a Central Commission on Food Supplies for the Army (*Tsekomprodarm*), consisting of two representatives of each commissariat under an independent chairman appointed by Sovnarkom. *Tsekomprodarm* was given exclusive powers over victualling the armed forces, existing requisitioning orders by military authorities were annulled and the latter were forbidden to engage in further requisitions without approval from *Tsekomprodarm*. Local organs of *Tsekomprodarm*, consisting of representatives of the Armed Forces and Food Supplies Commissariats under a chairman appointed by the Commission headquarters, were set up in the various military districts.[8]

This brief account scarcely conveys the complexity and confusion of administrative arrangements relating to military supplies,[9] but it should suffice to indicate the main trend during the summer and autumn of 1918: the creation of a succession of coordinating bodies which, despite the bewildering similarity of their titles, were possessed of ever broader scope and ever greater powers and were accountable at an ever higher level. And yet, as Pietsch points out, the existence of a plurality of such bodies each clothed with dictatorial powers over an ill-defined sphere, alongside the regular administrative machinery which retained 'residual' jurisdiction in various fields of economic administration, if anything only worsened the confusion. On 2 September, with the military situation deteriorating daily, the regime had been jolted by the attempt on Lenin's life into issuing a decree proclaiming Soviet Russia an 'armed camp': 'All the human and material resources of the Socialist Republic are placed at the disposal of the sacred cause of armed struggle against the aggressors. All citizens, irrespective of occupation and age, must unquestioningly fulfil whatever obligations for the defence of the country are imposed on them by the Soviet authorities.'[10] Yet three months later the administrative prerequisites for achieving the transformation of the country into an 'armed camp' were still not in existence. It was the creation of the Defence Council on 30 November that provided these prerequisites.

The Defence Council (its full title was the Council of Workers' and Peasants' Defence – *Sovet rabochei i krestyanskoi oborony*) was vested with 'full plenary powers in the matter of mobilising the human and material resources of the country in the interests of defence. The decisions of the Defence Council are unconditionally obligatory upon all agencies and institutions, central and local, and all citizens.' The decree placed all workers in transport, food supplies and the war industries under conditions of strict military discipline and made the 'unification' of administration in these fields the central concern of the Defence Council. This meant that the existing coordinating bodies and regular machinery of economic administration were now equally and unreservedly subjected to a single command enjoying powers effectively equal to those of Sovnarkom itself. To ensure that it could act expeditiously and authoritatively the Defence Council was given a small membership including three of the most powerful leaders: Lenin (as chairman of Sovnarkom), Stalin (to act as representative of the CEC rather than his Nationalities Commissariat) and Trotsky (as chairman of the Revolutionary Military Council). The other members were Railways Commissar

Nevsky, Deputy Food Supplies Commissar Bryukhanov, and chair-man of the Extraordinary Supplies Commission Krasin.[11]

The Defence Council went straight into action and beneficial results were very soon in evidence. However, it never fully solved the problem of overlapping responsibilities, cross-purposes and jurisdictional conflicts. With the creation of the Defence Council the agencies immediately responsible for production, procurement, transport etc., were now capped by a three-tiered coordinating superstructure, and a logical corollary would have been to reduce and simplify the intermediate coordinating bodies. In view of the critical military situation, it is perhaps understandable that the leadership did not give immediate attention to this, and it required some months of painful experience to bring home its necessity. For instance, at the end of January 1919 an official report by Stalin and Dzerzhinsky on the reasons for the fall of Perm laid particular stress on the breakdown of supplies resulting from administrative confusion between *Chrezkomsnab* and other bodies.[12] The solution, when it came in July 1919, took the form of appointing Rykov (who was also chairman of the NEC) as Extraordinary Plenipotentiary of the Defence Council for the Supply of the Red Army and Navy (*Chusosnabarm*), with an office superimposed over *Chrezkomsnab* and *Tsentrovoyenzag*, and with a network of subordinates located in the various fronts. On the face of it this looked like the addition of yet a fourth coordinating tier, but *Chusosnabarm* was empowered to reorganise the existing machinery so as to eliminate parallelism and superfluous echelons, and soon set about doing so.[13] In August it set up under its aegis a War Industries Council (*Promvoyensovet*) to centralise direction of all military production – something which, despite the efforts of the NEC and the various interdepartmental coordinating bodies over the past year, had still not been achieved. The success of the War Industries Council made it possible a few months later to abolish *Tzentrovoyenzag*.[14] Meanwhile on 4 October 1919 *Chrezkomsnab* was likewise abolished and its administrative machinery absorbed by *Chusosnabarm*.[15] Whether owing to such measures of administrative rationalisation or to Rykov's leadership, there is no doubt that *Chusosnabarm* radically improved the supply of manufactured goods for the front[16] and it is important in the present context to recall that this body reported direct to the Defence Council.[17] In the field of food supplies a similar dismantling of redundant coordinating machinery occurred. In August 1919

Tsekomprodarm was abolished and its responsibilities handed over
to a special directorate of the Food Supplies Commissariat, which,
as we have seen, was represented through Deputy Commissar
Bryukhanov in the Defence Council.[18]

Having been called into being essentially to coordinate the co-
ordinators, the Defence Council functioned in considerable part
through these more specialised inter-agency bodies. This, however,
did not exclude its dealing directly with individual commissariats or
with subdivisions or field officers of commissariats, with local bodies
or even individual enterprises, since, as we have seen, *all* agencies
at all levels were unconditionally subject to its authority. For
instance at its first meeting on 1 December 1918 the Council took
decisions relating to the Food Supplies, Railways and Army Commissariats, to two war production plants where a third shift was to
be introduced and workers' rations increased, and to rations and
clothing supplies for various categories of workers coming under a
number of separate agencies.[19] The range of issues dealt with was no
less broad and varied than the range of organisational units. In the
course of 1919, forty per cent of the published enactments of the
Defence Council related directly to military matters, thirteen per
cent to fuel supplies, ten per cent to transport, and eight per cent to
industry, while the remaining twenty-nine per cent covered fields as
diverse as posts and telegraphs, health, finance, agriculture and
education (see Table 2 below). The common theme running through
all the activities of the Council during its first year, however, was
the Civil War and its most pressing needs. It has often been argued
that a major and perhaps crucial advantage of the Bolsheviks in this
conflict was their control of a compact territory to which the White
forces were peripheral, so that they disposed of internal lines of
communication which their enemies lacked. For this advantage to
count, however, they had to be capable of organising themselves to
exploit it, to channel the meagre available resources into the raising,
arming, equipping, clothing and feeding of large military forces and
rapidly deploying and re-deploying them to meet the ever-changing
threats and opportunities around their perimeter of control. And
here the credit must go first and foremost to the Defence Council
which, while falling far short of achieving a fully coherent and
effective mobilisation for war, nevertheless played a vital part in
reversing that drift into administrative anarchy that threatened to
engulf the regime in 1918. Mikhail Frunze, the vanquisher of

Kolchak and Wrangel and later People's Commissar for the Army, speaking at a conference of Army political officers in 1924, made this point in unequivocal terms. 'The experience of the Civil War bears witness to the fact', he said, 'that if we had not possessed, in the shape of the Council of Labour and Defence, a body capable of embracing all fields of our Soviet life, we should scarcely have emerged the victors from that tussle which the course of our revolution faced us with.'[20]

By the beginning of 1920, however, the Civil War seemed virtually won, and the attention of the regime began to turn to the problems of reconstruction and restoration of the gravely weakened economy. The first major measure in this direction was a decision by the Defence Council on 15 January to convert one of the armies on the Eastern Front into a 'Labour Army' deployed in the Urals area and employed in such tasks as growing grain and fodder, collecting and transporting firewood, construction work and repairing agricultural equipment. Members of the Labour Army with special skills, insofar as they were not required for these priority tasks, could be detached to work in local industrial plants. To direct this work a Revolutionary Council of the Labour Army was formed, headed by a Plenipotentiary of the Defence Council and composed of representatives of the Revolutionary Military Council, the Commissariats of Food Supplies, Agriculture and Labour, and the NEC. These representatives were supposed to make decisions on matters coming within their field of primary jurisdiction and disputed matters were to be referred for final decision to the Defence Council. Disputes there were in plenty, some of them leading to confrontations between leading Bolsheviks, owing largely to Trotsky's deep commitment to the success of this undertaking. Meanwhile, a second Labour Army, functioning somewhat differently, was soon established in the Ukraine, and lesser ones in other areas, and, while in cost-benefit terms they can scarcely be adjudged a great success, the Labour Armies were a major feature of Soviet economic life during this first phase of reconstruction.[21]

The fact that the Defence Council was directly responsible both for the Labour Armies and the committee formed to administer the January 1920 decree introducing universal liability for labour service offers on the face of it sufficient explanation for the Council's change of name: though apparently no formal decision was taken, Lenin announced to the Ninth Party Congress on 31 March that it was now called the *Labour and* Defence Council (*Sovet truda i oborony* or *STO*).[22] In fact, however, this change reflected a more profound shift in both the administrative orientation of the Council and the preoccupations of the regime. In the course of 1918 and 1919 the Soviet bureaucracy had assumed more or less direct control over virtually all aspects of economic activity in the republic, but as yet no system of overall planning and coordination had been created. Since the free interplay of market forces had been suppressed, the economy thus lacked any mechanism to ensure the coherence and harmony of its parts. As we have seen, in 1919 the Defence Council had succeeded in cutting a swathe into the resultant chaos and disorder, so as to concentrate the human and material resources needed for the immediate tasks of war. Its very successes in this direction, however, could only aggravate the difficulties experienced by those needs and segments of society that were not assigned high priority, and this further exacerbated the confusion and constant wrangles. In the early months of 1920, with the pressures of war receding, the problem of how to instil some coherence into the economy became a major political issue, coming to a head at the Ninth Party Congress, which opened at the end of March. Trotsky, the *rapporteur* on this question, placed his main emphasis on the need for a comprehensive national economic plan[23] and, despite the reservations of certain leaders, notably Rykov,[24] this objective was duly proclaimed in the Congress resolution.[25] A more touchy question, however, was where responsibility for administering the plan, and providing overall managerial coordination, should lie. Should it lie with the NEC, several of whose leaders were pressing strongly for this solution? Rykov argued that a number of other economic commissariats could serve equally well as a coordinating centre, but that *one* of them would have to be given this authority. Lenin condemned all such proposals as attempts to form a bloc of the NEC and the economic commissariats outside the Defence Council and Sovnarkom,[26] thus indicating clearly enough where *he* thought the responsibility for economic coordination should lie. While in effect rejecting the pretensions of the NEC, the Congress failed to settle the issue definitively, its resolution merely instructing the Central Committee to work out a system of effective liaison between the economic branches of government,[27] and intermittent discussion continued in the following months. Meanwhile STO became more and more preoccupied with settling economic issues

thrown up by the commissariats and the specialised inter-agency
bodies, as scrutiny of its decisions reveals (see Table 2 below),
without, however, having its structure or powers revamped for it to
exercise planned and systematic coordination. In November Trotsky
published an article advocating just such a revamping. STO should
become 'predominantly', he argued, a Council on Labour, reorganised along the following general lines:

From a supreme inter-agency commission, which as a general rule inter-
venes in matters only in the case of conflicts between different administrative bodies, or in order to give a periodical shove to the work of one of
them in response to the pressing needs of the day...STO should be converted into a unifying and leading economic organ.[28]

Thus the concept was one of STO as virtually an economic cabinet.
Did this not, however, threaten to erect it into a parallel government
alongside and potentially rivalling the Sovnarkom? Meanwhile a
commission was now at work, chaired by Lenin and consisting of
Party Central Committee members but set up, interestingly enough,
by decision of Sovnarkom, to carry out the Ninth Party Congress
resolution on finding a satisfactory formula for liaison between the
economic departments of government. A variety of submissions was
received, including one from S. I. Gusev advocating a sharp upgrading of STO in terms of powers and personnel, and one from
Yu. Larin proposing the setting up of a new body, to be called
Tsentrokhozyaistvo (Centre for Managing the Economy).[29] This
commission worked out the solution that was put to the Eighth
Congress of Soviets by Lenin, and approved by the Congress in
December, a solution which in effect transformed STO along the
lines urged by Trotsky, but at the same time converted it into a
commission of Sovnarkom. The scope of STO was broadened, but it
was now placed in a clearly subordinate instead of a virtually
coordinate relationship with Sovnarkom. As this decree established
the character and position of STO for the remainder of our period
(and indeed for several years beyond) it is worth quoting here the
relevant paragraphs.

3. The reconciliation [*soglasovaniye*] and strengthening of the activity of
   agencies in the field of ensuring the defence of the country and economic
   construction appertains [*prinadlezhit*] to the Council of Labour and
   Defence.
4. For carrying out the task assigned to it the Council of Labour and

Defence issues regulations, ordinances and instructions and takes all [other] measures necessary for its correct and speedy fulfilment; in particular it establishes a unified economic plan for the RSFSR, presents it for the approval of the NEC, directs the work of the economic people's commissariats in conformity with this plan, supervises its fulfilment and in cases of necessity prescribes departures from this plan.
5. For all agencies and institutions both central and local the regulations of the Council of Labour and Defence are unconditionally obligatory.
6. The All-Russian Central Executive Committee and the Council of People's Commissars have the right to rescind or suspend regulations or decisions of the Council of Labour and Defence both on the protest of particular people's commissars and at their own discretion.[30]

Moving the adoption of this decree in his report to the Congress on the work of the CEC and Sovnarkom, Lenin had ridiculed as day-dreaming such proposals as Gusev's for sharply upgrading STO. Referring to the lack of clarity as to its constitutional position, he pointed out that possible conflicts with Sovnarkom had so far been avoided by the simple expedient of referring to the latter body matters on which STO had appeared to exceed its powers. Stating that a choice must now be made between making STO into either an economic cabinet fully separate from and equal to Sovnarkom or a commission with broad powers but nevertheless *under* Sovnarkom, he urged the latter solution, rejecting the former as being constitutionally difficult if not unworkable.[31]

A further decision of the Eighth Congress of Soviets provided STO with the basis for what was soon to become a complete hierarchy of regional and local bodies directly subject to its command. This decree established an Economic Consultative Board (*Ekonomicheskoye soveshchaniye*) in each gubernia (province), presided over by the chairman of the Gubernia Soviet Executive Committee and comprising the gubernia representatives of the NEC, the economic commissariats and the TUC.[32] This decree did not specifically place the Gubernia Economic Consultative Boards under the direct jurisdiction of STO, and indeed seemed to imply that their main channel to the centre would lie through the NEC. Recognising their value as a provincial *point d'appui*, however, STO quickly moved to bring them under its direct control, subordinating them by a decree of March 1921 to a group of Regional Economic Consultative Councils, whose chairmen it appointed and which functioned entirely under its command.[33] Three months later economic consultative boards were established at the uyezd and city levels (below the gubernias) and in plants and factories, while in the villages, committees (*sel'komy*) formed earlier by decision of the Eighth Congress of Soviets were now converted to serve as local organs of STO. On the face of it STO now disposed of a hierarchical 'apparatus' of its own stretching from the centre right down to the basic production units. Its power to command this apparatus, however, was not unqualified since the local economic consultative councils had the status of commissions of the corresponding soviet executive committees, which were empowered to rescind or suspend their decisions.[34] Moreover, the local economic consultative boards seem to have made very little mark and in many areas were not even formed, while even the gubernia boards were sometimes criticised as ineffective. Despite these limitations, the Regional Economic Councils and the subordinate boards were an important resource of STO in exercising its economic coordinating role.[35]

On 22 February 1921 the principle of overall national economic planning, the subject of so much discussion and of several weighty resolutions over the past year, was finally given institutional expression with the formation of a State General Planning Commission (*Gosudarstvennaya obshcheplanovaya Komissiya* – Gosplan). Gosplan was empowered to establish development priorities and to examine and reconcile the production objectives of all economic agencies, welding them into a coherent plan for the whole Republic and working out the measures required for the latter's fulfilment. It was to be attached to STO, which would also appoint its membership.[36]

Thus by the end of the Civil War STO had been equipped, both in terms of its powers and its planning and administrative machinery, to function as the general staff of a command economy of the kind we have come to associate with the Soviet system. Such a command economy, however, was not in fact to be realised for another decade for, within a few weeks of the decree establishing Gosplan, the Tenth Party Congress approved the momentous 'retreat' to NEP, which involved the dismantling of much of the centralised administrative direction of the economy built up under War Communism. Since market forces were once again called upon to play a major part in regulating economic life, and the attempt to control and direct everything bureaucratically from a single centre was for the time being abandoned, neither Gosplan nor STO's regional apparatus of economic consultative boards assumed the decision-making salience

they seemed destined for at the beginning of 1921, and the role of
STO itself proved in some respects a more modest one than had
been anticipated. Nonetheless it retained in the changed setting its
specialisation in economic matters, as Table 2 demonstrates. One
should beware of attaching too much weight to individual items in
this table, since a great many STO decisions were not published, and
the table analyses only those decisions that appeared at the time in
the government gazette (*Sobranie Uzakonenii*).[37] Nonetheless the
broad trends indicated are undoubtedly significant, and especially
the sharply accelerated shift to economic preoccupations from 1921
and the corresponding withdrawal from the field of military decision-
making. The increased salience of labour questions from 1920, the
changed balance as between transport and industry in 1920–1, and
the upsurge of concern with trade matters as NEP got under way in
1922 also deserve notice.[38] This picture will be amplified and modi-
fied somewhat in Chapter 9, but the important conclusion to observe
here is that STO, having played a crucial role in girding the country
for war in 1919, thereafter progressively transformed itself into the
economic work-horse of Sovnarkom, constituting, along with the
Little Sovnarkom, one of the twin supports of the Soviet government
leadership. An important Sovnarkom statement issued in August
1921, summing up the institutional implications of the transition to
NEP, confirmed STO in this role, characterising it as 'the general
leader of the economy'.[39]

How did STO operate? First we must recall an important point
of contrast with Sovnarkom itself – its compact membership. As we
noted, on its formation as the Defence Council in December 1918 its
numbers were limited to six. Two years later, when reorganised as
STO, it was increased only to nine: the Sovnarkom chairman, the
People's Commissars for Military Affairs, Labour, Railways, Agriculture and Food Supplies, the chairmen of the NEC and the
Worker-Peasant Inspectorate (the former Commissariat of State
Control), and a representative of the Central Committee of the
TUC. In addition, the Director of the Central Statistical Directorate was made a non-voting member. Thus in spite of its extension
to cover the whole economy, it remained a body of the same order
of magnitude. Moreover it retained the same three representatives
of the top Bolshevik leadership, namely Lenin, Trotsky and Stalin,
the last-named now as chairman of the Worker-Peasant Inspectorate
rather than as representative of the CEC. In September 1921 two

further members were added: the People's Commissars for Finance
and Foreign Trade.[40]

TABLE 2   *Subject areas of published decisions of STO 1919–22*

Subject area	1919 per cent	1920 per cent	1921 per cent	1922 per cent
Organisation of labour	2.0	9.8	12.3	10.4
Agriculture	2.0	2.4	9.3	3.1
Industry	8.1	4.8	18.5	9.6
Transport	10.1	24.5	12.3	14.2
Fuel	13.1	1.2	10.8	5.4
Food supplies	2.0	4.8	13.8	13.5
Raw material supplies	–	–	1.5	3.8
Trade	–	1.2	1.5	12.3
Finance	3.0	–	–	5.4
Foreign concessions	–	–	–	2.3
Total economic matters	*40.3*	*48.8*	*80.0*	*80.0*
Military matters	40.4	29.3	3.1	5.4
Control and accounting	2.0	1.2	–	4.2
Education, health, social security	8.1	6.1	7.7	2.3
Posts and telegraphs	4.1	2.4	1.5	2.7
Other matters	5.1	12.3	7.7	5.4

Source: Brodovich, p. 28.
(*Note*: the source shows incorrect totals for total economic matters in the years 1921
and 1922, corrected here.)

When one enquires, however, into who actually attended the
meetings of STO, the contrast with Sovnarkom begins to blur, since
STO, like the full Sovnarkom, 'did not confine itself to the narrow
circle of its members'.[41] To start with, STO members could have
deputies, formally appointed by Sovnarkom, serve in their place, and
most of them made extensive use of this right.[42] Secondly, most of
the 'authorised representatives' delegated by various agencies (see
Chapter 6) were assigned to attend STO meetings as well as those
of Sovnarkom. On top of these, the Sovnarkom practice of summon-
ing special *rapporteurs*, experts, and representatives of various departmental interests to attend for the discussion of particular issues,
seems to have been as widely used in STO.[43] Thus the attendance at
STO meetings tended to present the same crowded and kaleidoscopically changing aspect as that of its parent body. This is not to
mention the occasional 'extraordinary' meetings, like the one called

at the end of 1920 to consider the 1921 budget, to which Lenin summoned *all* people's commissars as well as all members of the Party Central Committee.[44]

To some extent this diffuse participation in STO decision-making was offset by Lenin's common practice of taking decisions in the name of STO after consulting the immediate membership (or their deputies) by telephone. Furthermore STO, like the Little Sovnarkom, soon started having 'administrative meetings' (*rasporyaditel'nye zasedaniya*) though it is doubtful if attendance at them was much more streamlined than at the regular meetings. They were usually chaired by V. A. Avanesov, Stalin's deputy in the Worker-Peasant Inspectorate, but sometimes by TUC Chairman A. A. Andreyev.[45] Their decisions became law when signed by Lenin. Moreover, if difficulty was encountered in reaching agreement on some urgent matter at such an 'administrative meeting', Lenin would sometimes agree to come in from his office next door and take the chair, thereby formally converting it into a 'plenary meeting'.[46]

At first the Defence Council was convened at irregular but frequent intervals, averaging over its first year almost two meetings a week, apart from a considerable number of extraordinary meetings and the telephone 'meetings' referred to above. As the practice of holding 'administrative' meetings became established the number of 'plenary' meetings declined to one a week and by 1921 a regular pattern had emerged of convening 'administrative' meetings on Wednesdays and 'plenary' meetings on Fridays.[47] Like the Sovnarkom, STO met in the evening, heavy agendas often keeping it in session till deep into the night.[48]

The standing orders governing its meetings also seem to have been much the same as used by Sovnarkom, although, if A. A. Andreyev's recollections are accurate, a shorter time was allowed for reports – three to five minutes instead of ten.[49] It also took its decisions by majority vote, though here it should be recalled that its voting membership was only half that of Sovnarkom.[50] In general, contemporary witnesses are unanimous in conveying the impression that meetings of STO were very similar to those of the full Sovnarkom in terms of participation, the way Lenin ran them, and the way they arrived at decisions. Although, as we have noted, this general impression needs to be qualified in some significant respects, there seems little foundation for the rather widespread view of STO as a tight-knit group of key leaders operating in flexible, streamlined manner in sharp contrast to the bumbling, hypertrophied Sovnarkom. What distinguished it was not so much its internal characteristics as its position in the complex pattern of decision-making relationships in the central government machine as a whole, a position whose origin and evolution we traced in the earlier part of this chapter. In the chapter that follows we shall try to grasp this pattern of relationships as a whole and to examine more closely the division of labour among the major elements in the Sovnarkom network.

PART THREE

OF MEN AND INSTITUTIONS

9

The system and the chief

We now have some idea of how the Sovnarkom and its two inner bodies emerged and developed in the years of revolution and civil war, how each operated and how they related to each other and to the administrative machine of the nascent Soviet state. In view of the constant flux and confusion and the dominating influence of Lenin's mind and will, the casual observer might be forgiven for seeing in the early Sovnarkom little more than the loosely-organised following of a triumphant charismatic leader. As the reader who has followed our analysis to this point will realise, however, this would be a profoundly misleading impression. From the very first weeks of its existence, Sovnarkom displayed an impulse towards articulation of its structures and regularisation and routinisation of its procedures: in other words towards *institutionalisation*. By the end of the Civil War it had evolved into a set of distinct but interlocking bodies operating closely together as a *system*, albeit a far from perfect one.

In 1921, despite the daunting problems of social disorder and economic collapse confronting the regime, the Sovnarkom system was for the first time able to function free of the overwhelming demands of daily military necessity. This, moreover, was the last year in which Lenin stood at its controls, although formally he remained chairman until his death in January 1924. Later we shall be considering the changes set in train by Lenin's illness, but let us now look more closely at how the system operated in 1921.

The first thing that strikes us is the regular pattern of meetings. With rare exceptions the Full Sovnarkom convened every Tuesday, while STO had a plenary meeting every Friday and an administrative meeting every Wednesday. The Little Sovnarkom also met at least twice a week, though frequently more often, and likewise distinguished plenary and administrative meetings. Nearly all meetings were held in the evening, with a substantial though manageable agenda: in the six months beginning November 1920 the Full Sovnarkom agendas averaged sixteen items per meeting, the Little Sovnarkom's thirteen, and those of STO twenty-two. Although documentation for meetings still left much to be desired, agenda items were now on the whole better prepared, so that meetings dragging on till midnight or beyond were no longer the pattern.[1]

The Sovnarkom bodies also spawned a constant stream of commissions, of which several dozen were normally in existence at any one time. Thus in the first four months of 1921 STO set up seventy-three commissions and the Full and Little Sovnarkoms seventy-four between them, and from then till the end of the year STO formed a further 103 commissions.[2] A number of these were standing bodies operating under special regulations, and a few, notably the State Planning Commission, the Supreme Arbitration Commission, and the Commission on Domestic Trade – all coming under STO – evolved in due course into government departments in their own right.[3] The great majority, however, were *ad hoc* groups of commissars and lesser officials charged with either putting decisions approved in principle into final form or with reconsidering unresolved matters and agreeing new proposals for submission to a later meeting. Of the 147 commissions set up in January–April 1921, forty-seven completed their tasks within two weeks and went out of existence, and altogether almost two-thirds were dissolved within the four months' period.[4] However, as these figures indicate, there was also a considerable number of *ad hoc* commissions that persisted for prolonged periods, either because of delays in resolving the matters referred to them or because they took on new issues. In addition to commissions set up by the Full and Little Sovnarkoms and STO, there were also many interdepartmental consultations (*mezhduve-domstvennye soveshchaniya*) created on the initiative of individual commissars or their deputies, or of the heads of such bodies as Chusosnabarm, the Vecheka or the Central Statistical Directorate.[5] The tendency of such bodies to proliferate and the difficulty of keeping track of them was a source of repeated concern, and in June 1920 a regulation had been adopted laying down rules for the creation and operation of interdepartmental committees and standing and *ad hoc* Commissions.[6] This seems to have been no more than partially successful, however, in keeping the numbers of such bodies down and controlling their operation.

Although a workable division of labour had evolved between
the Full and Little Sovnarkoms and STO, there never seems to have
been any precisely formulated delineation of functions. Generally
speaking, STO operated as an economic sub-cabinet, the Little
Sovnarkom dealt with more routine (especially financial) matters
and gave preliminary consideration to matters destined for the Full
Sovnarkom, while the latter dealt with more important or disputed
matters. These, however, were only rules of thumb and there was
much overlapping. The partial specialisation is revealed in Table 3,
but this unfortunately does not distinguish degrees of importance of
agenda items.

TABLE 3   *Subject areas of agenda items dealt with by Sovnarkom bodies,
November 1920–April 1921*

	Full SNK	Little SNK	STO
General and organisational	28.1	13.4	10.6
Finance	13.9	32.7	1.1
Supplies	8.9	5.8	24.8
Labour	6.6	8.9	18.0
Production	15.7	15.2	22.4
Others	26.8	24.0	23.1

Source: Durdenevsky 1922, p. 36.

The flexible relationship between the three bodies is also illustrated
by the considerable flow of business between them. For instance, in
1921 some ten per cent of matters coming before the Full Sovnarkom
were referred to it by the Little Sovnarkom, while in its turn it passed
fifteen per cent of its agenda items to the Little Sovnarkom for
decision. Nor, despite the special relationship of various commissariats and other agencies with one or other of the top bodies, was
there anything approaching a parcelling out of branches of the
government apparatus between them. For instance, the National
Economic Council, whose responsibilities linked it closely with STO,
provided twenty per cent of agenda items for the latter's meetings,
but it also supplied fourteen per cent of the Full Sovnarkom's agenda
items and eleven per cent of the Little Sovnarkom's.[7]

No outline of the operation of the Soviet government at this time
would be complete without considering the role of its Chancellery
(*Upravleniye delami* – literally 'Administration of Affairs'). This

body not only provided secretarial services but took on functions which made it a significant politico-administrative factor in its own right. As may be recalled from our account of the origins of Sovnarkom, Lenin had intended it to have some such role from the outset, and in this he reproduced Russian governmental practices that went back through the post-1905 Council of Ministers to the State Council and Committee of Ministers of the late nineteenth century. In particular, the Chancellery (*Gosudarstvennaya kantselyariya*) of the State Council had exercised *de facto* powers comparable with those of the Council itself, by virtue of its inter-departmental coordination responsibilities, its servicing of governmental committees and commissions, its research and legislative services, and its unique records system.[8] While the Chancellery of Sovnarkom and STO never matched this achievement, it nevertheless came to exercise major influence, for similar reasons.

Available information allows only a rough description of the structure of the Sovnarkom Chancellery. Its total staff in mid-1918 was sixty-one,[9] and it grew only modestly after that, reaching 102 in January 1921. The latter figure comprised sixty-five administrative officials, nine book-keepers and twenty-eight others including the telephonists and 'housekeeping' personnel.[10] There was some further expansion in the following months, as we shall note below. These figures include the officials of the Sovnarkom Secretariat, an organisationally discrete division of the Chancellery, which serviced meetings, recorded minutes, promulgated decisions, and handled the chairman's correspondence. Its staff numbered eight at the end of 1920, comprising the secretary, five assistant secretaries and two typists.[11] The Secretary, effectively the second most important person in the Chancellery, acted also as the chairman's principal private secretary, and seems to have been responsible for the General Office (*kantselyariya*) of Sovnarkom.[12] The Sovnarkom Chancellery and Secretariat also serviced STO, although certain staff members acquired specific responsibility for STO matters. In April 1921 the post of Assistant Head of Chancellery for STO was created; subsequently the position was renamed Assistant Head of Chancellery of Sovnarkom and STO for Economic Questions, and its responsibilities broadened to embrace certain categories of Full Sovnarkom business. A separate staff for the Little Sovnarkom had already hived off from the main secretariat in 1919.[13] The Chancellery was also responsible for Sovnarkom communications facilities which consisted of a telephone centre with direct lines to all central agencies, major provincial centres and military commands, located in a small room next to Lenin's office ('the booth' – *budka*), and the telegraph in the corridor outside it. Several Chancellery officials were employed in the Reception Office (*priyëmnaya*) which was originally located in the Sovnarkom offices proper but was later shifted on Lenin's initiative outside the Kremlin, and which had the task of answering citizen's questions and receiving and investigating their complaints.[14] Finally, the Chancellery had its own domestic staff of book-keepers, canteen personnel, cleaners, office messengers and guards.

The central responsibilities of the Chancellery were to prepare business for the meetings of Sovnarkom, the two lesser bodies and their commissions, and to check up on the execution of their decisions. All matters which commissariats and other agencies wished to bring before the government had to pass through the hands of its officers, who were supposed to ensure that proposals were properly formulated and documented and that any prior interdepartmental consultations it considered necessary had been carried out. They acquired considerable influence over priorities in dealing with government business, over which bodies matters were channelled to,[15] and the form in which they came up for decision. They were charged with convening commissions, facilitating interdepartmental consultation, collecting information, and ensuring that specified decisions were taken by various bodies. From the beginning senior Chancellery staff had been enjoined to follow up the implementation of Sovnarkom decisions, and Lenin frequently instructed them to check on the performance of particular agencies both with respect to routine procedures and specific decisions.[16] This responsibility was formalised in an instruction to the Head of Chancellery in January 1921,[17] and later a card index system was set up in an attempt to routinise this.

The scope and potential influence of Chancellery activities are well illustrated by a set of general instructions drawn up by Lenin in May 1921 for V. A. Smolyaninov, the recently appointed Deputy Head for STO. Smolyaninov was to put into proper form for the agenda of STO meetings all submissions on economic-related matters. He was to follow up the execution of all STO decisions and keep Lenin informed. He was to maintain a close watch on decision-making processes in economic-related commissariats, the State Planning Commission and other bodies set up by STO. He was to maintain constant contact with the Gubernia Economic Councils, checking up on their execution of tasks assigned by STO, and – with the chairman's knowledge or after consulting the commissariats concerned – giving the necessary instructions and explanations. All correspondence with the Gubernia Soviets and Economic Councils was supposed to pass through his hands (with the exception of the promulgation of Sovnarkom and STO decisions, which was handled by the Secretariat), and he was to inform Lenin of anything of importance that came up. He was also expected to keep himself *au fait*, through the medium of official reports and the press, with developments in all fields of the economy. Finally, he was empowered to take the initiative, subject only to Lenin's agreement, in bringing issues before the various commissariats or STO itself.[18] This was a tall order, but Smolyaninov was backed up by V. G. Zaks, a former official of the Commissariat of Finance, who was now also appointed Assistant Head of Chancellery for STO and, apart from a section of the junior administrative staff of the Chancellery, he was further assisted by three economists appointed in July 1921.[19] Although these instructions smack somewhat of Lenin's administrative perfectionism there is no reason to doubt that they roughly corresponded with the powers and responsibilities exercised by this senior Chancellery official.

The administrative ability of the leading Chancellery staff was clearly of a high order, and perhaps superior to that of most of the leading figures of the Soviet regime at that time. We have already observed the extraordinary organisational role of V. D. Bonch-Bruyevich, the first Head of Chancellery, in the months following the seizure of power. Bonch-Bruyevich's remarkable career combined almost lifelong service to the revolution with scholarly achievements of no mean significance. He was an ethnographer, whose interest in the study of Russian sectarian communities led him to accompany a party of Doukhobors on their migration to Canada in 1899, when he was twenty-six. Meanwhile, ten years previously he had been expelled from school and exiled to Kursk at the age of sixteen for involvement in student disturbances, and he had been active in Marxist circles in Moscow since 1892. He first met Lenin in 1894, and later worked closely with him for several years in Switzerland, assisting with the production of Lenin's newspaper *Iskra* ('The Spark') and subsequently organising the smuggling into Russia of illegal Bolshevik publications and looking after the Party's archive

in Geneva. Between the 1905 and 1917 Revolutions he was busy
initiating and managing legal Bolshevik publications in St Petersburg, and from 1912 worked on the Party newspaper *Pravda*. At the
same time, however, his reputation as a scholarly authority on the
sectarian movement was growing and he was even entrusted with
setting up a special section devoted to the ethnography of the
Russian religious sects in the Imperial Academy of Sciences.[20]

Bonch-Bruyevich served throughout the Civil War as Head of
Chancellery, retiring in October 1920 to devote himself henceforth
mainly to his scholarly activities.[21] He was succeeded by Nikolai
Gorbunov, whom we have met earlier as the first Sovnarkom Secre-
tary. Son of an engineer, Gorbunov graduated from the Petrograd
Technological Institute in 1917, joined the Bolsheviks after the
February Revolution, and from July 1917 headed the Information
Bureau of the SR- and Menshevik-dominated Central Executive
Committee of the First Congress of Soviets – where he must have
been a considerable asset to the Bolshevik cause. Here he came to the
attention of Bonch-Bruyevich, who sought him out in the first days
after the October coup and with Lenin's blessing installed him as
Secretary. In August 1918, however, he took over the Scientific and
Technical Department of the National Economic Council, and as
the Civil War developed joined the Red Army as a senior political
commissar. With Bonch-Bruyevich's departure in 1920, Lenin recalled the twenty-nine-year-old Gorbunov to Sovnarkom as Head of
Chancellery, and he retained this post till 1923.[22] From 1918
Gorbunov's successor as Sovnarkom Secretary was Lidia Fotiyeva
who, like Bonch-Bruyevich, had worked in Geneva with Lenin in the
early years of the Bolshevik movement: her task had been to help
Lenin's wife Krupskaya in maintaining clandestine contacts with the
Bolshevik underground inside Russia.

In the period following the Civil War, the most important Chancellery official after Gorbunov and Fotiyeva was V. A. Smolyaninov,
the Deputy Head for STO, who joined the Bolsheviks in 1908, at the
age of eighteen, took an active part in the seizure of power, and was
put in charge of the Smolensk Gubernia Economic Council. It was
the administrative abilities he demonstrated in this post throughout
the Civil War that earned him his transfer to the Sovnarkom
apparatus.

Our picture of the Sovnarkom staff would be incomplete without
mentioning the leading members of the Little Sovnarkom who,

although technically not Chancellery officials, were closely integrated with it in their day-to-day work. This applied even to certain
members who were formally officials of particular commissariats, but
in fact operated mainly from the Sovnarkom offices. A clear example
was M. Yu. Kozlovsky, the first regular chairman of the Little
Sovnarkom, who came to be identified almost entirely with the
Sovnarkom machine, rather than with the Justice Commissariat of
which he was a Board member. Maria Volodicheva, a Chancellery
stenographer, later recalled:

Vladimir Ilyich considered Kozlovsky his trusty assistant. Kozlovsky went
scrupulously into all details of matters and closely studied the nature of
disputes between different government departments. Vladimir Ilyich well
knew that [Kozlovsky], an outstanding lawyer, could quickly unravel any
matter, even a highly confused one. We officials of Lenin's Secretariat
were obliged to know at all times where [Koslovsky] was to be found, in
case it were necessary to put him in touch with Vladimir Ilyich. Instead of
the vagueness, lack of concreteness, and torrential verbosity which certain
people displayed, Kozlovsky always set out briefly, concretely, clearly and
precisely the essence of any matter, no matter how complex.[23]

Kozlovsky, an associate of Felix Dzerzhinsky and active supporter of
Lenin in the Polish Social Democratic Party since early in the
century, had headed the Investigation Commission of the Military
Revolutionary Committee – the precursor of the Vecheka – during
the first weeks of the Bolshevik regime.

The first full-time chairman of the Little Sovnarkom, A. S.
Kiselev, was a *rara avis* in Lenin's entourage: he came from the
working class. A fitter by trade, he had, however, spent years as a
professional revolutionary, gradually achieving prominence in the
Bolshevik underground and in 1914 being coopted to the Central
Committee. In 1917 he became chairman of the Ivanovo-Voznesensk
Soviet, in 1918 a leading official of the National Economic Council,
in 1919, after a short spell as a senior political officer in the Red
Army, was made a member of the Presidium of the CEC, and in
1920 President of the Union of Mineworkers. A member of the
Workers' Opposition in the period before the Tenth Party Congress,
Kiselev accepted the Congress decision disbanding his 'faction', and
threw his weight unreservedly behind Lenin. He remained chairman
of the Little Sovnarkom till 1923. The next most important official
of the Little Sovnarkom, who served as Vice-Chairman and substituted as Chairman during Kiselev's absences, was A. G. Goikhbarg.

A lawyer like Kozlovsky, Goikhbarg had been a Menshevik till 1917, but supported the Bolshevik seizure of power and in 1918 was appointed to the Justice Commissariat, to which he was attached, apart from a year or so during the Civil War, throughout the Lenin period, becoming a member of its Board in October 1920. However, there is no doubt that from 1921 onward Goikhbarg, like Kozlovsky before him, concentrated his energies on his Sovnarkom role, and worked closely in harness with the senior staff of the Chancellery.

These sketches of the leading officials of the Sovnarkom apparatus tell us much about the human ambience in which Lenin spent his working days. But a more immediate point is that these people, whether they had worked on Lenin's emigré staff in the past or had come to his attention through their services after the Revolution, were marked by unusual administrative capacity, which contributed greatly to the influence assumed by the Chancellery during this period.

A communications model of the Sovnarkom system of the early 1920s might be drawn as a diamond-shaped quadrilateral, with the base point representing the Chancellery, the lateral points STO and the Little Sovnarkom, and the apex the Full Sovnarkom. Communications between Sovnarkom and the multifarious agencies making up the government machine passed through the Chancellery, which on the one hand channelled down demands for action and information, and on the other received and processed requests for decision, filtering out those it could deal with itself and channelling the remainder up to the appropriate Sovnarkom body. At the STO and Little Sovnarkom level a further filtering took place, with a proportion of the business channelled to them passing up to the Full Sovnarkom. Clustered between and around the four points of the diamond was the kaleidoscope of standing and *ad hoc* commissions, each with its lines of communication running to the Chancellery and one or other of the Sovnarkom bodies.

This model might be further refined and elaborated, and shown as a diagram for the reader to puzzle and marvel over, but we will resist the temptation: for no attempt to represent Lenin's Sovnarkom diagrammatically, whether in terms of communication flows, or of the structure of power, or of the pattern of decision-making nodes, or even of the network of roles and role-relationships, could properly depict one basic and essential element – Lenin himself. We can illustrate this by asking where we would fit Lenin into a diagram of our communication model. The most immediate thought is to show him at the tip of the apex. But this would be to see him as interacting only at the Full Sovnarkom level, whereas there is abundant evidence (especially in his published correspondence) that he was constantly interacting with each of the points of the diamond. Perhaps, then, we should show him as an additional point in the middle of the diamond, with lines running to each of the corners. But this will not do either: for he was to be found in the corners as well, chairing both Full Sovnarkom and STO meetings, dominating the Little Sovnarkom through his vigorous scrutiny and control of its activities, and even, in a certain sense, being part of the Sovnarkom staff: for, alone of all members of the three decision-making bodies (apart from the chairman and deputy chairman of the Little Sovnarkom), he had his place of daily work, no less than any Chancellery official, *within* the Sovnarkom offices, and he, rather than the Head of Chancellery, was the ultimate boss of the Sovnarkom apparatus.[24] What cannot be indicated in any diagram was that Lenin pervaded the whole Sovnarkom system, his activity constantly entering it at all the nodal points, his methods stamped on its very structures and procedures and his attitudes and expectations 'internalised' to a greater or lesser extent in the working personalities of most of the individuals active in the system. This much is probably plain to the reader from what has gone before. It is time, however, to bring together the various aspects of Lenin's unique position in Sovnarkom, and to enquire what they add up to.

We must first remind ourselves how thoroughly Lenin's political and administrative activity was concentrated within Sovnarkom. The chairmanships of Sovnarkom and STO were the only formal positions he ever held within the Soviet regime. It is true of course that as the most authoritative member of the Party Central Committee he usually chaired its meetings and those of the Politburo and was its main spokesman at Party congresses. Yet unlike other Politburo members such as Stalin, Kamenev and Zinoviev, he never came to hold any formal position in the party giving him direct authority over any of its executive machinery. Discussing Lenin's preoccupation with his Sovnarkom duties, Adam Ulam has perceptively remarked that: 'The work in the Council was his life and it is clear that he neglected or much more willingly delegated authority in the Party in favour of tending to administrative details. *This* was business.'[25] The truth of this may be easily demonstrated. Despite

Lenin's lack of a formal executive post in the party, it would have been open to him to maintain an office in the party headquarters, or at least to locate a personal secretary there to help keep him in close touch with internal party matters; but he did neither of those things. As we know, his sole work-place was his office in the Sovnarkom Chancellery, and he had no secretarial staff apart from the secretary and assistant secretaries of Sovnarkom.

It might, of course, be thought that, while operating from the Sovnarkom offices and through the Sovnarkom staff, he nevertheless devoted his main attention to party matters and exercised some control over its machinery, or at least maintained sufficiently intense contact with a range of its officials to keep *au fait* with what was going on there. Here again, however, the evidence is negative. The impression consistently conveyed by both the reminiscences of members of his staff and the researches of Soviet scholars is that Sovnarkom matters typically took up the bulk of his working day. This impression gains weight from analysis of his correspondence. In 1921, for instance, sixty per cent of his surviving or recorded letters, memoranda and telegrams were addressed to central government agencies or officials and only fourteen per cent to central party agencies or officials.[26]

One feature of Lenin's correspondence with central party officials is that, apart from letters to individual Politburo members, he wrote only to the Central Committee secretary (in 1921 usually to Vyacheslav Molotov, sometimes to V. M. Mikhailov), and always in the tone of one making a request or a proposal, never a directive or demand. He scrupulously avoided giving the impression of claiming any personal authority to command the services of the party machine. For government officials he was the boss, but certainly not for party officials, however they might have looked up to him. His communications with those running the party machine, moreover, often betray a remarkable ignorance of what went on in the latter. For instance, in a note to Stalin in October 1921 commenting on proposals before the Orgburo for transferring officials to the Worker-Peasant Inspectorate (*Rabkrin*) from other commissariats, he wrote: 'The calculations seem exaggerated to me, but admittedly I am not familiar with the scale of the Orgburo's "assignment" work',[27] a remarkable confession, considering the vital importance and political sensitiveness of the Central Committee's 'cadres' activities.

There remains, however, a further question mark that might be

placed against this analysis: in comparing the attention Lenin paid
to government and to party business, must we not consider relative
quality and importance as well as quantity? This cannot be answered
in such unequivocal terms; nevertheless, it is not at all obvious from
the written record in Lenin's *Collected Works* that the matters he
dealt with through government channels tended to be more trivial
than those he dealt with through party channels. Many of his letters
to the Central Committee, for instance, were requests for help for
particular (often obscure) individuals, while others sought authorisations necessary for government officials to carry out various jobs.
More importantly, the bulk of his correspondence with the Central
Committee was in fact concerned with government business, with
minor issues predominating over larger policy issues. It is of course
true that both the broad lines of policy and the final adjudication of
disputed issues were the domain of the party, which usually meant
the Central Committee or its Politburo; and there is no doubt that
Lenin assented to this. But it seems no less true that he saw both the
identification of policy questions and the initiative for their solution
as normally arising within the government machine. Returning,
then, to Ulam's comment and asking ourselves *why* it was the
administrative details of Sovnarkom work that Lenin saw as 'business', the answer was not that administrative work was lacking in
the party machine, but rather that it appeared to him of less significance than government administration, less central to the cause of
the Revolution; that, at least, is the only conclusion that will make
sense of his conduct. He was, of course, tragically mistaken and this
we shall come back to later. The point here is that this 'mistake'
determined the character and impact of his work in Sovnarkom.
Unsurpassed among the Bolshevik leaders in ability and energy,
overshadowing all others in personal authority, he poured the
greater part of his abilities, energies and authority into his role as
Sovnarkom chairman. Small wonder, then, that Sovnarkom bore so
heavily the marks of his personality.

We have followed in some detail how Lenin consistently applied
the full force of his intelligence and will to establishing and maintaining effective operational procedures in Sovnarkom's decision-
making bodies and apparatus. Yet there is a dimension to this we
have not yet touched on. At the beginning of this chapter the concept 'charisma' was mentioned only to be promptly set aside. It is
clear however, that our picture of Lenin's role would be incomplete

without acknowledging something of this kind. The magnetic force of his personality and his capacity for commanding devoted support are not merely an artifact of official Soviet hagiography. They are also testified to by former comrades who had fallen out with him. Alexander Potresov, who knew Lenin from 1894 and collaborated with him on *Iskra*, but later became one of his leading Menshevik opponents, was to write of him after his death:

Only Lenin was followed unquestioningly as the indisputable leader, since it was only Lenin that possessed that rare phenomenon, especially in Russia: a man of iron will and indomitable energy, capable of instilling fanatical faith in the movement and the cause, and possessing an equal faith in himself. There was a time when I, too, was impressed by this will-power of Lenin's, which seemed to make of him a 'chosen leader'.[28]

Nikolai Valentinov, who was close to Lenin for a brief period in 1904, but soon suffered an estrangement, also confessed to falling under Lenin's 'hypnotic influence', but contested Potresov's attribution of it to his will-power and energy, since at the time he had succumbed to Lenin's spell the latter was going through a period of lassitude and indecision. 'It seemed to me', wrote Valentinov, 'that there was something extremely important about Lenin which I could not put my finger on. What was it? I could not have given a clear reply. I only knew that something attracted me to Lenin.'[29] Valentinov further recounts that Lenin, alone among the Russian emigré figures in Geneva, was surrounded by a whole circle of followers who had likewise fallen under his 'hypnotic influence', who referred to the thirty-four-year-old revolutionary as 'the old man', who addressed him by the affectionate-deferential name of 'Ilyich', and who created around him an 'atmosphere of worship'.[30]

Other accounts testify to the replication of this pseudo-filial bond in Lenin's entourage after the Revolution. Sergei Liberman, a non-Bolshevik who became a senior administrator under Lenin and occasionally attended meetings of Sovnarkom and STO, was able to observe this with a certain detachment:

At that time all the top-notchers of the Communist party were undoubtedly one close-knit family. Lenin was not merely a chairman but a recognised chief to whom everyone brought his thorny problems. The commissars quarreled among themselves in their daily work, but here Lenin had the last word; and all alike left these meetings reassured, as though their quarrels had been those of children now pacified by a wise parent.[31]

I shall not attempt to further analyse or explain this bond linking Lenin and his entourage and followers, for this would mean embarking on problems much disputed among social psychologists and political sociologists. Its existence, however, can scarcely be disputed on the evidence and it must figure prominently in our picture of Lenin's role in Sovnarkom. Nonetheless it would be gravely misleading to explain this role simply in terms of Lenin's 'charismatic' authority, for his 'charisma' was complemented by a prodigious capacity to get things done – and seems, indeed, to have partly originated in and been sustained by this capacity.

Lenin, then, was both a dominating (though not domineering) chairman and a revered leader; but he was also a dynamically effective *chief executive*. Lenin's executive style, moreover, was an essential element in the operation of the Soviet government machine under his chairmanship. It was a highly activist style, for Lenin was not content to interact with his immediate subordinates, the people's commissars, receiving and acting on their reports and initiatives, adjudicating between them and controlling their performance. He attempted to keep himself *au courant* with the execution of policy in all fields through contact by personal and telephone conversations and in writing with officials well down the line, identifying issues without waiting for the people's commissars concerned to bring them to his attention, and frequently taking the initiative in organising their solution. Moreover, there were at all times certain areas of government activity in which he was very deeply involved, and his prodigious working capacity and mastery of detail frequently allowed him to be at least as 'on top' of the problems concerned as the people's commissars concerned. This particularly applied to the taking over of industry in 1918, to military operations during the Civil War (though here his primacy was shared with Trotsky), to the restoration of the economy in 1921–2, and at all times to foreign affairs. The Foreign Affairs Commissar Chicherin was later to write: 'In the first years of the existence of our republic I spoke with [Lenin] several times a day by telephone, sometimes having quite prolonged conversations with him, apart from frequent personal discussions, and often discussed with him all the details of current diplomatic issues of any importance.' He added that in the course of these conversations Lenin frequently gave detailed recommendations on particular steps including the precise terms of diplomatic notes.[32] Other memoirs and the researches of Soviet historians convey a

A meeting of Sovnarkom in Smolny, early 1918

Left to right: I. Z. Shteinberg, I. I. Skvortsov-Stepanov, B. D. Kamkov, V. D. Bonch-Bruyevich, V. E. Trutovsky, A. G. Shlyapnikov, P. P. Proshyan, V. I. Lenin, I. V. Stalin, A. M. Kollontai, P. E. Dybenko, E. K. Koksharova, N. I. Podvoisky, N. P. Gorbunov, V. I. Nevsky (?), A. V. Shotman, G. V. Chicherin.

Lenin and Bonch-Bruyevich in the Kremlin grounds, 1918

Lenin with staff of the Sovnarkom Secretariat and Chancellery
Seated on Lenin's right is Secretary Fotiyeva and on his left Head of Chancellery
Bonch-Bruyevich

Sovnarkom Chairman Lenin at work in his Kremlin office, 1918 similar picture of his executive involvement in other policy areas.[33] Moreover he frequently acted on urgent issues of a kind that would normally be discussed in Sovnarkom or STO by taking a decision after collecting the opinions of other members by telephone, or if there were no time even for that, by acting personally and informing his colleagues at the next meeting.[34]

By the final phase of Lenin's leadership this 'activist' chief executive style was well entrenched,[35] and we shall illustrate his mode of operation with a few cases from this period. His handling of the problem of textile production, a matter of acute concern in the early months of 1921, provides a simple instance. Lenin tackled this by first meeting in his office on 9 April a group of factory representatives from the principal textile region of Ivanovo-Voznesensk, in order to establish the precise obstacles to their stepping up production. The same day he telegraphed I. I. Kutuzov, President of the Textile Workers' Trade Union, with copies to the heads of seven other bodies, in the following terms:

Please organise a meeting, today if possible, of representatives of the Chief Fuel Directorate, Chief Timber Committee, Chief Peat Directorate, Chief Textiles Directorate, the People's Commissariats of Railways, Finance, Food Supplies and Health, and the Commission on the Use of National Resources, with the participation of three comrades from Ivanovo-Voznesensk – Korolev, Korotkov and Manuilsky (telephone First House of Soviets, ext. 410).

On the question of urgent requirements of priority factories of the Ivanovo-Voznesensk Region.

Work to be completed on no account later than Tuesday for submission to Sovnarkom.

Decisions agreed on should be immediately implemented by order of the People's Commissars, but put through Sovnarkom.

If necessary in order to speed things up please arrange the meeting in bits to deal with particular questions.[36]

The meeting was promptly convened and a long list of measures agreed on (increasing fuel allocations, supplementing funds for wages, putting the region in the same supplies priority category as Moscow and Leningrad, etc.) and endorsed by Sovnarkom with minor amendments three days later.[37]

As inevitably happens to chief executives of the activist type, many proposals which might have been dealt with at lower echelons were brought to his attention by their initiators simply to ensure expeditious decision; in such cases his granting or withholding of support usually sufficed to determine the outcome. Again a particular example may be helpful, also dating from April 1921. The Chairman of the Chief Peat Directorate, I. I. Radchenko, in a move to increase the meagre food supplies to workers in the high-priority peat-processing industry, wrote to A. B. Khalatov, a member of the Food Supplies Board who chaired a Sovnarkom Commission on Supplies to Workers, proposing the allocation of three to five thousand poods of fats (1 Pood = c. 36 lbs or c. 16.5 kilos) in the form of a loan against supplies ordered from abroad through the Foreign Trade Commissariat. Radchenko sent a copy of his letter to Lenin, who immediately passed it on to Khalatov with the following note: 'This should be done. Judging by Lezhava's report (sent today, 22/4), this loan can be repaid from purchases abroad.'[38]

While there were many such cases where Lenin took direct action himself, he also made extensive use of Chancellery officials for this purpose. For example in May 1921 Lenin, N. P. Bryukhanov (Food Supplies Commissar) and A. I. Potyaev (Head of the Commissariat's Chief Fisheries Directorate) received a telegram from STO's 'pleni-potentiary' responsible for the Astrakhan fisheries, complaining of confusion in the supply of army labour and proposing measures to repair this, and Lenin passed his copy over to Smolyaninov, the Deputy Head of Chancellery, with the note: 'Investigate this and tell me the results. Take measures, which are urgent, in consultation with Potyaev.'[39] This case is also of interest as an example of Lenin's tendency to by-pass the relevant people's commissar in his concern to secure prompt action by one of the latter's subordinates.[40]

Another aspect of Lenin's chief-executive role to which he gave special emphasis was the pushing along of priority measures. His correspondence is replete with letters and telegrams to a great variety of officials instructing them to speed up implementation of particular decisions or programmes, requiring them to report to him personally or to his staff on the progress of implementation, or re-buking them for hold-ups.[41]

Earlier in this chapter we saw that one of the duties Lenin assigned to the Chancellery was to monitor the carrying out of decisions by Sovnarkom bodies. What should be added is that the action nor-mally required of them when failures, delays or evasions were detected was to report the matter to *him*. No doubt many of his 'rockets' to recalcitrant officials were the product of such Chancel-lery reports, but others evidently issued from complaints sent to him personally by officials of organisations which were disadvantaged by the dereliction in question. At the same time the success of Lenin's efforts to organise the systematic monitoring of the implementation of Sovnarkom programmes fell well short of his ambitions. As late as September 1921 we find him sending a long memorandum to Head of Chancellery Gorbunov enjoining him to put this work on an effective basis, to clarify with Smolyaninov which of them was responsible for following up which programmes, to establish proper files for the purpose, and so on.[42] Nevertheless, haphazard though it was, the possibility that it could bring one's sins to Lenin's attention and unleash his wrath upon one was probably a significant factor in galvanising effort in the upper ranks of the bureaucracy.

Before leaving the theme of Lenin as chief executive, we should recall his special relationship with the Little Sovnarkom – his 'chief assistant', to use his own words. This body, though later made responsible for the preliminary consideration of larger issues, was originally created – and this remained its central role throughout – to settle detailed matters in the implementation of policy. This was essentially an executive role and in the performance of it, as we saw in Chapter 7, it was closely supervised and steered by Lenin.

Lenin, then, as chairman, leader and chief executive: and now finally as politician. There is little need to amplify what has already been written by friends and foes alike about Lenin's formidable capacities as a practitioner of politics. He was, first, a superb tactician, capable of devising effective measures appropriate to his immediate goals, based on a realistic appraisal of the prevailing situation, including the strengths and weaknesses of his opponents as well as his supporters. Next came his remarkable powers of persuasion. 'No one', wrote Potresov, 'could sweep people away so much by his plans, impress them by his strength of will, and then win them over by his personality as this man...'[43] Along with his ability to fix on effective tactics and command support for them went an unusually clear grasp of the organisational resources necessary to carry his plans through, of which his creation of the disciplined, centralised Bolshevik Party was only one, albeit the most crucial, example. Finally, one should mention his seemingly instinctive understanding of the principles of effective coalition: striving always for the minimum winning alliance consistent with the maximum commitment to his goals, scorning wide coalitions that would confuse objectives and dilute organisational control, and ever ready to discard allies and supporters when their purposes diverged. We have seen ample evidence of these political abilities deployed within the sphere of Sovnarkom. Lenin's tactical skíll and powers of persuasion probably contributed as much as his 'charismatic' authority in ensuring his dominance of Sovnarkom's decision-making processes. His understanding of the crucial importance of organisational resources was reflected in his use of the inherited ministerial apparatus as well as his preoccupation with the internal machinery of Sovnarkom itself. His rigorous approach to coalition building found expression in his policies on the composition of the 'worker and peasant government' – his temporary alliance with the Left SRs and uncompromising opposition to a broad socialist coalition; one may also perhaps see evidence of it in his preference for taking decisions by majority vote rather than by consensus.

Thus as a practitioner of politics Lenin displayed in Sovnarkom the same impressive abilities that mark his performance on the wider political stage. At the same time, however, his standing at the head of an elaborate administrative machine and operating within a complex network of interlocking decision-making bodies called also for the more specific skills of 'bureaucratic politics', and there are indications that Lenin could hold his own here as well. In particular he evidently knew how to exploit his strategic advantages in the control of information, personnel and the flow of business in order to secure favoured administrative outcomes. Admittedly this is difficult to document in detail since it is in the nature of such politics that it leaves little trace in the public record, while Soviet memoirists and historians are unlikely to dwell on these aspects of Lenin's activity. We must therefore content ourselves with a few hints and glimpses.

The clearest evidence of Lenin's playing the game of bureaucratic politics relates to his management of the Little Sovnarkom, which we have analysed in Chapter 7. By concentrating, with the aid of the Chancellery staff, a great deal of business in this body, guiding its operations and vetting its decisions, personally endorsing them, returning them for amendment or taking them to the Full Sovnarkom, he acquired a valuable advantage over his colleagues in the party and government leadership in controlling the formulation and execution of policy. In general Lenin was uniquely placed to manoeuvre among the various Sovnarkom bodies and between them, the Politburo and the CEC. A simple illustration is his handling of a protest by Kamenev over a Little Sovnarkom decision in January 1920 to close one of the Moscow theatres – a decision which must have had Lenin's approval. As Chairman of the Moscow Soviet Kamenev sent a memorandum to Lenin objecting to the decision on the grounds that such matters were the province of local rather than central bodies. Probably with a view to heading off an appeal to the Politburo, of which Kamenev was a member, Lenin advised him to submit a formal protest to the Full Sovnarkom along with a draft resolution to the effect that the Little Sovnarkom should not lightly meddle with local matters and in any case not without consulting the soviets concerned. This duly came before the Full Sovnarkom at its next meeting, but the latter, while resolving that the Little Sovnarkom 'on matters relating to Moscow should be attended by representatives of the Moscow Soviet', endorsed the closure of the theatre. Thus Lenin's 'chief assistant' got its way, while Kamenev was left without an issue of principle warranting reconsideration of the matter by the Politburo.[44]

Without preempting the discussion in Chapters 12 and 14 of the larger issues of Sovnarkom–Politburo relations, we should note here that Lenin's approach to the respective jurisdiction of these two bodies was highly flexible and not unmarked by considerations of political expediency. Where possible he evidently sought to maximise the business settled within Sovnarkom, and there are reflections of this in his correspondence. For instance, in August 1921 when two senior officials protested to the Central Committee over a decision granting the Moscow Workers' Cooperative the right to purchase potatoes, and Lenin was asked along with other Politburo members to vote on the question, he told Central Committee Secretary Molotov that while he supported the protest, such matters should not go before the Central Committee without their prior consideration by Sovnarkom – whose decision of course would normally be final.[45] In another instance, in June 1921, the Cheka official responsible for security on the railways, V. V. Fomin, addressed a memorandum to the Central Committee, with a copy to Lenin, proposing that certain small factories be transferred from the NEC to the Railways Commissariat in order to produce goods against which to purchase foodstuffs for railway workers, and thus allay dangerous unrest; Lenin reacted by instructing Smolyaninov to immediately call a meeting of representatives of the relevant government bodies, with a view to dealing with the matter within the Sovnarkom network.[46] On the other hand, if a decision went against him in Sovnarkom, and he deemed the matter of sufficient importance, he would himself appeal it to the Politburo or the Central Committee. There were, moreover, some subtle variants of this course. In 1920, for instance, Sovnarkom took a decision opposed by Food Supplies Commissar Tsyurupa on the grounds that it violated his commissariat's monopoly on food matters. Tsyurupa appealed to the Politburo, whereupon Lenin, who had also voted against the decision in Sovnarkom, wrote a note to his Politburo colleagues saying that he deemed it 'inexpedient to countermand it immediately', but asking them to agree, without discussing the matter at a formal meeting of the Politburo, to certain concessions to Tsyurupa's objections and to having the matter reconsidered in a month or so.[47] Again, he might ask the Politburo to overturn a 'wrong' Sovnarkom decision not directly, but through the CEC. This happened in January 1922, for instance, in respect of a Sovnarkom resolution on support for the Bolshoi Theatre promoted by Lunacharsky.[48] On occasion he would also invoke the Politburo's authority to push through senior appointments encountering resistance in the relevant commissariat.[49]

Earlier in this chapter it was argued that the structures and procedures of Sovnarkom could not be viewed as simply outward forms cloaking what was essentially a personal following of the charismatic leader Lenin, and that on the contrary they constituted a substantially institutionalised system, which we attempted to analyse. The complex of roles performed by Lenin, however, made him an integral part of that system, and one of vital importance. We have attempted to identify and illustrate these roles – Lenin as chairman, as leader, as chief executive, as politician – but it must be realised that the roles were mutually reinforcing and in any actual situation liable to be intertwined. This is perhaps obvious, but an illustration or two might be in order.

The meetings of Sovnarkom provided opportunities for Lenin to operate simultaneously on the level of chairman and bureaucratic politician. For instance a dispute between Gosplan and the Finance Commissariat on the correct level of the note issue, a dispute in which Lenin obviously supported the latter, came to a head at a Sovnarkom meeting in November 1921. While Gosplan's representative was arguing his case Lenin passed a note to the Finance Commissariat representative Preobrazhensky reading: 'This is scandalous stuff! [*ved' on bezobrazit!*] He's *forgotten* inflation! Request the floor again immediately.' How the discussion went after that is not reported, but Lenin passed Preobrazhensky a second note saying 'If they drag it into the CEC, don't forget to insist it go to the Central Committee first' – evidently confident he could get a 'correct' decision from the latter body – in practice probably the Politburo.[50]

As commonly happens between the members and chairmen of executive bodies, Sovnarkom members would often consult Lenin beforehand on proposals they planned to place on the agenda, seeking to assure themselves of his support.[51] This had implications not only for what happened at the Sovnarkom session itself but for the preliminary politicking on the issue, since on the one hand Lenin could make his support conditional on the proposal's being amended as he saw fit, while on the other knowledge of Lenin's position strengthened the hand of the initiating commissar in negotiations with other departments. In such cases Lenin's personal authority and his roles as chief executive, bureaucratic politician and chairman might all be in play.

If, then, Lenin was such an important integral part of the Sovnarkom system, what if this element were to be removed? The operation of all governments and other executive bodies bears to a greater or lesser extent the imprint of their leaders' personalities, and the transition to a new leader always subjects the system to strain and sometimes to danger. In the case of the Sovnarkom system as it evolved in 1917–21, however, there were obviously special factors rendering it peculiarly vulnerable in the event of Lenin's withdrawal. It was not just a matter of the Chairman's overtowering personality; the system itself had been moulded from its very inception under his predominant influence and there was therefore something of a symbiotic relationship between Lenin's political personality and Sovnarkom. This contrasts sharply with the more usual situation where the leader has to adapt his political personality to working with a pre-existing system. Another aspect of the newness of Sovnarkom was that the legitimacy neither of its place in the wider political system nor of its internal structures and processes was deeply entrenched in the minds and attitudes of those operating it or of the population at large. This, moreover, was aggravated by the confused and fluid relationships between Sovnarkom and other leading political bodies, as well as by the scant significance which the Soviet leaders, as revolutionaries and as Marxists, attached to constitutional forms. While there could be argument over the weight to attach to these various reasons, the withdrawal of Lenin from the work of government, which began in the summer of 1921, did indeed lead to profound changes in the standing and operation of Sovnarkom. In Chapters 13 and 14 we shall describe these changes, and look at the arguments they provoked among the Soviet leaders. First, however, we must learn something more about the human and institutional context within which these changes occurred.

The people's commissars: recruitment

Nearly fifty men and one woman served for longer or shorter periods as members of Lenin's Sovnarkom. What sort of people were they? How were they chosen, and by whom? Were they selected for their party seniority and revolutionary services, or rather for the possesssion of appropriate qualifications and experience? What was their social and ethnic background, and what kind of education had they received? The answers to such questions should tell us much about the capabilities and position of Sovnarkom as an instrument of rule.

In this chapter and the next we shall be looking respectively at the recruitment and the background of the Sovnarkom membership and at how they changed over the Lenin period. There would be merit in widening our enquiry to include all the members of commissariat boards and others entitled to attend Sovnarkom meetings, some of whom, as we have seen, were more active in Sovnarkom affairs than were some of the people's commissars. Unfortunately, however, it is virtually impossible to establish a definitive list of such persons, and very little information is available about many of them. Moreover, questions of space oblige us to concentrate on the central core-group of government figures, and no objective criterion of such 'centrality' is available other than the admittedly imperfect one of formal people's commissar status.

The initial membership of Sovnarkom was thrashed out within some 36 hours in the heat and confusion attending the armed seizure of power and the Second Congress of Soviets. It was largely the work of Lenin, who had been authorised to prepare proposals on the make-up of the revolutionary government, at a Central Committee meeting some days earlier which had allocated responsibilities for the preparation of the Congress.[1] He probably brought some suggestions with him when he joined the other Central Committee

members in Smolny on the evening of 24 October, and that night
there was some preliminary discussion on the allocation of government posts.[2] According to Trotsky, Lenin proposed him as Chairman, on the grounds that it was he who headed the body that had
actually seized power, namely the Petrograd Soviet. At Trotsky's
insistence the proposal was dropped without discussion. Lenin then
suggested Trotsky be put in charge of Internal Affairs, but Trotsky,
with Sverdlov's support, managed to convince him that it would be
a liability to the revolution to have a Jew in this post. It was at
Sverdlov's suggestion that he was finally entrusted with Foreign
Affairs,[3] and Trotsky acquiesced, in the expectation that it would
leave him ample time to concentrate on party business.[4] How many
provisional nominees were agreed on at that meeting is not recorded,
but the next day Lenin was busy trying to convince leading Bolsheviks to take on various portfolios. 'I recall one little scene which
has sharply etched itself on my memory', Lomov was later to write.

In a far corridor of Smolny, on the second floor, in the semi-darkness,
Cde Lenin has caught his latest victim – I think it was Cde Menzhinsky.
Lenin had grasped Menzhinsky by his [coat] button, and despite all the
latter's efforts to slip away, would not let him go. Lenin was insisting that
Menzhinsky be immediately nominated as Commissar for Finance.[5]

All contemporary witnesses agree that it proved extremely difficult
to find leading Bolsheviks willing to serve on Sovnarkom – not
because they feared for their skins, but because they felt incompetent
and were afraid of making a mess of things.[6] Nonetheless by the
afternoon of 26 October, when the Central Committee convened
again, Lenin had a definitive list ready and according to Lomov,
there were no dissenters from his proposals.[7]

A few days later, when it became necessary to replace the people's
commissars who had resigned or had never taken up their duties,
the manner of selection was much the same. Again Lenin seems to
have played the dominant role, but consulting closely with Sverdlov
– as Trotsky's account indicates he had done from the outset.
Sverdlov's influence over government appointments resulted in part
from his responsibilities as Central Committee Secretary and (from
8 November) Chairman of the CEC, but perhaps primarily from
his generally-acknowledged encyclopedic knowledge of active Bolsheviks and his acute judgment of character and ability.[8]

According to Shlyapnikov, Lenin and the Central Committee also
entrusted him with helping to fill the vacant Sovnarkom posts. He

recalls that after Petrovsky's candidature for Internal Affairs Commissar was decided, he (Shlyapnikov) and Lenin had the difficult task of talking him into accepting.[9]

Latsis has left the following account of how a successor was found for Rykov as Internal Affairs Commissar, when Lenin's first candidate, Central Committee member Muranov, declined to serve:

Comrade Lenin decided to rummage around in the Petrograd organisation. And so one November evening Cde Podvoisky dashed up to me in the room of the Bureau of Commissars [of the Military Revolutionary Committee] and reported that Cde Lenin wanted to talk to me as a representative of the Petrograd organisation. In the room with Vladimir Ilyich I also found Ya. M. Sverdlov. They were engaged in a conversation about the missing people's commissars.

'So the Ministry of Internal Affairs is still not in our hands either?' asked Vladimir Ilyich.

'No', replied Cde Sverdlov, 'Muranov has locked himself in his house and won't come out.'

'Whoever would have suspected him of such pigheadedness! It is now obviously hopeless to expect we could talk him round.'

'Quite hopeless. We must appoint somebody else today. Let's ask Cde [Latsis] here', said Sverdlov, turning to me, 'which of the Petrograd workers might be picked for this job.'

We started going through the active [party] workers, one after another, beginning with the Vyborg district. But all the more prominent workers in the various districts turned out to be already installed in jobs...

It was getting to be a puzzle to find someone.

'But why don't we appoint Cde [Latsis]?' Lenin suddenly broke in.

My jaw dropped. Appointing me People's Commissar of Internal Affairs! After all, I didn't have the slightest conception of this job... I hastened to voice my disagreement.

'Vladimir Ilyich, this job is not for me: I've never once had the occasion to get familiar with this gigantic machine. No, I'm simply unsuitable.'

'And which of us *is* familiar with it?' [replied Lenin]...

At this point Cde Podvoisky bailed me out: 'This really would be a hard one for [Latsis].'

'But wouldn't it be difficult for any worker?' interposed Yakov Mikhailovich [Sverdlov].

I continued to demur: 'No, no, I'm not funking, but I simply wouldn't cope with this job. I'm just not as strong as people think.'

'All right then, let's put Cde [Latsis] down for the board', said Vladimir Ilyich, and took up a pencil to put me on the list.

'Now that will be fine', put in Cde Podvoisky.

'All right, we'll post Cde [Latsis] to the board', confirmed Cde Sverdlov.

I had no alternative but to keep quiet...

But where were we to get the people's commissar? After prolonged searchings, we came up with Cde G. I. Petrovsky...[10]

A large element of the fortuitous was present in many appointments at this time, as may be illustrated by the case of Tsyurupa.
The latter, who was in charge of food-procurement in the Ufa
region, visited Petrograd at the end of November after a Food
Supplies Conference, and called on Lenin. The latter, who had
known him since his revolutionary youth at the turn of the century,
discussed the food supplies situation with him and then urged him to
take a senior post in the commissariat. Tsyurupa reportedly resisted
the idea, on the grounds that his place was in the field, but Lenin
insisted and the next day he was made Deputy People's Commissar.
The Food Supplies Commissariat was already racked by the internal troubles that led in February to the resignation of Commissar
Shlikhter, when Tsyurupa took his place.[11]

As mentioned in Chapter 5, during this early period there was
frequent resort to the appointment of 'temporary deputy', i.e. acting,
people's commissars. One advantage of this was that some leading
Bolsheviks who were hesitant to accept formal appointment as
people's commissars could more easily be persuaded to assume responsibility on this qualified basis. Possibly, however, it was also
sometimes preferred because it did not require endorsement by
the multi-party CEC, but could be quietly enacted by decision of
Sovnarkom, which in practice sometimes meant by Lenin and one or
two colleagues, since such appointments were not necessarily discussed at formal meetings of Sovnarkom. Six acting people's commissars were appointed by Sovnarkom decision in the three weeks
beginning 30 October,[12] and only one of them seems to have been
discussed at a formal Sovnarkom meeting.[13] At the same time it
should be noted that Sovnarkom was not above publishing decisions
on its own authority appointing even fully-fledged people's commissars. It did so in the cases of Petrovsky (Internal Affairs) on
17 November, of Kolegaev (Agriculture) on 25 November, and
Shlikhter (Food Supplies) on 18 December.[14]

Of particular interest is the fact that the party Central Committee
seems to have taken little hand in Sovnarkom appointments in the
weeks following the seizure of power. At a meeting held on the night
of 4–5 November there was some discussion about replacing the
people's commissars who had resigned or not taken up duty, and
decisions may have been reached to approach particular individuals.[15] It is known that at that meeting Lenin proposed A. S.
Kiselev to replace Rykov as Internal Affairs Commissar, and that he

asked Central Committee member Bubnov to put the suggestion to Kiselev. Evidently, however, nothing came of this, since shortly thereafter we find Lenin urging Muranov to take on the job, and we have just seen how the matter was dealt with when Muranov declined. There is no evidence that these subsequent moves were specifically authorised by the Central Committee. In the course of a Central Committee meeting four days later, Teodorovich passed a note to Lenin suggesting Yelizarov be made acting People's Commissar for Railways, and Lenin wrote 'agreed Lenin' on the note, but there is no indication that the matter was formally discussed.[16] So far as can be established from the published record, none of the individual appointments made during this period was either originally decided by the Central Committee or subsequently put to it for endorsement after preliminary agreement had been reached elsewhere.[17]

The manner of selection of people's commissars does not seem to have changed greatly in the early months of 1918, when a number of further replacements became necessary, most of them precipitated by resignations over the Brest-Litovsk Treaty. The degree to which appointment procedures varied according to circumstances may be illustrated by three cases occurring in January. The appointment of Chicherin as Trotsky's deputy (and effective substitute) in the Foreign Affairs Commissariat was settled first at a Sovnarkom meeting held on 8 January, and endorsed the next day by the Central Committee.[18] On the other hand, when it was decided a few days later to replace Shlikhter as Food Supplies Commissar, this was first discussed in the Central Committee, which resolved that his successor should be either Bryukhanov or Tsyurupa, and three weeks later Sovnarkom adopted a decision to appoint the latter.[19] The appointment of Menzhinsky as Finance Commissar was handled differently again. On 19 January the Central Committee discussed 'the allocation of portfolios' between the Bolsheviks and Left SRs, and the minutes record 'the Left SRs are putting [a man] into Finance'.[20] This was reflected in a Sovnarkom decision taken later that day according the Left SR representative on the Board of the Finance Commissariat voting membership of Sovnarkom.[21] However the next day Sovnarkom resolved to appoint the Bolshevik Menzhinsky as People's Commissar for Finance, which does not appear to have been discussed by the Central Committee.[22]

Thus the Central Committee was an important factor in Sovnarkom appointments at the beginning of 1918, though not always a decisive one. The split in the party leadership precipitated by the Brest-Litovsk agreement, however, seriously damaged its effectiveness as a decision-making body and it does not appear to have played a part in choosing replacements for the Left Communist and Left SR commissars who resigned over the treaty. Again, the decision was primarily left to Lenin, in informal consultation with Sverdlov and other leaders, and to the extent that these appointments were the subject of collective discussion, this took place in Sovnarkom. On 18 March, at its first meeting held in Moscow, Sovnarkom was invited by Sverdlov to consider the whole question of replacements, and there was discussion on finding a new Chairman of the National Economic Council and new People's Commissars of Justice, Properties of the Republic, Agriculture, Trade and Industry, Navy, Welfare, and Posts and Telegraphs, but decision was reached on only a few of these vacancies at this meeting.[23] It is worth noting that the Central Committee had met three days before this but, although it had considered such matters as editorial appointments to *Pravda*, the Sovnarkom vacancies were not on its agenda.[24] In subsequent weeks three more appointments were agreed on at Sovnarkom meetings, those of Rykov as Chairman of the NEC, Sereda as Acting People's Commissar of Agriculture,[25] and Chicherin as Foreign Affairs Commissar.[26] The remaining vacancies, however, appear to have been decided on without formal discussion at Sovnarkom meetings.

Two appointments made during this period are of particular interest in affording apparent evidence of that 'close unity with the mass organisations of working men and women, sailors, soldiers, peasants and office-workers' which was envisaged in the decree of the Second Congress of Soviets establishing Sovnarkom (see Chapter 1). On 9 April Sovnarkom considered a submission from 'the commissars of the Moscow Posts and Telegraphs District', requesting the appointment of either N. P. Avilov or V. N. Podbelsky as People's Commissar for Posts and Telegraphs.[27] On the face of it, it was in response to this initiative from below that the leadership decided, in fact, to appoint Podbelsky. Closer examination of the case, however, shows that it is better understood in terms of intra-Bolshevik politics than of relationships between the regime and organisations representative of the 'masses'. Avilov, it may be remembered, was the original People's Commissar for Posts and Telegraphs who was stood aside for the Left SR Proshyan at the time of the share-out of portfolios in the previous December. The 'Commissars of the Moscow Posts and Telegraphs District' were a group of five prominent Bolsheviks who had taken charge of postal administration in Moscow at the time of the seizure of power and continued to run it in the early months of 1918. Podbelsky, a member of the Moscow Bolshevik Committee, was one of these and in March 1918, on the Government's arrival from Petrograd, it made him Commissar of the Moscow Posts and Telegraphs District. On the face of it, then, either he or Avilov would seem to have been the most obvious person for Sovnarkom to choose as People's Commissar anyway, without the need for prompting from below. However, it was precisely at this time that the party and government leadership were moving to liquidate the autonomy of local party and government officialdom in Moscow, while seeking to conciliate them by maximum consultation, respect for their wishes, and provision of suitable posts for their members. In this context, the opportunity of appointing a suitable Moscow Bolshevik as People's Commissar for Posts and Telegraphs, and ostensibly in response to local Moscow opinion, must have been particularly welcome to Lenin and his colleagues.

The other case, by contrast, undoubtedly involved a bid by the Bolshevik leadership to rally support within the relevant 'mass organisation', the Railwaymen's Union. It will be recalled that the union leadership, who wanted a broad coalition government of socialist parties, had mounted a severe threat to Lenin's regime within days of the seizure of power. Relations with the powerful and independent-minded union continued to be strained, and again reached crisis point in January 1918. At a congress of the union, Menshevik and Right SR members obtained a majority for their resolution declaring that all power properly resided in the Constituent Assembly, which was then in session – but about to be dispersed by Lenin's soldiers. The Bolsheviks and Left SRs and their supporters thereupon withdrew and convened separately as an 'Extraordinary All-Russian Railways Congress'. This assembly, which established a rival, 'loyal' union (known as Vikzhedor as against the old Vikzhel) acknowledged the authority of all decrees of the Soviet regime, agreed on new wage-scales for railway workers and officials, and approved a new scheme for the administration of the railways. The latter, agreed to if not inspired by Lenin and his colleagues, provided *inter alia* for Vikzhedor to elect an inner group of its members who would be collectively responsible for the running of the railways, and the CEC duly approved a formula under which this group would be recognised as the Board of the Railways Commissariat.[28] The Bolshevik Central Committee approved these arrangements at its meeting on 19 January, stipulating that a Bolshevik Board member must be designed to represent it on Sovnarkom, to act, in other words, as People's Commissar.[29] Yelizarov had meanwhile resigned as Acting People's Commissar (he was put in charge of insurance), but Nevsky remained, and probably out of respect for the presumed wishes of the Bolshevik leadership was elected by Vikzhedor to the Board, and nominated to represent it on Sovnarkom, i.e. to serve as People's Commissar. However, on 25 January Lenin spoke with Nevsky, asking him to stand aside in favour of one of the worker members of the Board, A. G. Rogov (a Bolshevik), and to serve officially as the latter's deputy. They then went on to discuss what needed to be done in the Commissariat.[30] A month later Lenin signed a Sovnarkom decree approving Rogov as People's Commissar and a Board of six, including Nevsky.[31]

It seems plain that Rogov was little more than a figurehead,[32] and that this sole case of the appointment of a people's commissar thrown up by a worker's mass organisation was motivated not by the principle proclaimed on the formation of Sovnarkom, but rather by the tactical consideration of securing the cooperation of leading Bolsheviks within the Railwaymen's Union in imposing essential discipline and centralised control over the railways against powerful opposition within the union itself and in regional soviet and other organisations.[33] However, Rogov quickly outlived his usefulness for this purpose, for the drive to establish centralised control and one-man management called for a strong hand at the top and on 9 May he was replaced by P. A. Kobozev, a people's commissar who was in many respects his antithesis. Though the son of a railway worker and himself a party member since 1898, Kobozev was an experienced railway engineer and administrator with an impressive record of imposing Soviet control in areas where it found itself under threat.[34] It was clearly the latter capacities that commended him to the Bolshevik leadership and he set to with a will to bring order to the railways. His zeal, however, proved counter-productive, provoking within three weeks a strike in the Tula railway workshops and a revolt against his 'dictatorship' at a further Railwaymen's Congress.[35] By this time, however, Kobozev was no longer in Moscow, having been despatched to quell the 'mutiny' of the Czechoslovak Legion, and he subsequently became Chairman of the Revolutionary Military Council of the Eastern Front. Nevsky, who combined dependability with a capacity to maintain reasonable relations with the railwaymen, was now in charge, and he was formally appointed Transport Commissar on 25 July.[36]

While we shall be examining the whole question of Sovnarkom's relationship with the CEC in a later chapter, something should be said here about the latter's involvement in Sovnarkom appointments. As we have seen, although Sverdlov had a major say in the selection of many people's commissars, this was due in only small part to his position as CEC Chairman. According to a resolution of the Third Congress of Soviets in January 1918,[37] all Government changes were supposed to be submitted for CEC approval, but the minutes of CEC meetings at this period make clear that it exercised this responsibility in a purely formal manner. For instance, in proposing the endorsement of Stuchka's appointment as Justice Commissar and of two acting people's commissars on 20 March 1918, the CEC Secretary Avanesov said: 'These comrades have already been approved by the Council of People's Commissars. In keeping with past practice, I shall not invite discussion of the question of these candidates and, if no one proposes to open discussion on their appointment I shall simply put it to the vote. Does anyone wish to engage in discussion of particular candidates? Then allow me to put it to the vote.'[38] Even this formality, however, was dispensed with after the break with the Left SRs and the adoption of the first Soviet Constitution by the Fifth Congress of Soviets in July 1918. The Constitution left the locus of responsibility for individual appointments in Sovnarkom (as for many other matters) unclear, merely stating that the CEC 'forms the Council of People's Commissars' (art. 35). In practice this was interpreted as not requiring CEC endorsement for specific changes of people's commissars.[39] At the Seventh Congress of Soviets in December 1919 the Menshevik Martov complained without suffering contradiction that it had become standard practice to appoint people's commissars without seeking approval by the CEC.[40] The latter's involvement in choosing the Government was henceforth limited to formal endorsement of Sovnarkom's current composition at the first CEC meeting after each Congress of Soviets.[41]

After the internal crises which shook the Soviet regime in its first

six months the turnover in Sovnarkom members slowed down
markedly, and its composition was relatively stable during the
Civil War. Thus there were altogether sixteen changes in 1918, but
only three each in 1919 and 1920, and four in 1921. Meanwhile the
process of filling Sovnarkom posts gradually took on a different
character.

Understandably, the chief criterion of selection at first was
prominence in the Bolshevik Party. Six of the fifteen original members of Sovnarkom were in the Bolshevik Central Committee (Lenin,
Trotsky, Stalin, Nogin, Milyutin and Lomov) and the rest were leading Bolsheviks involved in the seizure of power in Petrograd (Avilov,
Lunacharsky, Shlyapnikov, Teodorovich, Krylenko, Dybenko) or
Moscow (Rykov and Skvortsov-Stepanov). Of the three additional
commissars appointed in November 1917 Kollontai was a member
of the Central Committee and Essen Chairman of one of the district
Soviets in Petrograd, and only Yelizarov (formally Acting People's
Commissar) lacked senior political standing: his 'visibility' came
from his being Lenin's brother-in-law. As we have seen earlier in this
chapter, prominence in the Bolshevik organisation was still primarily
what drew the leaders' attention to possible replacements following
the resignations over the Brest-Litovsk Treaty.

Even at this period, however, the allocation of some portfolioes
owed much to the current responsibilities of those appointed. This
was most obviously the case with the members of the Committee on
Military and Naval Affairs: Antonov-Ovseyenko, as Secretary of the
Petrograd Military Revolutionary Committee, was a principal
organiser of the seizure of power; Krylenko, likewise a member of
the Petrograd MRC, was unique among Old Bolsheviks in the
authority which this 1916 conscript had achieved within the soldiers'
organisations; and Dybenko was the Red Sailor *par excellence*, and
Chairman of the Central Committee of the Baltic Fleet. But the
same might be said of Shlyapnikov (Labour), who headed the Metal-
workers' Union and Lunacharsky (Education), a leading party intellectual who had been serving as Deputy Head of the Petrograd
Duma responsible for cultural affairs. Three others could claim
experience particularly appropriate to their government appointments, namely Stalin (Nationalities), for some years the Party's leading spokesman on the national question; Yelizarov (Railways), a
transport engineer by profession; and Kollontai (Welfare), the most
influential Bolshevik writer on women's questions.[42]

As time went on a new factor emerged: relevant administrative experience under the Bolshevik regime itself. This can be seen as early as the appointment of Osinsky as Chairman of the National Economic Council in December 1917 for, apart from his prominence in the Moscow Party organisation before the seizure of power, he had meanwhile undergone his administrative 'blooding' as Director of the State Bank. From the second half of 1918 this factor came to the fore and, along with general experience and qualifications, tended to push party-political standing into the background. We shall be examining this development more systematically in the next chapter, but it is worth noting here insofar as it affected the way people came to be recruited to Sovnarkom positions. A good illustration is the appointment of Semashko as People's Commissar for Health in July 1918.

No Health Ministry had existed under the Provisional Government and, while Lenin and other Bolshevik leaders wanted a strong central instrumentality to coordinate their policies in this area, it took some time to achieve it. Health and hygiene directorates existed in a variety of commissariats and other agencies, and the first step was to establish a Council of Medical Boards in January 1918.[43] After the dust settled on Brest-Litovsk, further moves were initiated towards the establishment of a Health Commissariat, but these ran into strong resistance from entrenched departmental interests and from others who feared a bureaucratisation of medicine. In May Lenin discussed the tactics to be pursued with V. N. Velichkina, Deputy Chairman of the Council of Medical Boards (and wife of his Head of Chancellery Bonch-Bruyevich). It was decided to hold a Medical Workers' Congress and seek its endorsement for the Commissariat proposal. When this convened the following month the most effective advocate for a Health Commissariat proved to be N. A. Semashko, head of the Health Department of the Moscow Soviet. Although the Congress voted in favour of the creation of a Commissariat, departmental opposition continued and Sovnarkom had to discuss the matter at three separate meetings in the first half of July before reaching a final decision on the terms of its establishment.[44] Semashko, who was put in charge of the new Commissariat, had once been relatively prominent in the Bolshevik emigration, and was known to Lenin from his Geneva days. On his return to Russia in 1917 he had achieved sufficient standing in the Moscow Party organisation to be sent as a delegate to the Sixth Party Congress, but was not senior enough at the time of the seizure of power to land anything better than the Moscow Health Department, for which indeed as a qualified medical practitioner he commended himself. He was not among the dozen or so administrators originally chosen for the Council of Medical Boards, and was appointed to it only when the Government moved to Moscow. It may be that a chance meeting he reportedly had with Lenin about this time played a part in this appointment, but it was in any case a logical one once Moscow became the administrative capital. Between March and June he quickly made his mark as an advocate of centralised medical administration within the Council, most of whose members were committed to various departmental interests, and this led to the prominent role assigned him at the Medical Workers' Congress, while his successful performance at the latter made him an obvious choice to lead the group framing draft legislation on the Commissariat, and once this legislation was agreed, the natural candidate for People's Commissar.[45] What this story shows is that, while Semashko was far from being a nonentity in the Bolshevik Party, and Lenin's knowledge and good opinion of him evidently played a part, his 'visibility' as potential people's commissar was due primarily to the mark he had made in the administration and internal politics of the area of government concerned. This became more and more the pattern in the years that followed.

Of the five other Sovnarkom appointments in the second half of 1918, one, that of Central Committee member Krestinsky as People's Commissar for Finance, can be attributed primarily to party-political standing – although even he had done a stint as Deputy Chairman of the State Bank. Two others (Nevsky in Transport and Kursky in Justice) were essentially confirmations in office of administrators who had proved themselves as acting people's commissars. Shmidt, appointed People's Commissar for Labour in October, was a somewhat ambiguous case, since he had been a leading Petrograd Bolshevik for some years and was elected to the Central Committee in March 1918. His party standing, however, was mainly a function of his success as a trade union organiser, and it was primarily his position as Secretary of the All-Russian TUC that commended him for the Labour Commissariat. He was further qualified by having served on the Presidium of the National Economic Council and since June had represented the Labour Commissariat on the Little Sovnarkom.[46] However, the 1918 appointment that was most obviously due to qualifications and experience rather than party standing was that of Krasin as People's Commissar for Trade and Industry. Krasin, educated as an engineer, was a founding father of Bolshevism who achieved some prominence in the Party in the early years of the century, but then dropped out of politics and made a successful career in industrial management, during the war running various engineering plants owned by Siemens. It was not till December 1917 that he committed himself to serving the Soviet regime, and Lenin and Trotsky made immediate use of his unusual experience by including him in the team negotiating the peace treaty with the Germans. He was then placed on the Presidium of the National Economic Council and made Chairman of the Extraordinary Commission for Supply of the Red Army (*Chrezkomsnab*). From this it was a natural step to fill the long-standing vacancy in the Trade and Industry Commissariat. This commissariat, incidentally, came increasingly to concentrate on foreign trade, ceding its internal economic role to the National Economic Council, and in 1920 it was renamed the People's Commissariat for Foreign Trade, Krasin remaining in charge. Meanwhile in March 1919, with Nevsky's transfer to head the Central Committee Rural Work Department and to be Vice-Chairman of the National Economic Council, Krasin also took on the post of Transport Commissar.

In the second half of 1918 Sovnarkom itself continued to be the main institutional focus for the recruitment of people's commissars. The appointments of Semashko, Nevsky, Krestinsky and Krasin were all discussed and decreed by Sovnarkom and there is no record of their being considered by the Party Central Committee.[47] Kursky seems to have been appointed without formal consideration by either Sovnarkom or the Central Committee.[48] Shmidt's appointment as Labour Commissar was the sole government change in this period which can be shown to have been discussed and decided in advance by the Central Committee.[49]

Like Krasin's takeover of the Transport Commissariat, the other two appointments in 1919, those of Dzerzhinsky to Internal Affairs and Stalin to State Control, represented the acquisition of a second 'hat' by powerful and effective members of the government. It is noteworthy that the decisions on these two appointments were taken at a meeting of the Party Central Committee rather than of Sovnarkom,[50] though this probably reflected their political importance rather than a shift (as yet) in the locus of authority in such matters.

The Internal Affairs Commissariat had all along aspired to jurisdiction over 'the combating of counterrevolution', but Dzerzhinsky had stubbornly held out for the independence of his Vecheka. Since, however, the Commissariat had charge of the regular police (the 'militia'), and issued instructions on security matters to the gubernia soviets, conflicts between the two bodies were inevitable, despite the presence of mutual representation on each other's Boards. The solution, facilitated by the departure of Internal Affairs Commissar Petrovsky to head the Central Executive Committee of the new Soviet republic of the Ukraine, was to put Dzerzhinsky in charge of both bodies, while maintaining their separate identity.[51]

The logic of Stalin's holding both the State Control and Nationalities portfolios was not so obvious, although both did involve a watchdog role separate from the routine administration. For some time after the Bolshevik takeover of the old State Control Ministry it had been in something of a limbo, and only with its reorganisation and the appointment of Lander in May 1918 was it really set to work for the Soviet Government. Subsequently the growing administrative confusion, corruption and interdepartmental conflict enhanced its role and called for a more authoritative commissar. At the same time the Commissariat was reorganised along lines which foreshadowed (especially in the involvement of volunteer part-time inspectors) its transformation into the Commissariat of Worker-Peasant Inspection (Rabkrin) a year later.[52]

At the end of 1919 there was a shortlived merging of the Commissariats of Labour and Social Security under Labour Commissar Shmidt. To examine the politics of these changes would take us too far afield, but we should note here that the decisions on merging and subsequently splitting the commissariats were both taken by the Party Central Committee, and the latter decision was imposed against strong opposition from the Bolshevik leadership in the trade unions and the Labour Commissariat.[53] Vinokurov resumed the status of Social Security Commissar after the split in April 1920. A year later, with the expansion of trade union functions into the welfare area decreed by the Tenth Party Congress, the Social Security Commissariat again went into limbo, without, however, being formally abolished. Commissar Vinokurov, though not replaced till 1923, became full-time Chairman of a commission established for the relief of famine.

Early in 1920 yet another member of the inner leadership was given a second portfolio when Trotsky was put in charge of the Transport Commissariat. Well before this the disorganisation and decay of the railways had reached crisis point, dangerously hampering the movement of troops and equipment to the fronts and food to the towns. A strong hand was needed, and Krasin, increasingly taken up with the problems of foreign trade, was unable to provide it. Armed with a Politburo decision, Lenin telephoned Trotsky in the Urals inviting him to take over the Commissariat, and the latter agreed on the understanding that the appointment should be temporary in status.[54] Trotsky immediately threw himself into his new task, achieving considerable success by using the strict disciplinarian methods and the emphasis on technical competence that had paid such dividends in the armed forces.[55] He carried out a widespread purge and installed a new leadership in the Commissariat, handing over the portfolio at the end of the year to a man he had groomed for the task. 'The present People's Commissar of Transport, Cde Yemshanov', he told the Eighth Congress of Soviets,

formerly worked on the Perm line, and later at the centre, in particular serving on various consultative bodies and commissions which carried out surveys of our various lines and dismissed unsuitable officials, replacing them with officials sent out from the centre. Cde Yemshanov carried out this work along with the rest of us on the basis of methods laid down by me.[56]

The procedures followed on Yemshanov's appointment presented an illuminating contrast with the practices of two years earlier. The crucial decision was taken by the full Central Committee of the Party, and was duly adopted by Sovnarkom two days later in the form of a 'request' to the CEC. Incidentally in a note to Central Committee Secretary Serebryakov the day before the Central Committee meeting, Lenin had tentatively suggested a different candidate, but Trotsky's support probably clinched the issue in Yemshanov's favour.[57]

In February 1920 there occurred the first death in office of a Sovnarkom member – that of Posts and Telegraphs Commissar Podbelsky. The background of his successor, A. M. Lyubovich, was remarkably similar to Yemshanov's. Both had joined the Party only in 1917, first made their mark as union organisers and moved from there into the economic administration. Yemshanov had been committee chairman of the union of the Perm Railway Directorate, before being put in charge of the Directorate, then moved into the central administration of the Transport Commissariat and formally became People's Commissar. Lyubovich, aged 37 at the time of the Revolution, was an organiser of the Kronstadt Soviet and took part in the Bolshevik seizure of power, then became Chairman of the Central Committee of the Posts and Telegraphs Workers' Union, Deputy People's Commissar for Transport, and in March 1920 returned to Posts and Telegraphs as People's Commissar. These appointments mark a new departure in the recruitment of Sovnarkom members. The party standing of these men was negligible, but they had thrown in their lot with the Bolsheviks at the time of the Revolution, and then demonstrated their loyalty and leadership capacity in quasi-political, quasi-managerial roles in the economic administration.

In 1921 both these posts changed hands again. Lyubovich was sent to help strengthen the Soviet regime in Belorussia, becoming Deputy Chairman of its Sovnarkom and Chairman of its Planning Committee. His place was taken by V. S. Dovgalevsky, an Old Bolshevik and an electrical engineer by profession who had fought in the Civil War, then worked as a railway administrator, becoming Commissar of Communications in the Transport Commissariat, from which position he was transferred as People's Commissar for Posts and Telegraphs. Unlike his predecessor, Dovgalevsky lacked a base of support in the Postal Workers' Union, and Lenin, perhaps along with other leaders, having decided on him for the job but wishing to avoid subjecting their already difficult relations with the unions to further strain, evidently conceived the idea of giving him a spell in a union post before promotion as commissar. However, Lenin's confidant on the Posts and Telegraphs Board, A. M. Nikolaev, advised him that this would not work because TUC support would be lacking owing to Dovgalevsky's unacceptability to the Postal Workers' Union. The only way of getting him on to the Board, he argued, was 'from above', by decision of the Party Central Committee, but Party Secretary Molotov was hesitant to take this step for fear of offending TUC Chairman Tomsky. Lenin thereupon urged Nikolaev to submit the question to the next meeting of the Politburo, arming himself with as many written references on Dovgalevsky as possible, including one from Krasin. This was done, and the Politburo duly appointed Lenin's candidate a member of the Board and simultaneously People's Commissar.[58]

Meanwhile Yemshanov had seemingly not proved strong enough

for the Transport Commissariat, which was now taken over by Dzerzhinsky, who added it to his other two government posts. The combination was less strange than it might seem, since the Cheka had become closely concerned with the railways, whose security was of vital concern to the regime, and personnel of its Transport Department worked throughout the railway network. Furthermore the never-docile Railwaymen's Union, much influenced by the now outlawed Workers' Opposition, was proving uncooperative in the drive to restore the railways through tightening discipline and the employment of 'bourgeois' specialists. Dzerzhinsky's experience as 'Sword of the Revolution' would therefore come in handy. The appointment also reflected a partial switch of Dzerzhinsky's interest to problems of the economy, which led later (in 1924) to his assuming the chairmanship of the National Economic Council. The decision to appoint him was made not by Sovnarkom, but by the Party Central Committee, and according to Bonch-Bruyevich, without a formal meeting, but simply by the collection of signatures (presumably of Politburo members) on a decision drawn up by Lenin after an interview with Dzerzhinsky. His predecessor as Transport Commissar, incidentally, now became his deputy, and presumably continued to look after routine administration.[59]

Two other appointments in 1921 represented replacements for people's commissars promoted to be Deputy Chairman of Sovnarkom (see Chapter 13), in both cases made from within the department concerned. Thus in May Rykov was succeeded as Chairman of the NEC by P. A. Bogdanov, who had served in the latter body almost since its foundation, becoming Chairman of its Metals Division and a member of its Board; while in December Food Supplies Commissar Tsyurupa handed over to his deputy N. P. Bryukhanov, who had worked in the commissariat since February 1918.

The appointment of V. G. Yakovenko as Agriculture Commissar at the beginning of 1922 is an unusual case that deserves a closer look. The post had been vacant for almost a year. Sereda, the last incumbent, had written to Central Committee Secretary Krestinsky on 9 December 1920 asking to be relieved on grounds of ill-health, and he was duly released on 2 February 1921, being appointed Deputy Chairman of the newly-formed State Planning Commission (Gosplan). His deputy at the time he was preparing to leave was I. A. Teodorovich, the original Food Supplies Commissar. However,

early in 1921 an additional deputy people's commissar was appointed
in the person of N. Osinsky, the original Chairman of the NEC,
who had since been a leading figure successively in the Left Communist and Democratic Centralist oppositions. Osinsky had been
rusticated as Chairman of the Executive Committee of Tula Provincial Soviet where, however, he distinguished himself in 1920 by
achieving large-scale plantings of grain at a time when peasants
generally were drastically restricting their sowing. It was evidently
this, along with his good work as a member of the Board of the Food
Supplies Commissariat, that won him the strong support in party
circles which led to his senior appointment in the Agriculture Commissariat. Although the Commissariat was supposed to be run by a
troika of Osinsky, Teodorovich and Board member P. A. Mesyatsev,
Osinsky was treated by Lenin as effective head of the Commissariat
throughout 1921 and acted as its spokesman at important gatherings.
From the first Teodorovich and Osinsky seem to have been at logger-
heads, and as late as December 1921 we find them simultaneously
writing to Lenin complaining about each other. It is unclear whether
Osinsky was originally envisaged as taking over the commissariat but
the opposition he provoked caused the idea to be dropped; in any
case the conflict between him and Teodorovich seems to have delayed a decision on Sereda's successor.[60]

The resolution, when it came, took an unexpected form. From
early in 1921 Lenin had pressed for the recruitment of suitable
peasants to the Agriculture Commissariat,[61] as a move towards con-
solidating the new relationship with the peasantry that was the
cornerstone of NEP. Towards the end of the year the idea emerged
that what was needed was a '*muzhik* people's commissar' and the
search for a suitable candidate began. On 17 December Lenin
received a letter from Teodorovich recommending Yakovenko, who
was at that time Chairman of the Executive Committee of a district
(*uyezd*) Soviet in Siberia. A Siberian peasant who joined the
Bolshevik Party in his native village in July 1917, when he was on
leave from the army, Yakovenko had been active in local Soviet
organisations and became a partisan commander during the Civil
War. By December 1920 he had achieved enough prominence in the
Yenisei Province to be sent as one of its delegates to the Eighth
Congress of Soviets and a year later the provincial party committee
proposed to make him deputy chairman of the provincial soviet
executive committee. At this point Teodorovich remembered him,

having served with him during the Civil War, and immediately saw his potential for the agriculture commissariat. 'He is a massive, powerful *muzhik*', he wrote to Lenin, 'full-bearded and straight from the plough, in love with the "soil"...In my view he will be just the man for the post of *muzhik* people's commissar. His discipline and loyalty to the Soviet regime are beyond doubt.'[62]

Lenin's imagination was immediately captured.[63] The same day he sent a note to Kamenev, who was chairing Politburo meetings in his absence, and with whom he had recently discussed the matter, urging the necessity for as many Central Committee members as possible to get to know Yakovenko at the Congress of Soviets that was about to convene. Teodorovich's letter was to be shown first to the members of the Orgburo, and then the rest of the Central Committee.[64] Five days later he wrote to Central Committee Secretary Molotov urging him to speed up the familiarisation of all Politburo members with the contents of Teodorovich's letter 'regarding the Siberian peasant Yakovenko'. On 24 December he asked the Siberian Party Secretary Yaroslavsky to immediately obtain references on Yakovenko from all leading Siberian officials attending the Congress. Armed with three such references, he asked Molotov the next day to seek Politburo approval to summon Yakovenko to Moscow for the Politburo to meet him and consider his appointment as people's commissar.[65] On Yakovenko's arrival Lenin talked with him in his office for two hours and, having satisfied himself that he was all that Teodorovich claimed, proposed his appointment to the next meeting of the Politburo. The latter agreed – whether any doubts or alternative proposals were voiced is not recorded – and on 9 January the Presidium of the CEC endorsed the decision.[66]

While the new people's commissar was clearly more than the mere figurehead that Rogov had been in 1918, the Politburo decreed that all political decisions in the Commissariat were to be taken by a triumvirate of Yakovenko, Teodorovich and Osinsky, within which the last-named evidently enjoyed the special confidence of Lenin: certainly Lenin was not above addressing Osinsky on delicate matters over his ostensible superior's head.[67]

Apart from the addition of Kamenev as a third Deputy Chairman, there was only one new appointment to Sovnarkom in the course of 1922,[68] that of Sokolnikov as People's Commissar for Finance. His predecessor Krestinsky was made Soviet political representative (i.e. ambassador) in Germany in October 1921 but it was over a year before he was formally replaced. Sokolnikov's involvement in the administration of finance went back to 1918, when he had played a leading part in the nationalisation of the banks. The Civil War had taken him out of Sovnarkom activities, and 1920 found him head of the Soviet administration in Turkestan. On Krestinsky's departure the administration of the Finance Commissariat was at first in the hands of his deputy, A. O. Alsky, but then Sokolnikov joined the Board, was quickly promoted to deputy people's commissar, and by January 1922 had displaced Alsky as the chief spokesman for the commissariat.[69]

The Board was rife with personal antipathies and jealousies. On 31 December 1921 the Politburo resolved to appoint an additional deputy people's commissar in the person of A. M. Krasnoshchëkov, who had lived in America for 15 years, graduating from college in Chicago and gaining useful administrative experience, joined the Bolsheviks only in 1917, and in 1920–1 had headed the government of the pro-Soviet Far Eastern Republic. His appointment was bitterly opposed by the whole Board except Sokolnikov, and one of its leading members, E. A. Preobrazhensky, threatened to resign. On Lenin's initiative the Politburo insisted and on 10 January Sovnarkom formalised the appointment.[70] Later in the month the Politburo resolved that initial consideration of major policy questions in the field of finance should be entrusted to a *troika* consisting of Sokolnikov, Preobrazhensky and Krasnoshchëkov. To Lenin's fury, Sokolnikov 'rejected' this decision and the Politburo had to enforce it by a further decision a week later.[71] Krasnoshchëkov continued to suffer hostility within the Board, especially from Alsky, and in March he was sacked (on whose authority is not clear). He went to see Lenin, who was highly indignant at his treatment, and first proposed to the Politburo that he be found work in the NEC, but then a few days later wrote a secret letter to Sokolnikov in which he proposed that the 'good-for-nothing' Alsky be sacked and Krasnoshchëkov reinstated, since only he could put the administration in order. In the upshot, however, the Politburo transferred Krasnoshchëkov to the Presidium of the NEC, and at the same time revamped the Board, presumably removing Alsky as well.[72] Despite these troubles Sokolnikov remained effectively in charge of the commissariat, though they may have delayed the decision to formalise his position, and Lenin's long convalescence following his stroke in May further postponed the formal appointment for some months.

All this was a far cry from the feverish days of 1917–18. No longer were people's commissars made on the basis of hasty consultation among two or three leaders and a brief harangue to the astounded 'victim', frequently without formal discussion in any party or government body. It was now a deliberate and highly institutionalised process that might extend over several months. Although Lenin had not lost his central role, the institutional environment in which he operated was not only far more firmly structured, but had a changed centre of gravity. To the extent that formal bodies were involved in early Sovnarkom appointments, the crucial discussions more often than not took place in Sovnarkom itself; now it was the Politburo that decided all Sovnarkom appointments, while the CEC or its Presidium formalised them. Standing in the party had been the main criterion for early appointments, though some efforts were made to match the man to the job. As time went on qualifications and experience assumed ever greater importance, and increasingly this meant administrative experience working in the same department or some related one. Appointments according to the principle of bureaucratic seniority (deputies becoming people's commissars) now appeared, and bureaucratic politics both between and within commissariats began to influence the selection process.

The short-lived appointment of the Railwaymen's Union official Rogov as Transport Commissar in 1918 was clearly a political tactic and did not open a new era of consulting with the relevant 'mass organisations' in making Sovnarkom appointments. Similar tactical considerations evidently played a part in the appointment of Shmidt as Labour Commissar later the same year, and to a lesser extent of Yemshanov to Transport and Lyubovich to Posts and Telegraphs in 1920, all three of whom had a trade union background, while Yakovenko's appointment as Agriculture Commissar was undoubtedly aimed first and foremost at winning peasant support. Despite marked changes in the selection process, it remained entirely cooptative in character and confined within the ruling oligarchy, even if regard was occasionally taken of the impact of appointment decisions on relevant sectional opinion.

The people's commissars: personal background

The biographies of Sovnarkom members in Lenin's day show a wide diversity of social origin, education and life-experience. One might imagine this heterogeneity to have been moderated, if not negated, by the fact that they were all revolutionary Marxists. For was not participation in the Bolshevik movement the supreme formative experience for all of them, did not the fires of the revolutionary struggle melt the native ore of their original social personalities and identities and form them in a common mould? But this can scarcely be maintained either. Revolutionary Marxists who had achieved some prominence in the Russian Social-Democratic Labour Party they indeed all were, but their modes of being Marxists and of being revolutionaries were as varied as the other aspects of their biographies. Indeed, when one considers the many Sovnarkom members who found themselves amongst the supporters of multi-party government in 1917, the Left Communists in 1918, the Workers' Opposition or Democratic Centralists in 1920–1, or of the various opposition groupings of the middle and later 1920s, it is immediately apparent that those serving in Lenin's government had most diverse notions as to what the Revolution was about and how to create a socialist society. Behind this diversity of conviction lay the most varied political biographies.

It was a diversity that extended both to the experience and qualities of personality that first brought them into the revolutionary movement, and to the lives they led and the political positions they adopted after they had joined. The truth of this is immediately suggested by the starkly contrasting personalities and revolutionary careers of such dominating figures as Lenin, Trotsky and Stalin, and the contrasts appear no less when one considers the biographies of the lesser lights.[1] A systematic analysis of the political psychology of

Sovnarkom members would be beyond the capacities of the present author, and indeed in many cases the sources are far too fragmentary for such an undertaking. However, it is worth giving some samples of the varied factors which, on the face of it, may have contributed to their becoming revolutionaries.

It did not, of course, necessarily require unusual factors of personality or experience for a bright young man to be drawn into the revolutionary movement under the conditions prevailing in Tsarist Russia. Attracted by the natural curiosity, rebelliousness or idealism of youth into some clandestine radical circle at his grammar-school or university, he was then all too likely to suffer severe disciplinary action or even expulsion or arrest, thereby blighting his chances of a normal career and 'freezing' him in a revolutionary posture; thus did the autocracy create its own gravediggers. Almost two-thirds of the Bolsheviks who served on Lenin's Sovnarkom became revolutionaries in precisely this way – though no doubt other factors played a part in many of these cases, as we shall see. Early exposure to radical ideas in the family could also be important: Bryukhanov, Kamenev, Krasin, Krestinsky, Krylenko, Lenin, Lomov, Lunacharsky, Osinsky, Podbelsky and Vinokurov were all influenced in adolescence by the examples or ideas of radically-minded parents or elder brothers. The immediate family was not, of course, the only possible source of such early influences. Yelizarov developed a close friendship with Lenin's brother Alexander (executed in 1887 for plotting to assassinate the Tsar) and on wedding his sister married, as it were, into the Revolution. Dybenko was introduced to Marxist ideas by a teacher in his village school. Essen and a cousin seem to have provoked each other into ever more daring revolutionary ideas and associations.

Once we attempt to probe below such obvious influences, the search for revolutionising experiences becomes more speculative. Ethnic discrimination was evidently a factor in a few cases. Sokolnikov refers to the effect on him of harassment by his teachers because of his Jewishness. Such experiences may also have helped to radicalise the proud young Trotsky. Teodorovich came of a fanatically nationalistic Polish family and the Polish question was clearly an important influence in Dzerzhinsky's early political alienation as well,[2] as the Georgian question was in Stalin's. The humiliations attendant on being a clever boy from a lower class family, and either being denied suitable education or undergoing it in company with the pampered, arrogant sons of the rich, was one shared by Avilov,

Dybenko, Yelizarov, Lander, Nogin, Shlyapnikov, Shmidt and perhaps Trotsky. On a deeper psychological level, one is struck by the
number of people's commissars who had been deprived of their
fathers in their early years. Chicherin, Dzerzhinsky, Kursky, Lenin,
Nevsky, Rykov, Semashko and Stalin lost their fathers during their
childhood or adolescence. Teodorovich's father deserted the family
when he was five. Both Lander and Shmidt were sons of housemaids,
the former certainly illegitimate and the latter probably so. Lander,
it is true, spent a blissful early childhood with his maternal grand-
parents, but this came to an end when his mother married and his
stepfather took them away, while Shmidt was shunted between relatives and an orphanage.

Such factors, alone or in combination, would probably figure large
in any attempt to explain what lay behind our people's commissars
becoming revolutionaries in the first place. But numerous other
influences, as well as more or less fortuitous events, would also form
part of any full-scale analysis. Take Karl Lander, for instance. His
early family situation may have laid the psychological basis of his
alienation from the existing socio-political order, and the experience
of working as a labourer while studying at night to qualify as an
elementary school teacher probably reinforced it, but initially this
alienation took the form of a fanatical Tolstoyanism. Lander fell
under the influence of the well-known Tolstoyan, I. M. Tregubov,
who had been exiled by the authorities to his district, and for some
three years he carried on a correspondence with Tolstoy himself.
His enthusiasm led him to attempt a journey on foot from his Baltic
homeland to visit a Tolstoyan settlement in the Crimea. This turned
out to be his road to Damascus, for he was picked up by the police
as a vagrant and sent back home via various prisons and prison-
trains, a journey that lasted for months, and was then kept in prison
for several more months, this experience and the influence of various
Marxist revolutionaries who shared his cells along the way converting him to Social Democracy.[3]

Chicherin's adoption of revolutionary Marxism at the advanced
age of 32 followed an even more roundabout spiritual pilgrimage,
but again the seeds were evidently sown in childhood. His parents
had been converted to Christian pietism while Chicherin senior was
serving as a diplomat in Paris, and the latter, having violated the
social code of his class by declining to fight a duel, retired to his
estate, where the young Chicherin was surrounded by a sombre

atmosphere of constant bible-reading, prayers and hymn singing. This, he relates, implanted in him 'a certain messianism', while visits with his mother around the hamlets where she practised good works among the peasants induced 'an exalted romantic populism'. Then his father, foreseeing at last a way of proving his manhood, volunteered to be a stretcher-bearer in the Russo-Turkish war and died as a result of his privations – when Chichern junior was ten. Later, as a student in St Petersburg moving in establishment circles he suffered much humiliation due to his family's impoverished condition and 'disgrace'. For many years his alienation took purely personal forms before it found external expression in revolutionary activity.

Some other cases may be mentioned more briefly. Antonov-Ovseyenko, his father an impoverished nobleman, a reserve infantry officer, he himself short-sighted, weedy, sensitive and artistic, torn between his revulsion against the idea of military service and his sense of duty to the family to undertake it: in becoming an officer, he simultaneously became a revolutionary.[4] Alexandra Kollontai, for whom the revolutionary movement offered at the same time employment for her intellectual talents and generous spirit, and an escape from the constraints of Petersburg high society to a life of independence and freedom; Shlyapnikov, losing his father at three and spending his childhood in extreme want, subject to constant harassment because of his Old Believer background – 'Religious persecution, the persecution of the street, persecution in school, poverty and deprivation in the family, all this disposed my childhood dreams and aspirations towards struggle and martyrdom' – aspirations and dreams for which, as a seventeen-year-old worker involved in the 1891 St Petersburg strikes, he suddenly found expression and direction.

One could go on, but the examples already given should suffice to establish our main point: the crucial experiences forming the minds and personalities of those who were later to become people's commissars, and led them into the revolutionary movement, were extremely diverse. Little less varied, moreover, were their political biographies and patterns of life after they joined the movement. To start with, we should recall that Russian Social Democracy was a highly heterogeneous phenomenon, and several of the early Soviet leaders had spent long periods in other parts of it before throwing in their lot with Lenin and his Bolsheviks. Trotsky, of course, did so only on the eve of the Revolution, as likewise did Antonov-Ovseyenko, while Kollontai was a Menshevik till 1915 and Chicherin did not join the Bolsheviks till 1918, almost simultaneously with his appointment as people's commissar. Others again, having initially aligned themselves among Lenin's followers, subsequently broke with him for more or less lengthy periods on various issues. Lunacharsky, for instance, spent several years as a leader of the anti-Leninist *Vperëd* group, Osinsky was in the 'Otzovist' opposition (advocating withdrawal of the Bolshevik deputies from the Duma), Bogdanov was a 'defencist' supporter of the Russian war effort, while Krylenko temporarily deserted Bolshevism for syndicalism; Nogin was both a 'conciliator' in 1908–10 (favouring rapprochement with the Mensheviks), and a 'defencist' during the war. Others again more or less completely disengaged from the revolutionary movement and for many years were peacefully engaged in normal occupations. Krasin is the outstanding example. A leading collaborator of Lenin's in the early years of Bolshevism, he then moved to the *Vperëdist* opposition, and from 1910 till after the Revolution made a highly successful career as an industrial administrator. Bryukhanov seems to have had little contact with the revolutionary movement between 1907 and 1917, and Tsyurupa also dropped out for several years after the 1905 Revolution, resuming contact with his local Bolshevik organisation only in 1917.[5]

In analysing the variety of revolutionary experience that Sovnarkom members had behind them, perhaps the most fundamental distinction we should draw is that between the revolutionary at home and the revolutionary abroad, since life under the perilous, conspiratorial conditions of the Bolshevik underground in Russia clearly had little in common with life in the relatively safe but hothouse atmosphere of the Russian revolutionary 'colonies' of Geneva, Paris or Brussels. Many Bolshevik leaders enjoyed at least a taste of both, but most spent the decade or so before the Revolution predominantly either abroad (e.g. Lenin, Trotsky, Lunacharsky, Dovgalevsky, Kollontai) or in Russia (e.g. Stalin, Rykov, Dzerzhinsky, Krestinsky, Avilov). We should also distinguish degrees in the *intensity* of involvement in the movement. To think of the Bolshevik Party as made up wholly of 'professional revolutionaries' would be seriously misleading. Within the emigré movement, for instance, alongside leaders like Lenin and Trotsky whose time and energies were totally committed to the revolutionary cause there were others like Dovgalevsky or

Semashko, who combined their political activities with training for or practising a profession. Within Russia, the contrasts could be even greater between the conditions of life of a Stalin, Dzerzhinsky, Rykov or Podbelsky, operating for the most part as professional 'under-grounders' with false papers, and those whose contributions to the party cause were combined with the more or less peaceful pursuit of some regular employment. The latter category are represented by such as Sereda, who worked for some twenty years as an agricultural statistician while performing occasional tasks for the Bolshevik committees in various cities; or Bogdanov, who was employed by the Moscow City Council for six years before the War and in his spare time helped administer the Party finances; or Lenin's brother-in-law Yelizarov, whose main party function seems to have been supporting the Ulyanov family, while working as an insurance agent. Another critically differentiating factor in the political 'profile' of a revolutionary was his experience of prison, forced labour, or exile to the remote corners of the empire. A home-based Bolshevik like Essen could go through the whole period to 1917 without once suffering arrest. At the other extreme there was a Milyutin, who was arrested no less than eight times, a Teodorovich, who spent the years from 1909 to 1917 on hard labour, or a Dzerzhinsky, whose numerous stretches of prison, hard labour and exile totalled eleven years.

These various categories of experience were displayed in such a bewildering range of degrees and combinations that one cannot neatly classify the pre-revolutionary political biographies of Lenin's Sovnarkom members in terms of any simple typology. Nevertheless some attempt at a summary picture in quantitative terms may be justified, so long as it is understood that the boundaries are often blurred and the numerical relationships shown only roughly indicate the balance between different categories of experience. Table 4 is based on the political histories of Sovnarkom members between the beginnings of Bolshevism in 1903 and the October 1917 Revolution, grouping them in terms of two dichotomies: those living predominantly abroad or predominantly in Russia (emigration–Russia), and those working for the party predominantly on a basis of full-time commitment or predominantly on a part-time basis, i.e. combining party activity with some regular employment ('professional'–'amateur'). For the sake of the analysis 'predominantly' is taken to mean at least nine years out of the fifteen, and cases where the balance of time spent is closer than this are shown as classifiable with either alternative group, thus producing a range in most of the numerical values arrived at.[6] As in the other tables in this chapter, Sovnarkom members are analysed at three periods in time: immediately after the establishment of the regime, at the end of 1918 when the membership had emerged from its early shake-ups and assumed the relative stability it maintained during the Civil War, and at the end of 1922, when Lenin had his last burst of activity as Chairman. This procedure has the disadvantage of omitting a handful of people's commissars who came and went between those dates, but the great merit of revealing any trends there may have been over time.[7]

The trends revealed by this table are so marked that they command attention despite the imperfections of data and difficulties of classification. The 'professional revolutionaries' operating inside Russia made up a clear majority of the Sovnarkom formed in 1917, but by 1922 they had been reduced to a small minority, while all the other groups had grown. Taking our two dichotomies separately, we find clear trends in both. Sovnarkom members who had mainly lived

TABLE 4   *Predominant pre-revolutionary political experience of Sovnarkom members*

At least nine years between 1903 and 1917 spent as:	Original 1917 (N = 19)	End 1918 (N = 18)	End 1918 (N = 18)
'Professional' in emigration	5–6	4–6	6–8
'Amateur' in emigration	–	0–2	2–3
'Professional 'in Russia	10–11	7–8	3–5
'Amateur' in Russia	3	4–5	4–5
Total 'professionals'	16	11–14	10–12
Total 'amateurs'	3	4–7	6–8
Total in emigration	5–6	4–8	8–11
Total in Russia	13–14	11–13	7–10

abroad before the Revolution increased from under a third to about a half, while the ratio of 'professionals' to 'amateurs' declined from about 5 : 1 to about 3 : 2. Some partial explanations immediately suggest themselves. Before the Revolution full-time commitment as a 'professional revolutionary' was of course usually necessary to win leading status in the party. Moreover, in the early days of Sovnarkom, those on the spot, especially in the Petrograd and Moscow organisations of the party, enjoyed an obvious immediate advantage when people's commissars were being recruited. Other factors, however, also contributed to these trends, as will become apparent later in our analysis when we consider the training and work experience of Sovnarkom members.

The varied family origins of Sovnarkom members have already been alluded to, but this diversity was far from random. To start with, men of unequivocally proletarian background were very few, as likewise were those of peasant origin. Even at the beginning the majority of Sovnarkom members had been born into middle- or upper-class families, and the predominance tended to grow. In Table 5 we set out the occupation of Sovnarkom members' fathers,[8] and then aggregate them into two broad class groups. The largest group in this table, the officials, was also the most varied, but it included no really high-level civil *chinovniki*, and several seem to have been in bad odour owing to their political views. At the other extreme there were hardly any from the 'lower depths': perhaps Shlyapnikov comes closest. Thus the father of Yelizarov, though an ex-serf, was a solid and respected member of his community, serving as the village *starosta* or headman; Trotsky's father was a prosperous freeholder; Dybenko's was probably the only genuine poor peasant. The handful of urban workers did not include a single one who spent most of his working life in the industrial proletariat. The intelligentsia as traditionally understood in Russia was a category cutting across occupational boundaries and embracing those educated people who aspired to independent (and therefore often 'subversive') thinking. Many but probably not all of the ten professionals among our Sovnarkom members' fathers might be so classified, but several others who were employed in administrative jobs, judging by the accounts of their interests and life-styles given by their sons, were also evidently *intelligenty*. Altogether something like a quarter to a third of our people's commissars spent their childhood in intelligentsia families.

The estates (*sosloviya*) into which the society of Imperial Russia was officially divided, and which also cut across occupational categories, had declined greatly in importance by the time of the Revolution, but they retained some legal and political significance and still provided the basic framework for the social hierarchy. Unfortunately, data on the estates from which our people's commissars were drawn is very incomplete. One thing that is clear, however, is that the topmost estate of Tsarist society, the gentry (*dvoryanstvo*), provided far more than its share of Sovnarkom members. At least six,

TABLE 5　*Father's occupation*

Fathers of Sovnarkom members in:	1917	1918	1922
Government official	3	6	5
Army officer	2		
Engineer	1	1	2
Doctor			1
Teacher	2	3	2
Merchant–capitalist		1	1
Other upper or middle class occupation	3	1	2
Artisan	1	1	
Urban worker	1	1	2
Peasant/farmer	4	2	2
Other lower-class ocupation	1	2	1
	19	18	18
Total upper and middle class occupations	11	12	13
Total lower class occupations	8	6	5
Per cent upper- and middle-class occupations	58	67	72
Per cent lower-class occupations	42	33	28

and possibly eight, of the original people's commissars were from gentry families, although the gentry made up only some two per cent of the pre-revolutionary population. This means they were represented in Sovnarkom at upwards of fifteen times the rate of the population as a whole.[9] The number of Sovnarkom members in 1918 and 1922 whose estates have been established does not permit a direct comparison with 1917, but it seems likely that the proportion drawn from the gentry fell off somewhat. Of course the gentry varied greatly in rank, status, wealth, and source of income, and the families of our people's commissars formed a fair cross section, ranging from impoverished squires (*pomeshchiki*) to St Petersburg high society. If none were quite from the top drawer, at least some were from the second-top. Osinsky, whose correct family name was

Obolensky, was at pains to point out that he did not come from the ducal branch of the Obolensky clan. The Chicherins, on the other hand, were undoubtedly aristocrats, even if the people's commissar's immediate family was rather fallen from grace. Kollontai's father was a general. Essen's was a railway engineer, but the family was a distinguished one in St Petersburg, descended from Baltic counts of Swedish origin, and his uncle, Vice-Admiral N. O. von Essen, commanded the Baltic Fleet under Nicholas II and is accorded a longer entry in the Soviet Historical Encyclopedia than the people's commissar himself.[10] The break effected by revolutions in the social sources of recruitment to the political elite is rarely a complete one. In this respect the Bolshevik Revolution was no exception, and in its composition Sovnarkom provided substantial links between the old ruling strata and the new.

Although half the population of the Russian Empire were non-Russians, Russians formed the great majority of Sovnarkom members in Lenin's time. This partly reflects the composition of the pre-revolutionary party: as David Lane has shown, the Bolsheviks were most heavily concentrated in central Russian areas, in contrast with the Mensheviks and other Social-Democratic groups, who recruited more heavily in the borderlands.[11] Nevertheless non-Russians constituted about a third of the delegates to party congresses held between 1918 and 1922,[12] and Sovnarkom must therefore be regarded as ethnically one of the more homogeneous segments of the elite in this period. Those who can be definitely classified as non-Russians comprised a Georgian, a Jew and a Pole in 1917, a Georgian, a Jew and a Latvian in 1918, and a Georgian, three Jews and a Pole in 1922. To the 1918 group we should probably add a Ukrainian, if we regard Petrovsky as having been more Ukrainian than Russian. It is true that the antecedents of several others, to judge by their German, Polish or Ukrainian names, were at least partly non-Russian. However it would seem from their biographies that their families were more or less thoroughly assimilated, although there may have been three or four who retained some lingering identification with the nationality of their forebears.[13] With this qualification, it seems that Sovnarkom was three-quarters or more Russian throughout most of the Lenin period.

Let us now turn from the social and ethnic origins of the people's commissars to consider some other aspects of their lives and background. The Bolsheviks, like most revolutionary organisations, were a party of young men, and this is reflected in the membership of Sovnarkom. Kollontai was the only woman to serve in Lenin's government, and she only for four months. The people's commissars naturally tended to be older than the party membership as a whole, but they were still on average only 37 at the time of the seizure of power.[14] At the same time, they showed a wide diversity in age, ranging from the 28-year-old Dybenko to the 55-year-old Yelizarov. Lenin himself was aged 47 when he became Head of the Soviet Government.

TABLE 6   *Age of Sovnarkom members*

	1917	1918	1922
No. aged up to 29	2		
30–39	11	7	5
40–49	5	11	9
50 and over	1		4
Age of youngest	28	31	33
Age of oldest	55	49	52
Average age	37.4	41.5	43.4
Per cent under 40	69	39	28
Per cent 40 and over	31	61	72

As can be seen from Table 6, the age-range in Sovnarkom narrowed considerably between 1917 and 1922, from twenty-seven years to nineteen. At the same time the average age rose somewhat *faster* than the lapse of time, by six years over a period of five years. In other words, changes of people's commissars tended to bring in men who were *older* than their predecessors, an event rare enough in the membership of governments and executive bodies generally to call for some explanation. As we shall see shortly, it was a development that linked up with certain other trends in the characteristics of Sovnarkom members. Before leaving the topic, however, we may note that if forty can be regarded as the point of transition from young adulthood to early middle age, then Sovnarkom had crossed this Rubicon on a broad front before Lenin left the scene.

What kind of formal education had Sovnarkom members received? This is of interest for two reasons: first because it was the other main factor, along with family background, forming and defining their original social identity; and second, because it was a major ingredient in the intellectual equipment they brought to their work in Sovnarkom. It was not, of course, the only such ingredient, for all had drunk more or less deeply from the spring of Marxist thought, which sometimes contributed more to their knowledge of history, economics or philosophy than did their formal education. An obvious illustration is Avilov, who received only an elementary schooling and was already working in a printing shop at the age of twelve, acquiring most of his general education through the reading and study he did within the party, which included a year or so at the party school in Bologna. The preponderance of Marxism in their intellectual formation might be scarcely less marked, however, in the case of those with more extensive formal education. Skvortsov-Stepanov, for instance, graduated from Moscow Teachers' Institute, but the training he received there can hardly have contributed greatly to his later career as a Marxist publicist, in the course of which he wrote several books and translated Marx's *Capital* (together with V. Bazarov). This education in and through Marxism certainly varied greatly from individual to individual, but we propose to leave it aside in this discussion, since in most cases we know insufficient about what it involved to relate it meaningfully to their roles as people's commissars.

As we see from Table 7, the majority of Sovnarkom members received their schooling in the elite grammar schools (*gimnazii*) or modern schools (*real'nye uchilishcha*). In addition one (Kollontai) was educated at home by private tutors and a second (Antonov-Ovseyenko) went to cadet school. The proportion of Sovnarkom members who had enjoyed such select forms of schooling fluctuated between two-thirds and three-quarters throughout the Lenin period, and the predominance of graduates from the grammar schools, with their 'classical', literary-oriented programmes, over those from the more science-oriented modern schools, persisted undiminished.

However, for the majority of Sovnarkom members education had not ended with secondary school, and this applied particularly, of course, to the grammar school graduates. Several further points emerge when we turn to Table 8. Firstly, there was remarkable continuity in the educational composition of Sovnarkom over this period, in spite of the high turnover of members. The most significant change was the drop from four to two in the number of people's commissars whose education had not proceeded beyond elementary or 'city' school – a change which occurred already in 1918. Next, what stands out most is the persistent preponderance of members who had received some form of tertiary education, of whom half or more were holders of university or comparable degrees (*diplomy*).[15]

TABLE 7 *Highest pre-tertiary education received*

	1917	1918	1922
Private tutors	1		
Grammar school	8	9	10
Modern school	2	2	2
Either grammar or modern school	2	2	1
Cadet school	1		
Commercial school			1
Post-elementary 'city' (*gorodskoe*) school	2	3	2
Secondary church school	1	1	1
Elementary church school		1	
Elementary 'people's' (*narodnaia*) school	2		1
Total	19	18	18

The tertiary education received by Sovnarkom members was quite varied in character. Classification is complicated by the fact that several began their education in one institution and completed it in another, in some cases studying in more than one field. Lenin, for instance, was expelled from Kazan University at an early stage of his law studies but subsequently took his degree by external examination with St Petersburg University. Nevsky was expelled after two years in the Natural Science Faculty of Moscow University, and it was only after eleven years as a professional revolutionary that he managed to graduate from the University of Kharkov. Yelizarov, on the other hand, graduated in Mathematics and Physics when he was 24, but in his late thirties studied engineering for three years, being expelled, however, before graduation. Essen took a diploma in architecture from the Academy of Fine Arts in St Petersburg, studied law for a year, then Romance languages for a year, and finally studied art in Italy. Lunacharsky studied philosophy under Avenarius for two years in Zurich. Osinsky was enrolled in the universities of Moscow, Berlin and Munich, but without graduating from any of them. Krylenko was a graduate both of the History-Philosophy Faculty of St Petersburg University and the Kharkov Law Faculty, and also studied medicine for a year. Amongst the people's commissars appointed in 1917 St Petersburg was by far the most common place of tertiary education, but this predominance was lost in later years. In 1922 for the first time there were two graduates from foreign institutions – Sokolnikov who studied law and economics in Paris and Dovgalevsky who studied electrical engineering in Toulouse.

TABLE 8   *Highest education received*

	1917	1918	1922
Elementary	2	1	1
Post-elementary 'city' school	2	1	1
Modern school	1	1	1
Grammar school		1	1
Seminary	1	1	1
Agricultural college		1	1
Teachers' college	1	1	
Cadet college	1		
University – not graduating	4	2	4
University – graduating	7	8	5
Institute of technology		1	3
Total	19	18	18
Summarised			
Elementary	2	1	1
Secondary	3	3	3
Tertiary	14	14	14
(of whom university or institute graduates)	(7)	(9)	(8)
Total	19	18	18

Of those who completed their university studies, the overwhelming majority took professionally-oriented courses. About half were graduates in law or economics and half in science, medicine or engineering – and the balance did not change over the period. Of special interest is the emergence by 1922 of a significant minority of graduates from technological institutes.

Finally, what of the work experience acquired by Sovnarkom members before the Revolution? In many cases the answer was simple: they had no work experience, or none to speak of. An extreme example was Dzerzhinsky, who was expelled in the last year of grammar school for his revolutionary activities and at no time held a regular job. Another was Stalin, who never had occasion to practise the profession for which he trained in the Tiflis Seminary, and whose employment record was limited to a few months doing office work in the Observatory. Lenin's case was more typical. After taking his law degree, he worked half-heartedly as a solicitor for three or four years, but it was never his primary, full-time occupation, for he was already deeply involved in Marxist political activity. As we saw earlier in this chapter, however, there were other people's commissars who had worked more or less extensively in some trade or profession before the Revolution. Even some we have defined as 'professional revolutionaries' had enjoyed sufficient experience of some regular employment before 1917 for it to be of possible relevance to their later work as people's commissars. It is the nature and extent of such experience that we shall now examine more closely.

In Table 9 we have attempted a breakdown of Sovnarkom members in terms of their 'basic occupation', classifying those who worked seriously at some trade or profession for at least a brief period, as distinct from those who never seem to have had any calling or occupational identity other than that of revolutionary. The distinction is sometimes hard to draw with complete confidence, especially in the case of some lesser-known figures on whom biographical information is sketchy.[16] However, while there might be room for argument over some borderline cases, the picture conveyed by the table is certainly accurate enough to impart significance to any major trends it reveals. Two such trends do in fact appear. The first might have been anticipated from what was written earlier about 'professional' and 'amateur' revolutionaries: as time went on there was a marked increase in the proportion of people's commissars who had acquired some distinct occupational identity in the course of their lives before the Revolution. The second is a striking change in the balance of such pre-revolutionary callings, away from manual (mainly industrial) occupations and towards professional and administrative occupations. The proportion of people's commissars who had enjoyed substantial pre-revolutionary experience working in positions of some administrative or professional responsibility in large organisations trebled between 1917 and 1922 (from 11 per cent to 33 per cent).

TABLE 9   *Basic occupation*

	1917	1918	1922
Administrative or professional: government employer	2	4	4
Administrative or professional: private employer			2
Army officer	1		
Lawyer		1	1
Doctor		2	1
sub-total: non-manual	3	7	8
Manual worker	4	2	1
Peasant			1
Evidently none except revolutionary	12	9	8
Total	19	18	18

It is now time to draw together some of the threads of our discussion. Neither in terms of the origins and character of their revolutionary commitment nor of their crucial pre-revolutionary experiences were Lenin's people's commissars cast in a single mould. On the contrary, the characteristics they had in common were decidedly few. Almost without exception they were, indeed, *men*, and men in early maturity or early middle age. Predominantly, too, they were Great Russians, with a handful drawn from other nationalities of the Empire which were prominent in the revolutionary movement. The great majority of Bolshevik people's commissars appointed in 1917 had been full-time revolutionaries for many years, in the main within Russia itself, and they included a significant minority from humbler backgrounds. In subsequent years, however, there were several significant changes. The number of people's commissars who had spent long years abroad increased, and those whose commitment to the revolutionary cause in the decade or so before 1917 had been very much less than a full-time one increased even more. At the same time, while most Sovnarkom members were from the beginning relatively well educated, the minority lacking secondary education was halved and those with tertiary education (almost always professional in orientation) came to include a significant group with technological training. This was accompanied by a marked increase in Sovnarkom members who had the experience of exercising some trade or profession before the Revolution, with those who had worked in manual trades sharply declining and those who had been administrators or experts in large organisations rising to a third of the Sovnarkom membership. Along with these changes went a marked rise in the average age of Sovnarkom and an increased predominance of men from middle- and upper-class backgrounds.

Now it is obvious that all these changes were not the direct consequence of deliberate policy. Lenin and his colleagues did not consciously decide they wanted more older men in the government or less from working-class families. Nor did they make a conscious choice to include in Sovnarkom more men who had once been 'drop-outs' from the revolutionary movement. What, then, were the changes in the effective criteria for Sovnarkom membership to which most of these other changes were incidental? The answer evidently lies in the problem of matching the man to the office and changed conceptions of what office in Sovnarkom entailed.

As we saw in the previous chapter, the initial appointments to Sovnarkom were made predominantly on *political* grounds, which primarily meant standing in the party at the national level or in the local Petrograd and Moscow Committees. Matching the man to the job, where it was attempted, meant matching him *politically*, and was epitomised by the appointment of the union organiser Shlyapnikov as Labour Commissar and of the most successful Bolshevik leaders of the mutinous troops and sailors to the Committee on Military and Naval Affairs. Only the short-lived appointment of Yelizarov as 'Acting' Railways Commissar may be put down primarily to his technical and administrative experience. With time, however, the latter consideration came to matter more and more. Nothing could have been more purely political than Trotsky's appointment as Foreign Affairs Commissar. His successor Chicherin, by contrast, was a party nonentity, but he *had* worked in the old Ministry of Foreign Affairs (albeit only in its archives) and he possessed a social background and education fitting the 'technical' requirements of the post. Likewise the 'professional revolutionary' Essen was replaced as State Control Commissar by Lander, who had been employed for some years in the imperial State Control Ministry (the later appointment of Stalin reflecting a 'repoliticisation' of this post for reasons we have explained). Soon relevant administrative experience acquired *after* the Revolution also assumed importance in choosing government members, and more often than not those who commended themselves in this respect were men who had acquired appropriate training and experience before the Revolution – at the expense, as a rule, of their active commitment to the revolutionary cause. The change may be illustrated by comparing Lenin's first People's Commissar for Posts and Telegraphs, Avilov, whose pre-revolutionary years from the age of seventeen had been devoted to underground work in the Bolshevik cause punctuated by repeated arrests, with his last, Dovgalevsky, who spent the decade before the Revolution, in France, active in various Bolshevik groups, but finding time to qualify and then work as an engineer. After his brief spell as people's commissar Avilov was side-tracked into relatively more junior positions, while Dovgalevsky, serving first in the Red Army, then proved his worth in a succession of ever more senior adminis-trative posts. Even at the end of the Lenin period, political considera-tions of a kind could still determine Sovnarkom appointments, as the example of the *muzhik* people's commissar Yakovenko illustrates. But for the most part the 'politics' that now mattered was of the bureaucratic variety, involving personal and group rivalries within and between various segments of the administrative machine.

This transformation in the composition of Sovnarkom raises the question whether its functions within the system were also under-going changes. We have already seen indications of such changes when describing the evolution of decisions over Sovnarkom appoint-ments. In the chapters that follow these changes will move to the centre of our attention.

Government, soviets and party

Sovnarkom governed in the name of the soviets, but was also claimed to be an instrument of 'the dictatorship of the proletariat', which, as Lenin was to explain, meant 'in essence' the dictatorship of the Communist Party. These two bases of Sovnarkom's claim to legitimacy, though potentially in conflict, were harmonised in practice by the majorities which the Communists contrived to secure themselves in the soviets, and in particular in their all-Russian congresses, from October 1917 onward. At the same time this twofold legitimation had the effect of placing Sovnarkom in a complex network of relationships linking it, on the one hand, with bodies emanating from the congresses of soviets, and on the other, with bodies emanating from the congresses of the party. These relationships, which extended beyond the formal trappings of authority and the adoption of broad policy orientations to the details of day-to-day government, underwent marked changes over time. To properly understand the evolution of Sovnarkom, therefore, we need to know something about these supreme organs of the soviets and the party and their mutual interconnections.

The soviets, composed of deputies elected by open vote at places of work, originated during 1917 in the towns and military and naval units, and only gradually spread to the rural areas. Eventually a 'pyramid' of soviets was to be built up, at village, rural district (*volost*), town, county (*uyezd*), province (*gubernia*) and regional (*oblast*) levels and in the national republics, congresses of delegates at each level electing an executive committee – the administrative authority of the area – and delegates to the next higher congress. This pattern took some time to crystallise, however, and as late as the Sixth Congress of Soviets (November 1918) nearly ninety per cent of the delegates were elected direct by city, district or other lower level soviets.[1]

The All-Russian Congress of Soviets was defined in the 1918 Constitution as the 'supreme authority' of the Russian Socialist Federated Soviet Republic (RSFSR). Its convocations were vast gatherings ranging from 670 delegates at the Second Congress to over 2000 by the end of the Lenin period, remaining in session for from two days to over a week. The first few congresses were convened at roughly three-monthly intervals, and were mostly timed to provide endorsement for important political decisions. Thus the Third Congress in January 1918, which met immediately after the convening of the Constituent Assembly, gave its approval to the Bolshevik dispersal of the latter and voted to confirm the soviets and Sovnarkom as the only legitimate authorities in the land. The Extraordinary Fourth Congress in March endorsed the Brest-Litovsk Treaty and the Fifth Congress in July 1918 approved the Constitution of the RSFSR. After the Sixth Congress in November 1918, congresses were convened annually in December, their most important business being to discuss and approve a report on the work of Sovnarkom and the Central Executive Committee (CEC) during the intervening period and to elect a new CEC, though they also adopted resolutions on various matters of current policy and organisational structure.[2]

It is obvious from their brief and relatively infrequent meetings that the congresses of soviets could not be equated with a national parliament. Nevertheless in these early years they amounted to far more than the ritual displays of bogus unanimity which they were later to become. To start with, up to mid-1918 the Mensheviks, Right SRs and other parties opposed to the Bolshevik seizure of power attended the congresses in significant numbers and vigorously opposed the policies of the regime. During the same period major policy disagreements and power conflicts between the Bolsheviks and their Left SR allies also found open expression at congress sessions.[3] From the middle of 1918 the single party dictatorship rapidly entrenched itself, and the mounting repression of other parties made it extremely difficult for them to gain representation in the soviets. Thus, whereas the Fourth Congress in March 1918 comprised 797 Bolsheviks and their sympathisers, 275 Left SRs and their sympathisers, 132 representatives of eight other parties and twenty-two non-party delegates, by the Seventh Congress in December 1919, fully ninety-seven per cent of all delegates were members of the

Communist Party.[4] Even then, however, so long as the Civil War lasted the repressive measures against other parties were combined with some symbolic representation of those of their leaders who advocated support for the anti-White struggle.[5] At the same time, while party discipline normally constrained the Bolsheviks to display a united front against other parties within the soviets, this did not stop them criticising government practices and decisions, and proposing institutional and policy changes, and the all-Russian congresses of soviets provided one of the most significant settings for such real, if limited, unofficial political expression.[6] Consequently the congresses were treated by the Bolshevik leadership as serious events calling for the deployment of considerable resources of oratory, persuasion and manipulation.[7] Nevertheless the formal accountability of Sovnarkom to the all-Russian congress of soviets can scarcely be said to have acted as a constraint or even as a serious influence on Sovnarkom's operation. Its essential relevance was as a source of legitimacy of Sovnarkom's role and activity, and it had some secondary value in mobilising support for major policy decisions.

Sovnarkom's relationships with the All-Russian Central Executive Committee (CEC) were, however, considerably more complex. The Constitution of the RSFSR (see p. 129) vested the CEC with virtually all the powers of the Congress of Soviets between the latter's brief convocations. However, it was never intended to operate simply as a standing committee of the legislature, but, as its name implied, was imbued with executive functions. It was defined in article 31 of the Constitution as 'the supreme legislative, administrative [*rasporyaditel'nyi*] and controlling organ' of the RSFSR. Thus it embodied that rejection of the 'bourgeois' principle of division of powers which Lenin regarded as one of the great merits of the soviets, and was the formal equivalent of the executive committees of regional and local soviets which established themselves throughout the country as the key organs of government in the wake of the Revolution. However the same combination of legislative and executive powers was enjoyed by Sovnarkom as well. While its responsibilities were characterised in the Constitution (article 37) as those of 'the general administration of the affairs [*upravleniye delami*]' of the RSFSR, it will be recalled that it speedily asserted its authority also to promulgate decrees of a normative character. It was as early as 30 October that it published its decree stating that pending the con-

vening of the Constituent Assembly the compilation and promulgation of laws (*zakony*) would be done by the 'Temporary Workers'
and Peasants' Government' and attributing to the CEC only the
right to suspend, amend or revoke such laws.[8]

This absence of any clear formal delineation of functions between
Sovnarkom and the CEC both reflected and exacerbated the considerable overlap and confusion between them in practice, which
was marked, at least in the early months, with not a little conflict.
If to many it seemed superfluous to have two 'supreme' bodies under
the Congress of Soviets, both combining legislative and executive
powers, it was Sovnarkom which on the face of it was the spare
wheel. Essentially a committee of those directly responsible for the
various departments of administration, it had no parallel in the
soviets at lower levels, and the prompt suppression of the Sovnarkoms
set up by several regional and local soviets after the October Revolution served only to emphasise its anomalous character. Nor did such
a body seem in any way called for by the concept of proletarian
government held by Lenin on the eve of the Revolution (see Chapter
2). Yet it was this 'anomalous' body which the Bolshevik leaders,
and pre-eminently Lenin, invested with the effective powers of
government as they established and consolidated their regime. It is
highly doubtful that Lenin at any time envisaged the CEC as
genuinely sharing in Sovnarkom's policy-making and executive
functions, but he obviously saw the advantages of having, in
addition to a small body under his immediate direction where most
decisions were made, a larger, nominally superior body, which added
an aura of legitimacy to his regime, gave greater resonance to the
most important of its decisions and an opportunity to revise those on
which there were second thoughts. Other leaders, however, envisaged
a more central and active governing role for the CEC, were troubled
by the ascendancy of Sovnarkom, and considered it should be
effectively subordinated to the CEC if not absorbed by it. Such
attitudes were most strongly represented among the Left SRs, but for
a time extended to some prominent Bolsheviks as well. The ill-
defined and shifting relationship between the CEC and Sovnarkom
largely reflected the changing balance of such contradictory concepts, but was also conditioned by the low importance attached
by revolutionary Marxists to institutional structures, which they
saw as being shaped by, rather than shaping, the revolutionary
process.

The issue of Sovnarkom–CEC relationships was sharply posed within the very first days of the regime. During the conflict over the broadening of Sovnarkom to include members of the moderate socialist parties, which led to the first resignations of Bolshevik leaders from their party and government positions, accusations were pressed that Sovnarkom was exceeding its authority by issuing important decrees without first submitting them for the approval of the CEC. The 4 November meeting of the CEC that registered the defeat of the advocates of multi-party government also brought a vindication of Sovnarkom's right to act independently on important matters requiring urgent decision: 'The Soviet parliament [i.e. the CEC] cannot deny the Council of People's Commissars the right to issue, without prior discussion by the Central Executive Committee, urgent decrees within the framework of the general programme of the All-Russian Congress of Soviets.'⁹ In the future this decision was to be constantly quoted to justify the assertion of virtually dictatorial powers by Sovnarkom. To secure its adoption by a CEC in which he and his hard-line supporters could command only a precarious majority Lenin was also obliged to reaffirm in the same resolution the formal subordination of Sovnarkom to 'the Soviet parliament'. The CEC was to enjoy 'general control over the whole activity of the Council of People's Commissars and the possibility of changing the government or particular members of it'. At the same time the resolution expressed regret that the Left SRs were unwilling to join the government and thus denied themselves a say 'in the working out of all urgent decrees'. The connection between institutional relationships and the hard facts of power could be no more clearly expressed. After his earlier vacillations Lenin had decided to take power in the name of the soviets, a tactic that was fully vindicated after the event by the strength of opposition – even among some of his own supporters – to 'one-party dictatorship'. It was in fact just such a one-party dictatorship that he was determined to establish, but to hold and consolidate power required him to work through the soviets, and in particular through their supreme bodies, and even, so long as Left SR support could not be dispensed with, to admit the latter to a modest involvement in his government. At the same time he had no intention of allowing his freedom of action to be seriously fettered by a disputatious 'parliament' whose sixty-two Bolsheviks contained a number of dissidents and sat down with twenty-nine Left SRs and ten members of other parties.¹⁰ For his tactics to succeed, however, it was necessary to nourish in those who believed the CEC was the proper body to rule the illusion that it had the capacity to do so.

The CEC quickly established itself as a regularly operating institution, some weeks, in fact, ahead of Sovnarkom (see Chapter 3). On 2 November, a week after the seizure of power, it adopted a set of rules providing the means whereby, despite its unwieldy size, it might function as an executive as well as a legislative body. In addition to meetings of the full membership, which were to be held at least once every two weeks and to 'direct and guide' all CEC activity, there was provision also for 'narrow' meetings, which required a quorum of only twenty-five per cent, and for a Presidium, consisting of one-tenth of all CEC members. Furthermore, twelve departments (soon raised to fourteen) were set up to serve as the 'working organs' of the CEC under the direction of the Presidium. Some of these, like the Automobile and Printing Departments, were concerned simply with servicing the CEC's own operations, but others, like the Departments for Local Government and Nationality Affairs, were clearly intended to provide the CEC with a capacity for administrative action in the country at large independent of the machinery of Sovnarkom.[11] In the upshot there was little call for 'narrow meetings', since up to the middle of 1918 full meetings were held on average every four or five days, but the Presidium was quickly institutionalised, meeting every two or three days and at times even daily.[12]

Inevitably, the resolution of 4 November delineating the respective powers of Sovnarkom and the CEC provided no more than a brief respite in the conflict over their roles. In the following fortnight Sovnarkom's high-handed methods in disbanding the anti-Bolshevik Petrograd City Duma provoked a fresh dispute, resolved by the adoption, on Sverdlov's initiative, of an 'Instruction [*nakaz*] on Relations between the CEC and Sovnarkom', authorising the latter to take measures against 'counter-revolution' on its own authority for which it would be accountable to the CEC, while at the same time affirming that 'all legislative acts and likewise all regulations of major political significance' were to be presented 'for consideration and approval to the CEC'.[13] As Keep points out, this ambiguous phrase left open the question whether 'consideration and approval' were to be sought *before* or *after* Sovnarkom had enacted the measures concerned, and it was in the latter sense that the Bolsheviks interpreted it; hence again they had managed to take the fire out of the issue without conceding anything.[14]

It was no coincidence, however, that the Left SRs had brought the issue to a head at the very meeting of the CEC that approved their joining the government, and immediately after the more than threefold expansion of the CEC itself by the addition of 108 deputies chosen by the Left SR-dominated Peasant Congress, 100 deputies from the armed forces and fifty from the trade unions.[15] For the Left SRs clearly felt the Bolshevik retreat from absolute power which these changes signified must be pushed further and consolidated. Organisationally their position within the CEC was, moreover, soon to be further strengthened by the revamping of its internal arrangements; a new Bureau consisting of forty Bolsheviks and thirty-four Left SRs was set up and the Presidium was expanded to twelve Bolsheviks, seven Left SRs and one United Social Democrat.[16] On 24 November they went into the attack again, and failed only by the narrowest of margins to secure passage of a resolution conceding the possible expediency of the Sovnarkom action against the Petrograd Duma but nevertheless branding it as illegal.[17] The strength of the Left SRs at this period in the leading organs of the Soviet regime was in large part due to the Bolsheviks' need to keep them 'on side' in their continuing struggle with the moderate socialist opposition, now coming to a head with the convening of the Constituent Assembly in which the latter enjoyed a majority. The Third Congress of Soviets, convened to endorse the dissolution of the Assembly, elected a new CEC comprising 162 Bolsheviks, 122 Left SRs, and twenty-one members of other parties, which in turn chose a Presidium of seven Bolsheviks and five Left SRs. At the same time, while conflicts between the coalition partners persisted, and were soon to grow acute, the fact that the Left SRs were now entrenched both in Sovnarkom and the CEC meant that these conflicts tended to express themselves less than previously in jurisdictional disputes between these two bodies. Although complaints about Sovnarkom usurping the powers of the CEC never entirely ceased, the battleground now shifted mainly to the administrative level, with the Left SRs attempting to push their policies through those people's commissariats and those CEC departments which they controlled in conflict with commissariats and departments controlled by the Bolsheviks.[18]

The resignation of the Left SRs and Left Communists from

Sovnarkom in March 1918 over the Brest-Litovsk Treaty brought a further shift in political tactics. While the Left SRs continued to use their positions on the boards of the commissariats and in CEC departments to combat the Bolsheviks on the administrative level, the issue of Sovnarkom prerogatives *vis-à-vis* the CEC also resumed greater salience. However, since their representation in the CEC elected by the Fourth Congress of Soviets had dropped to under a quarter their complaints on this score no longer presented a danger to the Leninist oligarchy, even when backed by the Left Communists.[19] Moreover, with the regime's new emphasis at this period on centralised bureaucratic control and discipline, criticism tended to shift from the question of institutional relationships at the summit of power to that of central-local relationships and the repressive and highhanded behaviour of the 'exceptional organs'.[20] It was also perhaps to some extent damped down by the hope that the adoption of the Soviet Constitution now in preparation would lead to greater legality and curtail the arbitrary use of government power.

The arguments in the Constitution Drafting Commission and the Fifth Congress of Soviets centred around three distinct but overlapping issues, as Carr has pointed out:

It was a conflict between those who sought a weakening and those who sought a strengthening of state power; between those who desired a dispersal of state power and initiative through local authorities and those who desired a concentration of authority and discipline at the centre; and between those who sought to make federalism effective and those who, under whatever guise, sought to establish the 'one and indivisible' republic.[21]

In the upshot Lenin, though not a member of the Commission, obtained adoption of a text which basically reflected his position on these matters, one that provided for a strong, centralised state whose federalism merely granted a limited autonomy in non-Russian regions.

So far as the powers and mutual relationships of Sovnarkom and the CEC were concerned, all the ambiguities that had entrenched themselves in the previous months were, as we have seen above, fully reflected in the text of the Constitution. Both were attributed overlapping and poorly-defined legislative and executive prerogatives. Article 47 made the people's commissars and the commissariat boards 'wholly responsible' to *both* Sovnarkom *and* the CEC. It is true that under article 40 the CEC retained the power to annul or suspend Sovnarkom decisions, while article 41 prescribed that Sovnarkom was to submit for 'the consideration and approval' of the CEC all measured 'possessing major general political importance'. However, we have already noted the ambiguity of such provisions, and this was compounded by a note to article 41 which empowered Sovnarkom to implement on its own authority 'measures requiring immediate fulfilment'. In the existing conditions of mounting Civil War there were few decisions of any moment which could not plausibly be so qualified. This outcome, satisfactory as it was from the viewpoint of Lenin and Sovnarkom, was not, however, secured without a struggle. There was considerable support on the Constitution Drafting Commission for the view that there was no need to retain both the CEC and Sovnarkom, and for proposals either to replace the people's commissariats with boards of CEC members coordinated by a body consisting of their chairmen and the CEC Presidium members, or (less radically) to subordinate Sovnarkom more strictly to the CEC Presidium. Clever tactics by Sverdlov at a Party Central Committee meeting and at the Fifth Congress of Soviets sufficed to side-track such ideas, but they might have acquired more formidable momentum had not the Congress been conducted in a crisis atmosphere engendered by the Left SRs' attempted coup.[22]

Kamenev's resignation as Chairman of the CEC on 4 November 1917 was a piece of great good fortune for Lenin, for it enabled him to install Sverdlov, who proved his firmest, most reliable and organisationally most gifted collaborator in the year or so that followed. It was largely due to Sverdlov's superb capacity for managing men and meetings that the issue of CEC–Sovnarkom relations was prevented from becoming a serious threat to Lenin's regime during its formative period. For, while Sverdlov probably had no intention of reducing an instrument of power thus entrusted to him to a cipher, his essential commitment was of course to the Communist Party, of which he was also Secretary, and he fully realised that Sovnarkom and not the CEC was the only channel through which the party could effectively exercise governmental power at the centre. At the same time he worked vigorously to realise the potential of the CEC as an instrument through which the writ of the regime could be made to run throughout the country at large. For the ability of the people's commissariats to implement Sovnarkom measures through the field organs inherited from the old ministries was extremely limited and dependent on the cooperation of the soviets and their executive committees, in which effective power at the regional and local levels was now focused. It is true that the Bolsheviks quickly assumed control of most of these bodies, but the party had no machinery through which it could run things itself, as it was later to do, nor would this have been politically expedient at this period. The authority of the CEC, however, carried great weight with the lower-level soviets, since it was peculiarly 'their' organ at the centre, and standing as he did at the supreme command of both the soviet and the party hierarchies, Sverdlov was in a peculiarly strategic position to secure the compliance of local leaders with central government policies, and he exploited this position in masterly fashion. His main resource in doing so was not administrative machinery, there being no attempt to set up departments in the local soviets directly subordinate to those of the CEC (many of the latter were in fact abolished in the first half of 1918 on the grounds that they duplicated corresponding people's commissariats). Rather was it the obligation felt by leaders of the soviets to implement the decrees of the CEC by means of whatever machinery they disposed of locally, an obligation reinforced by the requirements of party discipline.[23] Thus the considerable legislative activity of the CEC during this period reflected not so much its own inner vitality as the advantage to Sovnarkom for getting its more important and sensitive decisions implemented locally of having them clothed in the authority of the CEC.

With the onset of the Civil War the significance of the CEC was sharply reduced. After June 1918 its meetings fell from about two a week to one a fortnight, and in the course of 1919 apparently ceased altogether.[24] The reasons were complex. On the one hand, with the transformation of the Left SRs from allies into enemies and the progressive reabsorption of the Left Communists into the government, the CEC largely lost its role as a forum within which a 'loyal opposition' could have its say, and in doing so shepherd their followers within the system even while criticising it.[25] From June 1918 to 1921 it consisted almost entirely of Communists. On the other hand its role as a focus from which the regime extended its authority to the provinces also lost much of its force. In part this was because the job of directing and controlling the regional and local soviets came more and more to be exercised through administrative channels, principally by the People's Commissariat for Internal

Affairs.[26] But more importantly it was because the influence of the soviets themselves declined drastically, since civil-war conditions soon revealed their inadequacies for effecting the decisive, flexible and disciplined executive action rightly deemed as essential by the Moscow leadership, who now quickly came to rely on the local organs of the Vecheka, the Revolutionary Military Council, the Food Commissariat, etc., with their centralised command and arbitrary powers.[27] A third factor was the death in March 1919 of Sverdlov, whose personal direction had been so vital to the early role of the CEC.

Complaints about the atrophy of the soviets were not long in coming, and they tended to be linked with accusations of bureaucratisation and to raise again the issue of Sovnarkom–CEC relationships. On 26 December 1918 a joint meeting of the Moscow District (*Okrug*) Committee of the Party and the Executive Committee of the Gubernia Soviet condemned the incursion of central government agencies into the affairs of the local soviets, characterising such practices as a revival of 'bureaucratic centralism'. The issue was pushed further at the Moscow Gubernia Party Conference on 2 March 1919 at which a resolution was adopted resuscitating the proposal that Sovnarkom be merged with the Presidium of the CEC.[28] Urging the adoption of this proposal at the Eighth Party Congress three weeks later, Osinsky presented a set of seventeen theses, for which he claimed the support of both the Moscow and Urals delegations,[29] and which envisaged, *inter alia*, the assumption by Sovnarkom of the functions of the CEC Presidium, the conversion of the People's commissariats into departments of the CEC, the grouping of the CEC membership into 'sections' which would control and direct the departments (i.e. the existing people's commissariats) and the firm subordination of the field units of central agencies to the local soviets. Zinoviev, as organisational spokesman of the Central Committee, rejected these proposals on the grounds that they would only import into the CEC the weaknesses of Sovnarkom, weaknesses which he admitted while yet defending Sovnarkom's record as a genuine government and an effective one. What was needed instead, he argued, was a completely new concept of the CEC, which should mainly comprise not, as at present, leading officials of central government agencies, but rather leaders of local soviets from the provinces. In this way the latter would acquire a political training while at the same time serving as communication channels between the regime and the worker and peasant masses.[30] The Congress resolution endorsed this concept, and also directed the next Congress of Soviets to clearly define the powers of the CEC Presidium and delineate its functions from those of Sovnarkom.[31]

This marked the end of the CEC as a body ostensibly manifesting at the apex of the new state system the original concept of the soviets as collectivities which both 'legislated' and 'administered', which adopted decisions and themselves implemented them. For it was precisely what Zinoviev now labelled the *chinovnik* character of the CEC – the fact that the majority of its members stood at the command posts in the central administrative machine – that gave this principle an appearance of reality. The appearance, as we have seen, had always been deceptive, since most decisions had from the beginning been taken elsewhere, mainly in Sovnarkom. Now, all serious effort to maintain this appearance was discarded, and the official argument that the new arrangements were more in keeping with the original concept of the Soviets, since the CEC members would now fan out into the provinces and implement its decisions on the spot, was a piece of sophistry which could deceive only the politically naive.

It was originally intended to hold a Congress of Soviets in May 1919 to implement these changes, but the Civil War now entered its most critical phase, and the Congress was not held till December, the CEC meanwhile drifting even further into the doldrums. Since the majority of CEC members were now to hold office in the provinces, one implication was that, instead of being in almost constant or frequent session, it would have to be convened for relatively brief periods at considerable intervals. Accordingly, it was resolved at the Seventh Congress of Soviets to hold sessions six times a year.[32] In fact five were held during the next year and four in each of the two succeeding years. A further implication was that if the CEC was to continue being extensively used to promulgate decisions which for symbolic reasons the regime wished to invest with its authority, and to legitimate changes in Sovnarkom membership, somebody – or some body – must represent it in exercising these functions between sessions. The CEC Presidium had already been employed for this purpose to some extent, although its main activities had previously been the organisation of CEC sessions and direction of its modest executive machinery. The Seventh Congress of Soviets now formally empowered the Presidium to act on behalf of the CEC in endorsing or suspending Sovnarkom decisions and appointing people's commissars.[33]

Since the CEC Presidium was a constantly functioning body, its new powers could be seen as potentially enabling it to establish its effective authority over Sovnarkom in a way that the CEC itself had never succeeded in doing. This potentiality was perceived by Bolshevik critics of the ruling oligarchy, and found advocates within the Presidium itself, whose efforts to actualise it soon led to conflicts. Nothing of the kind was envisaged by the oligarchy,[34] whose intentions were stated with remarkable frankness by Krestinsky in his organisational report to the Ninth Party Congress in March 1920:

Comrades may perhaps point out that by resolution of the Seventh Congress of Soviets the Presidium of the CEC was granted the right to approve on behalf of the CEC particular decisions of Sovnarkom and to suspend the implementation of these or those of the latter's regulations. Quite correct. Envisaged here are exceptional cases where the Central Committee of our party, in controlling and directing the work of our central organs, arrives at the conviction that this or that decree by virtue of its significance should be adopted by the CEC, but for technical reasons it is impossible to convene a plenary meeting of the CEC; in such cases, if the decree has already been adopted by Sovnarkom and if the Central Committee is in essential agreement with this decree and the Presidium of the CEC does not meet with any objections, the decree is put through the Presidium of the CEC and approved by it in the name of the CEC (after all the Central Committee does not preliminarily discuss all matters going through Sovnarkom). When it is necessary to revoke or suspend some regulation or other of Sovnarkom, the Central Committee does this through the Presidium of the CEC. This is the main aim of the right of approving and suspending, but not issuing decrees independently, which was granted by the Seventh Congress of Soviets to the CEC Presidium with respect to decisions of Sovnarkom.[35]

As the Civil War moved to its close a major task for the regime was the establishment of Soviet institutions in the vast newly-won territories to which its power now extended. There was an important role here for the CEC, which was called upon to project its symbolic authority in a way somewhat reminiscent of the weeks following the Revolution. Perhaps the most effective of the measures designed for this purpose was the despatch of 'agitation and instruction trains', manned by mixed teams of CEC members and central party and government officials but operating in the name of the CEC who, while manifesting the authority of the Soviet State, sought to win

the hearts and minds of the population in newly-incorporated territories, supervised the formation and staffing of the local soviet
administration, and sorted out difficulties and complaints on the
spot.[36]

With the end of hostilities the regime was faced with two major
problems which were destined to lead to greater prominence for the
CEC: the problem of administrative chaos and arbitrariness and
the problem of relations with the peasantry. Complaints over the
excesses of the 'extraordinary organs', especially the Cheka, the
disorder induced by the conflicting demands of various agencies
clothed with vast and ill-defined powers, and the atrophy of the
soviets, though never completely silenced, were muted so long as the
Soviet Republic was in danger. With victory, however, the pent-up
resentments and grievances of the people found massive and often
violent expression, and enjoyed powerful advocacy by oppositionists
at the Eighth Congress of Soviets in December 1920.[37] The leadership responded with a mixture of repression and conciliation –
conciliation which they found all the easier to undertake because
they themselves were profoundly convinced of the need to revive the
soviets and establish 'socialist legality', not only for purposes of
legitimating their authority but in order to provide a regular framework of law and government within which the work of reconstruction could proceed. Accordingly the years 1921 and 1922 brought a
constant flow of legislation curbing the 'extraordinary organs',
strengthening the soviets and clarifying their relationships with
central agencies, and establishing new law codes, and the CEC was
perceived as the appropriate organ through which this legislation
should be enacted. In the same period there was also a large increase
in legislation regarding relationships between the various Soviet
republics, changes in administrative-territorial divisions, and agree-
ments with foreign states, all of which constitutionally required
formal decisions by the CEC.

While the Russian peasantry suffered grievously at the hands of
both Civil War protagonists, it is probable that fear for their fresh-
won tillage in the event of a White victory was a major factor
enabling the Bolsheviks to prevail. Once this danger was passed,
however, peasant hostility to the exactions of Soviet officialdom,
and particularly to the ruinous grain requisitions, broke out into
widespread non-cooperation and violence, while food production
contracted disastrously. This was, of course, the main reason why

Lenin turned in 1921 to the New Economic Policy, the cornerstone of which was conciliation of the peasantry. Conciliation found its most essential expression in economic measures, but there were also efforts at appropriate changes on the level of political symbolism. While the image of Sovnarkom had become tarnished among the masses (especially in the countryside) through its association with the harsh and arbitrary methods of the 'extraordinary organs', that of the CEC was relatively unaffected, and the regime now attempted to capitalise on this by promulgating NEP-related measures through the CEC and encouraging the peasants to see in the latter a body peculiarly responsive to their concerns.[38] There is no doubt that these measures met with some success. As early as the first four months of 1921, ninety-five per cent of the complaints addressed by citizens to the CEC came from rural areas, compared with fifty-four per cent of those addressed to Sovnarkom.[39] An important role here was played by CEC Chairman M. I. Kalinin, who had succeeded Sverdlov on the latter's death in March 1919. Kalinin, himself one of the few Bolshevik leaders to come from a peasant family, enjoyed the *muzhik* appearance and simple, warm and sympathetic personality which encouraged many peasants to see him as one of them, and much effort was devoted in Soviet propaganda to representing him as 'the all-Russian village headman' (*vserossiiskii starosta*).

All this greatly enhanced the prominence of the CEC in 1921–2 and sharply increased the output of decisions promulgated in its name. In 1917–18 these amounted to sixteen per cent of the number of decisions promulgated by Sovnarkom, and in 1921 to forty per cent.[40] It did not, however, involve a notable expansion of the CEC's activity as a collective decision-making body: it met for a total of twenty days in 1920, ten in 1921 and twenty-four in 1922. Nor, it scarcely needs adding, did it resume its earlier role as a forum where alternatives to government policies might be seriously advocated, although dissent was still occasionally voiced on particular measures.[41] It was not in the CEC itself, but in its Presidium, that most of this new work was carried out. To facilitate this, the Eighth Congress of Soviets in December 1920 resolved that membership of the Presidium should henceforth be regarded as full-time work.[42] Seventeen full and twelve candidate members were elected to it by the Eighth Congress of CEC and fifteen full and twelve candidate members by the Ninth Congress CEC a year later.[43] In the first half of the year following the Eighth Congress the

Presidium met nineteen times, in the second half of 1921 sixty-two times, and in 1922 sixty-five times.[44] The Eighth Congress of Soviets also approved a substantial broadening of the Presidium's formal powers. It was now authorised to promulgate decisions on the implementation of existing legislation in the name of the CEC, reporting these at the next CEC session. Additionally it was empowered to revoke (and not just suspend) Sovnarkom decisions and to adjudicate in the conflicts between central and local government bodies.[45] Later legislation extended these powers even further. In particular at a meeting of the CEC in May 1921 the Presidium was required to hear regular reports from both the local soviets and central commissariats.[46]

There is no doubt that these enhanced powers gave a new edge to the issue of Sovnarkom–Presidium relations. As the Presidium began to exercise its new prerogatives there was bound to be uncertainty as to where the line should be drawn. This may be exemplified by a September 1921 decree clarifying that individual people's commissariats could not introduce draft decisions for CEC endorsement without prior discussion and approval in Sovnarkom.[47] Further, there can be little doubt that there was a certain amount of institutional patriotism among Presidium members, engendering an element of rivalry with Sovnarkom. However, it would be misleading to interpret their relations at this period essentially in conflict terms. There is little evidence that the Presidium ever amounted to much more than a subsidiary instrument of the party leadership as outlined by Krestinsky in 1920, even if more extensive use was now being made of this instrument.[48] In 1922–3 there was considerable disagreement among Soviet scholars as to what the greater prominence of the CEC Presidium betokened. One view was that the Soviet government consisted of two parts, functioning in parallel, a newer, growing part (the Presidium) which accorded with the spirit of Soviet constitutional development, and an older, declining part (Sovnarkom), which was a creature of the era of revolutionary transition. The advocates of this view saw the logical conclusion of the process in that favourite notion of Sovnarkom's critics: the CEC would replace it and take over the people's commissariats as its departments. Durdenevsky, rejecting this view, nevertheless saw the Presidium as now the senior party in the relationship with Sovnarkom in fact as well as law: the Presidium was 'the Government', and Sovnarkom 'a Cabinet of Ministers', by which he evidently meant a kind of executive committee of the government.[49] Finally, there was the view, which perhaps enjoyed the greatest authority, that 'Sovnarkom, which was the first supreme organ of administration, still plays the leading role up to the present day'.[50]

The lawyers' controversy on this issue was, however, somewhat unreal, for it left the key element in the pattern of central institutions out of the equation. There is no doubt that in terms of political salience and formal authority Sovnarkom yielded significantly to the Presidium at this period. At the same time it declined markedly in actual power, but here the chief beneficiary was not the Presidium, but the Party Central Committee and especially its inner bodies, the Politburo and Orgburo. It is to these that we must now turn.

Probably the two most familiar features of the Soviet political system as it operated under Stalin and has continued to operate since are the hierarchy of Communist Party organs in town, district, region and republic superordinated at each level over the corresponding organs of the state, and the concentration of supreme power in the central organs of the party, in particular its Political Bureau (Politburo) and Secretariat. The party is the focal, integrating mechanism in the whole system of governmental and non-governmental institutions, reserving for itself all their major decisions, directing, supervising and coordinating their operation and sorting out their problems and conflicts. It would be an easy assumption that these arrangements existed from the birth of the regime, embodying in the post-revolutionary context Lenin's original concept of the party as the directing and coordinating staff for all the organisations of the proletariat. Such an assumption, however, would be mistaken. In the first year or so after the Revolution there was no evidence that leading Bolsheviks believed the party should perform such a role, there was no attempt to equip it to do so, and it did not in fact do so. Before Lenin left the scene, however, the transformation of the party into the now familiar 'leading and directing force' in Soviet society was well advanced. This had profound implications for the standing and role of Sovnarkom, implications that were to become a central political issue during Lenin's last months in effective office.

Paradoxically, it was in the earliest period, before the Communist Party evolved the will and the machinery to directly manage the country, that its political influence was at its greatest. For in contrast with the political sterility of the mature Soviet system, the infant

Soviet Republic had a rich and turbulent political life, which was played out from the first largely within the Communist Party, and from mid-1918 almost entirely within it. Here we are giving the word 'politics' its conventional meaning which connotes the public canvassing of alternative policies and methods and criticism of incumbent leaders and their measures. The great issues facing the regime were vigorously debated at early party congresses, which were held in the spring of each year, and there were always enough critics of the leadership present to keep it on its toes defending its record and its policy proposals. Within the Central Committee as well there was frequent clash of opinion, policy-groups formed and reformed, and no leader, even Lenin, could be assured of an automatic majority. The same applied in the regional and local party organisations throughout the country. Granted that the dominant leaders rarely had to give way on major issues, granted also that factional manoeuvring and manipulation of meetings and elections was as much a feature of this early Soviet politics as the clash of high principle, and granted finally that the majority of party members participated only as followers of one group or another, there was yet a sense in which the party as such, and not just a hierarchy of officials acting in its name, actually ruled Soviet Russia during these years.

We are therefore not contending that the party was of little significance in the government of post-October Russia – quite the contrary. What must be realised, however, is that the tasks of embodying the party's will in concrete decisions and of getting these decisions implemented fell predominantly at the outset to organs not of the party, but of the State, and first and foremost to the Council of People's Commissars. In 1918 the Party Central Committee did indeed pre-decide the most momentous issues (like the Brest-Litovsk Treaty), settle some smaller but contentious ones, determine the tactics to be pursued in multi-party bodies, discuss the general orientation of policy, and decide *some* government appointments. But this is little more than is done in many Western liberal-democratic systems by the central executive or parliamentary caucus of the ruling party – and perhaps less than in some.[51] The Central Committee was involved at this time spasmodically but not systematically in the decisions of the government. As for the implementation of government policies at the provincial and local levels, we have seen that the demands of party discipline were an important factor, but these demands were for the carrying out of CEC and

Sovnarkom (not party) decisions by Communists working in local soviet (not party) bodies. At the time of the seizure of power, in fact, the local Bolshevik committee members usually formed themselves into the executive of the local soviet, and it was in this capacity that they soon came to make most of their decisions, so that the party committee as such tended to atrophy, becoming in effect, as some put it, merely the 'agitation department of the local soviet'.[52] At this time there were even suggestions that 'the party might be abolished now that there are soviets composed of communists'.[53]

This state of affairs persisted well into 1919. And yet by 1921 the Central Committee and its inner organs were well on the way to becoming the true government of the Soviet Republic, while the hierarchy of party officials was emerging as the key instrument of rule throughout the country. What had brought about this change? To explore this question properly would require a book in itself, and here we can only briefly consider some of the main forces at work.[54] These forces sprang from three distinct sets of relationships: those within the party leadership, those between the leadership and the party at large, and those among the various agencies and organisations through which the regime operated. Their final result was not the fruit of some grand design, but was rather the cumulative effect of many decisions with far more limited objectives and of more or less spontaneous adaptation to specific circumstances.

As early as the Seventh Party Congress in March 1918 there were expressions of concern over the party's tendency to atrophy as a working organisation, and Sverdlov urged that the centre of attention in the localities, and a good deal of executive activity, should be shifted from soviet to party bodies.[55] While modest and in some places substantial progress was achieved in this during the following months, the situation was still not radically different when the matter was raised again at the Eighth Party Congress a year later. One probable reason for this was preoccupation with the mounting Civil War. Perhaps no less important, however, was the dual role of Sverdlov, since as long as he was operating the soviet hierarchy with the one hand and the party hierarchy with the other, it seemed of secondary importance which of the two was bearing the greater weight. Despite the best of intentions to shift the emphasis to working through party channels, the natural tendency, given the great pressure for information and decision, was to rely mainly on the most effective machinery to hand, which at that time was the soviets.

Furthermore, though it was certainly an exaggeration to say, as some did at the time, that the Central Committee files were all in his head, and perished with him, it seems true that his prodigious memory and formidable organisational talent had to a large extent substituted for more formal arrangements. His death in March 1919 therefore precipitated the shake-up and accelerated the bureaucratisation of the party that followed, though the underlying causes lay elsewhere.

The resolution of the Eighth Party Congress on these matters[56] both reflected and stimulated the operation of forces at all three of the levels mentioned. At the leadership level there was to be a five-man Political Bureau and an Organisational Bureau within the Central Committee of nineteen voting and eight non-voting ('candidate') members. Such inner executive groups had existed more or less informally for some time. A seven-man Political Bureau (reduced to five by the dereliction of Kamenev and Zinoviev) had been set up a fortnight before the seizure of power, but there is no evidence that this body ever met.[57] Five weeks after the insurrection a Bureau was again formed, and empowered to take decisions that could not await the convening of the full Central Committee, on the understanding that such of the latter's members as happened to be in Smolny would participate. Again, however, this body did not become institutionalised, if it ever met.[58] There is further reference to a Bureau of the Central Committee shortly after the transfer of the leadership to Moscow and the Seventh Party Congress, but the evidence suggests it met only once.[59] During the following months party decision-making procedures were evidently informal in the extreme. The relatively small Central Committee elected in March 1918 was further diminished by the refusal of the Left Communist members to participate, so what with the frequent absence of other members from Moscow, especially as the Civil War got under way, it became difficult to meet with a quorum. Apart from special meetings to discuss the draft Constitution, it appears to have been convened only three times between late May 1918 and early January 1919.[60] Osinsky was probably justified in his contention that policy decisions issued in the name of the party were usually made by Lenin and Sverdlov acting jointly with or without consulting the (Communist) heads of the agencies involved.[61] This informal and expeditious mode of operation was hard to sustain, however, when the Left Communists began to take up their offices towards the end of the

year, and in so doing both made possible the regular convening of
the full Central Committee and ensured by their presence that its
meetings would be argumentative and cumbersome.[62] It was
probably these circumstances that led to the informal re-establish-
ment of a Political Bureau, which was functioning by December
1918, and this time never looked back.[63] A few weeks later, on
19 January, an 'Organisational Bureau' was also established by the
Central Committee.[64] With the formalisation of these two bodies by
the Congress the party now had at its disposal, for the first time since
the Revolution, an authoritative and streamlined executive, while
the expanded full Central Committee was able to concentrate on
larger policy questions and on matters of dispute within the bureaus.

On the level of intra-party relationships, the Eighth Congress
Resolution stressed the need for effective communications between
the centre and the provinces; this was to be fostered by the forwarding of regular reports and by personal inspections by a new corps of
Central Committee instructors. The Central Committee was to provide local party bodies with funds to cover their administrative
expenses. Most importantly, the Resolution envisaged a centralised
system of personnel control.

> The whole matter of assignment of party workers is in the hands of the
> Central Committee of the party. Its decision is obligatory for all. In each
> gubernia, gubernia forces are allocated by the gubernia party committee,
> and in the capitals by the city committees under the general leadership of
> the Central Committee. The Central Committee is instructed to wage the
> most determined struggle against any localism or separatism in these
> matters.
> The Central Committee is instructed to regularly reassign party workers
> from one field of work to another and one district to another with the aim
> of making the most productive use of them.

Finally, on the level of relations between the party and other
agencies of the regime, it was declared:

> The Communist Party sets itself the task of winning the decisive influ-
> ence and entire leadership in all organisations of the working people: in
> the trade unions, the cooperatives, agricultural communes, etc.
> The Communist Party especially strives for the execution of its pro-
> gramme and its complete dominance in the state organisations of today,
> which are the soviets.

To this end party caucuses were to be formed in all soviets and
other bodies, bound by party discipline to execute the decisions of

local party committees, which for their part must be kept separate and not let themselves be merged with the soviets.

All this required staff. Several specialised departments were established under the Central Committee Secretary and the number of full-time officials responsible to him rose from fifteen in March 1919 to eighty in December and to 150 by March 1920.[65] Progressively, corresponding departments were also set up in the gubernia and lower committees, headed by a full-time secretary, who soon became the dominant political figure in his locality and the chief link with the centre.

These changes did not occur without dislocation and resistance. At the centre the leadership was well aware of the apprehensions that its establishment of the bureaus would arouse, and sought to allay them by providing that other Central Committee members might attend their meetings and that they be wholly answerable to the Full Central Committee, which must meet regularly. Nonetheless, charges of usurpation of power by the bureaus were not long in coming. At the local level the establishment of effective and authoritative party organs was hampered by their continued financial dependence on the soviets (it was not till early 1920 that a system of funding by the Central Committee against the budget of the Internal Affairs Commissariat was operating)[66] and by the resentment of local Communist notables entrenched in the soviets at the pretensions of the party secretaries and their staffs, who were sometimes younger members of post-revolutionary vintage. Conflicts broke out between the two, prompting the Central Committee to issue a stern instruction in January 1920 'reminding all members of party caucuses of soviets and their executive committees of the need for their subordination to the directives of the local party centres'.[67]

The intention behind these measures was undoubtedly to effect considerable changes in the way power was exercised in post-revolutionary Russia. They were motivated by a serious concern over the party's lack of organisational cohesion and executive effectiveness, and over the 'bureaucratisation' of its cadres through their absorption in the day-to-day tasks of government administration. They betokened stricter discipline and centralised control within the party, the primacy over government bodies, and the provision of full-time executive machinery at each level of the party hierarchy. What happened, however, soon went far beyond what anyone seems to have intended, and the main underlying reason was the Civil War.

At the top the demands of war put a premium on the speedy and authoritative resolution of immediate problems. Broad political issues were shelved, and policy was largely made by default, through the cumulative impact of wide-ranging practical measures. In these circumstances it is not surprising that the Politburo and Orgburo quickly proved their usefulness, the former for expeditious handling of substantive issues and the latter mainly for personnel assignments and running the party machine. The full Central Committee remained important, but came to serve mainly as a kind of final court of appeal in disputed issues or a device to associate wider circles of the leadership with decisions espoused by the Politburo. The new division of labour was immediately reflected in the pattern of meetings of these bodies: in the eight months beginning April 1919 the Central Committee met at five or six week intervals instead of fortnightly as the party rules required, whereas the Politburo met on average every five days and the Orgburo every second day.[68] Although Central Committee Secretary Krestinsky in his report to the Ninth Congress in March 1920 spoke defensively about the infrequency of Central Committee meetings and the consequent handling by the bureaus of many matters that should normally have come before it, blaming these lapses on temporary circumstances,[69] the same pattern was repeated in the months that followed. From September 1920 to March 1921, when the leadership was divided by major policy disputes, the full Central Committee had a burst of roughly weekly meetings, but after these disputes were ended by the decisions of the Tenth Congress, it lapsed again into meeting at almost monthly intervals, while the Politburo met twice a week.[70]

The Politburo had now emerged as the crucial institutional embodiment of the ruling oligarchy. From the outset it was concerned as much, if not more, with decisions confronting the government as with matters arising within the party organisation itself. Up to a point this was to be expected: it was mainly through Sovnarkom that the 'proletarian dictatorship' operated and, now that there was a workable Central Committee executive capable of exercising the political primacy of the party, it would have been strange if important or disputed matters of government policy were not considered by it. But the ever-increasing flow of government business to the Politburo cannot be fully explained in these terms, and was clearly aided by the defects of Sovnarkom itself as a decision-making body.

Sovnarkom had been built by Lenin into a highly effective machine for dealing with the vast mass of administrative decisions constantly referred to it by the commissariats and other government agencies, but the relatively minor matters cluttering its agendas and the numerous second-flight officials attending its meetings seriously limited its capacity to deal with larger issues. Lenin, of course, was acutely aware of the problem but oversimplified its causes in blaming it on the 'bureaucratisation' of government officials and the avoidance of personal responsibility by people's commissars. Given the enormous range of government business, the novelty of much that was being done, and the overlapping jurisdictions of many agencies, innumerable problems demanding high-level rulings were bound to be generated.

The work of the Little Sovnarkom mitigated but did not cure the problem. What was needed was an inner cabinet of senior government members concentrating on the big questions and those that generated too much contention in the larger forum. To some extent the Defence Council was intended to perform this role, but it failed to break sufficiently with the organisational model of Sovnarkom itself to be more than partially successful in this (see pp. 95–8). From early 1919, however, a substitute for such an inner cabinet was available in the form of the Politburo, three of whose five members (Lenin, Stalin and Trotsky) were key figures in Sovnarkom.[71] Moreover, once the practice of having government matters considered by the Politburo was established, other characteristics of Sovnarkom ensured that it would be extensively resorted to. It will be recalled that, while at first people's commissars attended Sovnarkom meetings personally, the more senior of them, subject to enormous demands on their time, were soon taking advantage of their option to be represented by their deputies. With the onset of the Civil War, which placed extra burdens on the top leaders and frequently took them out of Moscow, this became the usual pattern, and once the Politburo was established they immediately began to use it to seek decisions which their deputies could not push through Sovnarkom and which required their personal intervention.[72] But once the value of the Politburo as a 'court of appeal' from Sovnarkom was demonstrated, lesser members began to use it too, seeking to have matters on which they could not secure a majority in Sovnarkom referred to the Central Committee, so that they could have a 'return bout' in the Politburo. Even Lenin, as we have seen, was not above resorting to this, despite his concern to contain business, wherever possible, within Sovnarkom.

But the expanding role of the party's central organs in the day-to-day work of government was due as much to forces at work in the provinces as to those at work in Moscow. In the early stages of the Civil War, owing to the exceptional powers vested in the organs of the Vecheka, the Revolutionary Military Council and the Food Supplies Commissariat and to the success of other central agencies in establishing direct control over their local offices, the effectiveness of the provincial and local soviets declined drastically and the Moscow leadership was thereby left without a unified network of authority and mechanism of local coordination. During 1919 and 1920 the local party committees moved into this vacuum. It is true that as long as the Civil War lasted the 'exceptional organs' remained to a considerable extent a law unto themselves.[73] Nevertheless, it was chiefly the party committees that Moscow relied on to strive for some coherence in the operation of agencies deployed in their areas, to serve as the focus of authority, to promote the general interests and priorities of the regime against narrow agency interests and priorities and to furnish systematic information about conditions and problems in the areas. Communications with the local party committees therefore became of increasing importance in securing the proper implementation of government policies and in providing information for evaluating their effectiveness. These communications passed through the departments of the Central Committee and converged on the Secretariat[74] and the Orgburo.[75] There was no mechanism for feeding this information directly into Sovnarkom, but both party and government information flows, as well as lines of command and control, culminated in the Politburo, which therefore enjoyed unique strategic advantages for taking effective decisions.

One further factor remains to be mentioned: personnel. Commitment and discipline were prime considerations in staffing the institutions of the regime during the Civil War, and party membership was the best criterion of these, albeit an imperfect one. The enormous demands thereby generated for party cadres were rendered insatiable by war losses, administrative reorganisations, the ebb and flow of Soviet-held territory, and later the extension of Soviet control to vast new areas. The centralised management of party job-assignments envisaged by the Eighth Congress Resolution was a response to this situation and was soon being exercised on a vast scale. By 1920

the offices of the Central Committee were making about 1000 postings a month.[76] At first these postings were rather haphazard, largely
taking the form of 'mobilisations' of Communists for personnel-
deficit agencies and districts. From 1921, however, as central
personnel records improved, the appointment process became far
more deliberate and individualised.

Personnel control was from the outset a powerful lever in the
hands of the central party machine. The capacity to reward loyal
service by promotion and to reassign 'awkward' Communists to less
sensitive positions did more than anything else to transform the
party itself into a passive instrument of a disciplined officialdom
and to politically disarm internal party critics of the ruling oligarchy.
But the personnel power of the party machine was not limited to the
party itself. Between April 1920 and February 1921, for instance,
the central party organs made 1715 postings to Sovnarkom positions
in Moscow and 202 to key trade union positions.[77] Subordinate party
organs exercised similar powers. In December 1920, following a
series of conflicts between people's commissariats and local party
committees over responsibility for appointments, the Central Committee Secretary issued an instruction forbidding government
agencies to transfer members of their own local staffs from one
gubernia to another without obtaining approval in each specific case
from the Central Committee, or to transfer personnel within
gubernias without the approval of the gubernia party committee.[78]
Thus, although members of Sovnarkom retained some say over
appointments in their commissariats, they could do little without the
cooperation of Central Committee officials. In the case of more
junior staff, this usually meant the Records and Assignment Department of the Central Committee (*Uchraspred*). More senior positions
were filled by the Secretariat or Orgburo, and a small number of
top appointments (including people's commissars) were evidently
reserved to the Politburo. Leaders could also appeal disputed
appointments from lower to higher bodies; Lenin, for instance,
would have cases transferred from the Orgburo to the Politburo
when he wanted a say in them.[79]

Thus between 1919 and 1921, the relationship between party and
state in Soviet Russia underwent a profound change, and in the
process Sovnarkom became increasingly dependent on the Party
Central Committee and its inner bodies in a variety of ways: for
policy guidance, for resolution of important and disputed matters,

for information necessary to effective executive action, for getting its programmes implemented in the provinces, for choosing its members, and for staffing its offices. The evidence available does not allow us to chronicle the evolution of this dependence in detail, but its broad outlines are clear enough.

Fairly full information is available on the matters dealt with by the top decision-making bodies of the party and government at their meetings up to November 1919.[80] By this time the Politburo and Full Central Committee were convening regularly and their agendas contained eight main categories of business: the military conduct of the War, foreign relations, disputes, senior appointments, propaganda, the political police, control of non-governmental organisations (particularly the trade unions) and relations with other parties. At this stage there was no sharp contrast between the matters handled by the two, although the Politburo tended to have more immediate executive issues on its agenda and the Full Central Committee more matters on which there was high-level conflict. Questions related to the economy or other aspects of domestic administration rarely came before them, the odd exceptions being issues of acute political importance (for instance the one such matter on the Central Committee's eighteen-item agenda on 26 September 1919 was the crisis in food supplies to Moscow).[81] The Defence Council had the longest agendas, its business covering a wide spectrum of activity but concerned in one way or another almost exclusively with war production and supplies. The Full Sovnarkom dealt with domestic administration generally, as well as personnel questions and conflicts between government agencies, and the Little Sovnarkom looked after the 'vermicelli'.

Unfortunately, precise information on agendas is lacking for later years, but some idea of where decisions were being made can be obtained by examining Lenin's published correspondence and seeing which bodies and officials he addressed on which kinds of matters. Beginning in 1920 we find increasing evidence of party involvement in economic questions and other aspects of domestic administration.[82] Three examples from the second quarter of 1921 will have to suffice. On 2 April we find Lenin asking a number of people's commissars to confer on the reduction of surplus labour employed in industrial establishments and to prepare proposals for consideration by the Politburo.[83] A fortnight later the Politburo discusses a report on the administration of the grain tax in the Kharkov gubernia.[84] Early in

June, Lenin writes to the Vice-Chairman of Rabkrin, Avanesov, urging him, in the event that the CEC Presidium fixes insufficiently punitive fines for the abuse by local functionaries of official transport, to appeal to the Central Committee, and promising to support him.[85]

The last of these cases indicates one of the factors making for greater party involvement: the enhanced authority and activity of the CEC Presidium and therefore the increased likelihood of conflicts with government agencies which could be resolved only by the Politburo or Central Committee. Another such factor was that, with the development of foreign trade and negotiations for foreign business 'concessions' in Russia, economic policy increasingly carried implications for foreign relations. A third was the extension of Soviet rule to nominally independent republics (the Ukraine, Belorussia, etc.), over which Sovnarkom had limited administrative control but whose Communist leaders were under party discipline to carry out decisions of the Central Committee and Politburo.

However, the basic reason appears to have been the authority as supreme decision-making bodies accumulated by the Central Committee and its bureaus during the Civil War and the effectiveness of the nation-wide machinery at their disposal. As the Civil War wound down the principal leaders of the party increasingly turned their attention from military issues to the problems of economic administration (several of them, as we have seen, took over economic-related commissariats) and it was natural for them to continue seeking decisions on their major problems, demands and conflicts from the leading organs of the party. The effect of this, however, was progressively to relegate Sovnarkom to a subordinate role in those wide areas of policy in which heretofore it had operated without close party direction.

This increased dependence of the top organs of the state on those of the party, however, also had a reciprocal aspect; for the machinery of Sovnarkom was crucial to the Politburo and Central Committee for both the formulation and execution of its decisions, especially in these new policy areas. A few further examples will help make the point. In September 1921 the Politburo resolved that no expenditure from the gold fund might be made without its specific sanction; to administer this, however, it required the co-operation of the Finance Commissariat, and Deputy Commissar Alsky was made personally responsible for keeping accurate records of all such expenditures and ensuring that none was approved by the

Sovnarkom, STO or the CEC Presidium without prior agreement of the Politburo.[86] The same month the Politburo considered a proposal for administrative cooperation between the statistical bureaus of the RSFSR and the Ukraine, and commissioned Sovnarkom to prepare a draft agreement on the matter. This was entrusted to a group formed by the Little Sovnarkom which then agreed its draft with the Secretary of the Central Committee.[87] The third example dates from March 1922. Lenin received a memorandum from the head of the Directorate of Technical Education on difficulties being experienced in the higher education system, and instructed his secretary to forward it to Central Committee Secretary Molotov with a request to place it on the agenda of the Politburo. The latter discussed the matter and commissioned the Education Commissar to negotiate with the Finance Commissar on new financial arrangements for higher education establishments.[88]

Recalling the Sovnarkom 'system' as described in Chapter 9, one must picture it as now capped by a new decision-making echelon – the Politburo and Central Committee. These had come to operate as the ultimate command centre of the government bureaucracy as well as that of the party. One consequence of this was that they were now conditioned by the 'bureaucratic' politics of the government machine no less than the internal politics of the party. Unfortunately a serious examination of this bureaucratic politics would take us too far afield, but we have seen many glimpses of it in the course of this book. Its ingredients were much the same as found in other bureaucratic systems.[89] Thus there was a politics of the budgetary process and of obtaining extra-budgetary finance; a politics of jurisdictional boundaries and of securing (or avoiding) responsibility for specific government programmes; a politics of personal and group loyalties and rivalries; a politics of senior appointments and of staff levels; a politics of controlling the upward flow of information so as to place favoured policies and officials in the best possible light and to discredit those not favoured; and finally a politics of discrimination in the implementation of measures so as to ensure that welcome ones succeeded while unwelcome ones were hamstrung by red tape or shortages of funds and staff. Such politics were played out not only within and between the top decision-making bodies of Sovnarkom, and their numerous standing and *ad hoc* commissions, but within and between the boards and the various divisions and echelons of individual commissariats and other agencies.

It would be misleading to conceive the motive force of such politics in terms purely of selfish personal, group or institutional advantage, for the participants frequently were, or believed themselves to be, primarily concerned with what they saw as the needs of society, the state, the Revolution, or at least the aspects of these administratively entrusted to them. As in other bureaucratic systems, however, the advancement of such altruistic concerns required coming to terms with the selfish ones which largely conditioned the operation of the system, and thus typically the two became inextricably intertwined. Meanwhile, the bureaucratisation of the internal life of the party and the suppression of heterodox ideas and groupings had left little of that politics in the other, more conventional sense mentioned earlier, in which policies of the regime were conditioned by the vigorous flow and clash of opinion within the party. It was bureaucratic politics that now mattered in the party no less than in the state, though the full realisation of this was to be some years in coming, and the central executive machinery of the party was where the two lines of bureaucratic politics converged.

Lydia Bach, an acute contemporary student of Soviet government, was of the view that most important decisions were still being taken by Sovnarkom at the height of the Civil War, but the drift of effective authority to the Central Committee, and more specifically to the Politburo and Orgburo, then accelerated rapidly. By 1922, she wrote, 'the Council of People's Commissars, having ceased to be a body with a will of its own, does nothing but register almost automatically decisions taken elsewhere and place its seal on them. Thus it has lost its importance and authority.'[90] This judgement, though a little bald, was not far from the truth. To trace the final stage in this shift of the effective focus of government, however, we need to consider the effects of Lenin's illness, to examine the measures taken in 1921 and 1922 to restore the effectiveness of Sovnarkom, and to observe Lenin's belated and vain efforts to reverse the process. These matters we turn to in the next two chapters.

13

Props for an ailing chairman

Although Lenin formally retained the post of Chairman of Sovnarkom until his death in January 1924, his active role had begun contracting a full two and half years before that. Towards the middle of 1921 his attacks of severe headache and insomnia became more frequent and intense. At first he resisted the urgings of his colleagues to rest, even ignoring an Orgburo decision of 4 June obliging him to take leave – for Lenin an extraordinary flouting of Party discipline. On 8 July, however, he gave way and himself applied for a month's leave, with provision for two to three visits to his office per week, each of two to three hours' duration, in order to attend sittings of the Politburo, Sovnarkom and STO. This was accepted by the Politburo the next day, but with the stipulation that he was to attend Politburo meetings only, not those of Sovnarkom. Lenin duly commenced his leave on 13 July, though he only partly observed the prescribed conditions. Already on the 15th, coming to his office to attend a meeting of the Politburo, he also chaired meetings of Sovnarkom and STO. Apart from transacting a good deal of other government business during this period, he chaired further meetings of STO on 19 July and 3 August. On 9 August, on the advice of his doctors, the Politburo took a further decision obliging him to extend his leave under more rigorous conditions, which Lenin accepted: he was not to attend *any* meeting without the specific prior approval of the Central Committee Secretariat. On 13 September, however, he resumed chairing Sovnarkom meetings, and for the next two and a half months maintained something like his normal pattern of work.

Early in December 1921 Lenin's health worsened, and he was obliged to take further leave, which he spent at his country residence in Gorki on the outskirts of Moscow. For the next three weeks his secretaries were forbidden to send him papers relating to current administration, but he was permitted to study those materials supplied by the commissariats which he needed for preparing his Sovnarkom–CEC report to the forthcoming Ninth Congress of Soviets. Although absent from the Eleventh Party Conference, held on 19–22 December, he did attend the Congress of Soviets on 23 December to personally deliver his report. During the next few days he was present at several other meetings, including one of the Party Central Committee, but his health was continuing to cause concern and on 31 December the Politburo again 'exiled' him to Gorki, prescribing that he could visit Moscow only with specific approval of the CEC Secretariat and restricting his telephone conversations to one hour a day. Further extensions of his leave were decreed on 2 and 28 February and 7 March. Nevertheless it is clear that Lenin managed to keep fairly well in touch with affairs during these early months of 1922, paying particular attention to the operation of Sovnarkom as well as to current economic administration and foreign policy issues: his some 200 letters, memoranda and telegrams surviving from January and February 1922 are largely concerned with these matters.

Lenin was finally permitted to take up his work in Moscow again in mid-March. At the end of March, he took part in the Eleventh Party Congress and in the next seven weeks regularly attended meetings of the Politburo, although he did not chair Sovnarkom or STO meetings during this period. On 23 May he left Moscow for a further rest, having two days before, however, written to the heads of all commissariats and other central government agencies asking them to keep him fully informed during his leave about all important aspects of their work. Then on 25 May he suffered his first stroke, which left him partly paralysed and with impaired speech. Struggling against his disabilities with remarkable courage and determination, Lenin after some weeks began to take up again the threads of current issues, and by the beginning of October he felt well enough to return to his Kremlin office with the intention of resuming, after ten months' interruption, the close direction of the operations of government he had exercised from 1917 to 1921. During the next few weeks he chaired seven meetings of Sovnarkom and five of STO, as well as participating in a plenum of the Central Committee and seven meetings of the Politburo. Again, however, the strain soon began to tell, and late in November his doctors forbade his participation in all executive meetings, though for a further fortnight he managed to keep up some work in his Kremlin office. In mid-December there was a grave deterioration in his condition, and from then on he took no further direct part in the business of government, although for some three months he continued writing and sought to involve himself in major political issues.

On 10 March 1923 Lenin suffered a further stroke which caused complete loss of speech and paralysis on the right side. Official medical bulletins, albeit concealing the true seriousness of his condition, now began to be published. By this point it must have been plain to those close to the summit of power that he would never again resume the effective leadership – Stalin was said to have been the first to recognise that Lenin was '*kaput*' – but there were no moves to release him from his government and party positions, and indeed he was elected Chairman of the USSR Sovnarkom when it was formed on 6 July. Although on the face of it his chairmanship was now merely symbolic, the thought that he might still struggle back to attempt a further active involvement in affairs as he had late in 1922 may have lingered in the minds of those running the Sovnarkom machine, and perhaps influenced their work and mutual relations. Indeed by the autumn of 1923 he had partly recovered his speech and taught himself to walk with a stick, and on 19 October he insisted on being driven to inspect the Agricultural Exhibition in Moscow and visited his Kremlin office where, according to one account, he sought in vain for a particular document in his desk drawer. His recovery never advanced beyond this point, however, and on 21 January he suffered his final, fatal stroke.[1]

As Lenin's involvement in the work of government progressively declined from the middle of 1921, he and his colleagues sought to fill the gap in two ways: by structural and procedural changes aimed at making Sovnarkom more of a self-operating system, not so dependent on the role of dominating leaders, and by bringing in deputies to take an increasing amount of work off Lenin's shoulders. These developments proceeded simultaneously and were closely interrelated, but they will be easier to follow if we consider them separately.

We have already described (see above pp. 78–80) the series of measures adopted in 1921 to augment the role and autonomy of the Little Sovnarkom. These measures limited the right of appeal from the Little to the Full Sovnarkom; added a chairman and other members independent of particular commissariats; channelled all

Sovnarkom business in the first instance to the Little Sovnarkom, with the exception of defence and foreign relations issues; then allowed even the latter to be referred to it at the discretion of the Full Sovnarkom or its chairman (which frequently happened);[2] authorised it to hold 'administrative' as well as 'plenary' meetings (like STO); and granted it considerable powers in supervising and enforcing the implementation of government decisions by commissariats and other agencies.

These innovations substantially changed the balance of power and functions as between the different Sovnarkom bodies and gave rise to frequent confusion and conflict, especially with STO.[3] Resolution of these difficulties was made all the more difficult in that they became acute precisely in the period – at the end of 1921 and early 1922 – when Lenin was forced to retire to Gorki. The first attempt to deal with them took the form of an instruction (*nakaz*) issued over the signature of Deputy Chairman Tsyurupa on 24 January, entitled 'On Demarcation between the Activities of the Council of People's Commissars, the Council of Labour and Defence and the Little Council of People's Commissars'. By listing various categories of business which were reserved for decision by the Full Sovnarkom or STO, this had the effect of setting limits to the expanding role of the Little Sovnarkom. Thus the Full Sovnarkom was given exclusive jurisdiction, subject to endorsement in some cases by the CEC, over all draft decrees involving changes in 'the general norms of political and economic life' or major changes in the operation of government institutions, over proposals for important policy changes, especially in the fields of foreign affairs and defence, over alterations to the tax laws, over introducing or amending law codes, over government staff establishments and over changes in the boards of commissariats. STO was authorised, at its 'plenary sittings', to approve state economic plans, to decide questions relating to the coordination of economic agencies, to consider regular reports from military and industrial commissariats and decide matters arising out of them, and to make appointments to its own standing commissions. Various more specific economic matters were placed under the jurisdiction of the 'administrative sittings' of STO.[4]

How far Lenin had been involved in the framing of this instruction is not clear, but on the same day that it was issued he wrote to Tsyurupa complaining that 'we are being dragged into the filthy bureaucratic bog of writing memoranda, gabbling about decrees, and writing decrees, and real [*zhivaya*] work is being drowned in this sea of paper', and proposing, first and foremost, that not less but *more* 'minor' business should be transferred from the Full Sovnarkom and STO to the Little Sovnarkom and STO's 'administrative sittings'.[5] Evidently Tsyurupa was not convinced that Lenin had grasped the main problem, since he wrote back focusing on the shortcomings arising from the greatly expanded role of the Little Sovnarkom. He also revealed that this body, in violation of its October 1921 statute, had already grown to twenty-two members, fifteen of them representing various commissariats and agencies and seven of them without departmental affiliation. It is quite clear that with the Little Sovnarkom's increased powers and importance everyone was trying to secure a voice in it. He proposed that its membership should be cut to five, its powers limited within the terms of the 24 January Instruction, and also that it should hand over financial allocations already provided for in the budget estimates to the Finance Commissariat.[6]

Lenin now replied agreeing to all these proposals (though he suggested the Little Sovnarkom membership should be seven rather than five) and urging Tsyurupa to embody them in a draft decree for submission to the Politburo.[7] But then a few days later, evidently with Tsyurupa's draft already to hand, he proposed it be supplemented by a separate resolution to the effect that the central responsibility of the Little Sovnarkom was 'to strictly supervise' the activity of the people's commissariats, ensuring that they carried out all their tasks, observed the laws, avoided red tape, etc. etc.[8] Tsyurupa was dismayed by this proposal, and wrote back the same day arguing that it 'would reduce the whole undertaking to nothing' since it would 'open up a limitless field of action' for the Little Sovnarkom, whose constant badgering of the commissariats would bring work to a standstill.[9] Lenin, despite considerable common ground on the need for people's commissars to assume greater personal responsibility, for the Little Sovnarkom to be reduced in size, and for Sovnarkom staffs to be cut generally, considered there was a 'radical disagreement' between himself and Tsyurupa, and persisted in his efforts to convince the latter that the essential thing was 'verification of fulfilment' rather than the formal structure and powers of particular Sovnarkom bodies. His last letter on the matter was dated 27 February. Tsyurupa's draft proposals on the reorganisation of the Little Sovnarkom were down for discussion by the Politburo on

4 March but no decision was reached at that meeting[10] or, presumably owing to continued disagreements, for several more weeks. The matter was deemed important enough to be placed on the agenda of the first meeting of the new full Central Committee elected by the Eleventh Party Congress on 3 April.[11] Whether complete agreement was reached even then, however, is not entirely clear, as it was only on 22 April that the relevant decree was promulgated.[12]

The decree provided for a membership of six, which might be regarded as a compromise between Tsyurupa's and Lenin's original suggestions.[13] In other respects it represented a complete victory for the Little Sovnarkom's critics. It was no longer to hold 'administrative sittings' or to form commissions. It was to lose its executive and expert staff, its secretariat being restricted to the keeping of minutes. Its jurisdiction was to be limited as prescribed in the Instruction of 24 January. The Finance Commissariat would henceforth handle authorisations of expenditures within the bugetary estimates, the Little Sovnarkom confining itself to considering requests for funds surplus to estimates. Finally, the decree stated the urgent necessity of revising the Little Sovnarkom statute of October 1921.

In the following months the Little Sovnarkom seems to have played a far more modest role than in its heyday of 1921. A revised draft statute was prepared in the period in which Lenin was recuperating from his stroke, but was promulgated (reportedly with a number of changes) only on 31 October, when he was back in the Chairman's office.[14] The new Statute incorporated some of the limitations on the Little Sovnarkom introduced by the January 1922 Instruction and the April 1922 decree, while softening or removing others. The subordinate role of the Little Sovnarkom was emphasised in clause 1 of the Statute where it was described as operating 'with the powers of a Commission of the Council of People's Commissars' – thus reviving the modest formula of its early years which had been conspicuously absent from the October 1921 Statute.[15] Nevertheless its jurisdiction was defined in very wide terms, the business specifically reserved to the Full Sovnarkom being limited to foreign affairs and defence matters and budget estimates (both of which could still be referred to it by Sovnarkom or its chairman), appeals against STO decisions and personal decisions of the Sovnarkom chairman, and appointments of deputy people's commissars and members of the boards of central government bodies. Otherwise all matters were still to go in the first instance to the Little Sovnarkom, except that both

the Sovnarkom and Little Sovnarkom chairmen were given discretionary power to refer matters directly to the Full Sovnarkom.
The membership was increased to eight by the addition of representatives of the trade unions and the local soviets. The prohibition on
the Little Sovnarkom's forming commissions was dropped, and it was
authorised to employ a secretariat of its own capable of preparing
business for consideration as well as keeping the minutes. The
quorum for meetings was fixed at four (as compared with seven
under the old Statute when the full membership was ten), including
either the chairman or deputy chairman. For the first time the
powers of the Little Sovnarkom chairman were listed and he was
authorised to make various categories of administrative decisions
obligatory on the government agencies concerned *and* the Little
Sovnarkom members. While the practice of holding 'administrative
sittings' was not revived, the fixing of a more modest quorum and
the independent executive role of the chairman provided a partial
substitute allowing much Little Sovnarkom business to be transacted
without full-scale meetings.[16] The powers of the Sovnarkom chairman *vis-à-vis* the Little Sovnarkom, also specified for the first time,
corresponded with those Lenin had earlier come to exercise in
practice (see pp. 80–3). He was made responsible for 'general
supervision' of it; its decrees, in the absence of appeal within the
prescribed period and sanctioned by the Justice Commissar, passed
into force with the same authority as Full Sovnarkom decrees once
he had signed them – and he was empowered to return them for
further consideration or refer them to the Full Sovnarkom; executive
decisions of the Little Sovnarkom entered into force immediately on
his countersigning the minutes.

The October 1922 Little Sovnarkom Statute thus appears to have
reflected a concern by Lenin, as he resumed for the last time the
reins of government, to restore the Little Sovnarkom's position
sufficiently for it to serve again as his 'first assistant', without
encouraging a repetition of the hypertrophy it had undergone in the
months following the October 1921 Statute. But in giving binding
legal form to arrangements that previously had enjoyed the flexibility of conventional working rules it also reflected the current
concern to institutionalise and depersonalise the operations of
government.

A second major question that attracted the rule-makers at this
period was the procedures for preparing and introducing agenda

items for Sovnarkom and STO meetings. A decree on this matter published on 11 April 1922 codified existing practice, while introducing a number of additional prescriptions. It listed the officials and institutions entitled to introduce agenda items; stipulated arrangements for prior consultation with other interested departments; laid down schedules for forwarding agenda proposals to the secretariat, for interdepartmental consultation, for the receipt of departmental comments, for the provision of documentation, and for the distribution of agenda papers; and listed the discretionary powers of the Sovnarkom and STO Chairman and the Head of Chancellery in determining when, in what form and by what body agenda submissions were dealt with. The concern to have commissars and their departments take more responsibility and refer up less questions for Sovnarkom to decide was reflected in a clause of the decree prescribing that agenda proposals would only be accepted if the matter extended beyond the jurisdiction of the department concerned, if there was irreconcilable conflict on it between affected departments, if the department had been specifically entrusted by higher bodies with introducing proposals on the matter, if the proposal would require amendment of existing legislation, or if it were by way of protest against decisions of other government officials.[17]

Three months later a supplementary decree was promulgated. This included one or two provisions of substance, such as the need for departments to refer all draft statutes and decrees to Sovnarkom's legislative draftsman *before* consideration by Sovnarkom or STO, but otherwise reaffirmed existing rules about such matters as prior interdepartmental consultation and the timely provision of documentation – which indicates that departments were still lax about such procedures – and laid down formal rules for a number of additional, and quite minor, procedural aspects.[18]

Then there was the question of procedures for departmental appeals against decisions of Sovnarkom bodies. In April a decree was published regarding appeals against Full and Little Sovnarkom decisions on financial allocations: they had to be made within twenty-four hours, signed by the head of the agency concerned or his deputy, and so on.[19] In August a second decree was promulgated, this time covering protests against all categories of decisions by the Full and Little Sovnarkoms and STO. Appeals against Full Sovnarkom decisions were to go to the Presidium of the CEC and those

against Little Sovnarkom and STO decisions to the Full Sovnarkom.
The time limit in all cases was set at seven days.[20]

In July new standing orders for Sovnarkom meetings were promulgated. These also seem to have confirmed the procedures evolved
under Lenin and their interest lies primarily in the fact that it was
felt necessary at this time to reaffirm them formally and *publish*
them. Interestingly, the standing orders retained provision for additional agenda items to be proposed at the beginning of the meeting,
which cannot have failed to weaken observance of the elaborate
rules for notice and documentation of agenda proposals and prior
interdepartmental consultation.[21] Finally, a decree was issued in
August 1922 regarding the oral statements (*doklady*) made on introducing agenda items at Sovnarkom and STO meetings and on who
might be entrusted with them. In line with previous practice such
statements might be made by board members of people's commissariats and other agencies as well as the people's commissars themselves. Attendance of departmental experts to introduce items or
speak to them was to be limited to exceptional cases or matters of a
highly technical character, their names were to be given the secretariat in advance, and their participation did not absolve attendance
during the discussion by the people's commissar concerned or his
authorised representative.[22]

Soviet scholars tend to attribute this spate of legislation about the
internal arrangements of Sovnarkom to the current concern for
greater legality, and certainly this was a time of codifying laws,
greater observance of constitutional forms, and of curbing arbitrary
action by the political police and other bodies. However, there can
be little doubt that it primarily reflected the dislocations caused by
the inability of anyone to substitute for Lenin in his harmonising,
enforcing and energising role, and efforts to make up for this by
finding optimal internal arrangements and then embodying them in
formal, binding decisions.

We shall now turn to the parallel efforts to provide Lenin with
deputies who would ease the burden for him and take over during
his absences. The first such deputy was appointed on 27 May 1921,
in the person of Alexei Rykov.[23] Having combined throughout the
Civil War the posts of Chairman of the National Economic Council
and Extraordinary Plenipotentiary of the Defence Council for
Supplies to the Red Army (*Chusosnabarm*), he had been the
Council's key economic administrator, and with its transformation

into essentially an economic coordinating body he was thus the obvious choice for Deputy Chairman. At the time of this appointment Lenin clearly wished to divest himself of some of the detailed business of government, but hardly anticipated that his health would repeatedly take him away from his work in the next few months. During these absences Rykov came to deputise for him in Sovnarkom as well,[24] and although this never seems to have been formalised, he was soon being referred to as Deputy Chairman of *Sovnarkom* and STO.[25] By general consent Rykov was an outstanding economic administrator. According to Liberman:

All, but especially Lenin, carefully considered Ryckov's [sic] opinion on each economic matter in question, although the vice-chairman had received no formal training in economics and, to boot, had boasted of no practical business experience. He had a great deal of common sense – what in America is called 'horse sense' and in Russian *russkaya smekalka* or 'Russian shrewdness' – and his remarks, either in formal debates or in informal conversation were meaty, to the point, and, by and large, very valuable.[26]

Towards the end of 1921 Rykov himself fell ill, but owing to the excellent medical treatment he received in Germany, was able to resume work some three months later.[27] Rykov's absence precipitated (or perhaps caused) the appointment of a new deputy chairman in the person of A. D. Tsyurupa. A foundation member of STO, Tsyurupa had distinguished himself during the Civil War as Food Supplies Commissar. Though always ailing, he was the only administrator whom Lenin invested with the same degree of trust and reliance as he placed in Rykov.[28] Lenin's original proposal, approved by the Politburo on 1 December 1921, was that Tsyurupa should be made Second Deputy Chairman of *STO*. However, the Politburo met again four days later and resolved that he should be appointed Deputy Chairman of Sovnarkom as well. Since Soviet sources, and specifically the editors of Lenin's *Collected Works*, go out of their way to identify decisions taken on Lenin's initiative and do not so identify this latter resolution on Tsyurupa,[29] it looks as if Lenin's Politburo colleagues may have deemed it necessary to go further in this matter than Lenin intended, probably with the Chairman's health in mind and his impending departure for Gorki the following day.[30] Certainly, Lenin had no reservations about Rykov and Tsyurupa *acting* as his deputies in Sovnarkom. His original draft motion on the deputies had listed among their proposed powers 'voting membership of Sovnarkom and STO, and chairing [them] in the Chairman's absence' and '*all* the powers of the Chairman of Sovnarkom with respect to participating in all collegial bodies and institutions [*kollegiyakh i uchrezhdeniyakh*]'.[31] However, he seems to have been reluctant to formalise this position and one wonders why. It was surely not from fear that his own status would be diminished thereby, as such vanity was not in his character; nor that the faithful workhorses Rykov and Tsyurupa might come to challenge his leadership. In fact the clue is probably to be found in the modest political status of the deputies themselves. At this stage Lenin was still just looking for assistants to ease his load, but *not* to substitute for him. The fact that neither of the men chosen as deputies was a Politburo member presupposed that Lenin would actively persist in his Chairman's role, continuing to serve as the linch-pin between Sovnarkom and the Politburo. In this context, as Lenin evidently perceived, it was anomalous to make them deputy chairmen of *Sovnarkom* when it was impossible for them to deputise in this most vital aspect of the Chairman's role, and no less anomalous for them to enjoy a formal status in Sovnarkom superior to that of those people's commissars, namely Trotsky and Stalin, who were members of the Politburo. The other obvious consideration was the limitation of their competence, in both the administrative and psychological senses of the term. Both of them had enjoyed authority up to this time only within the economic administration, and there was no chance therefore that the Politburo would invest them with wide prerogatives in such fields as foreign affairs or internal security, or over commissariats headed by Trotsky (Army and Navy) and Stalin (Nationalities and Worker-Peasant Inspectorate). This explains why Lenin's draft resolution on the deputies, in stating that they should exercise the Chairman's powers in participating in 'all collegial bodies and institutions', specifically limited the 'power to give directives [*ukazaniya*] subject to immediate fulfilment with respect to the practical work of people's commissars and the members of their boards', to 'questions of unifying and directing the work of the economic people's commissariats'.[32]

This, however, raises a further question. Who served as the 'linch-pin' during Tsyurupa's first three months as deputy, when Lenin was attending meetings neither of Sovnarkom nor the Politburo? There is no evidence that either Trotsky or Stalin contributed significantly to this function. Neither of them was by this time a regular

participant in the work of Sovnarkom and, apart from overall supervision of their respective commissariats, they seem to have been content to limit their involvement in government business to those
matters that found their way onto the Politburo agenda. In fact, the
gap seems to have been mainly filled by Kamenev – in spite of his
not actually being a member of Sovnarkom. Kamenev was Chairman of the Moscow Soviet, as well as acknowledged leader of the
Moscow party organisation, and the numerous issues that arose involving relationships between central and local bodies in Moscow
made him and his assistants frequent participants in meetings of the
Full and Little Sovnarkoms and STO and their commissions. By
1921 this seems have blossomed into a more general involvement in
Sovnarkom business, and Liberman refers to him as being 'in charge
of a number of economic agencies'.[33] No doubt owing to his Politburo membership, he came further to the fore during Lenin's
absences of July–September 1921. On 26 October Lenin wrote to
him: 'Cde Kamenev, tariffs are coming up in Sovnarkom. Will you
come on Tuesday? *For sure?* Furthermore, it would be better to put
you on to Sovnarkom formally.'[34] Though no such formal appointment was to transpire at this stage, Kamenev's responsibilities in
Sovnarkom continued to grow. He chaired the government's important Economic Commission,[35] and retained this position when the
Politburo resolved on 1 December to upgrade it, under the title of
'Unified [*Yedinaya*] Economic Commission', with powers 'to unify
[consideration of] all economic and financial questions'.[36] Thus
Kamenev assumed Sovnarkom responsibilities in precisely the field
of government activity in which the deputies were most directly
engaged (in practice this meant Tsyurupa alone from December
1921 to February 1922), and it was probably this which led to his
becoming the main link between Sovnarkom and the Politburo.

At this point we must back-track a little to trace more closely the
evolution of Lenin's ideas on what his deputies should do and how
they should organise their work. These ideas were first outlined in
his letter to Tsyurupa on 28 November 1921, the main points of
which we have already noted. In this letter his primary concern for
the deputies to take over from him the main burden of overall
economic direction was quite specific: 'The task is to unify in practice, to tighten up and improve *economic* work AS A WHOLE...'
(emphasis in original). To this end Tsyurupa and Rykov were to pay
special attention to the role of Gosplan and the State Bank, they

were to keep personally *au courant* with what the economic people's commissars and all members of their boards were currently doing, to sit in on important board meetings in these commissariats, and so on. As to whether it was a job that needed doing for only three or four years or more like thirty, 'we will see', he wrote.[37]

Between 24 January and 27 February 1922 Lenin exchanged several letters with Tsyurupa on the internal workings of Sovnarkom.[38] A central issue under discussion here was the role and operation of the Little Sovnarkom, and this we have already examined. But these letters were primarily intended by Lenin as guidance and instruction to his deputy on the central problems of managing and improving Sovnarkom. There was no serious effort at this point to set out his ideas systematically, and it would serve little purpose to detail all his comments and suggestions. It is possible, however, to distil from these letters three main injunctions:

(1) people's commissars should take more personal responsibility and not be allowed to overload the agenda of the Full and Little Sovnarkoms and STO with 'vermicelli';
(2) new decrees and resolutions should be minimised and control over implementation of existing ones maximised;
(3) far more attention should be paid to choosing better officials and vetting their work.

These were by no means new concerns for Lenin, but they now moved to the centre of his attention and remained there during the months of active work that remained to him. He summed them up in the last of these letters as follows:

...the vice-chairmen of Sovnarkom, cdes Rykov and Tsyurupa, should exert all their efforts to free themselves of trifles and commissions; should struggle against being dragged into questions which should be decided by the people's commissars; should devote two to three hours a day, as a minimum, to personally familiarising themselves with responsible officials – not the 'big shots' [*sanovniki*] – in the most important commissariats (and later all of them) for the purposes of checking and selecting personnel; should employ the apparatus of the Sovnarkom Chancellery and some of the members of the Little Sovnarkom, and also Rabkrin, to check the actual work and its effectiveness; in a word, they should become practical instructors in state work...[39]

The schoolmaster, ever an aspect of Lenin's personality (and perhaps implanted there by the image of his father), was now coming very much to the fore. 'You and Rykov', he wrote to Tsyurupa, 'should summon – or drop in on them yourselves – not the "big shots", but board members and those a bit lower, the working officials of commissariats X, Y and Z – and check their work, dig down to the essence, school them, teach them, and give them a good thrashing.'[40]

Following the Eleventh Party Congress – which itself brought important decisions affecting Sovnarkom, as we shall see – Lenin set about getting a systematic statement of his deputies' responsibilities and methods of operation worked out and agreed. The basis of this was a memorandum submitted by Tsyurupa, on which Lenin first obtained Rykov's comments, added a number of points of his own, and then edited and rearranged this material into a thirty-one-paragraph draft Statute on the Work of the Deputies. Although Tsyurupa's memorandum has not been published, there is a summary of it in Lenin's working notes for the draft decree printed in his *Collected Works*, from which, with the aid of a useful editorial note, it is possible to reconstruct the original ingredients of the Statute and the manner in which they were put together.[41] From this it is clear that Lenin's known priorities for his deputies formed the *point de départ* for Tsyurupa's memorandum: the stress on avoiding petty issues and commissions, on checking the fulfilment of decisions, on fighting red tape, and so on. With two minor exceptions Lenin incorporated all Tsyurupa's points and Rykov's additions (which characteristically enough dealt with such practical matters as the Chancellery, the Little Sovnarkom, the Regional Economic Councils, and relations with the soviets). The points added by Lenin himself were headed by the injunction that the deputies should devote nine-tenths of their time to the economic commissariats, and included such matters as the reduction of staff establishments and the switching around of Communists working in government departments, as well as proposals relating to particular agencies.

Lenin's final product was an awkward, wordy combination of general principles, working rules and guidelines on specific policy questions. At the one extreme we have such provisions as:

Divesting Sovnarkom and STO to the maximum degree of minor questions, the settling of which should take place partly (and predominantly) in the process of departmental administration, and partly (specifically in cases not permitting of delay or of exceptional importance) by ordinances issued directly by the deputies themselves [para. 3].

At the other extreme were paragraphs on such matters as the payment of officials in the Trade Commissariat by a bonus system depending on turnover and profits, or editorial policy for the STO journal *Economic Life*. There is little point in summarising the Statute here in detail, since many of its provisions cover familiar ground or were of purely ephemeral relevance. One further general point should be noted, however, since it reflects Lenin's concern to uphold through the role of his deputies the prerogatives of Sovnarkom. The first of the responsibilities assigned them was:

Observation to ensure that the consideration of soviet [i.e. governmental] matters in other institutions, both of the soviets and the party (the Presidium of the CEC, the Politburo and Orgburo of the CC of the R[ussian] C[ommunist] P[arty] and so on without any exception) should not take place other than with the knowledge and participation of the deputies [para. 2].

Of particular interest were the provisions for cooperation and sharing responsibilities between the deputies. They were to confer on the most important issues, to exchange copies of their more important decisions and keep a stenographic record of their verbal instructions. In case of disagreement they were to refer the matter to the Chairman (i.e. Lenin) and only in his absence to the Politburo. Tsyurupa was to chair meetings of the Full Sovnarkom, and hand over to Rykov at the end of two hours; the latter was to chair meetings of STO, and both were to attend all meetings of these bodies. Tsyurupa was to sign decrees and instructions of the Full and Little Sovnarkoms, and supervise the work of their commissions, of the Little Sovnarkom itself, and the Sovnarkom Chancellery and Secretariat. Rykov was to supervise the work of STO and that part of the Sovnarkom staff handling STO business. Tsyurupa's supervisory and executive responsibilities were to embrace the commissariats of Agriculture, Transport, Posts and Telegraphs, Justice, Internal Affairs, Nationalities, Education and the National Economic Council, while Rykov's were to cover the commissariats of Finance, Foreign Trade, Labour (including the Trade Union Council), Social Security, Food Supplies, Army, Foreign Affairs and Health, the Commission on Domestic Trade, the Central Consumer Cooperative Council, the Central Statistical Directorate, the Regional Economic Councils, Gosplan and the Committee on Foreign Concessions. Interestingly, the one agency not allocated to either was Stalin's Rabkrin. At the same time they were to make use of Rabkrin in exercising their checking role.

Lenin signed the draft, marked 'Top Secret', and distributed it

'for information' to members of the Politburo.[42] During the next
few days a number sent their comments and on 21 April these were
distributed in a further information document to Politburo members.[43] Stalin and Zinoviev made no comment, while Kamenev and
Molotov confined themselves to the words 'agree with Cde. Lenin'.
Tomsky wrote briefly to the effect that the Statute was too long and
contained internal contradictions, and registered his disagreement
with the bonus system for trade officials on the grounds that Soviet
functionaries lacked the necessary sense of responsibility and personal interest – it would only lead to plundering the state. Trotsky
wrote a long comment on 18 April and followed it up with another
the following day. His basic criticism was that the Statute tried to
cover so much that it was equivalent to covering nothing: 'The
deputies should strive to ensure that in all fields and in all respects
everything should be fine', he parodied. More specifically, he argued
that Rabkrin was hopeless as a control instrument of the deputies
since, as 'the whole country' knew, it was packed with officials who
had made a mess of some 'real' job and it was riddled with intrigues.
What disturbed him most, however, was that no organ was provided
that could give effective guidance to the economy, and he rehearsed
his earlier views, which had been rejected by Lenin and his other
colleagues, that Gosplan should be given extensive executive powers
for this purpose.

Rykov's comments were briefer, but to the point. He confessed
that, despite having been consulted on the draft, he was apprehen-
sive about aspects of it. Sharing Trotsky's scepticism about Rabkrin,
he feared that using its staff for control purposes would lead to
arbitrary harassment of officials over trifles and disrupt the normal
chain of command. Both he and Trotsky were concerned about the
dangers of disharmony between the deputies. Rykov put the point
tactfully but firmly:

The whole draft is based on the assumption that peace and light will
prevail between Cde Tsyurupa and myself. Up to now the work has begun
fine and harmoniously, and there are reasons to think this will continue.
But from the organisational point of view, and the constitutional for that
matter – given there will be personal changes – can one count on successful
work by people with equal powers in one and the same job? I fear that this
will turn out to be as rare an event as Siamese twins.

It was a further two weeks before Lenin responded to these strictures (he had been undergoing an operation to remove the bullet

left by the assassination attempt of 1918). In a letter written on 5 May, also for distribution to the Politburo, he said that Rykov's criticisms were too vague to require answer, he briefly refuted Tomsky's views on the bonus system, and reserved most of his barbs for Trotsky's strictures on Rabkrin and Gosplan. He also took the opportunity to object to a further letter Trotsky had written on 23 April in which he had criticised a Politburo decision to set up a *Fintroika*, a commission of the two deputies and Finance Commissar Sokolnikov, on the grounds that this would act as a 'brake' between the Little and Full Sovnarkoms.[44]

And here, it would seem, the matter rested. So far as can be determined from available sources, the differences over Lenin's draft were not further discussed and it was never formally approved at Politburo level. It was apparently not placed on the agenda for the next two Politburo meetings[45] and on the day fixed for the third, 25 May, Lenin suffered his stroke, and the issue was evidently shelved. Presumably the more concrete provisions of Lenin's draft were more or less faithfully observed in the initial stage, but both the working rules and the allocation of functions were constantly being adapted to changing circumstances, and there was evidently a good deal of improvisation. As we have seen, the decrees adopted in April 1922 – while the Deputies Statute was being drafted – on several aspects of Sovnarkom procedure, such as the preparation and introduction of agenda items and appeals against Sovnarkom or STO decisions, were radically amended or supplemented in July–August, and there is no reason to believe that other internal arrangements approved by the Chairman were treated as any more sacrosanct.

In the middle months of 1922, though never so massively buttressed by formal arrangements and support staff, the whole Sovnarkom edifice was visibly sagging. Only the chief's return could hope to put it to rights.

14

The last months

We are now approaching the final stage in the history of Lenin's
Sovnarkom – indeed we have already glimpsed one aspect of it in
observing the partial revival of the Little Sovnarkom after the
Chairman's return to his office in October 1922. To appreciate the
dramatic significance of his last acts as Sovnarkom Chairman,
however, we shall need to broaden our focus and again retrace our
steps somewhat. It will already be plain that decisions about internal
arrangements in Sovnarkom, and especially such matters as the role
of different bodies and the personalities and powers of the deputy
chairmen, were closely bound up with the great question of party–
state relationships, and specifically the relationships between Sovnarkom and the Politburo.

Lenin's repeated absences from the middle of 1921 had accelerated a trend that was already well under way during the Civil War:
the shift from Sovnarkom to the Politburo as the end-point of the
decision-making process over an ever-widening range of government
business and on ever more detailed matters. We have already glanced
at the underlying factors making for this trend (see Chapter 12), and
we have also seen how Lenin contributed to it himself by appealing
matters to the Politburo where he was dissatisfied with the way
Sovnarkom had dealt with them. Evidence has also been cited,
however, of his concern for the executive prerogatives of Sovnarkom,
and there can be little doubt that as long as he stood firmly at the
helm the drift of business to the Politburo was at least moderated.
Whether he could, and would, have contrived to reverse the trend
is a question we shall attempt to probe in the following pages.
The reasons for its acceleration from mid-1921 are easy enough to
see. On matters other than current economic administration his
deputies simply did not possess the political standing and relevant

experience to have final decisions taken at Sovnarkom level. Even within the economic sphere they lacked the personal authority and other qualities which usually enabled Lenin to secure agreement within the Sovnarkom network on issues of importance or those involving interdepartmental conflict.

When Lenin took up the threads again in the spring of 1922 he showed himself fully aware of what was happening and determined to do something about it. It is clear, moreover, that his misgivings were shared by at least one other member of the leadership, and the issue was raised in the Central Committee in the course of preparations for the Eleventh Party Congress. When Zinoviev submitted his draft congress report on Party organisational matters Trotsky circulated a letter, on 10 March, on the question of party–state relations, arguing for a sharper differentiation of their functions. Evidently Stalin and Kamenev were entrusted with drafting a new section on this question for inclusion in the Congress resolution, for on 21 March Lenin wrote to them accepting their draft 'in the main', registering his support, again 'in the main', for Trotsky's position, and mentioning his intention of including in his draft report a number of additional points of his own. His report, which was approved by the Central Committee on 25 March, thus incorporates the work of several hands, but there is no doubt that it fully expressed his own convictions.[1]

The Congress opened two days later and this is what Lenin had to say on the issue:

An incorrect relationship has come into existence between the party and soviet [i.e. governmental] institutions, and on this score we are completely unanimous...A formal way out of this is difficult, because we are administered by a single government party, and one cannot forbid a party member making complaints. That is why everything gets dragged from Sovnarkom into the Politburo. A large part of the fault here has been mine, since a great deal of the linking-up between Sovnarkom and the Politburo has been borne by me personally. And when I was obliged to be away it turned out that the two wheels [i.e. Rykov and Tsyurupa] did not work in unison, and Kamenev had to do a third job in order to maintain these links. Since in the near future I will scarcely be able to return to the job, all hopes are transferred to the fact that we now have two deputies as well...

But...regarding the basic directives. There is complete agreement here in the CC, and I hope that the congress will give great attention to this question and approve the directives along the lines that it is necessary to free the Politburo and CC of trifles and heighten the work of the officials responsible. It is necessary that the people's commissars should be responsible for their own jobs and not the way it is – first take it to Sovnarkom and then to the Politburo. We cannot formally abrogate the right to appeal to the CC, because our party is the sole government party. What we must nip in the bud is any attempt to appeal over trifles, rather must we heighten the authority of Sovnarkom, the people's commissars should take more part in it instead of their deputies, and it is necessary to change the character of Sovnarkom's work in a way that I have not managed to do over the past year: to pay a great deal more attention to checking up on implementation. We will have two deputies as well – Rykov and Tsyurupa. Rykov, when he worked in Chusosnabarm, managed to pull things together, and the job went well. Tsyurupa set up one of our best people's commissariats. If the two of them together pay the maximum attention to straightening out the people's commissariats in the matter of their implementation and responsibility, we will make at least a small step forward. . .Comrade Rykov should be a member of the CC Bureau [i.e. Politburo] and a member of the CEC Presidium, because there should be a link between these institutions, since without this link the main wheels sometimes run idle.[2]

Lenin's diagnosis of the problem and his suggested remedies raise a number of questions, some of which we shall consider right away. We may first note in passing his twice going out of his way to claim that the leadership was unanimous on the issue of Politburo–Sovnarkom relations: evidently he thought his audience of some 700 leading Communists would take some convincing on this point. We observe his confirmation of our analysis regarding the key role assumed by Kamenev in linking Sovnarkom with the Politburo: but then, no suggestion that this role should continue, let alone be formalised by Kamenev's nomination as a deputy chairman or even a member of Sovnarkom. Instead, all hopes now resided in Rykov and Tsyurupa, and the former was to be made a full member of the Politburo, so that he could serve as the link that Kamenev had been called on to provide up to that point. In the light of Lenin's urgings some five months earlier that Kamenev should be more actively involved in Sovnarkom and that his position there should be formalised, one wonders whether in the meantime he had been disappointed by Kamenev's performance. Alternatively one might speculate that Kamenev lacked sufficient support within Sovnarkom itself, that other top leaders were uneasy about his taking this additional powerful position, or indeed that he himself rejected it. It seems unlikely, in fact, that Lenin originally intended Kamenev's increased involvement in Sovnarkom to develop into the Politburo-link role, since in October–November 1921 he clearly anticipated continuing to perform this role himself. According to Liberman,

'Lenin did not hold too high an opinion of his [Kamenev's] practical sense. He preferred to entrust Kamenev merely with the drawing-up of projects, resolutions, decrees, etc. – a well-nigh mechanical task, not requiring much originality.'[3]

Of Lenin's other recommendations, the priority urged for checking up on the implementation of decisions reflected one of his constant preoccupations, as we have seen.[4] However, his stress on the people's commissars taking more personal responsibility, and his linking of this with the *institutional* role of Sovnarkom – its 'authority' should be raised and the commissars themselves participate in it instead of delegating it to their deputies – struck a new note. In this context he further urged less reliance on decision-making by commissions, and finding ways to improve the quality of commissars.[5]

Neither Lenin's diagnosis nor his prescriptions went uncriticised at the Congress, which was the scene for a display of plain speaking now unusual in the Russian Communist Party and no doubt unwelcome to the ruling oligarchy. The former Central Committee Secretary, Preobrazhensky, now a leading financial administrator, while welcoming Lenin's advocacy of drawing a sharper line between the work of party and government bodies at the top, was abusively scornful of Rykov's capacity to give effective leadership to economic administration in Sovnarkom: since willy-nilly issues would continue to be referred for party decision, he urged the creation of a Party *Ekonomburo*, alongside the Politburo and Orgburo, and consisting of officials free of departmental affiliation to particular commissariats.[6] Preobrazhensky persisted with this proposal to the point of moving it as an amendment to the official resolution on the Central Committee report, but his was the sole vote in favour.[7]

Another delegate, the former 'Democratic Centralist' Osinsky, now serving as Deputy People's Commissar for Agriculture, contested Lenin's assertion that the practice of referring every trifle to the Politburo had only developed during his illness; on the contrary, as he had mentioned at the previous congress, this practice had long been endemic. He put it down to the attempt of Sovnarkom to function as a legislative as well as an administrative body. His solution, a characteristically 'constitutional' one, was to place the legislative function firmly in the hands of the CEC and turn Sovnarkom into a proper executive 'cabinet'.[8] His use of this latter term, with its associations of bourgeois parliamentarianism, provided a convenient cudgel for Lenin to belabour and ridicule him.[9]

The official proposals which Lenin was advancing in the name of the outgoing Central Committee envisaged that party bodies at all levels, and not only those at the centre, should be divested of a substantial part of the decision-making prerogatives that they had assumed during the Civil War. Among the large contingent of provincial party officials attending the Congress, such ideas must have been received with a mixture of cynicism and apprehension, but on the whole they were too 'disciplined' to demur. The most outspoken reaction was voiced by A. I. Mikoyan, Secretary of the Nizhny-Novgorod gubkom, and soon to emerge as one of Stalin's leading supporters. Mikoyan argued that the interests of the proletariat were involved in many purely administrative matters, and party officials must therefore continue to concern themselves with them.[10]

Despite these and other critical voices, Lenin's proposals were duly incorporated into the Congress Resolution, which deemed it 'possible and necessary to unburden the party of a range of questions of a purely soviet [i.e. governmental] nature, which it came to assume in the pre-congress period'. To this end the responsibilities of both the local soviets and the CEC were to be heightened, and:

With the same objectives of unburdening the supreme organs of the party of questions of a purely soviet nature and of introducing the maximum level of planning and answerability into the activity of the soviet apparatus at the centre and in the localities, it is necessary to heighten and strengthen the activity of Sovnarkom as an organ of systematic leadership and co-ordination [*soglasovaniya*] of the work of all organs of state administration.[11]

Furthermore, Rykov, as Lenin proposed, was elected to the Politburo at the first meeting of the Central Committee following the Congress.

Here, perhaps, were the elements of a solution to Sovnarkom's drastic decline as a decision-making body. But to transform it into reality would require the political skill, authoritative leadership, and energetic attention to detail that only Lenin could provide, and this was no longer available. As already noted, in the weeks separating the Eleventh Party Congress from his first stroke he did not attend a single meeting of Sovnarkom. Obviously he was placing his primary reliance on Rykov, but Rykov was not of the political calibre to carry through such a programme against the powerful forces pushing in the opposite direction – and this was a major political miscalculation by Lenin himself.

During the next three months, with Rykov and Tsyurupa totally absorbed in their efforts to operate the government machine as effectively as could be without Lenin's guiding hand at the controls, the trend to refer matters of substance or of interdepartmental disagreement for resolution by the Politburo became even more intense than before. This further shift of business from the government to the party executive was accompanied by a marked expansion of the activity of the Orgburo and Central Committee Secretariat into areas of administrative decision formerly reserved to Sovnarkom and the commissariats. This placed enormous power in the hands of Stalin, who had enjoyed the position of General Secretary since April 1922 but in practice had dominated the party machine since a year before that when he was made the only member of the Politburo serving on the Orgburo. The same period saw the beginnings of that alliance between Stalin, Zinoviev and Kamenev which in 1923 was to blossom into a ruling triumvirate dominating the Politburo and the whole political life of the country.

During August and September, as he strove to catch up with what had been happening during the acute stage of his illness, Lenin clearly recognised that the measures he had sponsored at the Eleventh Congress to restore the authority and effectiveness of Sovnarkom had failed, and on 11 September he made a dramatic move aimed at repairing the damage or at least patching it up till he could himself resume active direction of affairs. This took the form of a note to Stalin proposing that the Politburo appoint Kamenev and Trotsky as additional deputy chairmen of Sovnarkom.[12] The basic intention here is obvious enough: the investing of two additional Politburo members with deputy chairmen's powers and responsibilities would enable far more matters, and more important matters, to be settled within Sovnarkom, both by virtue of the individual executive authority they would exercise and of the enhanced collective authority Sovnarkom would acquire. The requirement that the deputies should consult on important and disputed issues would have the effect of creating an 'inner cabinet' of four, of whom three would be members of the Politburo. Together with Lenin, these would form a majority in the Politburo, so that the likelihood of a successful appeal to the latter body against their decisions would be small. Provided the deputies could act with sufficient cohesion – and here lay the obvious weak point of the proposal – this could have led to a radical change in the Sovnarkom–Politburo relationship.

Why Kamenev and Trotsky? As we have seen, Kamenev's local responsibilities in Moscow and his role on important economic bodies of party and government made him a logical choice, despite Lenin's reservations about his administrative abilities, and there is no need to assume that at this stage Lenin was consciously aiming to drive a wedge between Kamenev and Stalin, though a little later such a design might have been feasible. The logic of Trotsky's nomination is not so obvious. Although his direct executive responsibilities were confined to the Army Commissariat Trotsky was indeed constantly involved in major policy decisions in all areas of domestic and foreign affairs. However, this policy-making role was focused on the Politburo and he seems to have scorned any personal participation in the work of Sovnarkom bodies. Furthermore Trotsky had for some time been odd man out on important issues of economic administration, with Lenin himself and the majority of Politburo members ranged against him.[13] Of course policy disputes within the leadership were inevitable, and every leader found himself outvoted from time to time, but in Trotsky's case such disputes acquired a special edge because of the legacy of reserve and resentment towards him lingering from his years of virulent opposition to Bolshevism, in some cases reinforced by personality clashes during the Civil War.

Lenin must have had very strong reasons for proposing Trotsky as a deputy chairman of Sovnarkom in the face of such considerations, and two such reasons were probably paramount. The first was the enormous authority he would bring to the job. Despite the relative coolness towards him in the upper ranks of the party, no leader other than Lenin himself had higher standing in the eyes of the party rank-and-file and the population at large. The second reason was his robust opposition to the encroachments of the party machine on the executive and administrative prerogatives of the state. In common with Lenin, he differed from Stalin, Zinoviev and Kamenev in holding no executive position within the party. As we noted he himself raised the question of party–state relations on the eve of the Eleventh Congress, and during the Congress itself no one had more strongly and outspokenly supported Lenin's proposals on divesting party bodies of most of the governmental business they were transacting.

It is quite clear that the party, even in the person of the party organisations, cannot decide all questions. Any economic question is complicated.

However there is a widespread view that if you introduce this complicated question into the gubkom [provincial party committee], the Orgburo, or the Politburo of the CC, it will immediately become simple. It is considered that the very economic administrator who could not cope with his economic duties when he was in charge of the provincial economic council would be anointed with grace should he be appointed gubkom secretary...An official lacking the necessary character and sense of responsibility will himself rush to the gubkom, the ukom [district committee] or the Politburo, in order to shed the responsibility...A ruling party does not in the least mean a party directly administering all details of the job.[14]

Nine-tenths of the matters dealt with by party bodies, he said, should properly be left to the government administration.[15] These views provoked a sharp riposte from Mikoyan. 'I am not surprised', he sarcastically stated, 'that Cde Trotsky said this. He has no idea about gubkoms, he is a military man.'[16] If Trotsky was seen as a leading opponent of the party machine, he was no great friend of its master either. The hostility generated by Civil War disputes had been kept alive by later policy clashes and Trotsky's open disdain for Stalin's Rabkrin, another question on which up to now he had been at odds with Lenin. It is therefore difficult to escape the conclusion that Lenin now realised something like a direct confrontation with the party machine would be unavoidable if a proper party–state relationship were to be restored, and was seeking to marshal his biggest guns for this purpose.

In this, however, he was disappointed, for while Kamenev accepted the nomination, Trotsky declined. His reasons were probably complex. The excuse he offered at the time – that Lenin had timed the nomination with a view to Rykov's impending leave whereas he himself had been granted leave to prepare for the Comintern Congress – was obviously disingenuous.[17] The reason he later gave – that what was wanted was greater authority and responsibility for the people's commissars rather than multiplication of deputy chairmen – was probably quite genuine.[18] But Deutscher is almost certainly correct in suggesting the further motive that 'his pride may have been hurt by an arrangement which would have placed him formally on the same footing as the other vice-Premiers who were only Lenin's inferior assistants'.[19] Moreover, Trotsky may have been justly sceptical about the prospects of a workable 'inner cabinet' which included such incompatible personalities as himself, Rykov and Kamenev.

The upshot was that an 'inner cabinet' did indeed emerge and begin to operate in the following weeks. Consisting of Rykov, Kamenev and Tsyurupa, and referred to as the 'Conference of Deputies' (*soveshchaniye zamov*) and later as the 'Board [*Kollegiya*] of Deputies', it became an extra echelon in the hierarchy of authority without, however, stemming the flow of business to the Politburo in any significant degree.[20]

Lenin now clearly realised that only *his* hand at the helm presented any prospect of restoring Sovnarkom. No other conclusion is possible if one compares his behaviour in the weeks preceding his first stroke when he was attending Politburo and other meetings but *not* those of Sovnarkom, with his behaviour when he returned to the Kremlin early in October. He now resumed working daily in his Sovnarkom office, chairing all meetings of Sovnarkom and STO, vetting the decisions of the Little Sovnarkom, and supervising the work of the Chancellery and Secretariat: in other words, performing the full-time chief executive role he had exercised up to mid-1921. As we have seen, he also found time to revise the draft Little Sovnarkom Statute to bring it in line with his requirements.[21] When one bears in mind his depleted physical resources, and the fact that he also participated in Politburo meetings during this period and sought to give a lead on all major policy issues, the central importance he now assigned to reviving Sovnarkom becomes plain.

While it is obvious that Lenin could not long maintain such a workload, even barring a serious relapse, it was perhaps essential for him to totally immerse himself for a time in the Sovnarkom operation before he could move effectively to setting it to rights. Looking ahead, Lenin seems to have perceived that what was needed was *both* himself on the spot exercising general leadership and supervision, *and* the kinds of arrangements for devolving some of his duties on his deputies and for rendering the operation of Sovnarkom bodies more effective and self-sustaining, which were earlier seen as substitutes for his direct personal participation. Within a few weeks he was beginning to address himself to devising patterns of activity that would combine these two aspects. At a meeting of Sovnarkom on 3 December he presented his proposals for revising the procedures for preparing and submitting matters for Sovnarkom consideration.[22] On the following day he distributed to his deputies some initial proposals for reallocation of work amongst them: one was to take special responsibility for STO and the other two for Sovnarkom, switching around monthly; a list assigning executive responsibility for the various commissariats among the deputies was to be drawn up, as in the previous April; Kamenev was nonetheless to continue with certain tasks he had already undertaken; and each deputy was to have a systematic programme of checking sections of the government machine.[23]

Five days later he distributed further proposals which included an outline of institutionalised 'sittings' (*zasedaniya*) of the chairman and deputies, i.e. the 'inner cabinet'. They were all to be at work in the Sovnarkom offices between eleven and two and between six and nine on Mondays, Tuesdays, Thursdays and Fridays. At such times, provided Sovnarkom, STO or the Politburo were not in session, special meetings of the 'inner cabinet' (the term was never used by Lenin or his contemporaries) might be called whenever urgent or contentious issues came up, and in any case at least two such meetings of an hour's duration should be held each week. In addition the Chairman and deputies were together to agree the agenda and priority of business for all Sovnarkom bodies. The deputies were to keep close watch on the work of the Little Sovnarkom and the 'administrative sittings' of STO – the latter had been discontinued but should now be revived. All three deputies should attend meetings of Sovnarkom's Finance Committee – which had become an important instrument of administration in recent months – along with Finance Commissar Sokolnikov, his deputy, and Little Sovnarkom Chairman Kiselev. Lenin also raised the question whether there should not be one meeting of the Finance Committee weekly under his own chairmanship. He now suggested that the group of commissariats for which each deputy would have supervisory and executive responsibilities should be changed every two months, so that they all could become familiar with the whole government machine. And finally he reiterated the importance of the deputies' setting aside time to study the work of middle and lower level officials.[24]

These proposals were obviously just the beginning of a programme of reorganising and revivifying Sovnarkom which, to have any hope of success, would require constant effort for a considerable time. But time was just what Lenin was not given to enjoy. Within a few more days a further relapse caused him to give up once more, and this time for good, the active direction of affairs. Meanwhile, in a discussion with his deputies on 12 December the latter submitted to him their agreed proposals for the sharing of responsibilities. Lenin found them very unsatisfactory. Replying the next day, he argued that the deputies had failed to take account of their personal strengths and weaknesses in allocating responsibilities. In particular Kamenev should specialise in chairing meetings and seeing that decisions were expressed in proper legal form, while Rykov and Tsyurupa should do the actual administrative work. Since he himself had insisted on a periodical circulation of roles, this criticism must have left his deputies somewhat nonplussed. However, he did not press his counter-proposals which, as he said, had no immediate practical significance since he had to take further sick leave. At the same time he agreed to their implementing their proposals only until such time as he resumed duty, if this should be sooner than the three months they suggested.[25]

And this, in effect, is the end of our story, for he never did resume duty, as we have observed. There is, however, a postscript. For the recurrence of Lenin's illness in December 1922 coincided with a profound crisis of confidence in the regime he had created and led over five years, and the writings in which his doubts and remedies were expressed held great potential implications for the future of of Sovnarkom. These doubts had been building up for a year or more, and we have seen some of the symptoms of them in his growing preoccupation with bureaucratic red tape and muddle, his constant tinkering with the Sovnarkom machine, and his increasingly resolute efforts to restore the business of day-to-day government from the Politburo and other central party organs to Sovnarkom. Up to the autumn of 1922, however, he seems to have assumed that the problems, though serious, were not fundamental, and would respond in time to intelligent and persistent counter-measures. It was what he saw after he came back to his office in October that imbued his doubts with a new and sickening urgency: bureaucracy rampant, confused and divided counsels, and policy drifting in a dangerous direction on a whole range of issues. The 'Georgian Crisis' of December 1922 brought his personal crisis to a head. This was occasioned by the high-handed and dictatorial manner in which Stalin and his agents forced Georgia into a Transcaucasian Federation against the will of the majority of Georgian Communists and their local leaders. Although Lenin considered the idea of such a federation correct in principle, the way it was imposed brought home to him not only how far his regime had become infected by the brutal high-handedness and Great Russian chauvinism of its

Tsarist predecessors, but that the chief focus of infection was the apex of the Communist Party organisation itself.[26]

The tragic irony was that the agitation induced in him by this realisation almost certainly precipitated the medical relapse that incapacitated him for active counter-measures.[27] Nevertheless, with his characteristic courage and tenacity, he sought yet again, in the only way open to him, to impose his will on the course of history, beginning to dictate, within days of his stroke, the series of memoranda, notes and articles that later became known as his 'Testament'.[28] If historians differ considerably in their exegesis of these documents and their evaluation of their political significance,[29] this is due not only to their own divergent political perspectives but also to the many ambiguities, contradictions and changes of mind in the documents themselves. There is no need here to examine these writings in detail, but part of their content, seen in relation to certain other letters and conversations of Lenin at this time and placed in political context, bears closely on the fate of Sovnarkom and therefore claims our attention.

The central burden of Lenin's 'Testament' was his intention to introduce 'a number of changes in our political regime' at the party congress due in April 1923. These were to embrace both the structure and the personnel of the party leadership. While conceding that the long-term survival and stability of the regime would depend on successful maintenance of the worker-peasant alliance, he argued that 'considerations of a purely personal character' faced it with immediate instability and a possible split if the measures he recommended were not urgently taken. A confessed Marxist could stress in no stronger terms the fundamental nature of the problems as he now perceived them. His major structural proposal was that the Central Committee should be increased to 50–100 members by the addition of worker and peasant communists drawn from the lower echelons of the party. These would have the right of attending meetings of the Politburo as well as the Central Committee, they were to see all party documents, and their task would be not only to control but to *remake* the apparatus.[30] Later he envisaged also expanding and reinforcing the powers of the Central Control Commission, the party's internal disciplinary body, linking it closely with a revamped Rabkrin, and prescribing that a certain proportion of its members should also attend all Politburo meetings.[31] The intention here was obvious: the arbitrary power of the Politburo oligarchy would be checked, the entrenched leadership diluted, and the independence of the party machine from the party as a political organism curbed.

The need for these structural changes Lenin linked directly with the relationship between Stalin and Trotsky, which he saw as constituting 'a good half of the danger of the split which could be avoided and the avoidance of which, in my opinion, should be contributed to, amongst other things, by the increase in the number of CC members to 50 or 100'.[32] Let us therefore look a little more closely at the evolution of Lenin's relations with his two most powerful colleagues. The sharpened concern that Lenin showed in the autumn of 1922 over Sovnarkom's position *vis-à-vis* the Central Committee does not seem, at first, to have been directly linked with apprehensions about Stalin personally. Between October and December, however, a whole series of issues arose on which Lenin felt that policy was disastrously off-course, and at the centre of most of them stood Stalin. The most important of these were measures to dilute the state monopoly of foreign trade, and the arrangements envisaged for the non-Russian national areas in the draft USSR Constitution, the erroneous character of which was dramatised for Lenin by the Georgian crisis. On these matters Lenin found himself at one with Trotsky, and as his critical attitude to Stalin grew, he also came to accept the validity of Trotsky's disdain for Stalin's Rabkrin. The one thing that still divided them was Trotsky's conviction that Gosplan should be vested with extensive executive powers over the economy, but by the end of December Lenin had reached the conclusion that on this matter, too, Trotsky was basically correct.[33] An early expression of their rapprochement had been the renewed proposal by Lenin, evidently made in November, that Trotsky should become a deputy chairman of Sovnarkom. Trotsky replied that he would accept if the Central Committee made it a matter of party discipline, but he was against the proposal, on the grounds that the multiplication of deputies was organisationally ill-advised. There was no place for a 'Board of Deputies', though he could see the necessity of *one* Deputy Chairman of Sovnarkom and possibly another for STO. Perhaps he was hinting here at the terms on which he himself would be prepared to accept the Deputy Chairmanship, but if so Lenin never took it up.[34] After Lenin's relapse, with his eyes now thoroughly opened to Stalin by the Georgian crisis, he moved into a closer alliance with Trotsky, relying on him to act on his behalf on both the foreign trade monopoly issue and the Georgian question. As Lenin's correspondence shows, this reliance on Trotsky, and on him alone amongst his Politburo colleagues, continued right up to Lenin's further stroke and loss of speech on 10 March.[35]

So far as Stalin was concerned Lenin's plans for restructuring the party leadership had as their keystone his removal from the position of General Secretary. This was broadly hinted at in the second of his memoranda, dictated on 25 December, and proposed unequivocally in his third, dictated ten days later.[36]

Lenin's final campaign to put his regime to rights came to naught. For reasons on which we can only speculate Trotsky failed to confront Stalin on the Georgian and other issues at the Twelfth Congress in April 1923. Stalin found a convenient excuse for suppressing Lenin's memoranda to the Congress containing his proposals for restructuring the central party organs and removing Stalin from the General Secretaryship. The Central Committee and Central Control Commission were indeed expanded as Lenin had suggested, but with Stalin still running the Secretariat the newcomers were inevitably drawn predominantly from his provincial adherents, and the move only strengthened the oligarchy rather than diluting it.[37]

The implications of these developments for Sovnarkom will be obvious. Since December it had returned to operating in the crippled fashion established during Lenin's previous absences, and with the latter's failure to have the Twelfth Congress shake up the existing arrangements the subordination of government to party machine became permanently entrenched. True, at the end of 1922 Rabkrin had been transferred from Stalin to Tsyurupa, but it is doubtful if this caused the General Secretary much concern so long as he retained control of the party machine.[38] There were also other developments related to the formation of the USSR and the adaptation of Sovnarkom to serve in form (and not just in practice) this wider federation. In this connection Stalin shrewdly revived in January 1923 the proposal that Trotsky become a deputy chairman and suggested also that there be a further deputy chairman representing the Ukraine. There was obviously no chance that Trotsky would consent to serve as one of five deputies with Sovnarkom's overall status unchanged, and after a considerable recriminatory correspondence in which Trotsky was forced to defend his earlier refusals to serve as deputy, he summed up his objections as follows: 'The work of a deputy under the present set-up wholly contradicts all my habits and concepts on properly organised work. My appointment to such a job would signify, in my eyes, my liquidation as a Soviet official.'[39] About the same time Zinoviev suggested that the work of the Politburo be reorganised to make each of its members responsible for a group of commissariats and other government agencies. Trotsky opposed this on the grounds that it would turn them all into Sovnarkom deputy chairmen, and the proposal was defeated. However, the idea was revived in June 1923 and this time adopted, much to Trotsky's disgust.[40]

But we are now speaking of a period when Sovnarkom was no longer in any real sense the government of Lenin, despite the grotesque farce of his election as Chairman of the newly formed USSR Sovnarkom on 7 July, and are thus exceeding our brief. The one question that remains is why Lenin's efforts to restore Sovnarkom and to repair his regime generally proved so singularly inept. It is tempting to put it down simply to the deterioration in his mental capacities, but there is probably more to it than this. His most consistent error, given the obvious uncertainty of his health, lay in devising arrangements, in April 1922 as much as December 1922 and January 1923, whose chances of success depended on his personal involvement in carrying them out. In retrospect it is easy to argue that he should have handed over the Sovnarkom chairmanship to someone else in 1921 or 1922, limiting himself to chairing the Politburo and from that position working to ensure that the new Sovnarkom Chairman had the same freedom of action that Stalin, for instance, was permitted in his management of the party machine. But there was the rub – *who* was to be the new Chairman? In his memorandum of 24 January 1923, Lenin ran through the qualities of nearly all the principal leaders, whom he rightly perceived as unsuitable for some reason or other for top office. Even Trotsky, his current ally, although 'the most capable person in the present CC', was 'excessively given to self-confidence and gets too carried away with the purely administrative side of work'. Rykov and Tomsky, the two Politburo members exempt from his strictures, were obviously not of the political calibre to step into his shoes – Rykov, despite his great administrative talents, was to demonstrate this when he was made Sovnarkom Chairman following Lenin's death. As Schapiro has pointed out, the very qualities that commended his Politburo colleagues to Lenin as instruments of his revolutionary will unfitted them to fill the unique role built up around his own exceptional personality over two decades of revolutionary leadership.[41] In early 1923 he evidently still hoped there might be time to train a new generation of leaders from whom suitable successors would emerge.[42] His moves to this end, however, had come two years too late.

A memorandum signed by Stalin, Kamenev, Zinoviev, Tomsky and Rykov in March 1923, on the eve of the Twelfth Congress, and intended to rally support in the Central Committee against Trotsky's criticisms of the Politburo, contains a passage which can be read as an off-handed valediction for Lenin's Sovnarkom: 'Now, when the Politburo, in connection with the illness of Vladimir Ilyich, is even more required to perform the role of the actual government, it is indubitably necessary to improve the work of the Politburo.'[43] The implied condition for the Politburo to withdraw from this role, namely that Lenin should be back in command, was of course never to be met, and the appointment after his death of a relatively junior member of the Politburo as the new Sovnarkom Chairman ensured that the existing relationship between the two bodies would be perpetuated.

15

Some historical reflections

For the first three years or so of its existence the Council of People's Commissars was the government of the embattled Soviet Republic in fact as well as name. If it subsequently became something less than this it nevertheless remained a key political and administrative body second in importance only to the Political Bureau of the Party Central Committee. Moreover, despite its great expansion since the 1930s, its many reorganisations, its renaming as the Council of Ministers in 1946, and its several changes of leadership, its modern structures and processes have evolved organically out of those established under Lenin, and have manifested a remarkable level of continuity. Many of its parts, including several of the present Soviet ministries, had their origins as people's commissariats or other Sovnarkom agencies formed in the Lenin period, and in some cases beyond that as imperial ministries established well back in the nineteenth century. This legacy is a monument to the achievement of those who built up Sovnarkom from the old and new materials at their disposal and launched it as a functioning institution.

In evaluating this achievement, moreover, it is important to realise how advanced many of Sovnarkom's institutional features were for its time. As a government executive Sovnarkom invites closest comparison with cabinet systems of the British type,[1] since, like them it consisted of 'ministers' individually responsible for the various branches of the administration and collectively responsible for the government as a whole, and headed by a 'prime minister' who orchestrated and more or less dominated its decision-making activities but whose executive authority derived from his role *within* the collective body (rather than from a superordinated 'presidential' position) and who could be overruled by the latter.[2] Considering Sovnarkom in this comparative context, it is striking that in such matters as the conduct of meetings according to prepared agenda, the compilation and advance circulation of relevant documentation, the keeping of minutes, and the creation of a secretariat for maintaining records, preparing meetings, promoting interdepartmental consultation and following up decisions, Sovnarkom had attained a point within its first few months which the British Cabinet was reaching only at about the same time, after some two centuries of experience; in fact in these respects the machinery and procedures elaborated by Sovnarkom by the end of the Civil War were to be matched by the British Cabinet only during and after the Second World War.

The reasons were perhaps largely functional. It was only in the course of the First, and especially the Second, World War that the scope and pressure of business facing the British Cabinet necessitated such arrangements, while Sovnarkom was faced with a similar, or greater, scope and pressure of business from its very inception. Doubtless cultural factors also played a part. The informality of British Cabinet procedures was long valued as one of its essential characteristics, so much so that there was strong pressure in the early 1920s to abolish the new Cabinet Secretariat as unconstitutional, and such attitudes undoubtedly delayed its development. By contrast, the Soviet government was heir to a continental bureaucratic tradition which in Russia, no less than in France or Germany, linked decision-making with ample documentation, formal rules and secretarial support staff. In fact models for the machinery and procedures adopted by Sovnarkom had already been provided by its predecessors in the Tsarist and Provisional Governments.

If, however, both the need and the models for such arrangements were present, it was still necessary that both should be perceived, and the latter adapted and applied. And here the credit must go first and foremost to Lenin himself, to his first Head of Chancellery, Bonch-Bruyevich, to such second-line officials as Bogolepov and Kozlovsky, and almost certainly (though much harder to document) to a handful of senior officials, such as P. M. Trokhimovsky, carried over from the old regime. It is remarkable, and perhaps unprecedented, that Lenin, a man approaching fifty who had spent his whole youth and adult life as professional revolutionary, could apply himself so single-mindedly and persistently to such humdrum matters, especially when one recalls the critical and chaotic circumstances in which he did so. This relates, moreover, not only to his contribution to the creation and running of the Sovnarkom machine, but to his exercise of the 'prime-ministerial' role. In such matters as the management of agendas, the clarification of issues and judicious injection of his influence on them before they came up for formal consideration, the guidance, stimulation and focusing of discussion, the crystallisation of clear decisions embodied in his summings-up, the use of standing and *ad hoc* committees, and the exercise of his executive authority in taking, facilitating or ensuring administrative decisions, Lenin quickly displayed a mastery that would have done credit to a politician who had served a long apprenticeship in a mature system of cabinet government.

Nevertheless, we must come back to the fact that Sovnarkom in a sense 'failed', that it proved incapable in the end of maintaining itself as *the* government of the Soviet Republic. Without retracing in detail already familiar ground, let us recall some of the reasons for this, and briefly explore some of its wider causes and implications.

We might start with the observation that most of Lenin's colleagues lacked his facility in adapting their patterns of thought and action to the tasks of running a government rather than fighting one. Liberman recalls the 'peculiar atmosphere' that prevailed at the meetings of Sovnarkom and other government bodies chaired by Lenin. 'Despite all the efforts of an officious secretary to impart to each session the solemn character of a cabinet meeting, we could not help feeling that here we were, attending another meeting of an underground revolutionary committee.'[3] As he pointed out, the attitudes of mind of the participants found outward expression in their leather jackets and heavy topcoats and the random way they scattered their chairs around the room rather than sitting tamely at the cabinet table. How far this atmosphere militated against effective decision-making by Sovnarkom is hard to judge, but the dissonance between the efforts of Lenin to conduct an orderly cabinet meeting and the free-wheeling style of most of his colleagues must have contributed to the impatience of the more senior of these with Sovnarkom meetings and encouraged them to make their own contributions to policy in the more congenial ambience of the Party Central Committee. Paradoxically, then, the greater Lenin's success in moulding Sovnarkom into a smoothly-working organ of government, the greater the tendency for crucial policy-inputs to be directed elsewhere. One suspects, too, that in time this problem acquired another dimension: as Sovnarkom was more and more imbued with Lenin's political style and dominated by his personality, it came to be perceived as something like *his* bailiwick, just as the Revolutionary Military Council was Trotsky's, the Orgburo was Stalin's, and the Vecheka Dzerzhinsky's, Moscow Kamenev's and Petrograd Zinoviev's. While on the one hand this meant that he, like they, should be left by and large to run his 'bailiwick' in his own way, the corollary was that *his* should be subject just as the others were to the same superordinated level of authority, where ultimate policy would be determined, coordination achieved, and disputes adjudicated – namely the Party Central Committee.

Obviously, this problem might have been averted had people's commissars not been free to absent themselves from Sovnarkom sessions and be represented there by deputies or more junior members of their boards. Such formal arrangements sometimes have much to do with the fate of institutions. Other formal weaknesses were the generous attendance provisions which allowed meetings to become too large, and the convention that non-agenda questions might be raised as a matter of urgency. One might also argue that a more effective committee structure would have made a lot of difference. The Little Sovnarkom did an invaluable job as a general purposes committee for second-order business, and STO was of crucial importance in directing production and distribution, especially during the Civil War. But what if Sovnarkom had developed a system of specialised committees covering all major policy areas, analogous to those supporting the post-war British Cabinet, and each chaired by a senior member of the government? Of course such devices may work in one country and not in another,[4] but the establishment of an influential Finance Committee at the end of the Lenin era perhaps points in the direction Sovnarkom might have moved. Such a committee system might have brought policy back under the umbrella of Sovnarkom, while ensuring that Full Sovnarkom agendas were limited to the most important and contentious issues. As an alternative or complement to such arrangements Sovnarkom might have formed an inner cabinet of its most authoritative members to deal with major policy questions, as we have suggested earlier, and as Lenin seems to have belatedly considered from September 1922. There is little profit, however, in speculating on such might-have-beens.

One might also raise the question whether Lenin's prime-ministerial qualities, despite their manifest strengths, did not also possess their fatal flaws. Could it be that the withdrawal of Lenin's senior colleagues from active participation in Sovnarkom was not entirely unwelcome to him, if not because it cleared the way for him to dominate it, at least because it made it easier to get on with the job without time-consuming wrangles? If he did not at least subconsciously derive satisfaction from their absence, why did he not take firmer measures against it? Such suspicions are not unreasonable, but it is difficult to find positive evidence to support them. Moreover it goes against what we know of Lenin's concern to see that officials affected by decisions had a say in them, and seems to impute to him an improbable level of percipience and control over the behaviour of his senior colleagues.

A more realistic candidate for the 'fatal flaw' is Lenin's preoccupation with detail, which was discussed in Chapter 9. As we saw, his mastery of detail was an important source of his influence over policy, but did he allow it to consume too much of his time and also contribute to the cluttering of Full Sovnarkom agendas with minor matters, despite the existence of the Little Sovnarkom? Some of his colleagues evidently thought so. At the Eleventh Party Congress Preobrazhensky, while warmly supporting Lenin's strictures on the drift of government business to the Politburo, put part of the blame on to Lenin's total absorption, year after year, in 'Sovnarkom vermicelli', which was ruining his health and preventing him from attending to larger questions.[5]

Be this as it may, there was one way in which Lenin contributed profoundly to the eclipse of Sovnarkom: his failure to make satisfactory arrangements for its leadership when he fell ill. Despite the factors we have mentioned, despite the importance already assumed by the party machine, despite the expansion of Politburo attention to domestic administration at the end of the Civil War, Sovnarkom's eclipse had still not reached the point of no return before Lenin's prolonged absences began in 1921. The 'prime-ministerial' role, with its sub-roles of leader, chairman, chief executive and politician, was not an expendable part of the Sovnarkom system. Thus the measures taken to deal with his partial and then virtually complete withdrawal were fundamentally misconceived; what was wanted was not institutional arrangements and deputies to take over the minor details of the prime ministerial role, but a vigorous and authoritative *Acting* Chairman to take over its central aspects. The headlong decline of Sovnarkom once these stopped being performed should have made this apparent. Yet Trotsky alone among the leading Bolsheviks gave evidence of realising it, although others may have perceived it too but kept it to themselves out of deference to Lenin or for more self-serving reasons.

If Lenin himself grasped the problem, his failure to deal with it may have been due to his belief, suggested in Chapter 14, that there was no one suitable to take his place. Yet one recalls his conviction that men can grow to meet the demands of high office – an argument he often used to persuade reluctant Bolsheviks to accept appointment as people's commissars. There thus seems a curious myopia if not a dog-in-the-manger attitude in his behaviour: unable to perform the prime-ministerial role himself, he would not give any of his colleagues a chance to perform it. Someone – perhaps Rykov, perhaps Kamenev – might have coped, particularly if backed by Lenin's support at Politburo level. The prime-ministerial role would have to be adapted to the strengths and weaknesses of its new incumbent, but if the move had been made early enough Lenin might have had time to ensure that it worked. Simple greed for power does not seem to have been in Lenin's character, and the explanation for his behaviour may have had more of a tragic quality. Throughout his political career he repeatedly formed the conviction that erstwhile comrades were leading his cause astray and only his guidance could confirm it on the right path. While the capacity to do this again, when necessary, was not something he could easily concede, and effective leadership resources must therefore be kept in his hands, it was the resources embodied in the Sovnarkom chairmanship which had been crucial to his leadership position since the Revolution. Meanwhile, the more the leading bodies of the party became dependent upon the latter's bureaucratic machinery, in which he had never been involved, the less could he view his position in these bodies as offering adequate substitute for his role as Head of Government. Paradoxically, however, it was his failure to entrust the resources of the Sovnarkom chairmanship to another that disastrously accelerated their dissipation and confirmed his party on the mistaken path from which, all too late, he sought to deflect it.

Without assuming the omniscience to rank all these factors and reveal all their interconnections, we would argue that they should figure in any analysis of the early evolution of Sovnarkom. Even taken together, however, they remain seriously incomplete, and now we must turn to a whole new dimension of the question. We may best approach this by recalling our comparison of Sovnarkom with a British-type cabinet, and observing that the discussion here was limited to matters of structure and procedure, without touching seriously on larger questions of power, authority and legitimacy. These questions were broached, though not systematically explored, in the arguments at the Eleventh Party Congress provoked by Lenin's proposals for reversing the drift of government business from Sovnarkom to the Politburo. They were perhaps most clearly posed by Osinsky, who, as we saw, contended that the crux of the problem was 'the inappropriate system of government' in which Sovnarkom, vested with both legislative and executive powers, was unable effectively to exercise either. Legislative functions should be the monopoly of the Central Executive Committee of the Congress of Soviets, and Sovnarkom should become a 'Cabinet of Commissars', the executive arm of government, its members nominated by its Chairman and with him collectively responsible to the CEC. This appears to have been the last occasion on which a prominent Bolshevik advocated essentially a cabinet–parliamentary system of government, in which by implication the ruling party would be limited to the role of formulating overall policy – the sort of system, in fact, that showed signs of emerging in the first months of the Soviet regime. These signs, as we know, were illusory, and would have proved so sooner or later even had the realities not been pre-cipitately exposed by the circumstances of the Civil War. For the principle of legitimacy which this approach implied, one in which authority derived from the freely-chosen representatives of the people whose will, freely formulated and freely expressed, should be the basis of government policy, was not one that Lenin or his colleagues of like mind could ever accept. Government policy was an expression of class interest, and the interest of the victorious pro-letariat was best known to its conscious vanguard, the Communist Party. The responsibility of this vanguard to the class it led, and through it to History, was not to be met by deriving its policies from opinion welling up from below and expressed through formal insti-tutions, but by leading the class and the masses to pursue their true interests, if possible by education and persuasion, if necessary by coercion. Furthermore, if error based outside the party had no rights, error inside the party was also intolerable if it threatened to deflect it from the true path perceived by the leadership. Hence the Tenth Congress ban on 'factionalism' and the use of the party machine to suppress groups critical of the dominant oligarchy and their policies. Against this background, it is not surprising that Lenin should have dismissed Osinsky's views as beneath criticism, merely expressing regret that such a capable official should reveal himself, in proposing 'the changeover to a cabinet system', as politically completely defunct – and by a 'cabinet system' he clearly meant what we have termed a 'cabinet–parliamentary system'.[6] For him it was unthinkable for a Bolshevik to question the principle that ultimate authority must be kept in the hands of the leading organs of the party. Despite the difficulties it created for a rational distribution of work between Sovnarkom and the Politburo, 'we cannot revoke the right to appeal to the Central Committee, since our party is the single government party'.[7] Even when, some months later, Lenin's growing dismay at the state of his regime led him to contemplate an assault to transform those very leading organs of the party, he gave no sign that he had come to doubt this principle of authority. Lenin wanted to have his cake and eat it. He wanted an effective cabinet but not a 'cabinet system'. Its members were to do the work of government but the power was to lie elsewhere. There was to be one locus of legitimacy for the governed (the soviets and their Central Executive Committee) and another for the governors (the Party Central Committee). What he long shrank from accepting was that the burden of decision would necessarily accumulate where final authority lay, the divorce of power and responsibility would unfit the government to govern, and the regime would become a self-perpetuating oligarchy of party bosses on whose personalities and relationships the revolutionary society would fatally depend.

And here we must broaden our historical focus. For this was not the first time in Russian history that the shoots of a cabinet–parliamentary system had appeared, only to be choked in the profuse and robust weeds of a bureaucratic authoritarianism before they could mature. The failure of the Council of Ministers–Duma experiment after 1905 is an obvious parallel. There were, however, precursors to these institutions whose character and experience are also highly relevant, and these deserve at least a brief glance.[8]

The trend from absolute monarchy to cabinet–parliamentary forms of government, completed in Britain in the eighteenth century, extended in time to most of Europe, though in many countries the transition was retarded, distorted and still incomplete in the early twentieth century: and Russia, of course, was one of these. Typically the 'cabinet' developed out of some kind of advisory–executive committee of the monarch's top officials, and the 'parliament' out of some wider consultative body representative mainly of the rich and powerful. The former could only be a 'true' cabinet when it had command of all branches of government business and dealt collectively with the monarch through a 'prime minister'. The 'parliament' could only be a 'true' one when executive action was obliged to conform to its predominant opinion and top executives were answerable to it for their performance. Although initially often contraposed, they could mature only in symbiosis. For both had to contend with the absolute claims of the monarch and the arbitrary actions of his agents and, while cabinet served parliament as a device for achieving the answerability of the administration, parliament provided cabinet with its support base for asserting its collective will *vis-à-vis the* monarch.

These generalisations, like all such essays at historical synthesis along ideal-typical lines, are highly vulnerable to objections on both theoretical and empirical grounds. We would argue, however, that they have sufficient basis in actual historical tendencies in Europe to throw useful light on the evolution of Russian institutions. The first 'protocabinet' in Russia was the Senate established by Peter the Great which, however, after a chequered career in the eighteenth century, subsequently evolved into a large body lacking executive powers but exercising broad functions of judicial administration and administrative 'control' (in the continental sense of the term). The Committee of Ministers (*Komitet ministrov*), formed by Alexander I in 1802, gave early promise of evolving into a cabinet, especially under Count Saltykov's chairmanship during Alexander's preoccupation with the war with Napoleon, when it exercised something like full collective responsibility for domestic government. After 1815, however, falling under the control of Alexander's reactionary adviser Arakcheyev, and lacking any wider institutionalised base from which it might have gained support, the Committee of Ministers declined in importance, and, although it survived till 1905, did so essentially as an administrative committee processing 'vermicelli'. The next 'protocabinet' was Alexander II's Council of Ministers (*Sovet ministrov*). Functioning unofficially from 1857 and given official standing in 1861, the Council of Ministers served initially to consolidate the work of various *ad hoc* commissions preparing proposals for reform in the confused, quasi-revolutionary atmosphere of

Alexander's early years, although it also took up issues requiring interministerial coordination and considered the annual reports of ministers and their proposals for major legislation. The institutional autonomy and identity of the Council of Ministers was weakened, however, by the fact that the monarch attended and chaired its meetings, and by the continued existence of the Committee of Ministers, with which it overlapped in membership and whose Chancellery (*upravleniye delami*) it shared. As social order and discipline were reestablished and the impulse to reform played itself out, the Council declined in importance, rarely meeting in the 1870s.

At the beginning of Alexander III's reign, however, in 1881–2, the Council of Ministers suddenly revived and seemed to some, in fact, to be on the point of a breakthrough to cabinet rule. For it had been agreed, apparently with the Tsar's approval, that in order to ensure that the Government maintained a united front in the face of the 'nihilist' threat, henceforth no minister should make recommendations for action to the Tsar without the collective agreement of his colleagues in the Council. The possibly revolutionary implications of this ostensibly modest procedural innovation were most strongly emphasised by an acute foreign observer, Anatole Leroy-Beaulieu: such a unified and collectively responsible ministry would be able to deal from a position of strength with the Emperor, who would be constrained to give it wide scope for independent action, so that gradually it would come to see itself as responsible to the public at large as much as to the Emperor. 'The Tsar would find himself reduced almost to the role of a constitutional monarch, [even] without a constitution or a parliament.'[9] If such expectations may have been exaggerated, they were shared, alas, by Alexander's conservative adviser Pobedonostsev, on whose initiative, and without prior warning to his ministers, the Tsar issued a proclamation reasserting the full force of the autocratic principle, 'against all encroachments'. While agreeing that there should be unity of outlook in the ministry, Pobedonostsev took steps to ensure that this would be a reactionary and not a reforming unity, and that it should not acquire institutional expression that might threaten the Tsar's prerogatives. This in effect spelt the demise of the Council of Ministers which, although not officially abolished, held only one further meeting.

On one point, however, Leroy-Beaulieu's analysis was incomplete:

for if the Council of Ministers could be seen as a protocabinet, there also existed a protoparliament in the form of the State Council (*Gosudarstvennyi sovet*). Originally intended by Alexander I to substitute for a parliament in considering legislation and the overall control of government, the State Council had failed to develop an autonomous political role, largely owing to the purely official character of its membership. At the end of Alexander II's reign, proposals were presented by the relatively liberal General Loris-Melikov to bring in under the State Council certain policy-formulating commissions composed of elective members and experts as well as government officials, and to add some elected members to the State Council itself. Alexander II approved the first proposal and the second was still under consideration at the time of his assassination. In the following months there was strong support among the majority of ministers to implement these proposals, and it was against this, as well as the initiative for collective responsibility of the ministry, that Alexander III's proclamation was directed. Nevertheless, despite the defeat of the reform proposals, the State Council did operate as something of a protoparliament under Alexander III, subjecting many government proposals to close scrutiny, delaying the enactment of quite a few measures and even causing certain of them to be dropped.

Meanwhile, with the replacement of some of the more liberal ministers and the paralysis of the Council of Ministers, the Committee of Ministers underwent something of a revival as a vehicle for the Tsar's policy and an instrument of coordination. At the same time, the Tsar jealously preserved his prerogative of dealing separately with his ministers, as did his successor, Nicholas II. While both the Council of State and the Committee of Ministers were significant institutions during this period, their autonomy was severely limited and they tended to offset rather than reinforce each other's influence.

The institutional changes following the 1905 Revolution marked a big step towards a cabinet–parliamentary system of government. A bicameral legislature was formed, the State Council (partly reformed) constituting the upper house and a new fully-elective assembly (the Duma) constituting the lower. The Committee of Ministers was abolished and the Council of Ministers revived, now chaired by a 'prime' Minister, and the change was seen by many as portending a genuine cabinet, exercising collective responsibility for the whole work of government.

However, if these reforms marked the end of untrammelled absolutism, its heritage remained powerful enough to severely cripple both 'parliament' and 'cabinet'. The amended Fundamental Laws reasserted the autocratic power of the Tsar. The ministers were responsible directly to him (not through the Council) rather than to the Duma, which enjoyed only the power of interpellation. All laws had to be submitted to the Duma and State Council when they were in session, but Article 87 allowed laws to be enacted while they were in recess, subject to their subsequent endorsement by the legislature. Furthermore the monarch's 'sovereign commands' (*vysochaishiye poveleniya*), countersigned by a single minister without submission to the State Council or Duma, offered in effect an alternative channel of legislation. The suffrage, relatively democratic at first, was soon made highly unequal, and supporters of the autocracy were thus ensured a comfortable majority in the Duma.

Whether the post-1905 Council of Ministers *could* have evolved into a genuine cabinet is a matter of opinion, but that it failed to do so in the twelve years of its existence is generally agreed. The persistence of the Tsar's power to deal directly with individual ministers, taking separate advice from them and issuing commands on their recommendation, a power extensively used by Nicholas, represented a fatal defect in its cohesion and authority. Furthermore, under paragraphs 16 and 17 of the Statute on the Council of Ministers, those ministers responsible for defence and foreign affairs, as well as the imperial court and domains, were not required to refer matters to the Council except where this was stipulated by a sovereign command or where other ministries were affected. In effect, as some contemporaries recognised, the government was divided into council and non-council (*sovetskiye i nesovetskiye*) ministries.

Thus the 'prehistory' of the Council of People's Commissars as a protocabinet goes back at least to 1802, if not to a century earlier. Even from the sketchy account above some parallels between Sovnarkom and its precursors will be obvious. When the Bolsheviks took over the old ministries, they inherited not only certain structures and personnel, but also certain models for a 'government' to cap and unify them. Although they were far from attaching any mystique or even legitimacy to such models, neither did they bring to the task of setting up a government any blueprints of their own or any disposition to emulate the models of 'bourgeois' governments abroad. Thus it was natural to slip into patterns which were well entrenched in Russian 'political culture'.

No less important as a source of such parallels was the like commitment of the imperial and Bolshevik regimes to a principle of absolute power focused outside and above the executive organs of government. If Divine Providence vested the Autocratic Power in the hands of the Tsar, History vested the Dictatorship of the Proletariat in the hands of the party leadership. This produced similar *direct* effects on the way the executive organs of government themselves operated, which we shall consider in a moment. But they also affected it *indirectly*, through the impact of absolutism on the 'protoparliament', and the relations of this to the 'protocabinet'. The Tsarist regime conceded to the State Council, and especially later to the Duma, a certain role in checking the work of government, in legislation, and in representing sectional opinion, but resisted the notion that the government should be responsible to these bodies, since this would be to encroach on the sovereign's prerogatives. The role assigned by the Bolshevik regime to the Central Executive Committee of the Congress of Soviets, and the limitations of this role, were in practice essentially the same, despite the relevant enabling documents which proclaimed otherwise. In both cases 'protoparliament' and 'protocabinet' became *alternative* instruments available to the sovereign power for dealing with the business of government, combining (albeit in different mixes) 'legislative' and 'executive' functions. In neither case did they evolve the level of mutual dependence and mutual interest over against the sovereign power necessary for the transition to a genuine cabinet–parliamentary system.

Both the absolute ruler of Tsarist Russia and the absolute oligarchy of Bolshevik Russia rightly saw it as an essential condition of maintaining their position, as the final authority in the land, that they could deal directly with particular members of the government and not only with the government as a whole through its 'prime minister'. This entailed the power not only to take advice from individual ministers (or people's commissars) but to issue decisions on that advice and have these decisions carried out, even when they lacked the support of a majority of government members. While the purpose of this was to retain for the sovereign power the overall direction of policy, it had the unintended effect of burdening it with deciding many relatively minor matters, on which individual ministers (or people's commissars) found themselves at odds with the majority of their colleagues. Paradoxically, this did not lead to a lightening of the 'protocabinet's' own decision-making load. For on the one hand matters referred to the sovereign power had usually been before the 'protocabinet' first, and on the other the situation was obviously inimical to unity and coherence in the 'protocabinet', and the constant friction and cross-purposes this entailed generated a surfeit of vexatious 'vermicelli'.

It is true that much 'vermicelli' dished up to the government was the product of another feature shared by the Tsarist and Bolshevik regimes, namely the vast range of social activity which they sought to direct and control through ponderous and inefficient bureaucracies, whose lower reaches combined arbitrariness of action with the evasion of responsibility and whose upper levels manifested an exaggerated sense of departmental interest. The 'bureaucratic politics' to which all complex administrative systems are prone was exacerbated in both the Tsarist and Soviet systems by their tolerance of disunity within the 'protocabinet', itself a consequence, as has been suggested, of the superordinated absolute power. Minor issues thrown up in profusion by the bureaucracies were invested by interdepartmental rivalries with exaggerated importance and found their way onto the 'protocabinet's' agenda paper or necessitated the convening of yet another interdepartmental commission. As we have seen, the flow of 'vermicelli' prompted Lenin's Council of People's Commissars to set up a 'Little Council' to deal with it, just as Stolypin's Council of Ministers had done eleven years previously. However, this could not stop the Full Council, too, from being bogged down in masses of minor matters, and this, in combination with its lacking the final say on more important issues, tended to depress it to the status of a 'vermicelli commission' itself. Thus in this respect Sovnarkom recapitulated under Lenin the experience of Alexander I's Committee of Ministers nearly a century earlier.

A further parallel was the virtual exclusion of certain major policy areas from the province of the 'protocabinet', in particular foreign affairs, defence and internal security. This placed additional strains on the unity of government which only the absolute ruler or oligarchy could meet. The latter, to help cope with these demands, and to make effective use of the power to deal directly with branches of the administration, clearly needed a bureaucratic machine of their own, separate from that run by the 'protocabinet'. We have seen how the Bolshevik leadership acquired such a separate bureaucracy and the interplay of its growth with the decline of Sovnarkom. There was no real equivalent in late Tsarist Russia but a partial one operated through most of the nineteenth century in the form of the Emperor's Personal Chancery, divided under Nicholas I and Alexander II into four functional departments.

To point to such parallels is not to question the vast differences between the Tsarist and Communist regimes. The values informing them were fundamentally opposed. The former was an absolutism to prevent change, the latter an absolutism to make it. The former sought to suppress or minimise mass participation, the latter to stimulate, mobilise and canalise it. The locus of absolute power was structurally quite different: a single ruler and his court of personal advisers and confidants on the one hand, an oligarchy embodied in a formal institution on the other, the 'prime minister' being excluded from the absolute power in the former case and included in it in the latter. The pathologies of absolutism, moreover, were undoubtedly aggravated by the personalities of individual Tsars, especially Nicholas II, with his passivity, irresoluteness and preference for first ministers who were nonentities.

It is true that some of these contrasts appear less than total when examined closely. Divisions within the Politburo could paralyse action no less than the divisions within Nicholas II's soul, and the Soviet oligarchy was of course long displaced by a personal ruler more absolute and more arbitrary than any Tsar since Peter the Great. The leaderlessness of the Council of Ministers in its final years due to the appointment of weak first ministers was matched by the leaderlessness of Sovnarkom due to Lenin's illness. Nor – to mention an aspect which we have no space to examine in depth – was the gap between the *operative* values of Russia's rulers before and after the Revolution ever quite as great as their public manifestation would suggest, and it became progressively less so with the entrenchment of bureaucratic structures, the emergence of new privileged strata, and the revival of Russian patriotism.

Notwithstanding such qualifications, however, the differences between the Tsarist and Communist systems were undoubtedly many and profound, and especially in some respects in Lenin's time. This makes the similarities in the structure of political and administrative behaviour all the more striking and significant. We have suggested that these similarities derived partly from the functional requirements they shared as absolutist systems operating through large centralised bureaucracies, partly from continuities in political culture, and partly from the carry-over of specific procedures and machinery. Without venturing to weight these factors, we would view them all as important and as normally operating in combination.

There was clearly something in Lenin's view that the ills of his regime were due to 'bureaucratism' perpetuated in the structures and personnel inherited from the Old Regime. As a total explanation, however, it was profoundly misleading. On the one hand the underlying causes lay not in the bureaucracy itself but in the structure of power and authority. On the other hand, the pathologies of bureaucracy, the analogies with that repressive *chinovnik* apparatus which the Revolution was to have swept away, were most apparent not in the segments of the government machine directly inherited from the imperial regime, which in fact were the main repository of those elements of modern economic and social administration that Lenin had deemed worthy of preservation. Rather were they to be found in those new bureaucratic juggernauts which had been created to support the new absolutism: the party apparatus and the Vecheka. It was *here* that was focused that arbitrariness, overbearing boorishness, abuse of power and obscurantism that so disturbed the failing Lenin, and it was no accident that when a new personal despot established himself a few years later, it was from the Central Committee Secretariat that he emerged and the key agents of his power were the corps of regional party secretaries and the NKVD, just as those of the nineteenth century Tsars were the provincial governors and the Okhrana. The eclipse of Lenin's Sovnarkom helped to pave the way for this.

Appendix A

Composition of Sovnarkom 1917–1922

Note In cases where decrees establishing precise official dates of appointments are unavailable, month of taking up office is indicated. In a few cases appointments were made in an acting or temporary capacity but quickly became substantive without formalisation by further decree; these are marked with an asterisk. No termination date is shown for members still in office at the end of 1922.

CHAIRMAN
Lenin, V. I.   26 October 1917

DEPUTY CHAIRMEN OF SOVNARKOM AND/OR STO
Rykov, A. I.   26 May 1921
Tsyurupa, A. D.   December 1921
Kamenev, L. B.   September 1922

PEOPLE'S COMMISSAR FOR FOREIGN AFFAIRS
(*po inostrannym delam*)
Trotsky, L. D.   26 October 1917–18 February 1918
Chicherin, G. V.   30 May 1918 (Acting from 18 February 1918)

PEOPLE'S COMMISSAR FOR INTERNAL AFFAIRS
(*po vnutrennym delam*)
Rykov, A. I.   26 October 1917–4 November 1917
Petrovsky, G. I.   17 November 1917–30 March 1919
Dzerzhinsky, F. E.   30 March 1919

PEOPLE'S COMMISSAR FOR LOCAL GOVERNMENT
(*po mestnomu samoupravleniyu*)
Trutovsky, V. E.   12 December 1917–16 March 1918

PEOPLE'S COMMISSAR FOR NATIONALITIES
(*po delam natsional'nostei*)
Stalin, I. V.   26 October 1917

PEOPLE'S COMMISSAR FOR JUSTICE
(*yustitsii*)

Lomov, G. I.   26 October 1917 (did not take up appointment)
   Deputy P. I. Stuchka in charge during vacancy.
Shteinberg, I. Z.   12 December 1917–16 March 1918
Stuchka, P. I.   20 March 1918–4 September 1918
Kursky, D. I.   4 September 1918

PEOPLE'S COMMISSAR FOR STATE CONTROL
(*gosudarstvennogo kontrolya*)

   Becomes Rabkrin February 1920
Essen, E. E.   20 November 1917*–9 May 1918
Lander, K. I.   9 May 1918–9 April 1919
Stalin, I. V.   9 April 1919–7 February 1920

PEOPLE'S COMMISSAR FOR RABKRIN

(Worker-Peasant Inspectorate – *raboche-krestyanskoi inspektsii*)
Stalin, I. V.   7 February 1920–27 December 1922
Tsyurupa, A. D.   27 December 1922

PEOPLE'S COMMISSAR FOR FINANCE
(*finansov*)

Skvortsov-Stepanov, I. I.   26 October 1917 (did not take up appointment)
Menzhinsky, V. R.   20 January 1918 (Acting from 30 October 1917) –
   March 1918
Gukovsky, I. E.   21 March 1918*–16 August 1918
Krestinsky, N. N.   16 August 1918–December 1922 (in practice till
   October 1921)
Sokolnikov, G. Ya.   December 1922 (in practice January 1922)

PEOPLE'S COMMISSAR FOR LABOUR
(*truda*)

Shlyapnikov, A. G.   26 October 1917–October 1918
Shmidt, V. V.   October 1918

PEOPLE'S COMMISSAR FOR WELFARE
(*gosudarstvennogo prizreniya*)

   Becomes Social Security April 1918
Kollontai, A. M.   30 October 1917–23 February 1918

PEOPLE'S COMMISSAR FOR SOCIAL SECURITY
(*sotsiyal'nogo obespecheniya*)

Vinokurov, A. N.   20 March 1918–December 1919 (Merged in Labour
   Commissariat 8 December 1919–21 April 1920)
Vinokurov, A. N.   21 April 1920 – (in practice only till 1921; later Deputy
   Commissar V. P. Milyutin effectively in charge)

PEOPLE'S COMMISSAR FOR EDUCATION
(*prosveshcheniya*)

Lunacharsky, A. V. 26 October 1917

PEOPLE'S COMMISSAR FOR HEALTH
(*zdravookhraneniya*)

Semashko, N. A. 11 July 1918

PEOPLE'S COMMISSAR FOR POSTS AND TELEGRAPHS
(*pocht i telegrafov*)

Avilov, N. P. 26 October 1917–22 December 1917
Proshyan, P. P. 22 December 1917–16 March 1918
Podbelsky, V. N. 11 April 1918–25 February 1920
Lyubovich, A. M. March 1920–28 May 1921
Dovgalevsky, V. S. 28 May 1921–30 December 1922

PEOPLE'S COMMISSAR FOR PROPERTIES OF THE REPUBLIC
(*imushchestv rossiiskoi respubliki*)

Karelin, V. A. 12 December 1917–16 March 1918

PEOPLE'S COMMISSAR FOR AGRICULTURE
(*sel'skogo khozyaistva*)

Milyutin, V. P. 26 October 1917–4 November 1917
   Deputy A. G. Shlikhter in charge during vacancy
Kolegaev, A. L. 25 November 1917–16 March 1918
Sereda, S. P. 28 March 1918*–2 March 1921
   Deputy N. Osinsky effectively in charge during vacancy.
Yakovenko, V. G. 9 January 1922

PEOPLE'S COMMISSAR FOR FOOD SUPPLIES
(*prodovol'stviya*)

Teodorovich, I. A. 26 October 1917–18 December 1917 (in practice
   November 1917)
Shlikhter, A. G. 18 December 1917 (Acting from 19 November 1917)–
   25 February 1918
Tsyurupa, A. G. 25 February 1918–11 December 1921
Bryukhanov, N. P. 11 December 1921

PEOPLE'S COMMISSAR FOR TRANSPORT
(*putei soobshcheniya*)

   Called Railways (*po delam zheleznodorozhnym*) during
   first few weeks
Yelizarov, M. T. 8 December 1917*–7 January 1918
Rogov, A. G. 24 February 1918–9 May 1918
Kobozev, P. A. 9 May 1918–25 July 1918
Nevsky, V. I. 25 July 1918–17 March 1919
Krasin, L. B. 17 March 1919–23 March 1920

Trotsky, L. D.   23 March 1920*–December 1920
Yemshanov, A. I.   December 1920–14 April 1921
Dzerzhinsky, F. E.   14 April 1921

PEOPLE'S COMMISSAR FOR TRADE AND INDUSTRY
(*po delam torgovli i promyshlennosti*)
Becomes Foreign Trade June 1920
Nogin, V. P.   26 October 1917–4 November 1917. A. G. Shlyapnikov in
charge during vacancy
Smirnov, V. M.   25 January 1918–16 February 1918. Deputy M. G.
Bronsky evidently in charge during vacancy
Krasin, L. B.   13 November 1918–11 June 1920

PEOPLE'S COMMISSAR FOR FOREIGN TRADE
(*vneshnei torgovli*)
Krasin, L. B.   11 June 1920

CHAIRMAN OF NATIONAL ECONOMIC COUNCIL
(*Vysshii Sovet Narodnogo Khozyaistva*)
Osinsky, N.   12 December 1917–28 March 1918
Rykov, A. I.   28 March 1918–28 May 1921
Bogdanov, P. A.   28 May 1921

COMMITTEE ON MILITARY AND NAVAL AFFAIRS
(*Komitet po delam voyennym i morskim*)
Split into Army and Navy Commissariats November 1917
Antonov-Ovseyenko, V. A. ⎫
Krylenko, N. V.   ⎬ 26 October 1917–November 1917
Dybenko, P. E.   ⎭
Podvoisky, N. I.   27 October 1917–November 1917

PEOPLE'S COMMISSAR FOR THE ARMY
(*po voyennym delam*)
Podvoisky, N. I.   November 1917–28 March 1918 (in practice February
1918)

PEOPLE'S COMMISSAR FOR THE NAVY
(*po morskim delam*)
Dybenko, P. E.   November 1917–28 March 1918 (in practice February
1918)

MILITARY COMMISSAR FOR ARMY AND NAVY AFFAIRS (WAR COMMISSAR)
(*Voyennyi komissar po voyennym i morskim delam*)
Responsible for separate Army and Navy Commissariats
Trotsky, L. D.   28 March 1918 (in practice February 1918).
Also Chairman of Revolutionary Military Council of the
Republic.

Appendix B

Checklist of Sovnarkom members 1917–1922

Note (A): initial Bolshevik appointees to Sovnarkom positions 1917
(B): member 31 December 1918
(C): member 30 December 1922
Names shown are those usually employed as Sovnarkom members. Where these are 'party' names and their original family names are sometimes used in documents relating to their Sovnarkom positions, these are shown in brackets.

Antonov-Ovseyenko, V. A.	(A)	Nogin, V. P.	(A)
Avilov, N. P. (Glebov)	(A)	Osinsky, N. (V. V. Obolensky)	(A)
Bogdanov, P. A.	(C)	Petrovsky, G. I.	(B)
Bryukhanov, N. P.	(C)	Podbelsky, V. N.	(B)
Chicherin, G. V.	(B, C)	Podvoisky, N. I.	
Dovgalevsky, V. S.	(C)	Podvoisky, N. I.	
Dybenko, P. E.	(A)	Proshyan, P. P. (Left SR)	
Dzerzhinsky, F. E.	(C)	Rogov, A. G.	
Essen, E. E.	(A)	Rykov, A. I.	(A, B, C)
Gukovsky, I. E.		Semashko, N. A.	(B, C)
Kamenev, L. B.	(C)	Sereda, S. P.	(B)
Karelin, V. A. (Left SR)		Shlikhter, A. G.	
Kobozev, P. A.		Shlyapnikov, A. G.	(A)
Kolegaev, A. L. (Left SR)		Shmidt, V. V.	(B, C)
Kollontai, A. M.	(A)	Shteinberg, I. Z. (Left SR)	
Krasin, L. B.	(B, C)	Skvortsov-Stepanov, I. I.	(A)
Krestinsky, N. N.	(B)	Smirnov, V. M.	
Krylenko, N. V.	(A)	Sokolnikov, G. Ya.	(C)
Kursky, D. I.	(B, C)	Stalin, I. V. (Dzhugashvili)	(A, B, C)
Lander, K. I.	(B)	Stuchka, P. I.	
Lenin, V. I. (Ulyanov)	(A, B, C)	Teodorovich, I. A.	(A)
Lomov, A. (Oppokov, G. I.)	(A)	Trotsky, L. D. (Bronshtein)	(A, B, C)
Lunacharsky, A. V.	(A, B, C)	Trutovsky, V. Ye. (Left SR)	
Lyubovich, A. M.		Tsyurupa, A. D.	(B, C)
Menzhinsky, V. R.		Vinokurov, A. N.	(B)
Milyutin, V. P.	(A)	Yakovenko, V. G.	(C)
Nevsky, V. I.	(B)	Yelizarov, M. T.	(A)
		Yemshanov, A. I.	

In addition the Left SRs Algasov, V. A. and Mikhailov (initials not identified) served as People's Commissars without Portfolio in the Internal Affairs Commissariat.

Notes

CHAPTER I: THE ORIGINS OF SOVNARKOM

1 For a detailed account of the Bolshevik seizure of power, see Robert V. Daniels, *Red October: The Bolshevik Revolution of 1917*, New York, 1967 (cited hereafter as Daniels, 1967). The relevant literature is of course enormous; its 'classics' are: John Reed, *Ten Days that Shook the World*, London, 1926, new edition, Harmondsworth, 1966; N. N. Sukhanov, *Zapiski o revolyutsii*, Vol. 7, Berlin, 1923 (there is an excellent abridged translation by Joel Carmichael, *The Russian Revolution 1917*, London, 1955, Part VI); and W. H. Chamberlin, *The Russian Revolution 1917–1921*, New York, 1935, Chs. XIII–XIV. See also the recent valuable study by John L. H. Keep, *The Russian Revolution: a Study in Mass Mobilization*, New York, 1976, Part IV.

2 *Istoriya Sovetskoi Konstitutsii (V Dokumentakh) 1917–1956*, Moscow, 1957, p. 42.

3 *Dekrety Sovetskoi vlasti* (cited hereafter as *DSV*), Vol. 1, Moscow, 1957, pp. 20–1. A curious legalism in this decree was the use of real rather than 'party' names, the latter being given in brackets, e.g. Ulyanov (Lenin), Bronshtein (Trotsky), Dzhugashvili (Stalin), etc. This practice persisted in many official documents for some time.

4 Of the people's commissariats established at the time of the seizure of power the following were based on former Tsarist ministries: Internal Affairs, Agriculture, Trade and Industry, Education, Finance, Foreign Affairs, Justice and Transport. Three other Tsarist departments, namely State Control, Army and Navy, were revived within weeks of the Revolution. Of the four remaining people's commissariats, namely Posts and Telegraphs, Labour, Food Supplies and Nationalities, the first three had been established by the Provisional Government and only the last was a Bolshevik innovation. The two Tsarist departments dropped were the Ministry of the Imperial Court and the Procuracy of the Holy Synod. The Bolsheviks initially renamed the Tsarist Transport Ministry (*Ministerstvo Putei Soobshcheniya* – literally 'communications') the Railways Commissariat, but this change was also very shortlived.

5 *DSV*, Vol. 1, p. 20.

6 V. D. Bonch-Bruyevich, *Vospominaniya o Lenine*, Moscow, 1969, p. 129.

7 See Ye. N. Gorodetsky, *Rozhdeniye Sovetskogo gosudarstva 1917–1918gg.*, Moscow, 1965, p. 150; M. P. Iroshnikov, *Sozdaniye sovetskogo tsentral'nogo gosudarstvennogo apparata. Sovet Narodnykh Komissarov i narodnye komissariaty oktyabr' 1917g.–yanvar' 1918g.*, Moscow, Leningrad, 1966 (cited hereafter as Iroshnikov, 1966), pp. 43, 46; and E. V. Klopov, 'Pervyi den' deyatel'nosti V. I. Lenina na postu Predsedatelya Soveta Narodnykh Komissarov', *Istoriya SSSR*, 1961, no. 2 (cited hereafter as Klopov, 1961), pp. 26–7. At a meeting of the Bolshevik Central Committee held on 21 October, various leaders had been made responsible for preparing proposals on the major issues now made urgent by the decision to take power immediately and requiring action at the forthcoming Second Congress of Soviets. As might be expected, the question of 'power' was allocated to Lenin, along with 'the war' and 'the land': see *Protokoly Tsentral'nogo Komiteta RSDRP (b), Avgust 1917–fevral' 1918*, Moscow, 1958 (cited hereafter as *Protokoly TsK*), p. 118. The reference to 'power' (*vlast'*) in the laconic Central Committee minutes was clearly intended to cover the character and structure of the revolutionary government. The night of 24–5, when most of the Bolshevik leadership was closeted in room no. 38 in Smolny, was the first opportunity Lenin had to discuss his ideas with the Central Committee, and the last occasion to do so before the Congress opened. No minutes of these discussions seem to have survived, and perhaps none were kept.

8 *Leninskii sbornik*, Moscow, 1924– , xxi, pp. 91–2. Lenin abbreviated many words, in several cases giving initials only; our translation follows the interpretation given by the editors of *Leninskii sbornik*, except for the word 'commissions' in the phrase 'commissions of people's commissars', where, according to Klopov, who checked it with the original, there is a misprint in the *Leninskii sbornik* version, an *i-kratkii* being printed as an *-i*, thus turning a plural into a singular. (See E. V. Klopov, *Lenin v Smol'nom. Gosudarstvennaya deyatel'nost' V. I. Lenina v pervye mesyatsy sovetskoi vlasti, oktyabr' 1917–mart 1918g.*, Moscow, 1965 (cited hereafter as Klopov, 1965), p. 27). Failure to note this misprint has led more than one scholar into dubious interpretations of this document; see e.g. Gorodetsky, p. 151. Cf. Iroshnikov 1966, p. 46. We have attempted to reproduce the exact layout as printed in *Leninskii sbornik*.

9 The assumption of some writers that a *Commission* of People's Commissars was planned at this time evidently arises from the misprint in *Leninskii sbornik* referred to in footnote 8.

10 Bonch-Bruyevich, now a district Bolshevik leader in Petrograd, had many years previously served as Lenin's main administrative assistant in his emigré headquarters. See below, Chapter 9.

11 The early history of the commissariat boards (*kollegii*) still awaits systematic study. They emerged in rather haphazard fashion in November–December 1917 and initially varied greatly in size,

composition, mode of operation and effective powers. In the first few months, moreover, confusion was compounded by frequent changes of membership, the manifold other commitments of most board members, the loose rules about their attendance at Sovnarkom meetings, and the frequent conflicts between Bolshevik and Left SR board members. Although no uniform legislation defining the structure and powers of commissariat boards was enacted during the Lenin era, by the end of 1918 a fairly uniform formula had emerged, according to which the board operated as essentially an advisory body, under the people's commissar, empowered to appeal to Sovnarkom against his decisions but not to overrule or suspend them. See I. L. Davitnidze, *Kollegii ministerstv. Pravovoye polozheniye i organizatsiya raboty*, Moscow, 1972, Chapter 1. Nevertheless the political and administrative role of individual board members continued to vary greatly, as a function largely of their individual capacities and their relationships with their people's commissars and top party and government leaders. When and by whom the title of these bodies was changed so soon to 'boards' from 'commissions' as envisaged in the Second Congress of Soviets decree on Sovnarkom has not been established. Is it mere coincidence that the various departments of the Russian government were run by boards (*kollegii*) before the establishment of ministries under Speransky at the beginning of the nineteenth century? Be this as it may, these collegial bodies under Sovnarkom were seen as performing functions previously shared between the minister and his deputies (*tovarishchi ministra*) under the Tsarist Council of Ministers; for a formula explicitly equating the two, see the CEC decision on the Commission of Public Education, *Protokoly zasedanii Vserossiiskogo Tsentral'nogo Ispolnitel'nogo Komiteta Sovetov rabochikh, soldatskikh, krestyanskikh i kazachikh deputatov, II sozyv, 27 oktyabrya–29 dekabrya 1917*, Petrograd, 1918, p. 49.

12 N. K. Krupskaya, *Vospominaniya o Lenine*, Moscow, 1968, p. 337.

13 A. Yoffe, 'Pervoye proletarskoye pravitel'stvo', *Kommunisticheskii internatsional*, 1919, no. 6, col. 777.

14 E.g. Gorodetsky, p. 151.

15 Krupskaya, p. 337.

16 See N. N. Sukhanov, *Zapiski o revolyutsii*, Vol. 7, pp. 237–8.

17 See below, Chapter 5. See also R. M. Savitskaya, *Ocherk deyatel'nosti V. I. Lenina. Mart-iyul' 1918g.*, Moscow, 1969, pp. 352–8.

18 *The Trotsky Papers 1917–1922*, edited and annotated by Jan M. Meijer, Vol. 1 (1917–1919), The Hague, 1964, p. 2.

19 *Leninskii sbornik*, XXI, p. 92. The term 'ministry' sometimes also found its way into official decrees at this time. For instance a Sovnarkom decree on legislative procedures issued on 29 October stated that 'Each draft law is submitted for the consideration of the Government from the appropriate Ministry over the signature of the People's Commissar concerned'. See *DSV*, Vol. 1, p. 29.

20 See L. A. Fotiyeva, *Iz zhizni V. I. Lenina*, Moscow, 1967 (cited hereafter as Fotiyeva, 1967), p. 141.

21 V. I. Lenin, *Polnoye sobraniye sochinenii. Izdaniye pyatoye,* Moscow, 1958–1965 (cited hereafter as *PSS*), Vol. 41, pp. 43–4.

22 Cf. E. H. Carr, *The Bolshevik Revolution 1917–1923,* 1st edn., Vol. 1, London, 1950, pp. 109–23; L. B. Schapiro, *The Communist Party of the Soviet Union,* 1st edn., New York, 1960, pp. 180–1.

CHAPTER 2: 'THE FIRST PROLETARIAN GOVERNMENT'

1 Lenin, *PSS,* Vol. 33, p. 117.

2 *Ibid.,* Vol. 34, p. 312.

3 *Ibid.,* p. 303.

4 *Ibid.,* p. 307.

5 *Ibid.,* p. 311.

6 See Yoffe, Col. 777–82.

7 *Izvestiya,* 10 October 1917, p. 7. In this initial decision it was referred to as a 'Committee of Revolutionary Defence'.

8 *Petrogradskii Voyenno-Revolyutsionnyi Komitet. Dokumenty i materialy v trëkh tomakh,* ed. D. A. Chugayev and others, Moscow, 1966–7 (cited hereafter as *Petrogradskii VRK*), Vol. 1, pp. 40–4.

9 See Trotsky, in 'Vospominaniya ob oktyabr'skom perevorote', *Proletarskaya revolyutsiya,* no. 10 (October) 1922, p. 52f. Cf. K. Meshekhonin, 'K vospominaniyam tov. Trotskogo', *ibid.,* pp. 85–8.

10 *Protokoly TsK,* p. 104. On Trotsky's role, see I. Deutscher, *The Prophet Armed. Trotsky: 1879–21,* London, 1954, pp. 297–312 and Daniels 1967, p. 217. Cf. L. Trotsky, *Moya Zhizn': Opyt Avtobiografii,* Berlin, 1930, Vol. 11, pp. 41–9. As Stalin consolidated his power Trotsky's vital role in the seizure of power began to be denigrated, and it is still passed over in silence by Soviet writers. However, Stalin himself wrote on the first anniversary of the Revolution:

> The whole work of the practical organisation of the rising was under the direct leadership of the Chairman of the Petrograd Soviet, Comrade Trotsky. One can say with certainty that, for the rapid movement of the proletariat to the side of the soviets and for the skilful, unceasing work of the Military Revolutionary Committee, the party is obliged first and foremost to Trotsky. His chief assistants were Comrades Antonov-Ovseyenko and Podvoisky (I. Stalin, 'Oktyabr'skii perevorot', *Pravda,* Nov. 6–7, 1918).

Daniels' view of the MRC as essentially a 'front' for the Bolshevik Military Organisation, which had been in existence for several months, seems justified for the period up to and immediately after the insurrection, though subsequently it greatly transcended these origins, as we shall see. Cf. N. I. Podvoisky, 'Voyennaya organizatsiya TsK RS-DRP (b) i voyenno-revolyutsionnyi komitet 1917g.', *Krasnaya letopis'* 1923, Nos. 6 and 8.

11 Leo Trotzki, *Von der Oktober-Revolution bis zum Brester Friedensvertrag,* Belp-Bern, 1918, pp. 53–4.

12 MRC headquarters was originally divided into seven departments: defence, supplies, communications, information bureau, workers'

militia, reporting section (*stol donesenii*) and commandant's office (*komendatura*) (see *Petrogradskii VRK* Vol. I, p. 41). On 20 October a department of revolutionary air services was added, and on 24 October a motor transport allocation section: see S. Piontkovsky, 'Voenno-revolyutsionnyi komitet v oktyabr'skie dni', *Proletarskaya revolyutsiya*, 1927, no. 10 (69), p. 116.

13 See Piontkovsky, pp. 121, 128.

14 An invaluable source for studying the activities and mode of operation in the MRC is the three-volume documentary collection *Petrogradskii VRK*, which has already been cited. Also important are G. A. Belov et al. (eds.), *Doneseniya komissarov Petrogradskogo Voenno-Revolyutsionnogo Komiteta*, Moscow, 1957; *Bol'shevistskiye Voenno-Revolyutsionniye Komitety*, comp. G. D. Kostomarov and N. I. Tolokonsky, Moscow, 1958; and *Velikaya Oktyabr'skaya Sotsialisticheskaya Revolyutsiya: Dokumenty i Materialy. Oktyabr'skoye vooruzhennoe vosstanie v Petrograde*, G. N. Golikov et al. (eds.), Moscow, 1957.

15 *Petrogradskii VRK*, Vol. I, p. 9.

16 Gorodetsky, p. 117.

17 Piontkovsky, p. 133.

18 *Ibid.*, p. 128.

19 Iroshnikov 1966, pp. 67–9. Certain early Sovnarkom decisions, including even decrees appointing Deputy People's Commissars, were issued under MRC letterheads. See Gorodetsky, p. 122.

20 Gorodetsky, pp. 122–8, Piontkovsky, p. 133.

21 Piontkovsky, p. 128.

22 The decree (*DSV*, Vol. I, p. 24) caused strong misgivings among a section of the Bolshevik leadership. See Chamberlin, Vol. I, p. 352.

23 Gorodetsky, pp. 133–5, Piontkovsky, pp. 122, 129.

24 Piontkovsky, pp. 131–2, Gorodetsky, pp. 119–22.

25 Yoffe, Col. 780.

26 See *Petrogradskii VRK*, Vol. I, p. 116, Vol. III, p. 177.

27 Piontkovsky, pp. 122–5.

28 Gorodetsky, pp. 130–2.

29 See e.g. *Petrogradskii VRK*, Vol. II, p. 516.

30 *Ibid.*, *passim*. This body was sometimes referred to simply as the *Sledstvennaya komissiya* (see e.g. *Ibid.*, Vol. I, p. 456). On 15 November it was proposed to entrust it with independent powers of arrest without reference to the MRC (*Ibid.*, Vol. III, p. 5), but it is not clear from the documents whether this proposal was implemented.

31 See *Bol'shevistskie Voenno-Revolyutsionnye Komitety*, Parts II and III, *Petrogradskii VRK*, *passim*. The latter collection contains documents on Petrograd MRC contacts with twenty-eight military revolutionary committees. These contacts demanded increasing attention from the MRC in the course of November and the importance assumed by MRC channels in controlling the provinces may be illustrated by a letter addressed to it by the Party Central Committee

about 26 November, asking the MRC to supply arms for the support of the local Bolshevik committee in the Urals town of Nizhny-Tagil. See *Petrogradskii VRK*, Vol. III, p. 392. Throughout its period of existence the MRC despatched altogether 644 commissars to the provinces. See *ibid.*, p. 366.

32 Piontkovsky, p. 130.

33 *Petrogradskii VRK*, Vol. I, p. 275.

34 *Ibid.*, p. 362.

35 Piontkovsky, p. 115.

36 Listed in *Petrogradskii VRK*, Vol. III, pp. 663–4. In addition the editors of this work have identified fifteen other persons referred to by historians or memoirists as MRC members, but without confirmatory evidence in the MRC documents.

37 Piontkovsky, p. 115.

38 Gorodetsky, p. 115.

39 Apart from the Investigation Department, the most important departments set up after the insurrection were those for Food Supplies and Agitation. A vital role was played by the Bureau of Commissars, which was primarily responsible both for selecting commissars and coordinating their work in the post-insurrection period. (See *Petrogradskii VRK, passim.*)

40 Gorodetsky, p. 114; *Petrogradskii VRK*, Vol. III, p. 537.

41 *Petrogradskii VRK*, Vol. I, pp. 58, 408, 532; Vol. II, p. 277; Vol. III, p. 285. There is also one reference in the available documents to a Presidium of the MRC but we have no evidence as to its functions, and it was probably a very ephemeral body; see *Petrogradskii VRK*, Vol. III, p. 663. Cf. Gorodetsky, p. 114.

42 Podvoisky in *Krasnaya letopis'* 1923, No. 8, p. 17.

43 Following the insurrection, Lenin naturally took a close interest in MRC activities (see, e.g., Piontkovsky, pp. 115–16), but the tendency of some writers to attribute to him a dominating influence (e.g. Gorodetsky, p. 110) finds little support in the available documents.

44 *Petrogradskii VRK*, Vol. I, p. 198, G. Kramarov, *Soldat Revolyutsii: O Sergeye Ivanoviche Guseve*, Moscow, 1964, p. 59.

45 Yoffe, Col. 780.

46 Gorodetsky, p. 142.

47 *Petrogradskii VRK*, Vol. III, p. 5. Walter Pietsch, in *Revolution und Staat*, Cologne, 1969, p. 62, gives considerable weight to current demands of the Executive Committee of the Peasants' Congress for the abolition of the MRC in explaining Lenin's agreement to its dissolution.

48 *Ibid.*, p. 349.

49 *Ibid.*, pp. 569–70.

50 *Ibid.*, p. 232. This presumably was the basis of Latsis' proposal at the Sovnarkom meeting four days later, referred to above.

51 P. G. Sofinov, *Ocherki istorii Vserossiiskoi Chrezvychainoi Komissii (1917–1922gg.)*, Moscow, 1960, p. 17.

52 *Ibid.*, p. 18.

53 See Carl Leiden and K. M. Schmitt, *The Politics of Violence: Revolution in the Modern World*, Englewood Cliffs, N.J., 1968, p. 63. Several recent comparative studies have done much to enhance our understanding of the patterns and processes of revolution, and warrant careful study in relation to the developments discussed here. See especially John Dunn, *Modern Revolutions: An Introduction to the Analysis of a Political Phenomenon*, Cambridge, 1972, and Peter Calvert, *A Study of Revolution*, Oxford, 1970.

54 The discussion of Sovnarkom here could also apply in large part to the CEC.

55 Tom Burns and G. M. Stalker, *The Management of Innovation*, London, 1961.

56 *Ibid.*, p. 5.

57 *Ibid.*, p. 6. The two models are explained at length in Chapter 6, and their characteristics summarised systematically on pp. 119–22.

58 It is somewhat surprising that more scholars have not recognised the relevance of Burns and Stalker's findings and analysis for understanding political decision-making structures under conditions of stability or revolutionary change. One scholar who has is Victor A. Thompson who, in his paper, 'Bureaucracy and Innovation', *Administrative Science Quarterly*, Vol. x, 1965–6, pp. 1–20, makes use of the concepts of Burns and Stalker in analysing the problems of effecting change in developing countries and advocates an organic model of administration. See also R. S. Milne, 'Mechanistic and Organic Models of Public Administration in Developing Countries', *Administrative Science Quarterly*, Vol. xv, 1970, pp. 57–67, where it is argued against Thompson that such countries lack some of the essential conditions for organic systems to be effective.

59 Pietsch, p. 44.

CHAPTER 3: SOVNARKOM TAKES OVER

1 See Carr, Vol. i, Chapter 5.

2 See Schapiro, p. 170. There is no doubt that the efforts to form a multi-party socialist government were frustrated by the intransigence of the other socialist parties as well as by Lenin's. For an account which puts the blame mainly on the former, see Marcel Liebman, *Leninism under Lenin*, transl. Brian Pearce, London, 1975, p. 231f.

3 Krupskaya, p. 337. The metaphor was borrowed from one of I. A. Krylov's fables.

4 As Trotsky has it, 'No minutes were kept or they have not been preserved. Nobody was bothering about future historians, although a lot of trouble was being prepared for them right there.' Leon Trotsky, *The History of the Russian Revolution*, Vol. iii, *The Triumph of the Soviets*, London, 1933, pp. 316–17.

5 Details of structural and membership changes in the Council will be found in Chapters 5 and 10 and Appendix A.

6 A major motive of the Left SRs in joining the government was to restrain the arbitrary use of their power by the Bolshevik leadership. Their decision to do so was evidently precipitated by the exacerbation of their relations with the 'rump' SR party during the campaign to elect delegates to the Second Peasant Congress. See Oliver Henry Radkey, *The Sickle under the Hammer: The Russian Socialist Revolutionaries in the Early Months of Soviet Rule*, New York and London, 1963, pp. 146–8. In the present work space is lacking for serious discussion of the important role of the SRs in the early Soviet regime, and for this the reader is referred to Radkey's excellent study.

7 *DSV*, Vol. 1, p. 102.

8 *Ibid.*, pp. 200, 215. None of the available sources indicates Mikhailov's initials.

9 See Carr, Vol. 1, pp. 119–33 and Schapiro, pp. 180–1.

10 Sverdlov proposed the dropping of the 'provisional' from Sovnarkom's title and the acceptance as permanent of its 'temporary' legislation in the closing minutes of the Congress, and the proposal was accepted without discussion and with acclamation. See *Syezdy sovetov soyuznykh i avtonomnykh sovetskikh sotsialisticheskikh respublik. Sbornik dokumentov v trëkh tomakh 1917–1936gg.*, Vol. 1, Moscow, 1959, pp. 46–7.

11 See Iroshnikov 1966, pp. 56–8; M. P. Iroshnikov, *Predsedatel' Soveta Narodnykh Komissarov V. I. Ulyanov (Lenin). Ocherki gosudarstvennoi deyatel'nosti v 1917–1918gg.*, Leningrad, 1974 (cited hereafter as Iroshnikov 1974), p. 78; Gorodetsky, pp. 207–8; M. Latsis, 'Tov. Dzerzhinsky i VChK,' *Proletarskaya revolyutsiya*, 1926, no. 9 (cited hereafter as Latsis 1926), p. 85; M. Latsis, 'Vozniknoveniye Narodnogo Komissariata Vnutrennykh Del', *Ibid.* 1925, no. 2 (cited hereafter as Latsis 1925), pp. 150–5; I. N. Steinberg, *In the Workshop of the Revolution*, London, 1953, pp. 65–73; James Bunyan, *Intervention, Civil War and Communism in Russia*, Baltimore, Md., 1936, pp. 259–60; James Bunyan and H. H. Fisher, *The Bolshevik Revolution 1917–1918. Documents and Materials*, Stanford, Calif., 1934, pp. 580–1. See also *Leninskii sbornik*, xxi, pp. 110–17.

12 V. S. Orlov, 'V. I. Lenin i sozdaniye apparata pervogo v mire raboche-krestyanskogo pravitel'stva', *Voprosy istorii* 1963, no. 4, p. 17

13 Bonch-Bruyevich, p. 129.

14 Iroshnikov 1966, p. 95.

15 Orlov, pp. 17–18; Iroshnikov 1966, p. 96. It seems likely that there was also a meeting on 29 November. Cf. Iroshnikov 1974, p. 169.

16 Bunyan and Fisher, p. 185. See also N. Gorbunov, 'Kak sozdavalsya v Oktyabr'skiye dni rabochii apparat Soveta Narodnykh Komissarov', *Pravda*, 6–7 November 1927.

17 Iroshnikov 1966, pp. 62–3. Gorbunov had previously worked with Bonch-Bruyevich in the Petrograd party organisation.

18 Gorbunov *op. cit.*; on 7 November Sovnarkom's work suffered a setback when the typist failed to report for duty, and Gorbunov had to

send an urgent message to the Military Revolutionary Committee to let him have one of their typists for a few hours.

19   Iroshnikov 1966, pp. 65–7.

20   *Ibid.*, pp. 70–2.

21   *Ibid.*, p. 63.

22   A. Kollontai, 'Lenin v Smol'nom', quoted Iroshnikov 1966, p. 65.

23   Iroshnikov 1966, p. 73.

24   Larin in Bunyan and Fisher, p. 185; Iroshnikov 1966, p. 96; Bonch-Bruyevich, p. 129.

25   Yoffe, col. 777. As Professor Roger Pethybridge (personal communication) has reminded me, the very 'geography' of the Smolny Institute fostered this 'organic' mode of operation, as is borne out by the testimony of many contemporary participants. The nuclei of the people's commissariats and other institutions were scattered in small rooms ranged along the building's corridors, and individual Bolshevik leaders were constantly popping in and out of each other's open doors and improvising small conferences with whoever was at hand.

26   *Triumfal'noye shestviye sovetskoi vlasti, Chast' pervaya*, D. A. Chugaev *et al.* (eds.), Moscow, 1963, pp. 94–5.

27   There is disagreement among Soviet historians on this point. Cf. Gorodetsky, pp. 146–8, Iroshnikov 1966, pp. 201–2.

28   Gorodetsky, pp. 147–8, 156–7.

29   Iroshnikov 1966, p. 96.

30   *Ibid.*, p. 100.

31   See S. Piontkovsky, 'Lenin v Sovnarkome (ot II do III Syezda Sovetov)', *Bor'ba klassov* 1934, no. 1, p. 108.

32   Deputy Finance Commissar Bogolepov has left a description of the early Sovnarkom meetings held in Lenin's office when no agenda was prepared in advance and all board members of the various commissariats had the right to attend. See D. Bogolepov, 'Finansovoye stroitel'stvo v pervye gody Oktyabr'skoi Revolyutsii', *Proletarskaya revolyutsiya* 1925, no. 4, pp. 159–60.

33   It may occasion little surprise that Stalin was the most constant attender – he missed only two meetings, and Lenin three. Stalin also chaired the meetings during the two days Lenin was 'on leave' from the Council. Our statement that Sverdlov was normally present reflects the consensus of Soviet historians, but Maria Skrypnik, a leading official of the Sovnarkom Secretariat, gives a somewhat different picture. Referring to the earliest period, she writes: 'Ya. M. Sverdlov attended Sovnarkom meetings infrequently, but he was always prominent when he did.' See her *Vospominaniya ob Ilyiche (1917–1918)*, Moscow, 1965, p. 39.

34   Piontkovsky, p. 108.

35   Gorodetsky, p. 158. This resolution was also intended to ensure that *at least* one spokesman for a commissariat should be present when questions affecting it were under discussion.

36   *Leninskii sbornik*, XXXV, p. 15.

37   *Triumfal'noye shestviye sovetskoi vlasti. Chast' pervaya*, p. 140.

38 See Lenin, *PSS*, Vol. 34, p. 384.

39 Iroshnikov 1966, pp. 101–2.

40 Gorodetsky, pp. 157–8.

41 Iroshnikov 1966, pp. 103–4.

42 Piontkovsky, p. 109. See also Iroshnikov 1974, pp. 189–91.

43 Iroshnikov 1966, p. 104.

44 *Ibid.*

45 *Ibid.*, pp. 104–5. It is possible, however, that a body known as the 'Little Sovnarkom' had at least a shadowy and intermittent existence some weeks before this. V. S. Orlov pointed out in 1963 (p. 26) that the Sovnarkom minutes had mentioned the referral of a matter to the Little Sovnarkom on 17 November. Iroshnikov originally contested that this was 'the' Little Sovnarkom rather than some *ad hoc* body, but he later changed his mind. Cf. Iroshnikov 1966, p. 105 and 1974, p. 197. Cf. Ye. Korenevskaya, 'V. I. Lenin i organizatsiya raboty sovetskogo pravitel′stva v 1917–1922gg., *Voyenno-istoricheskii zhurnal* 1968, no. 4 (cited hereafter as Korenevskaya, 1968(2)), p. 101.

46 Quoted Iroshnikov 1966, pp. 105–6.

47 V. Durdenevsky, 'Sovet Narodnykh Komissarov', *Sovetskoye pravo* 1922, no. 1 (cited hereafter as Durdenevsky, 1922), p. 38. In Durdenevsky's view, the Little Council, like the Council of Ministers itself, came to exercise legislative powers, though their decisions did not possess the formal status of 'laws'. See also N. P. Yeroshkin, *Ocherki istorii gosudarstvennykh uchrezhdenii dorevolyutsionnoi Rossii*, Moscow, 1960, p. 353. After the February Revolution, the Provisional Government also set up a Little Council of Ministers. See Paul P. Gronsky and Nicholas J. Astrov, *The War and the Russian Government*, New York, 1973 (first published 1929), p. 82.

48 See *Vladimir Ilyich Lenin. Biograficheskaya khronika* (cited hereafter as *Lenin: khronika*), Vol. 5, Moscow, 1974, p. 108. Cf. Bogolepov, pp. 159–60. Bogolepov, a finance specialist who had been a Bolshevik member of the Fourth State Duma in 1914–15, was himself probably not entirely ignorant of government administrative procedures under the old regime.

49 Iroshnikov 1966, pp. 105–7. Cf. K. G. Fedorov, *Istoriya sovetskogo gosudarstva i prava*, Rostov, 1964, p. 35.

50 *Lenin: khronika*, Vol. 5, p. 230.

51 See Iroshnikov 1974, p. 199. Between 9 January and the transfer to Moscow on 10 March the Little Sovnarkom held eleven meetings, but most of these were evidently concentrated in the early part of this period.

52 *Leninskii sbornik* XXI, p. 98.

53 Klopov 1961, p. 431; Iroshnikov 1974, p. 188. Trotsky mentions this short-lived body, giving the correct date for its formation. See Leon Trotski, *Stalin. An Appraisal of the Man and his Influence*, edited and translated from the Russian by Charles Malamuth, London, 1947, p. 241. Isaac Deutscher, citing this reference by Trotsky, misleadingly implies that this 'inner cabinet' functioned throughout the

period of the Bolshevik–SR coalition government. See his *Stalin: A Political Biography*, London, 1961 (first published 1949), p. 180, and *The Prophet Armed. Trotsky: 1879–1921*, London, 1970 (first published 1954), p. 341.

CHAPTER 4: ACQUIRING A BUREAUCRACY

1 Iroshnikov 1966, pp. 173–4.
2 *Ibid.*, pp. 175–8.
3 P. A. Koz'min, in 'Vospominaniya ob oktyabr'skom perevorote', *Proletarskaya revolyutsiya*, 1922, no. 10, pp. 44–52.
4 *DSV*, Vol. 1, p. 62.
5 Iroshnikov 1966, pp. 156–7.
6 There is an interesting analysis of the varied factors influencing different categories of officials to participate in opposition and passive resistance in Z. Serebryansky, 'Sabotazh i sozdanie novogo gosudarstvennogo apparata', *Proletarskaya revolyutsiya*, 1926, no. 10, pp. 8–11.
7 See Chamberlin, Vol. 1, p. 351.
8 Iroshnikov 1966, pp. 158–61. How far the composition of this body actually coincided with the Little Council appointed by the Provisional Government has not been established.
9 *Ibid.*, p. 168.
10 See e.g. Lenin, *PSS*, Vol. 35, p. 308. Cf. Ya. Peters, 'Vospominaniya o rabote v VChK v pervyi god revolyutsii', *Proletarskaya revolyutsia*, 1924, no. 10, p. 7.
11 Iroshnikov 1966, pp. 159–60.
12 *Ibid.*, pp. 161–7.
13 *Ibid.*, pp. 168–9. Cf. V. Polyansky, 'Kak nachinal rabotat' Narodnyi Komissariat Prosveshcheniya', *Proletarskaya revolyutsiya*, 1926, no. 2, pp. 56–7. There were also cases where ministerial officials established 'underground' offices outside the ministerial buildings, issuing circulars and instructions in competition with those emanating from the commissariats. See A. Shlyapnikov, 'K Oktyabryu', *Proletarskaya revolyutsiya*, 1922, no. 10, pp. 38–9, and Sheila Fitzpatrick, *The Commissariat of Enlightenment: Soviet Organisation of Education and the Arts under Lunacharsky*, Cambridge, 1970, p. 16.
14 'Vospominaniya ob oktyabr'skom perevorote', 1922, no. 10, pp. 62–3; and Iroshnikov 1966, p. 195.
15 Iroshnikov 1966, pp. 185–8.
16 *DSV*, Vol. 1, pp. 107–8; Iroshnikov 1966, pp. 188–92, 250–2.
17 *DSV*, Vol. 1, pp. 91–2; Iroshnikov 1966, p. 196.
18 Iroshnikov 1966, pp. 198–200, 235.
19 *Ibid.*, pp. 201–2, 204.
20 *Ibid.*, pp. 214–15.
21 *Triumfal'noye shestviye sovetskoi vlasti. Chast' pervaya*, pp. 94–5.
22 Latsis 1925, p. 144. In this case, however, despite the best efforts of the messengers, it was immediately apparent that further information and assistance would be needed from some of the senior officials of

the Ministry, and in the days that followed the few such officials who could be found were forcibly brought to their offices, an operation which proved very disappointing in its results.

23 Iroshnikov 1966, pp. 246–7.

24 *Ibid.*, pp. 166–7 and Trotsky in 'Vospominaniya ob oktyabr'skom perevorote', *Proletarskaya revolyutsiya*, 1922, no. 10, pp. 59–61.

25 The politics of the Food Supplies Commissariat at this period were highly complex and revealing and deserve more detailed treatment than has been possible here. See Pietsch, pp. 59–60; 'Vospominaniya ob oktyabr'skom perevorote', pp. 46, 50–1; D. S. Baburin, 'Narkomprod v pervye gody sovetskoi vlasti', *Istoricheskie zapiski*, Vol. 61, 1957, pp. 333–43; A. Shlikhter, *Na barrikadakh proletarskoi revolyutsii*, Kiev, 1927, esp. p. 148; Yu. K. Strizhkov, 'V. I. Lenin – organizator i rukovoditel' bor'by za sozdanie sovetskogo prodovol'stvennogo apparata, oktyabr' 1917g.–mai 1918g.' in S. S. Khesin (ed.), *Bor'ba za pobedu i ukrepleniye sovetskoi vlasti, 1917–1918. Sbornik statei*, Moscow, 1966, esp. pp. 261–3.

26 'Vospominaniya ob oktyabr'skom perevorote', pp. 51–2.

27 *Ibid.*, p. 51; Iroshnikov 1966, pp. 182–4; A. Shylapnikov, 'K oktyabryu', p. 24f.

28 Iroshnikov 1966, pp. 211–13. See Chapter 12.

29 *Ibid.*, pp. 184–5, 206–20. This author, on whose researches we have relied heavily in this section, gives a valuable commissariat-by-commissariat account of the chief sources of staff recruited to work in the central government offices in November–December 1917 (*ibid.*, pp. 221–39). See also Iroshnikov 1974, pp. 117–36.

30 Iroshnikov 1966, p. 249.

31 *Ibid.*, pp. 198–200.

32 There seems to have been no general policy on the part of the Soviet government to guarantee their existing jobs to collaborating officials, but this was evidently the practice in at least some departments. Thus a decision of the Commissariat for Internal Affairs issued on 20 November stated that 'Officials remaining at their jobs are to retain their former posts.' *Triumfal'noye shestviye sovetskoi vlasti, Chast' pervaya*, p. 103.

33 This was also reflected in salary provisions. While the salary of people's commissars and other senior Bolshevik officials was limited to 500 roubles a month, departmental heads could be paid up to 800 and, where they were regarded as irreplaceable specialists, their salary was fixed by negotiation. Iroshnikov 1966, p. 259. See also S. A. Fedyukin, *Sovetskaya vlast' i burzhuaznye spetsialisty*, Moscow, 1965, Chapter 1.

34 Iroshnikov 1966, pp. 253–67; Latsis 1925, pp. 157–9.

35 *DSV*, Vol. 1, pp. 172–4. Its first Chairman, Osinsky, was given the title of People's Commissar for the Organisation and Regulation of Production, *ibid.*, Vol. 1, p. 216.

36 V. Z. Drobizhev, *Glavnyi shtab sotsialisticheskoi promyshlennosti (Ocherki istorii VSNKh, 1917–1932gg.)*, Moscow, 1966, Chapter 1;

Iroshnikov 1966, pp. 226–9, 244–6. The National Economic Council also took over part of the staff of the wartime commissions and conferences: see Iroshnikov, 1974, pp. 130–1.

37 *DSV*, Vol. 1, pp. 124–231, 252.
38 *Ibid.*, pp. 185, 234; Iroshnikov 1966, p. 205.
39 Lenin, *PSS*, Vol. 45, p. 383.
40 On the 'spoils system', see e.g. Austin Ranney, Wilmoore Kendall and Earl Latham, *Democracy and the American Party System*, New York, 1956, Ch. 16, and James Bryce, *The American Commonwealth*, 3rd ed., London, 1895, vol. II, Ch. LXV.

CHAPTER 5: THE MOVE TO MOSCOW

1 Bonch-Bruyevich, pp. 216–26.
2 See L. Kuznetskaya, K. Mashtakova and Z. Subbotina, *Kabinet i kvartira Vladimira Ilyicha Lenina v Kremle*, Moscow, 1968; A. Andreyev, B. Pankov and E. Smirnova, *Lenin v Kremle*, Moscow, 1960; and Bonch-Bruyevich, pp. 227–31. The Sovnarkom and Lenin's quarters were on the third floor of a large building now known as the *Zdaniye Pravitel'stva SSSR* (Building of the USSR Government) and originally housing the imperial judicial offices, built in classical style by the distinguished architect M. F. Kazakov in 1788, and located near the Spassky Gate which opens on to Red Square. Lenin shared his flat, which consisted of three main rooms, a maid's room, kitchen and bathroom, with his wife Nadezhda Krupskaya and his sister Maria. The CEC was located on the ground floor of the same building.
3 Fotiyeva 1967, pp. 140–1.
4 *Leninskii sbornik*, XXXI, p. 96.
5 Fotiyeva 1967, p. 140.
6 Fitzpatrick, p. 18.
7 Carr, Vol. 1, p. 18.
8 *DSV*, Vol. 2, p. 5.
9 Trotsky, *Stalin*, p. 256.
10 Pestkovsky, as reported by Trotsky, *Stalin*, pp. 256–7.
11 Bogolepov, pp. 171–2, 176.
12 For examples in the Education Commissariat, see Fitzpatrick, p. 17.
13 Bonch-Bruyevich, p. 228.
14 *DSV*, Vol. 2, pp. 403–4. Pokrovsky himself, an old associate of Lunacharsky, had already joined the latter as Deputy Commissar for Education in May and took with him several of his adherents. See Fitzpatrick, pp. 6–7, 18.
15 See M. Latsis, 1926, pp. 56–7, and A. N. Tishkov, *Pervyi Chekist*, Moscow, 1968, pp. 26–7.
16 Dybenko, fretful of discipline and influenced by his mistress, Alexandra Kollontai, soon to become a leading Left Communist, had fallen foul of the leadership and gone into limbo even before his

resignation over Brest-Litovsk. He subsequently redeemed himself by his exploits during the Civil War.

17 Trotsky's official title, as conferred by the CEC on 28 March 1918, was 'Military Commissar for Army and Navy Affairs'.

18 Iroshnikov 1974, p. 146.

19 *Ibid.*, Part III, and M. P. Iroshnikov, 'K voprosu o slome burzhuaznoi gosudarstvennoi mashiny v Rossii', in Yu. S. Tokarev *et al.* (eds.), *Problemy gosudarstvennogo stroitel'stva v pervye gody sovetskoi vlasti. Sbornik statei*, Leningrad, 1973 (cited hereafter as Iroshnikov 1973).

20 Iroshnikov 1973, pp. 54–5.

21 A special sub-group here were the wives and other relatives of leading party members; these were particularly numerous, for instance, in the upper echelons of the Education Commissariat. See Fitzpatrick, p. 19.

22 See A. V. Krasnikova, 'Studencheskaya organizatsiya pri Peterburgskom komitete RSDRP (b) i ee vklad v sovetskoye gosudarstvennoye stroitel'stvo v pervye posleoktyabr'skiye mesyatsy 1917g.', in Yu. S. Tokarev, pp. 76–82.

23 Figures derived from Iroshnikov 1974, pp. 390–3, Tables 10 and 11.

24 Derived from figures and calculations in *ibid.*, pp. 404–6. Precise figures on the length of time officials had been in the party are not available, but the percentages given here may be regarded as very close approximations. Unfortunately the data do not separate those joining before and after the February Revolution.

25 See T. H. Rigby, *Communist Party Membership in the USSR 1917–1967*, Princeton, 1968 (cited hereafter as Rigby, 1968), Chapter 1.

CHAPTER 6: SOVNARKOM IN SESSION

1 Fotiyeva, 1967, p. 141.

2 Korenevskaya, 1968 (2), p. 103.

3 E. B. Genkina, 'O dokladakh V. I. Lenina v Sovnarkome, Sovete Oborony i Sovete Truda i Oborony (1917–1922gg.)', *Istoriya SSSR*, 1973, no. 4 (cited hereafter as Genkina, 1973), p. 69.

4 Korenevskaya, 1968 (2), p. 103.

5 Genkina, 1973, p. 69.

6 Korenevskaya, 1968 (2), p. 103: G. Leplevsky, *O rabote V. I. Lenina v Sovnarkome v 1921–1922gg.*, Moscow, 1971, pp. 2–4.

7 *DSV*, Vol. 1, p. 566.

8 Trotsky, *Moya zhizn'*, Vol. 2, p. 84. Trotsky's Army Commissariat was normally represented in Sovnarkom by Deputy People's Commissar Sklyansky.

9 Leplevsky, p. 23.

10 The most succinct statements on attendance at Sovnarkom meetings are in Ye. I. Korenevskaya, *Pervoye sovetskoye pravitel'stvo (pravovye osnovy organizatsii i deyatel'nosti Soveta Narodnykh Komissarov, Soveta Truda i Oborony i Malogo Soveta Narodnykh Komissarov v 1917–1922gg.)*, Avtoreferat kandidatskoi dissertatsii, Moscow, 1968

(cited hereafter as Korenevskaya, 1968 (1)), p. 2. See also Korenevskaya, 1968 (2), p. 103.

11 Fotiyeva, 1967, p. 112.
12 E. B. Genkina, *Lenin – Predsedatel' Sovnarkoma i STO*, Moscow, 1960 (cited hereafter as Genkina, 1960), p. 30.
13 Bonch-Bruyevich, p. 361.
14 Leplevsky, p. 23.
15 L. A. Fotiyeva, *V. I. Lenin – rukovoditel' i tovarishch*, 2nd ed., Moscow, 1973 (cited hereafter as Fotiyeva, 1973), p. 41. The minutes were evidently brief and no attempt was made to record the details of reports or discussions. See also Genkina, 1973, pp. 71–2 and Iroshnikov, 1974, pp. 171–3.
16 Leplevsky, p. 14.
17 Fotiyeva, 1967, pp. 103–4. At first *rapporteurs* often sat right through Sovnarkom meetings, but later Lenin objected to this, and instructed Sovnarkom secretary Gorbunov to ensure that such 'outsiders' should be present only while matters affecting them were under discussion.
18 Savitskaya, p. 184.
19 Leplevsky, p. 12.
20 *Leninskii sbornik*, XXXV, p. 15.
21 See Fotiyeva, 1967, p. 144.
22 *Ibid.*, p. 224.
23 *Ibid.*, p. 143; *Leninskii sbornik*, XXI, pp. 96–7.
24 Fotiyeva, 1967, p. 142. It should be recalled that meetings were being held on most days of the week at that period.
25 *Ibid.*, p. 143.
26 *Ibid.*, p. 99.
27 Durdenevsky, 1922, p. 55.
28 See Iroshnikov, 1974, pp. 180–3, and Ye. I. Korenevskaya, 'Organizatsionno-pravovye formy deyatel'nosti SNK RSFSR (1917–1922gg.)', *Sovetskoye gosudarstvo i pravo*, 1968, no. 7 (cited hereafter as Korenevskaya, 1968 (3)), pp. 94–6. It was not till April 1922 that a comprehensive regulation on the preparation of Sovnarkom agenda was adopted. See *Sovetskoye pravo*, 1922, no. 1, pp. 66–7.
29 See *DSV*, Vol. 2, pp. 570–1.
30 See Leplevsky, pp. 3–4. The reports of Lenin's conduct of Sovnarkom meetings in Lenin: *Khronika*, Vols. 5–7 *passim*, mention innumerable cases of amendments to the printed agenda approved at the outset of meetings.
31 See Fotiyeva, 1967, pp. 100–1.
32 Leplevsky, p. 15.
33 *DSV*, Vol. 5, pp. 425–6. The rules were drafted by Justice Commissar Kursky, but closely followed an outline handed to him by Lenin. See Lenin, *PSS*, Vol. 50, p. 274.
34 Fotiyeva, 1967, p. 107.
35 See Ya. Gindin, *Vospominaniya o Vladimire Ilyiche*, Moscow, 1973, p. 9.
36 In one case on record an item was introduced by a twenty-minute

report by a senior 'military specialist', which Lenin found so badly presented that he summoned the *rapporteur* to his office the following morning to instruct him in the art of preparing reports. See Fotiyeva, 1967, pp. 107–8.

37 This is testified to by all contemporary witnesses. Leplevsky (p. 3) states that in the two years he was attending Sovnarkom meetings under Lenin's chairmanship he cannot recall a single occasion on which the latter opened proceedings even a trifle after the appointed time. Cf. Fotiyeva, 1973, p. 36.

38 *Sobraniye uzakonenii i rasporyazhenii raboche-krestyanskogo pravitel'stva RSFSR*, Petrograd–Moscow, 1917–, 1920, no. 32, art. 156 (cited hereafter as SU).

39 See E. B. Genkina, *Gosudarstvennaya deyatel'nost' V. I. Lenina 1921–1923gg.*, Moscow, 1969 (cited hereafter as Genkina, 1969), p. 372.

40 See *ibid.* and *Leninskii sbornik*, xx, pp. 209, 342.

41 Fotiyeva, 1967, p. 107 and Fotiyeva, 1973, pp. 39–40.

42 Leplevsky, p. 8. Cf. Genkina, 1969, p. 375.

43 Leplevsky, p. 11.

44 Fotiyeva, 1967, p. 143.

45 For examples, see Genkina, 1960, pp. 38–40. For a more systematic discussion, see Genkina, 1973.

46 Fotiyeva, 1967, p. 145; Leplevsky, p. 8; Genkina, 1960, pp. 36–7.

47 See *Vospominaniya o Vladimire Ilyiche Lenine*, no. 2, Moscow, 1957, p. 35. It is extremely difficult to establish with precision who at any particular time had the right to vote at Sovnarkom meetings. Generally speaking, it was limited to people's commissars or their authorised proxies and a small number of other 'accredited representatives'. In the earliest period there seems to have been some confusion about voting rights and apparently some members were allowed a vote on matters of one kind and not of another. This applied, for instance, to the People's Commissar for State Control, who could speak on political questions but vote only on economic and financial questions. See *Obrazovanie i razvitiye organov sotsialisticheskogo kontrolya v SSSR (1917–1975). Sbornik dokumentov i materialov*, Moscow, 1975, p. 44. (Certain sources, e.g. *DSV*, Vol. 1, p. 180, print a different wording of this decree, which limits the vote to political matters; if this is accurate, its logic is difficult to grasp, in view of this commissariat's responsibilities.) Other anomalous decisions were taken during the period of the Bolshevik–Left SR coalition, reflecting the political balance of the time. For instance in February 1918 Left SR member of the Finance Board, Brilliantov, was given voting membership of Sovnarkom. See *Lenin: khronika*, Vol. 5, p. 220. The granting of voting rights to people's commissars' proxies was supposed to require specific resolution of Sovnarkom, and such resolutions were at least sometimes taken at Sovnarkom meetings. See, e.g., *ibid.*, p. 368 and Vol. 7, p. 171.

48 See Leplevsky, p. 23.

49 Fotiyeva, 1967, pp. 97–8. See below, Chapters 11 and 12.

50 N. A. Semashko, 'Ilyich vedët zasedaniye', *Leninskiye stranitsy*, Moscow, 1960, p. 108.

51 A. V. Lunacharsky, 'Lenin v Sovnarkome', in *Vospominaniya o Vladimire Ilyiche Lenine*, no. 2, p. 295.

52 Andreyev, p. 34. After Lenin's lung wound in August 1918 smoking was forbidden around the Sovnarkom table, but members were allowed to smoke beside the airvent of the stove. According to Andreyev there were sometimes more gathered round the stove than participating in the meeting.

53 A. Yelizarova, 'Stranichka vospominanii o Vladimire Ilyiche v Sovnarkome', *Proletarskaya revolyutsiya* 1929, no. 11, p. 89. One cannot help recalling here Parkinson's account of what happens at committee meetings once they have got too large. 'Amid all this drivel the useful men present, if there are any, exchange little notes that read, "Lunch with me tomorrow – we'll fix it then".' (C. North-cote Parkinson, *Parkinson's Law or the Pursuit of Progress*, London, 1965, p. 41).

54 Yelizarov, after serving briefly as Commissar for Railways, was put in charge of state insurance early in 1918 and subsequently became a board member of the Commissariat for Trade and Industry; both of these posts entitled him to attend Sovnarkom meetings. He died of typhus in 1919.

55 Yelizarova, pp. 88–9. Other contemporary witnesses and Soviet historians provide much evidence confirming the importance of these informal levels of activity at Sovnarkom sessions and Lenin's capacity simultaneously to control and guide the meeting, to confer by notes with others present and to work on documents relating to other, connected matters. Cf., e.g., Iroshnikov, 1974, pp. 235–7. The reports of Sovnarkom meetings in *Lenin: khronika*, Vols. 5–7, *passim*, contain many references to notes exchanged in the course of discussions.

CHAPTER 7: 'THE MINUTE HAND'

1 A vast amount of government business was of course settled at the level of the constituent commissariats and other agencies by decisions promulgated in their name. Our concern here, however, is with those decisions issued in the name of the Government as such.

2 *Leninskii sbornik*, xxxv, p. 18. The prime mover in the revival of the Little Sovnarkom, as apparently in its original establishment, was D. P. Bogolepov. See *Lenin: khronika*, Vol. 5, pp. 328, 341. Although its official title was still 'The Commission of Sovnarkom', the term 'Little Sovnarkom' was used informally and soon passed again into official usage. *Ibid.*, Vols. 5 and 6, *passim*.

3 See Iroshnikov, 1974, pp. 199–204.

4 See, for example, *Lenin: khronika*, Vol. 7, p. 486, where reference is

made to the Little Sovnarkom's handling of a complaint from the Justice Commissariat that the Internal Affairs Commissariat and Vecheka were trespassing on its jurisdiction.

5 See Iroshnikov, 1974, pp. 206–7; Latsis, 1926, p. 89.

6 Iroshnikov, 1974, pp. 200–3.

7 Durdenevsky, 1922, p. 45.

8 Korenevskaya, 1968 (1), p. 24. Among the bodies represented in this way were the Army Commissariat and *Chusosnabarm* (see Chapter 8).

9 See Korenevskaya, 1968 (2), p. 101; Durdenevsky, 1922, p. 45; N. Zubov, *Pervyi predsedatel' Malogo Sovnarkoma*, Moscow, 1975, pp. 169–75. For some time beginning in October 1918, Kozlovsky was officially authorised to exercise the Chairmanship alternately with A. V. Galkin of the State Control Commissariat. See Iroshnikov, 1974, p. 202.

10 *Spravochnik tsentral'nykh i mestnykh uchrezhdenii RSFSR, partiinykh organizatsii i professional'nykh soyuzov*, 2nd ed., Moscow, 1920, p. 9.

11 See *DSV*, Vol. 4, p. xi. See also Fotiyeva, 1967, p. 101. This procedure had already been practised unofficially for some months. See Iroshnikov, 1974, p. 206.

12 This regulation does not seem to have been published, but it is outlined in Korenevskaya, 1968 (1), p. 24. See also Lenin, *PSS*, Vol. 51, pp. 205, 428, and Genkina, 1969, p. 445.

13 See Leplevsky, p. 17.

14 *Ibid.*, p. 18.

15 *SU* 1921, 68/532.

16 The two deputy chairmen at this period were A. G. Goikhbarg of the Commissariat of Justice and G. M. Leplevsky of the Commissariat of Internal Affairs.

17 *SU* 1922, 1/19.

18 Korenevskaya, 1968 (2), p. 103. In the course of 1921 it seems to have had three meetings a week. Its meetings commonly lasted until after midnight, sometimes until as late as 3 a.m. See Gindin, p. 8.

19 Gindin, p. 8.

20 For examples of Lenin's reference back of Little Sovnarkom decisions for further consideration, see Lenin, *PSS*, Vol. 51, p. 240; Vol. 52, pp. 17, 273; Vol. 54, pp. 32–3, 106–8.

21 Leplevsky, pp. 16–17; Gindin, p. 8. See also *Leninskii sbornik*, xxvIII, p. 365.

22 See Genkina, 1960, p. 46. The June 1920 regulation on the Little Sovnarkom, as originally approved, stated that, apart from budgetary matters, which were automatically referred to it, and other matters which it decided to consider at its own discretion, the Little Sovnarkom was obliged to consider matters referred to it by decision of the Full Sovnarkom. The day after the regulation was adopted, however, Lenin initiated the amendment that 'matters may also come up for consideration of the Little Council on the proposal of the Chairman of the Sovnarkom'. See Lenin, *PSS*, Vol. 51, pp. 205, 428. For examples of matters referred by Lenin to the Little

Sovnarkom, see *ibid.*, Vol. 51, pp. 227, 257, 263, 271, 323; Vol. 52, pp. 18, 56, 72, 171; Vol. 54, pp. 38–9, 159.

23   Gindin, pp. 8–9.
24   Leplevsky, p. 28.
25   Leplevsky, pp. 24–7. For other cases of Lenin's management of the Little Sovnarkom to achieve desired policy objectives, see Genkina, 1960, pp. 45–7. For an example of Lenin's supporting the Little Sovnarkom and its Chairman Kiselev against an objection by a people's commissar to one of its decisions which had his support, see Lenin, *PSS*, Vol. 53, pp. 91–2.
26   Durdenevsky, 1922, p. 46.
27   Gindin, p. 21.
28   N. A. Milyutin in *Vospominaniya o V. I. Lenine*, Vol. 4, Moscow, 1969, p. 193.

CHAPTER 8: SOVNARKOM'S 'ALTER EGO'

1   For an example, see *The Trotsky Papers*, Vol. 1, pp. 240–4.
2   See Durdenevsky, 1922, p. 47.
3   The council running the Central Supplies Directorate was headed by a Chief of Supplies (*Glavnachsnab*) assisted by two military commissars. See A. V. Venediktov, *Organizatsiya gosudarstvennoi promyshlennosti v SSSR*, Vol. 1, Leningrad, 1957, p. 478.
4   *SU* 1918, 83/875. The Central Department of Military Procurements proceeded to set up its own network of subordinate departments in the provincial economic councils under the National Economic Council.
5   This body was called the Commission for Investigating the Organisation and Activity of Organisations for Supply of the People's Commissariat for Military Affairs (*Komissiya dlya obsledovaniya organizatsii i deyatel'nosti organov snabzheniya Narodnogo komissariata po voyennym delam*). See *DSV*, Vol. 3, pp. 290–1.
6   *DSV*, Vol. 3, pp. 515–16.
7   See *The Trotsky Papers*, Vol. 1, p. 583, note 8.
8   *DSV*, Vol. 3, pp. 313–14. For the structure and powers of this body, as subsequently elaborated by the Defence Council, see *SU* 1919, 19/216. The full name of *Tsekomprodarm* was *Tsentral'naya komissiya po uporyadocheniyu i pravil'noi postanovke dela snabzheniya armii prodovol'stviyem i produktami pervoi neobkhodimosti* (Central Commission on the Regulating and Correct Arrangement of the Matter of Supplying the Army with Foodstuffs and Essential Items). The decree also required local military authorities to nominate representatives to the boards (*kollegii*) of the provincial food supplies committees, which had been set up in May to administer the food requisitioning programme.
9   Cf. Pietsch, pp. 104–7.
10   *DSV*, Vol. 3, p. 159.

11   *Ibid.*, Vol. 4, pp. 92–4; Krasin was also People's Commissar for Trade and Industry and a member of the Presidium of the NEC.

12   See I. Stalin, *Sochineniya*, Vol. 4, *Noyabr' 1917–1920*, Moscow, 1947, pp. 218–20.

13   The decision to make Rykov super-coordinator of military supplies was taken at a meeting of the Party Central Committee on 3 July 1919, as part of a package of measures most of which were contrary to Trotsky's policies and organisational interests. See *The Trotsky Papers*, Vol. 1, pp. 578–85. For the political background and consequences of these measures, see Deutscher, *The Prophet Armed*, pp. 432–6. The establishment and powers of *Chusosnabarm* were embodied in a decree of the CEC published on 8 July: see *SU* 1919, 35/349 and Venediktov, Vol. 1, p. 489. On Rykov in the role of *Chusosnabarm*, see Samuel A. Oppenheim, *Aleksei Ivanovich Rykov (1881–1938): a Political Biography*, Ph.D. Dissertation, Indiana University, 1972, pp. 203–10.

14   Venediktov, Vol. 1, pp. 490–2.

15   *SU* 1919, 48/474.

16   See Oppenheim, pp. 208–9.

17   At the same time it would be an exaggeration to claim that *Chusosnabarm* entirely put an end to jurisdictional wrangles in the field of military supplies, and its representatives at the front were often in conflict with the local Revolutionary Military Councils. See Oppenheim, p. 208.

18   See *SU* 1919, 41/391 and 55/533.

19   *Leninskii sbornik*, XVIII, pp. 243–4. For other examples illustrating the variety of bodies receiving the direct attention of the Defence Council, see Venediktov, Vol. 1, pp. 485–6.

20   M. V. Frunze, *Sochineniya*, Vol. 2, 1926, p. 135, quoted by N. A. Kulikova, 'Deyatel'nost' Soveta Truda i Oborony v period vtoroi mirovoi peredyshki' in I. G. Ryabtsev *et al.* (eds.), *O deyatel'nosti V. I. Lenina v 1917–1922 gody; Sbornik statei*, Moscow, 1958, p. 156.

21   Venediktov, Vol. 1, pp. 494–8. On the inconsistencies in the composition of the Revolutionary Councils of the various Labour Armies and the confusion as to their powers and accountability, see S. Brodovich, 'STO i Ekoso RSFSR', *Vlast' sovetov* 1924, no. 5, pp. 38–9.

22   Lenin, *PSS*, Vol. 40, p. 273. The last decree of the Council published under its original title appeared on 3 April 1920. On 7 April its decrees began to be published as from the *Defence and Labour Council*, and on 16 April as from the *Labour and Defence Council*. See *SU* 1920, 26/130, 27/132 and 29/146. Henceforth we shall follow the Soviet convention of referring to it by its initials – STO.

23   *Devyatyi Syezd RKP (b), Protokoly Mart–Aprel' 1920*, Moscow, 1960 (cited hereafter as *Devyatyi Syezd RKP(b)*), p. 95f.

24   Oppenheim, pp. 199–200.

25   *Devyatyi Syezd RKP(b)*, p. 405.

26   Lenin, *PSS*, Vol. 40, p. 273. The dispute is summarised in Brodovich, pp. 23–4.

27 *Devyatyi Syezd RKP(b)*, p. 417.
28 *Ekonomicheskaya zhizn'* 1920, no. 151, p. 3.
29 See B. M. Shekhvatov, 'Bor'ba V. I. Lenina za posledovatel'noe osushchestleniye printsipa demokraticheskogo tsentralizma v upravlenii narodnym khozyaistvom pri perekhode k NEPu', in Ryabtsev, pp. 239–40, *Leninskii sbornik*, XXXV, pp. 160–1, *Izvestiya Tsentral'nogo Komiteta RKP(b)* 1920, no. 26, p. 4. The Commission was established at a Sovnarkom meeting on 26 October 1920. Gusev was at that time in the Chief Political Directorate of the Red Army; Larin, a former Menshevik, now working in the economic administration, was soon to become a member of Gosplan.
30 *SU* 1921, 1/2, reprinted in *Istoriya Sovetskoi Konstitutsii (v dokumentakh) 1917–1956*, p. 258.
31 See Lenin, *PSS*, Vol. 42, pp. 155–6.
32 *Direktivy KPSS i sovetskogo pravitel'stva po khozyaistvennym voprosam*, Vol. 1, Moscow, 1957, pp. 188–90.
33 *SU* 1921, 27/153. Venediktov, Vol. 1, pp. 28–9. The Regional Economic Consultative Councils operated both through the gubernia boards and through regional offices of the various commissariats whose representatives constituted the councils' membership. The ambiguous position of these representatives was a fertile source of conflict, which a decree of June 1922 sought to relieve, by affirming unequivocally their obligation to carry out 'their' council's decisions but giving the right to lodge a protest to STO through 'their' commissariat. See *SU* 1922, 42/500. This STO decree was reaffirmed two months later by the CEC; see *SU* 1922, 52/669. With the setting up of the Regional Councils the Revolutionary Councils of the Labour Armies were disbanded, as were, about the same time, several other inter-agency coordinating bodies of the Civil War period.
34 See *SU* 1921, 44/223 and 57/364. See also B. M. Shekhvatov, in Ryabtsev, pp. 240–51. On the origins and subsequent operation of the Economic Consultative Councils under NEP, see L. M. Drobizheva, 'Razrabotka i realizatsiya Leninskogo "Nakaza ot STO mestnym sovetskim uchrezhdeniyam"', *Voprosy istorii* 1962, no. 6, pp. 17–32.
35 See Brodovich, p. 41.
36 *Direktivy KPSS i sovetskogo pravitel'stva po khozyaistvennym voprosam*, Vol. 1, pp. 203–4.
37 The low figures shown for supply matters, especially in 1919–20 – probably due in large part to the fact that many decisions in this field were promulgated as ordinances of the various subordinate inter-agency bodies – seriously understate the STO concern with this area.
38 For further developments in the first half of 1923, see Brodovich, p. 29.
39 'Nakaz Soveta Narodnykh Komissarov o provedenii v zhizn' nachal novoi ekonomicheskoi politiki', in *Direktivy KPSS i sovetskogo pravitel'stva po khozyaistvennym voprosam*, Vol. 1, p. 258.
40 Durdenevsky, 1922, p. 48.

41 Yu. S. Kukushkin, *V. I. Lenin – predsedatel' soveta rabochei i krestyanskoi oborony*, Moscow, 1962, p. 26.
42 The practice began in the early days of the Defence Council and was specifically provided for in the decree transforming the latter into STO.
43 See Korenevskaya, 1968 (2), pp. 103–4 and Genkina, 1960, p. 30.
44 Gindin, p. 14.
45 Korenevskaya, 1968 (2), p. 103; Genkina, 1960, p. 30; Fotiyeva, 1967, p. 102; Brodovich (p. 31) claims on the basis of information from an STO official that a clear distinction between the powers and membership of 'plenary' and 'administrative' meetings was never established. The first known decree formalising the status of STO 'administrative meetings' dates from 10 March 1920.
46 Gindin, p. 6; Fotiyeva, 1967, p. 102.
47 Korenevskaya, 1968 (2), p. 103; Genkina, 1960, p. 31 and 1969, p. 368; Leplevsky, p. 3; N. N. Akimov and M. G. Vlasova, 'V. I. Lenin – predsedatel' soveta rabochei i krestyanskoi oborony', *Voprosy istorii* 1955, no. 1, p. 34.
48 Korenevskaya, 1968 (2), p. 103; agendas of 'administrative meetings' tended to be especially long, sometimes comprising up to 50 items; see Leplevsky, p. 15.
49 A. A. Andreyev in *Vospominaniya o Vladimire Ilyiche Lenine*, Vol. 2, p. 34.
50 *Ibid.*, p. 35.

CHAPTER 9: THE SYSTEM AND THE CHIEF

1 Genkina, 1969, p. 368; Korenevskaya, 1968 (2), p. 103; Durdenevsky, 1922, p. 55. The Little Sovnarkom held seventy-seven meetings in the six months November 1920–April 1921, i.e. an average of almost three a week.
2 Durdenevsky, 1922, p. 55; Brodovich, p. 35.
3 A. A. Nelidov, *Istoriya gosudarstvennykh uchrezhdenii SSSR. Chast' I (1917–1936)*, Moscow, 1962, p. 211; Korenevskaya, 1968 (1), p. 26.
4 Durdenevsky, 1922, p. 55.
5 See L. I. Antonova, 'Organizatsionnye formy pravotvorcheskoi deyatel'nosti Soveta Narodnykh Komissarov (1917–1922gg.)', *Pravovedeniye* 1968, no. 3, p. 104.
6 *SU* 1920, 59/269.
7 Durdenevsky, 1922, p. 57.
8 See George L. Yaney, *The Systematization of Russian Government. Social Evolution in the Domestic Administration of Imperial Russia, 1711–1905*, Urbana Ill.–Chicago–London, 1973, pp. 256–8.
9 Fotiyeva, 1967, pp. 140–1. The most detailed available account of the organisation and staff of the Chancellery relates to the Smolny period: see Iroshnikov, 1966, Chapter 2.
10 Genkina, 1969, p. 381.

11   V. A. Lyubisheva, 'Organizatsiya truda v sekretariate V. I. Lenina v
     SNK', in Ye. N. Gorodetsky *et al.* (eds.), *Stroitel'stvo Sovetskogo
     Gosudarstva*, Moscow, 1972, p. 204.

12   Lenin, *PSS*, Vol. 53, pp. 193, 416.

13   *Ibid.*, Vol. 52, pp. 199–200, Vol. 53, pp. 162–3; Korenevskaya, 1968
     (1), p. 26. The first Secretary of the Little Sovnarkom was S. V.
     Svirskaya: see N. Zubov, *Pervyi predsedatel' Malogo Sovnarkoma*,
     Moscow, 1975 (cited hereafter as Zubov, 1975), p. 180. Sometimes
     the staffs servicing STO and the Little Sovnarkom were referred to
     in official documents as separate secretariats, sometimes not. For an
     example of the former, see *SU* 1922, 1/19.

14   Fotiyeva, 1967, pp. 90–3.

15   However, in 1920 the Little Sovnarkom had been given final respon-
     sibility for determining which matters proposed for the Sovnarkom
     agenda were considered by which bodies.

16   Lenin's correspondence for this period is replete with cases illustrat-
     ing the various responsibilities of Chancellery staff mentioned. See
     Lenin, *PSS*, Vols. 50–4, *passim*. The Chancellery's authority within
     the whole central government network is illustrated by a decision of
     December 1921 empowering it to bring formal charges against senior
     officials who failed to provide within three days (or twenty-four hours
     in cases of urgency) information requested by the Chancellery. See *SU*
     1922, 1/19.

17   Lenin, *PSS*, Vol. 52, pp. 53, 361.

18   Lenin, *PSS*, Vol. 52, pp. 199–200. The appointment of Smolyaninov
     and Lenin's instructions to him evidently formed part of a general
     stocktaking and partial reorganisation of the Chancellery at this time.
     An order (unfortunately unpublished) was issued in May 1921
     specifying the duties of each staff member (see Lyubisheva, p. 201)
     and in the following two months several additional senior appoint-
     ments were made. This reorganisation was probably connected in
     some way with the appointment of Rykov as deputy chairman of
     STO, on which see below, Chapter 13.

19   The Little Sovnarkom also obtained the services of three new
     officials with economic training and experience at the same time.
     See B. M. Shekhvatov, *Lenin i Sovetskoe gosudarstvo. Deyatel'nost'
     V. I. Lenina po sovershenstvovaniyu gosudarstvennogo upravleniya,
     1921–1922*, Moscow, 1960, p. 212. See also *Leninskii sbornik*, xxxvii,
     p. 312.

20   *Bol'shaya sovetskaya entsiklopediya*, 1st edn., Vol. 7 (1927) (cited
     hereafter as *BSE*), p. 126.

21   Although his first job was to manage a state farm near Moscow which
     was intended both as a model farm and a support-base for a network
     of official 'rest homes' for senior Bolsheviks (see Bonch-Bruyevich,
     pp. 391–401, 479). The farm, which came under the Moscow Health
     Department (Lenin, *PSS*, Vol. 53, p. 394), bore the idyllic name of
     'Forest Glades' (*Lesnye polyany*). The circumstances of his resigning
     his vital work in the Sovnarkom apparatus remain unexplained,

although there are stories of improprieties. The usually reliable Nikolay Valentinov (*Encounters with Lenin*, London, 1968, p. 169 n.) says he 'fell into disfavour with Lenin over some misdemeanors', while S. V. Dmitrievsky (*Sovetskiye portrety*, Berlin, 1932, p. 22) claims he was removed for 'abuses'.

22 See Gorbunov, in *Pravda*, 6–7 November 1927. Party Secretary Krestinsky evidently suggested Gorbunov's brother Pavel for the job of Head of Chancellery (perhaps acting on behalf of the Orgburo). However, Lenin pressed for N. P. Gorbunov, and the Central Committee agreed, appointing brother Pavel to head their own Chancellery. See *Leninskii sbornik*, xxvii, pp. 269–70. This particular combination of posts in the hands of two close relatives raises some intriguing questions on which, unfortunately, the published record sheds no light. Very soon, however, Pavel was transferred to the Foreign Affairs Commissariat to head its Chancellery. See *ibid.*, p. 323.

23 Zubov, 1975, p. 172.

24 This was reflected administratively and symbolically in various ways, such as the fact that he was on the payroll of the Sovnarkom – unlike the People's Commissars, who were on those of the various Commissariats – or the photographs of Lenin in the midst of the Sovnarkom staff. But it is best illustrated by the constant attention, attested to both in his correspondence and in memoirs, that Lenin paid to the work of staff members, instructing them on improved methods and personally admonishing them for carelessness or inefficiency as well as concerning himself with their welfare.

25 Adam Ulam, *Lenin and the Bolsheviks*, London, 1966, p. 536. Sovnarkom Secretary Gorbunov drew attention to the same characteristic in the following terms:

> While concerning himself with the most important political issues, often of a world scale, Vladimir Ilyich never cut himself off from current matters, was exceptionally accessible and reacted vigorously to hundreds and thousands of comparatively minor questions... Vladimir Ilyich sometimes devoted greater importance to the carrying through to completion of some minor question of a practical character than to dozens of 'decisions of principle' adopted and subsequently just remaining on paper.

See *Vospominaniya o Lenine*, Vol. 2, p. 58.

26 Based on calculations reported in Genkina, 1969, pp. 378–9, 402, and the author's own analysis of material in Lenin, *PSS*, Vols. 43, 44, 52–4. Ambiguous cases have been identified as party-related correspondence. Communications with Politburo members on matters involving party bodies, even in a secondary or purely formal way, are likewise treated as party correspondence. Of the total of 1460 items of correspondence, 574 were addressed to people's commissariats or other central government agencies of equivalent status. Most of the 140 communications addressed to local bodies also went to government rather than party organisations. One difficulty in evaluating

this data is that we do not know what proportion of his correspondence has survived: some, at least, has undoubtedly been lost or destroyed, and some may still be suppressed. However, given the four-to-one ratio of government to party addressees in the surviving correspondence, it is hard to imagine that the balance would be much changed if the missing correspondence were available. In fact, a greater proportion of the often scribbled 'in house' memoranda to Sovnarkom officials is likely to have eluded the voracious files of the Marx–Lenin Institute. The contrast looms even larger when one considers that the pattern of Lenin's daily contacts would have required him to rely far more on written rather than verbal communications in his dealings with party officials than in those with government officials. Of course Lenin also had recourse to the telephone, but there is no evidence that the pattern here differed radically from that found in his correspondence.

27 Lenin, *PSS*, Vol. 53, p. 300. Lenin insisted on a reduction in the number slated for transfer, especially from the economic commissariats. In another note to Stalin proposing the necessary authorisation and arrangements for Gosplan Chairman Krzhizhanovsky to visit Germany for medical treatment, he confesses ignorance as to whether this comes within the competence of the Orgburo or Secretariat. See *PSS*, Vol. 54, p. 243. He never revealed the slightest doubt as to where competence lay as between central government bodies.

28 A. N. Potresov, quoted from the journal *Die Gesellschaft*, in Valentinov, p. 42.

29 Valentinov, pp. 42–3.

30 *Ibid.*, pp. 39–40.

31 S. Liberman, *Building Lenin's Russia*, Chicago, 1945, p. 13. Liberman also noted the significance of the patronymic form of address, 'Ilyich', applied to Lenin alone of the Bolshevik leaders, and conveying the mixture of fondness and respect, the 'personal attachment' which every Bolshevik had for Lenin, which 'could be sensed at any meeting of either of the two councils', and which partly accounted for the authority he was able to exercise in the business of government. See *ibid.*, p. 79.

32 *Vospominaniya o V. I. Lenine*, Vol. 3, Moscow, 1969, pp. 483–4.

33 See especially Iroshnikov, 1974, pp. 210–29.

34 See Kukushkin, p. 27.

35 See Genkina, 1960, Chapter 2, and Genkina, 1969, Part II, Chapter 9.

36 Lenin, *PSS*, Vol. 52, pp. 137–8.

37 *Ibid.*, p. 386; Genkina, 1960, p. 52.

38 Lenin, *PSS*, Vol. 52, pp. 160, 394.

39 *Ibid.*, pp. 222, 415. For a similar example, dating from 1919, see *Lenin: khronika*, Vol. 7, p. 149.

40 For other examples from 1921 of Lenin's use of Chancellery officials

to assist him in performing his *executive* role, see Lenin, *PSS*, Vol. 52, pp. 36, 46, 53, 56, 57, 203, 208, 231, 236, 237, 257, 259, 277; Vol. 53, pp. 162, 199.

41 The following letter addressed to the Electricity Department of the NEC in September 1921 will exemplify the flavour of these communications:

> You are expected to carry out with complete precision and maximum adherence to the schedule laid down for completion of construction, the supply of electrotechnical equipment to the Kashira construction project. I categorically demand that in this matter there should not be the slightest delays, which could lead to the non-completion of the project in· terms of the prescribed schedule. You are to keep STO (Comrade Smolyaninov) informed of progress with supplies.

See Lenin, *PSS*, Vol. 53, p. 187.

42 Lenin, *PSS*, Vol. 53, pp. 162–4.

43 Potresov, quoted Valentinov, p. 42.

44 See Lenin, *PSS*, pp. 122, 304. The following year Kamenev had occasion to protest against a further Little Sovnarkom decision on a related issue, whereupon Lenin wrote the following highly revealing minute to the Little Sovnarkom: 'In view of the objection against this decision placed by Cde Kamenev, a member of the Politburo, I propose this decree be reconsidered with Cde Kamenev present.' See Lenin, *PSS*, Vol. 53, p. 188.

45 Lenin, *PSS*, Vol. 53, pp. 150, 407.

46 See *Ibid.*, Vol. 52, pp. 259, 427. For other cases of issues transferred on Lenin's initiative from the Politburo to Sovnarkom, see *ibid.*, pp. 408–9, note 303; and Vol. 54, pp. 250, 641.

47 *Ibid.*, Vol. 51, pp. 114, 401.

48 The actual phrasing of his proposal to the Politburo was 'to instruct [*poruchit'*] the Presidium of the CEC to revoke the decision of Sovnarkom', which reveals much about the Bolshevik leadership's attitude towards constitutional forms. See Lenin, *PSS*, Vol. 54, p. 110.

49 For an example in the Finance Commissariat, see *ibid.*, pp. 106, 592.

50 *Leninskii sbornik*, XXVIII, p. 401.

51 See Iroshnikov, 1974, p. 179.

CHAPTER 10: THE PEOPLE'S COMMISSARS: RECRUITMENT

1 See Chapter 1, note 7. See also Iroshnikov, 1966, pp. 42–6.

2 See Krupskaya, p. 320; Iroshnikov, 1966, pp. 46–7.

3 Trotsky, *Moya zhizn'*, Vol. II, pp. 62–3. Partial confirmation of Trotsky's claim that Lenin pressed him to assume the Chairmanship is the report by A. A. Yoffe, who attended the meeting, that Lenin at first categorically refused the post himself. Yoffe states that it was morning by the time the meeting came to consider the composition of the Government. See Iroshnikov, 1974, p. 41.

4 S. Pestkovsky, 'Ob oktyabr'skikh dnyakh v Pitere', *Proletarskaya revolyutsiya*, 1922, no. 10, p. 99.

5 G. Lomov, 'V dni buri i natiska', *Proletarskaya revolyutsiya*, 1927, no. 10, p. 172.

6 *Ibid.*, A. G. Shlyapnikov, p. 31; Krupskaya, p. 320; A. V. Lunacharsky, 'Smolnyi v velikuyu noch'' in *Vospominaniya o V. I. Lenine*, Vol. 1, Moscow, 1956, p. 628.

7 Lomov, p. 172. Cf. Iroshnikov, 1966, p. 47 and Iroshnikov, 1974, p. 41. This Central Committee meeting was held in conjunction with the Bolshevik caucus of the Congress of Soviets. It approved the principle of a single-party government as well as the actual list to be presented to the Congress. It may be that not all the future people's commissars were consulted in advance. This is implied by Shlyapnikov, whose first intimation that he was to be Commissar for Labour evidently came immediately after the Central Committee meeting of 26 October, when he was told that he must go and take charge of the Labour Ministry. Another appointee, Skvortsov-Stepanov, who was in Moscow at the time and remained there, never actually taking up his duties as people's commissar, must also have been chosen without his knowledge.

8 Sverdlov's widow has assembled an impressive array of testimonies to these abilities; see K. T. Sverdlova, *Yakov Mikhailovich Sverdlov*, Moscow, 1957, pp. 377–87.

9 Shlyapnikov, p. 31.

10 Latsis, 1925, pp. 138–40. In the original, Latsis' party nickname *Dyadya* (Uncle) is used.

11 Strizhkov in Khesin, pp. 250–1. See also Iroshnikov, 1974, p. 93.

12 See *DSV*, Vol. 1, pp. 581–4. Details are: Menzhinsky (Finance) 30 October; Yelizarov (Railways) 8 November; Shlikhter (Agriculture) 13 November; Stuchka (Justice) 16 November; Shlikhter again (now Food Supplies) 19 November; and Essen (State Control) 20 November.

13 The evidence for this is the outline of matters dealt with at Sovnarkom meetings contained in *Lenin: khronika*, Vol. 5. The exception was the last of these appointments, that of Essen.

14 See *DSV*, Vol. 1, pp. 583, 585–6. The cavalier attitude towards formal procedure at this time, exemplified by the manner of these appointments, was particularly blatant in the case of Petrovsky, whose appointment was simply embodied in an order (*prikaz*) of Sovnarkom relating to the Ministry of Internal Affairs (see *Lenin: khronika*, Vol. 5, p. 66). At least the other decisions were given the dignity of resolutions or decrees (*postanovleniya*) of Sovnarkom. Moreover, Petrovsky's appointment was anomalously described as 'commissar' rather than 'people's commissar'.

15 See *Lenin: khronika*, Vol. 5, p. 33. The minutes of this meeting are not contained in the *Protokoly TsK*.

16 *Ibid.*, pp. 33, 41. At the same meeting Lenin received a note from Podvoisky proposing Nevsky as acting Railways Commissar, to which

he also agreed, and later that day he signed Sovnarkom decisions appointing both Yelizarov and Nevsky (*ibid.*, p. 41). It would seem, however, that Nevsky did not take up this work immediately and for the time being Yelizarov was in charge of the commissariat.

17 The main source of information on the matters dealt with by the Central Committee during this period is the collection of official minutes published in *Protokoly TsK*. Unfortunately, no minutes were evidently made of certain meetings or, if made, were lost. This applied, for instance, to the meetings of the night of 24–5, 26 October, and 4 November. However, some information is available about such meetings in later memoirs and in Vol. 5 of *Lenin: khronika*, the editors of which have sought to identify from archival and published sources details of all meetings attended by Lenin.

18 See *DSV*, Vol. 1, p. 588; *Lenin: khronika*, Vol. 5, p. 191; *Protokoly TsK*, p. 165. Chicherin was initially appointed to look after the commissariat during Trotsky's preoccupation with negotiations with the Germans. This is reflected in the Central Committee minutes, which referred to the appointment as temporary.

19 *Protokoly TsK*, p. 180; *Lenin: khronika*, Vol. 5, p. 281. Although Shlikhter's achievements in this post were highly regarded by Lenin and other leaders, he had become a liability through alienating the 'bourgeois specialists' in the central offices of the commissariat whose cooperation was regarded as necessary.

20 *Protokoly TsK*, p. 180.

21 See *Lenin: khronika*, Vol. 5, pp. 220–1.

22 *Ibid.*, p. 223; *DSV*, Vol. 1, p. 588.

23 *Lenin: khronika*, Vol. 5, pp. 323–4. This source mentions specifically only the appointment of Stuchka as People's Commissar of Justice (with Krasikov to act temporarily in his place), of P. P. Malinovsky as acting People's Commissar for Properties of the Republic, and of Vinokurov as Deputy People's Commissar of Welfare, but it is possible that one or two other decisions were taken at this meeting. Five days earlier Lenin had signed a Sovnarkom decision described by this same source as relating to 'new appointments to the Army Department and the People's Commissariat of Foreign Affairs' (*Ibid.*, p. 314). The text of this decision has not been located, but it almost certainly refers to Trotsky's transfer from the post of People's Commissar for Foreign Affairs to that of People's Commissar for the Army, and to Chicherin's confirmation as Acting People's Commissar for Foreign Affairs. Trotsky had told a stormy Central Committee meeting on 24 February that, while resigning as Foreign Affairs Commissar and withdrawing from the work of Sovnarkom and the CEC, he agreed to this not being made public for the time being, in contrast with the Left Communists, who sought the maximum publicity for their resignations. See *Protokoly TsK*, p. 225. The question of the Navy Commissariat posed by Dybenko's resignation was solved by the transfer of this portfolio to him as well, and this may have been agreed on at the Sovnarkom meeting of 18 March.

On 24 March the CEC approved Trotsky's appointment as 'Military Commissar for Army and Navy Affairs'. See *Protokoly zasedanii Vserossiiskogo Tsentral'nogo Ispolnitel'nogo Komiteta IV-go sozyva. Stenograficheskii otchët*, Moscow, 1920 (cited hereafter as *VTsIK IV: Protokoly*), p. 4.

24 *Lenin: khronika*, Vol. 5, p. 318.

25 *Ibid.*, p. 356. Officially Sereda was appointed Deputy People's Commissar, but his choice as People's Commissar for Agriculture was probably settled by this time. There were evidently technical difficulties to formalising this, connected with delays in Kolegaev's vacating the post (*ibid.*, p. 384). By mid-May at the latest, he was being referred to as people's commissar (*ibid.*, p. 460), although no formal decision on this has been located. In relation to our estimate of the minor role of the Central Committee in Sovnarkom appointments at this time, it should be noted that the Bureau of the Central Committee (see Chapter 12) may have discussed some of them. It evidently did in the case of Rykov, but only to the extent of approving his appointment on the day *after* it had been decided by Sovnarkom. See Iroshnikov, 1974, p. 101.

26 *Ibid.*, p. 498.

27 *Ibid.*, p. 368.

28 See *Protokoly TsK*, pp. 284–5.

29 *Ibid.*, p. 180.

30 *Lenin: khronika*, Vol. 5, p. 234.

31 *Ibid.*, p. 277. It is impossible to do justice here to the complexities of the regime's relationships with the Railwaymen's Union during this period. See Jay B. Sorenson, *The Life and Death of Soviet Trade Unionism 1917–1928*, New York, 1969, pp. 45–54.

32 Lenin had only one recorded contact with him during his period as commissar, compared with eight with his ostensible deputy, Nevsky (*Lenin: khronika*, Vol. 5, *passim*). Soviet historical and general encyclopedias usually pass over Rogov in silence, while referring to Nevsky as People's Commissar for Railways 'from the October Revolution', without mentioning his serving as Deputy People's Commissar under Rogov and the latter's immediate successor, Kobozev. Nevsky makes the same claim in his autobiographical sketch in the Granat Encyclopedia (Vol. 41, chast' 1, Col. 80). However, two articles about him appearing in Soviet journals in the mid-1960s mention that he served as Deputy before becoming People's Commissar (*Voprosy istorii KPSS*, 1966, no. 5, p. 101 and *Istoriya SSSR*, 1967, no. 1, p. 107).

33 See *DSV*, Vol. 2, pp. 12–21. The disorganisation of transport was one of the most serious problems facing the regime at this time, and Lenin indicated the exceptional importance he attached to the issue in his article 'Current Tasks of Soviet Power'. See Lenin, *PSS*, Vol. 36, p. 198ff.

34 For brief biographies of Kobozev, see *BSE*, 3rd edn., Vol. 12, p. 353, and Lenin, *PSS*, Vol. 50, pp. 533–4. The latter makes no mention of

his serving as Transport Commissar. More detailed information about his activities in 1918 is contained in *Lenin: khronika*, Vol. 5, *passim*. Between January and May 1918 he was entrusted by Sovnarkom with 'exceptional powers' to suppress political and armed opposition in the Urals, Central Asia and the Baku area. It seems that Lenin interviewed him shortly before his appointment as Transport Commissar, since there is a record of his writing Kobozev's address and telephone number on the latter's visiting card and requesting his secretary to enter it in his address book. See *Lenin: khronika*, Vol. 5, p. 438.

35 See *VTsIK IV: Protokoly*, pp. 366–73. At a meeting of the CEC held significantly while the Railwaymen's Congress was in session, a report on the railways was delivered by Nevsky, who made faint efforts to defend Kobozev, but the latter's methods were vigorously assailed in a co-report by M. F. Krushinsky, a Bolshevik railwayman who was on the Board of the Transport Commissariat. An even sharper attack on his 'dictatorship', however, came from an unidentified 'voice from the hall' when the discussion on Nevsky's report was gagged (*ibid.*).

36 See *Lenin: khronika*, Vol. 5, pp. 665–6. Cf. Iroshnikov, 1974, p. 101.

37 'The Government of the Federation, the Council of People's Commissars, is elected and replaced, as a whole or in part, by the All-Russian Congress of Soviets or the All-Russian Central Executive Committee.' *Istoriya Sovetskoi Konstitutsii. Sbornik dokumentov 1917–1956*, p. 57.

38 *VTsIK IV: Protokoly*, p. 40. To take another example, on 9 May CEC Secretary Avanesov proposed the endorsement of Lander's and Kobozev's appointments in the following terms: 'I place before you for approval two People's Commissars proposed by Sovnarkom, Cde Lander as Commissar for State Control and railway engineer Kobozev as Transport Commissar, and propose them for approval in the usual way. Who is for the proposal and who against? Two against. So the proposal is carried.' (*Ibid.*, p. 241.) The formality of securing CEC approval of Government appointments was normally (though not invariably) observed during this period. For endorsement of the appointments of Trotsky, Rykov and Podbelsky, see *ibid.*, pp. 4, 107. However, as in the period before the Fourth Congress of Soviets, persons approved as Deputy (i.e. Acting) People's Commissar continued on occasion to assume the duties and title of People's Commissar without specific endorsement as such by CEC. This was evidently the case, for instance, with Sereda (see above, n. 25).

39 Not one of the six people's commissars appointed between the Fifth and Sixth Congress of Soviets was presented for endorsement by the CEC. See *Pyatyi sozyv Vserossiiskogo Tsentral'nogo Ispolnitel'nogo Komiteta rabochikh krestyanskikh, kazachikh i krasnoarmeiskikh deputatov. Stenograficheskii otchët*, Moscow, 1919, *passim* (cited hereafter as *VTsK V: Sten. otchët*). However, it seems likely that

appointments began to be formalised by the CEC Presidium from this time. On 25 July, just after the Fifth Congress of Soviets, Sverdlov sent Lenin a note asking him to be sure to put Nevsky's appointment as Transport Commissar through Sovnarkom at its meeting that evening, so it could be approved by the CEC, and Lenin duly complied (*Lenin: khronika*, Vol. 5, pp. 665–6). Since there was to be a further Sovnarkom meeting before the next meeting of the CEC on 29 July, and Nevsky's appointment was not in fact mentioned in the protocols of any CEC meeting, it seems likely that it was a meeting of the CEC Presidium that Sverdlov had in mind in his note to Lenin.

40 *Sed'moi Vserossiiskii Syezd Sovetov rabochikh, krestyanskikh, krasnoarmeiskikh i kazachikh deputatov. Stenograficheskii otchët*, Moscow, 1920 (cited hereafter as *VII Syezd Sovetov*), p. 61.

41 See *Sessii Vserossiiskogo Tsentral'nogo Ispolnitel'nogo Komiteta VIII Sozyva. Stenograficheskii otchët*, Moscow, 1921 (cited hereafter as *VTsIK VIII: Sten. otchët*), p. 20, and *I i II Sessii Vserossiiskogo Tsentral'nogo Ispolnitel'nogo Komiteta IX Sozyva. Stenograficheskii otchët*, Moscow, 1923 (cited hereafter as *VTsIK IX: I i II sessii*), p. 4.

42 Biographical information on Sovnarkom members cited in this chapter and the next has been culled from a wide range of sources, of which the single most valuable one was the collection of biographies and autobiographies *Deyateli Soyuza Sovetskikh Sotsialisticheskikh Respublik i Oktyabr'skoi Revolyutsii*, Moscow, n.d., published as Vol. 41 of the *Entsiklopediya Granat* and photo-reprinted by Univercity Microfilms, Ann Arbor, Mi., 1970. Other sources included the three editions of the *Bol'shaya sovetskaya entsiklopediya*, the *Sovetskaya istoricheskaya entsiklopediya*, and biographical notes appended to Lenin's *PSS* and to the stenographic reports of party congresses. It would be unwieldy to give specific references for each item of information obtained from these sources, but where additional information is provided by other authorities is used, these are cited.

43 See *DSV*, Vol. 1, pp. 403–4. It was originally proposed to Sovnarkom that the Council Chairman have the status of People's Commissar, but instead he was merely granted the right to attend Sovnarkom meetings in a consultative capacity. See also *Lenin: khronika*, Vol. 5, p. 230. The Council was chaired by the Bolshevik A. N. Vinokurov, a doctor by profession who later succeeded Kollontai as People's Commissar for Social Security.

44 See *Lenin: khronika*, Vol. 5, pp. 559, 581, 593, 627.

45 See N. A. Semashko, *Prozhitoe i perezhitoe. Vospominaniya*, Moscow, 1960, Chapter IX; A. I. Nesterenko, *Kak byl obrazovan Narodnyi Komissariat zdravookhraneniya RSFSR. Iz istorii sovetskogo zdravookhraneniya (Oktyabr' 1917–iyul' 1918g.)*, Moscow, 1965, Chapters I–II, IV–V; Z. Tikhonova, *Narodnyi Komissar Zdorovya (O N. A. Semashko)*, Moscow, 1960, pp. 17–21, M. Chachko, *Povest' o narodnom komissare*, Moscow, 1972, pp. 183–5; M. I. Barsukov, *Velikaya Oktyabr'skaya sotsialisticheskaya revolyutsiya i organizatsiya*

sovetskogo zdravookhraneniya (*Oktyabr' 1917g.–iyul' 1918g.*), Moscow, 1951.

46 See *Lenin: khronika*, Vol. 5, p. 516. As Labour Commissar Shmidt was to prove on the whole a dependable agent of the party–government leadership in their delicate and conflict-ridden relationship with the unions, in contrast with his predecessor Shlyapnikov, who became a leader of the Workers' Opposition. See Sorenson, pp. 91–2.

47 This statement is based mainly on the reported agenda of Sovnarkom and Central Committee meetings in *Lenin: khronika*, Vols. 5 and 6, *passim*. See also V. V. Anikeyev, *Deyatel'nost' Tsentral'nogo Komiteta RSDRP(b)–RKP(b) v 1917–1918 godakh. Khronika sobytii*, Moscow, 1974, *passim*. For the decree embodying Semashko's appointment see *DSV*, Vol. 3, pp. 3–4; this in fact appointed him *Acting* (*ispolnyayushchii dolzhnost'*) People's Commissar, pending endorsement by the CEC but, as we have noted, the CEC ceased dealing with individual government changes from about this time and in fact Semashko began to be referred to almost immediately as 'People's Commissar'; there is no record of this being formalised by any further Sovnarkom meeting.

48 Kursky had served as Acting Justice Commissar in April–May 1918 during an absence of the recently appointed People's Commissar Stuchka, and on the latter's return was his principal deputy. In August Stuchka was relieved of his portfolio at his own request, serving briefly on the Board of the Foreign Affairs Commissariat and then heading the short-lived Soviet government of his native Latvia. (See *DSV*, Vol. 2, p. 634; *Lenin: khronika*, Vol. 5, pp. 354, 371, 430, 560 and Vol. 6, p. 88.) Kursky's biographies refer to his assuming the role of People's Commissar from this time, but there is no record of this being decided at the meeting of any official body.

49 See Anikeyev, pp. 408–9, *Lenin: khronika*, Vol. 6, p. 129. The Central Committee decided on 16 September that Shmidt should become Labour Commissar, but according to his biographies he did not formally take up the post until November. The first decree signed by him as Labour Commissar is dated 27 October. See *SU* 1918: 79/830. There is no record, however, of Sovnarkom's considering the appointment in the meantime. The decision to transfer the Labour portfolio to Shmidt was taken against the background of ructions in the commissariat which culminated in the despatch of his predecessor Shlyapnikov to the first of what proved to be a series of Civil War military-political commands.

50 See *Lenin: khronika*, Vol. 6, p. 598.

51 Latsis, 1926, p. 94. The reasons attributed by Dzerzhinsky's lieutenant, Latsis, for his resisting the incorporation of the Vecheka into the Internal Affairs Commissariat were that the former was an 'exceptional' organ which should not form a permanent part of the Soviet government apparatus, and that it would look bad for the revolutionary regime to emulate its Tsarist predecessor in combining within the one government department central control over local

government and the regular and political police. These views acquire a certain irony in the light of the subsequent history of the political police in the USSR.

52 For the decree on the 1919 reorganisation, see *DSV*, Vol. 5, pp. 46–51, and for that establishing Rabkrin, see *DSV*, Vol. 7, pp. 208–15. On the early period of the State Control Commissariat and the formation of Rabkrin, see G. A. Dorokhova, *Raboche-krestyanskaya inspektsiya v 1920–1923gg.*, Moscow, 1959, Introduction and Chapter 1, Section 1; S. N. Ikonnikov, *Organizatsiya i deyatel'nost' RKI v 1920–1925gg.*, Moscow, 1960, Chapter 1, and V. I. Turovtsev, *Gosudarstvennyi i obshchestvennyi kontrol' v SSSR*, Moscow, 1970, pp. 63–5.

53 See *Vysshiye organy gosudarstvennoi vlasti i organy tsentral'nogo upravleniya RSFSR (1917–1967gg). Spravochnik*, Moscow, 1971, pp. 438–9; *Devyatyi syezd RKP(b)*, pp. 40–1, 492. Sovnarkom had long been plagued by the problem of jurisdictional boundaries between the Labour and Social Security Commissariats. See, e.g., *Lenin: khronika*, Vol. 7, p. 23.

54 See *The Trotsky Papers*, Vol. II, p. 117. Though Trotsky was duly appointed *Acting* Transport Commissar (*Izvestiya*, 23 March 1920), he was soon being referred to simply as People's Commissar (The Trotsky Archive, doc. 519, *The Trotsky Papers*, Vol. II, p. 308). Nevertheless, Krasin was still regarded as at least formally in charge, and was only released on the appointment of Yemshanov. See *Leninskii sbornik* XXXVII, p. 270. Cf. *The Trotsky Papers*, Vol. II, p. 334.

55 Trotsky himself makes no bones about the 'administrative methods' he used in the railways. See his *Moya Zhizn'*, Vol. II, pp. 197–201.

56 *Vos'moi Vserossiiskii Syezd Sovetov, rabochikh, krestyanskikh, krasnoarmeiskikh i kazachikh deputatov. Stenograficheskii otchët*, Moscow, 1921 (cited hereafter as *VIII syezd sovetov*), p. 174.

57 See *Leninskii sbornik*, XXXVII, pp. 270–1. Lenin also proposed to Serebryakov that the key Board member Lomonosov be required to enter into a written obligation 'to make no changes either in Trotsky's system or his decisions' (*ibid.*).

58 *Ibid.*, XXXVII, p. 295.

59 See Lenin, *PSS*, Vol. 52, p. 140, Bonch-Bruyevich, *Vospominaniya o Lenine*, pp. 271–2; N. Zubov, *F. E. Dzerzhinskii. Biografiya*, Moscow, 1963, pp. 266–7; A. V. Tishkov, *Pervyi Chekist*, Moscow, 1968, pp. 110–11.

60 This account is based mainly on analysis of correspondence and notes in Lenin, *PSS*, vols. 52 and 53, *passim*. See also Yu. A. Polyakov, *Perekhod k NEPu i sovetskoye krestyanstvo*, Moscow, 1967, pp. 369–370. Lenin came stoutly to Osinsky's defence when he encountered criticism soon after his appointment to the Agriculture Commissariat (Lenin, *PSS*, Vol. 52, p. 61). Osinsky was *rapporteur* on agricultural matters at meetings of the CEC, e.g. on the spring sowing campaign on 19 March 1921 (*VTsIK VIII: sten. otchët*, p. 98ff.) and also at

the Ninth Congress of Soviets in December 1921 (*Devyatyi Vseros-siiskii Syezd rabochikh, krestyanskikh, krasnoarmeiskikh i kazachikh deputatov. Stenograficheskii otchët*, Moscow, 1922, p. 97ff.). At the first session of the CEC following the latter, the list of Sovnarkom members presented for endorsement included him as Deputy Commissar for Agriculture (*VTsIK IX: I i II sessii*, p. 4) and as late as the Eleventh Party Congress in March 1922 Lenin referred to him as leading the Commissariat (*Odinnadtsatyi syezd RKP(b), Mart–aprel' 1922 goda. Stenograficheskii otchët*, Moscow, 1961 (cited hereafter as *Odinnadtsatyi syezd RKP(b)*), p. 144.

61 See *Leninskii sbornik*, XXXVI, p. 163, and Lenin, *PSS*, Vol. 52, p. 85–6.
62 Yu. V. Zhurov, 'V. G. Yakovenko', *Istoriya SSSR*, no. 3, 1969, p. 112ff.
63 In May 1921 Yakovenko had been one of the authors of a memorandum addressed jointly to Lenin, the Central Committee and the CEC, complaining about the strongarm methods of the Siberian Food Supplies Commissar, P. Kaganovich, in violation of the new NEP approach to the peasantry (see Polyakov, p. 244). However, it seems unlikely that Lenin remembered this or that it was a direct factor in Yakovenko's appointment.
64 Lenin, *PSS*, Vol. 54, pp. 80–1.
65 *Ibid.*, pp. 85, 92–4.
66 Polyakov, p. 370, dates the Politburo decision to appoint Yakovenko to 26 December, but according to the editors of Lenin's *PSS* (Vol. 54, p. 587) it was only on 26 December that the Politburo approved Lenin's proposal to summon Yakovenko to Moscow. In the course of Yakovenko's interview with Lenin, he extracted a promise from the latter to provide funds to assist the peasants of his native district, who had been ruined (like millions of others) during the Civil War, if he would agree to serve as People's Commissar. See Zhurov, p. 120.
67 See Lenin, *PSS*, Vol. 54, p. 262; Polyakov, p. 370. Osinsky and Teodorovich continued to feud, and the former was removed from the commissariat in January 1923, to be replaced by A. P. Smirnov, who took over from Yakovenko as People's Commissar six months later. Yakovenko was transferred to the less sensitive post of Social Security Commissar.
68 The transformation in February 1922 of Vecheka into the Chief Political Directorate (GPU) attached to (*pri*) the People's Commissariat of Internal Affairs involved no change in the membership of Sovnarkom, since Dzerzhinsky remained in charge.
69 Based on analysis of Lenin's correspondence with representatives of the commissariat in *PSS*, Vols. 53 and 54.
70 See Lenin, *PSS*, Vol. 54, pp. 106, 592.
71 *Ibid.*, pp. 137–8, 601.
72 *Ibid.*, pp. 219, 224, 634. The evidence suggests that most of the leadership were less enthusiastic about Krasnoshchëkov than was Lenin, who saw him as a practical administrator with a sympathetic understanding of commerce, qualities of particular importance under NEP and rare among Bolsheviks.

CHAPTER II: THE PEOPLE'S COMMISSARS:
PERSONAL BACKGROUND

1 For sources of biographical information used in this chapter, see
   Chapter 10, note 42.
2 See Zubov, 1963, p. 10.
3 Lander tells part of this story in his autobiography in the Granat
   Encyclopedia, and a fuller account may be found in V. Ye. Baranchenko, 'Karl Lander', *Voprosy istorii*, 1971, no. 1, pp. 200–4.
   Tolstoy's influence was evidently instrumental in securing his release
   after a later arrest. After the Revolution Tregubov became the leading spokesman for a curious 'party' of Communist-Sectarians, and as
   such addressed the Seventh and Eighth Congresses of Soviets, appealing at the latter for a halt to persecution of his members. See *VII
   syezd sovetov*, pp. 274–6 and *VIII syezd sovetov*, pp. 226–8.
4 See Anton Rakitin, *V. A. Antonov-Ovseyenko: Dokumental'nyi
   biograficheskii ocherk*, Leningrad, 1975, Chapter 1.
5 In general, the period from about 1907, when the Tsarist government
   had regained firm control of the country and begun to crack down
   again on the revolutionaries, was one of deep disillusionment that
   affected particularly the middle-class intellectuals in the party, many
   of whom reduced or totally ceased their involvement in political
   activity.
6 Periods spent in prison, hard labour or exile are classified as 'professional' years, while periods of total withdrawal from political
   activity are treated as 'amateur' years, as are periods spent on full-
   time courses of professional training. In the few cases where available
   biographical sources leave some doubt as to the precise periods
   involved, the closest possible estimate is made and in classifying
   'borderline' cases an attempt is made to balance such uncertainties.
7 The 1917 list comprises, as well as those approved by the Second
   Congress of Soviets, the Bolsheviks appointed to additional Sovnarkom
   posts in the ensuing weeks (Kollontai, Essen, Osinsky and Yelizarov),
   and is thus a list of *initial* Bolshevik appointments, even though
   certain of the Second Congress of Soviets appointees departed before
   certain of the additional members were installed. Yelizarov is included because he came to be treated and referred to as People's
   Commissar, though formally appointed only as Acting ('Temporary
   Deputy') People's Commissar. Similarly the 1922 list includes
   Sokolnikov, who had been exercising the responsibilities of People's
   Commissar for over a year, though not yet formally appointed as
   such. For names, see the full list of Sovnarkom members, showing
   period in office, in Appendix A, and the checklist in Appendix B.
8 In the cases of the fatherless Lander and Shmidt, their mothers'
   occupation is used. The 'other upper and middle class' and 'other
   lower class' categories comprise fathers holding miscellaneous known
   positions as well as a few whose precise occupations are unknown.

The dichotomising by class presented little difficulty except for two borderline cases: a white-collar employee in a factory, whom we classified as middle-class, and a shop assistant, classified as lower class.

9　The 1897 census showed that 1.2 million out of a total population of 126 million were members of the hereditary gentry, while a further 600,000 were persons enjoying conferred gentry status by virtue of service, usually in the upper ranks of the state bureaucracy. The latter group had roughly doubled by 1917. It is uncertain what proportion of the gentry fathers of our people's commissars had hereditary and what proportion conferred status.

10　*Sovetskaya istoricheskaya entsiklopediya*, Vol. 16, Moscow, 1976, col. 602–3. On people's commissar Essen, see 'Ob E. E. Essene', *Krasnaya letopis'*, 1931, no. 3, pp. 142–56.

11　See David Lane, *The Roots of Russian Communism: a Social and Historical Study of Russian Social-Democracy 1898–1907*, Amsterdam, 1969, pp. 39–46.

12　See T. H. Rigby, 'The Soviet Political Elite 1917–1922', *The British Journal of Political Science*, Vol. I, Part IV, October 1971 (cited hereafter as Rigby, 1971), p. 267.

13　Here we might distinguish between a Vasilii Vladimirovich Shmidt, whose impeccably Russian Christian name and patronymic belie the German surname, and an Eduard Eduardovich Essen, whose family, though assimilated into the Russian elite, manifested in their children's names a continued attachment to their Baltic German (originally Swedish) roots. Essen, incidentally, dropped the parental 'von'. Kollontai writes of her parents: 'My father was a Russian General, Ukrainian by birth. My mother was a native of Finland, of a peasant family.' Yet her lifelong friend Elena Stasova describes her unequivocally as a 'wonderful Russian woman' (see A. M. Itkina, *Revolyutsioner, tribun, diplomat: ocherk zhizni Aleksandry Mikhailovnoi Kollontai*, Moscow, 1964, p. 3), and there seem no grounds for disputing her Russianness. Or, for that matter, Lunacharsky's or Kursky's, though both were born in the Ukraine and the latter had a Ukrainian mother. In the cases of Podbelsky, Semashko, Sereda and Tsyurupa, however, available information leaves it unclear as to how completely their families were assimilated. The question of assimilation also arises in the case of the Jewish members of Sovnarkom, none of whom came from traditional Jewish families: Trotsky's father was a farmer well outside the Pale of Settlement, Sokolnikov's was a doctor and Kamenev's an engineer. The last-named certainly grew up in a predominantly Russian milieu.

14　For comparison with the overall party membership, see Rigby, 1968, Chapter 11, and with the inner circles of the party, see Rigby, 1971, p. 265.

15　Some doubt attaches to two of the people's commissars classified here as graduates. Milyutin attended St Petersburg University and was later employed as an economist, but available sources do not state whether or not he had completed his university studies. Sereda evidently held some post-secondary qualification, since he was employed by public bodies as a statistician, but no details have been established.

16 In identifying basic occupation, spells of casual work undertaken for 'cover' or living expenses between bouts of arrest or 'underground' activity are discounted, as also are brief periods of intermittent or part-time work after graduation where the person concerned (as in Lenin's case) is already firmly set on the path of revolution. Also discounted is employment up to the age of sixteen, as well as military service as a wartime conscript. Several people's commissars had extensive journalistic experience but, as this took the form of writing for revolutionary publications, it is not treated here as an occupation separate from that of 'revolutionary'.

CHAPTER 12: GOVERNMENT, SOVIETS AND PARTY

1 See T. D. Ionkina, *Vserossiiskiye syezdy sovetov v pervye gody proletarskoi diktatury*, Moscow, 1974, p. 200. The best account of the soviets in the revolutionary and Civil War periods is Oskar Anweiler, *Die Rätebewegung in Russland 1905–1921*, Leiden, 1958, Chapters IV and V.

2 A useful collection of documents relating to the early all-Russian congresses will be found in *Syezdy sovetov SSSR, soyuznykh respublik i avtonomnykh sovetskikh sotsialisticheskikh respublik. Sbornik dokumentov*, Vol. 1, Moscow, 1959, at pp. 3–242.

3 At the Third Congress criticism was focused on the Bolshevik proposals for the federal structure of the Soviet Republic. Martov assailed these on behalf of the Mensheviks and there was also Left SR criticism, albeit somewhat muted, which resulted in a number of amendments to the legislation in the direction of strengthening local powers. See *Tretii Vserossiiskii Syezd Sovetov rabochikh, soldatskikh i krestyanskikh deputatov* (no place or date), pp. 75–82. At the Fourth Congress opposition to the Brest-Litovsk treaty was voiced by representatives of the Left and Right SRs, the Mensheviks, the United Internationalists and the Anarchists. See *Stenograficheskii otchët 4-go Chrezychainogo Syezda Sovetov rabochikh, soldatskikh, krestyanskikh i kazachikh deputatov*, Moscow, 1920, pp. 23–47. This Congress was also the scene of the breach of party discipline by the 'Left Communists', who read their declaration opposed to the treaty, *ibid.*, p. 67. The Fifth, which opened shortly after a decision had been taken to expel all Mensheviks and Right SRs from the soviets, opened with an assault by the Left SRs on the Bolsheviks' conciliation of the Germans and their repressive and exploitative policies towards the peasants. The attempted Left SR coup in the course of the Congress led to the arrest of most SR members, after which there were few

deputies left to criticise, only the Maximalist Polyansky managing to urge against excessive centralisation. See *Pyatyi Vserossiiskii Syezd Sovetov rabochikh, krestyanskikh, krasnoarmeiskikh i kazachikh deputatov. Stenograficheskii otchët*, Moscow, 1918, pp. 191–3; Chamberlin, Vol. II, pp. 49–56. There was no dissent at the Sixth Congress in November 1918.

4   See Ionkina, pp. 118, 225.

5   See Carr, Vol. I, pp. 179–83. At the Seventh and Eighth Congresses the Menshevik leaders Martov and Dan displayed great courage in criticising the repressive arbitrariness of the regime against the constant abuse and catcalls of the massed Bolshevik delegates. See, e.g. *VII syezd sovetov*, p. 6off.; *VIII syezd sovetov*, pp. 33–42, 54–7. Cf. Israel Getzler, *Martov. A Political Biography of a Russian Social Democrat*, Cambridge–Melbourne, 1967, Chapter 8.

6   Bolshevik criticism was most outspoken at the Seventh Congress (see especially Sapronov's speech in *VII syezd sovetov*, pp. 196–202), was more restrained at the Eighth, and from the Ninth on was extremely mild.

7   This may be illustrated by the fact that when Lenin was granted sick leave at the end of 1921 and forbidden to work, an exception was made for his preparing and delivering his report to the Ninth Congress of Soviets.

8   *DSV*, Vol. I, pp. 29–30.

9   *DSV*, Vol. I, p. 41. See John L. H. Keep, *The Russian Revolution. A Study in Mass Mobilization*, New York, 1977, pp. 317–19. For the arguments in the CEC on 2 and 3 November over the coalition issue, see *Protokoly zasedanii Vserossiiskogo Tsentral'nogo Ispolnitel'nogo Komiteta Sovetov rabochikh, soldatskikh, krestyanskikh i kazachikh deputatov, II, sozyv, 27 oktyabrya–29 dekabrya 1917*, pp. 21ff., 135ff.

10 The party composition of successive convocations of the CEC is tabulated in K. G. Fedorov, *VTsIK v pervye gody sovetskoi vlasti 1917–1920gg.*, Moscow, 1957, p. 40.

11 See *DSV*, Vol. I, pp. 36–9; Pietsch, pp. 63–4.

12 See *Vysshiye organy gosudarsvennoi vlasti i organy gosudarstvennogo upravleniya RSFSR (1919–1967gg.) Spravochnik*, p. 37.

13 *DSV*, Vol. I, p. 102; Pietsch, p. 64. The instruction also prescribed that people's commissars were to make weekly reports to the CEC and that questions signed by at least fifteen CEC members were to receive immediate reply, but the published record affords little evidence that these provisions were implemented.

14 See Keep, pp. 322–3.

15 *DSV*, Vol. I, p. 88. The 101 original members of the CEC had meanwhile been increased by cooption to 108, so the total membership was now 366.

16 Keep, p. 321. A similar Bureau had operated within the First (pre-October) CEC. The Bureau does not seem to have established itself as a regularly functioning body, and the unwieldiness of the full CEC was mitigated by the relatively low attendance levels. Decisions, even

important ones, were not infrequently taken without the legal quorum of fifty per cent.

17 *Protokoly zasedanii Vserossiiskogo Tsentral'nogo Ispolnitel'nogo Komiteta rabochikh, soldatskikh, krestyanskikh i kazachikh deputatov, II sozyv*, p. 85. Lenin hastily interrupted a Sovnarkom meeting in order for its members to dash over to the CEC to register their votes on this issue. See *Lenin: khronika*, Vol. 5, p. 81.

18 See p. 28. At the same time the coalition parties did not always maintain a united front at CEC meetings in this period. For instance, the left SRs opposed the Bolshevik decree suppressing the Cadet party at the meeting of 28 November, the vote on this measure reportedly being 150 for and ninety-eight against. See Steinberg, pp. 57–61. Unfortunately stenographic reports of the meetings of the CEC elected by the Third Congress of Soviets were never published.

19 At this Congress the CEC membership was reduced to 207, of whom 141 were Bolsheviks, forty-eight Left SRs and eighteen from other parties. The introduction of revised CEC rules at the meeting of 15 April was one issue provoking vigorous criticism from Left SR, Menshevik and Anarchist delegates over existing relationships between Sovnarkom and the Soviets but none of the many amendments proposed were accepted by the Bolsheviks. See *VTsIK IV: Protokoly*, p. 128ff.

20 See, e.g., *VTsIK IV: Protokoly*, pp. 110–11, 137, 403–12. Despite the safe majority enjoyed by Lenin's supporters in the CEC elected by the Fourth Congress of Soviets, its meetings were often very lively affairs. On less contentious issues its debates sometimes led to Sovnarkom spokesmen accepting amendments to legislation they were introducing, e.g. on the law on the consumer cooperatives discussed on 4 April (*ibid.*, pp. 106–9). It also served as a forum in which aggrieved groups could register their protests against actions of the regime; e.g. the Anarchists assailed the violent destruction of their headquarters by the Cheka (*ibid.*, pp. 109–10). Furthermore, there were reports by commissariats on their activities, which sometimes came in for vigorous criticism; e.g., the debate on the Finance Commissar's report (*ibid.*, pp. 117–52), which was assailed by Bukharin on behalf of the 'Left Communists' as well as by representatives of other parties. At the Fifth Congress of Soviets Sverdlov was to claim that Left SRs had been relatively mild in their opposition in the early days of the outgoing CEC, but towards the end had opposed the Government on all major issues, making common cause with the opposition parties. See Sverdlov, Vol. 2, p. 236.

21 Carr, Vol. 1, p. 136. Chapter 6 of this work is one of the two most useful non-Soviet discussions of the making of the 1918 Constitution, the other being Pietsch, Chapter VI. The most valuable Soviet source is G. S. Gurvich, *Istoriya Sovetskoi Konstitutsii*, Moscow, 1923. The Commission was chaired by Sverdlov, and its fifteen members included two Left Communists, two Left SRs and one Socialist-Revolutionary-Maximalist.

22 See Pietsch, pp. 83–4. A symbolic gesture to the proponents of merging Sovnarkom with the CEC was a reference to the people's commissariats as departments under the CEC. This never possessed any practical significance since relations between the commissariats and the CEC were always mediated through Sovnarkom.

23 At the same time the CEC under Sverdlov's direction made considerable use of 'plenipotentiaries', chosen from CEC members or officials and despatched to regional and local soviets where central policies were not being properly implemented. See Fedorov, Chapter 2, Section 1. The main channel for this up to April 1918 was the CEC's Other Cities Department, which was headed by Sverdlov himself. *Ibid.*, pp. 82–4.

24 There is some uncertainty as to just how early in 1919 the CEC stopped convening. Cf. M. Kareva, 'Vserossiiskii Tsentral'nyi Ispolnitel'nyi Komitet (1918–1922gg.)', *Bor'ba klassov*, 1936, no. 12, p. 66; L. I. Antonova, 'VTsIK i ego Prezidium v 1917–1922gg.', *Sovetskoye gosudarstvo i pravo* 1967, no. 10, p. 33; Pietsch, pp. 111, 119. However, when at the Seventh Congress of Soviets in December 1919 Martov claimed that the CEC had not met over the past year this was not denied by the Bolsheviks, Trotsky simply interjecting, 'They were at the front!' See *VII syezd sovetov*, p. 60. No stenographic reports of meetings of the CEC elected by the Sixth Congress of Soviets were published, and it is clear that decrees issued in the name of the CEC at this period were usually adopted by its Presidium on the initiative of Sovnarkom.

25 Only two cases of dissent from Government policies have been discovered in the reports of the CEC elected by the Fifth Congress. See *VTsIK V: Sten. otchët*, pp. 100–2, 287–8.

26 The Internal Affairs Commissariat began to play a part in this from the end of 1917 and in the first half of 1918 its role grew rapidly, owing largely to its control of funds allocated to subsidise local government services. See 'K istorii organizatsii sovetskogo gosudarstvennogo apparata (1917–1918gg.)', *Istoricheskii arkhiv*, 1956, no. 5, pp. 64–87. In April 1918 it took over from the CEC the latter's Other Cities Department, with its function of sending out 'plenipotentiaries' to the provinces. See Fedorov, p. 84.

27 See Pietsch, Chapter VII. These bodies made their greatest inroads into the role of the soviets during 1919, but the process began earlier. As early as May 1918 when the Food Supplies Commissariat had been authorised to use armed detachments to seize 'surplus' grain from the peasants the relevant decree empowered it to dissolve all local bodies which resisted or 'disorganised' its work, and to arrest their officials. See *DSV*, Vol. 2, pp. 264–6. During the debate in the CEC on this decree Tsyurupa added the gloss that any local soviets that did not fully cooperate would be dealt with by armed force as enemies in the Civil War. See *VTsIK IV: Protokoly*, p. 260. Likewise the local Military Councils accepted the authority only of Trotsky's Supreme R.M.C. in Moscow, and the manner in which this

led to the reduction of the executive committees of the soviets to a cipher though this had never been intended by the leadership, was clearly described by Sapronov at the Seventh Congress of Soviets. See *VII syezd sovetov*, p. 198. In the second half of 1918 the machinery of the soviets in the rural areas had been left hanging in the air through the replacement of the Left SR-dominated village soviets by Poor Peasants Committees (the village soviets were later revived). Moreover, even those local departments over which the soviets had nominal control were progressively converted into field offices of the corresponding commissariats in Moscow. See *VII syezd sovetov*, pp. 197–200.

28 *Vos'moi syezd RKP(b). Mart 1919 goda. Protokoly*, Moscow, 1959, p. 543, note 71 (cited hereafter as *Vos'moi syezd RKP(b)*).

29 *Ibid.*, pp. 191, 194–7. Other delegates shared his views on the drift to 'bureaucratisation' and the usurpation by central agencies of the rights of local soviets, especially his fellow-Muscovite Sapronov. See *ibid.*, pp. 201–3.

30 *Ibid.*, pp. 222–3.

31 *Ibid.*, p. 427.

32 *SU* 1919, 64/578.

33 *Ibid.* The Seventh Congress resolution 'On Soviet Construction' was the first authoritative formulation of the Presidium's position and powers – the 1918 Constitution had merely mentioned its existence incidentally. This resolution – which also embodied the decision on CEC sessions referred to as well as provisions regarding the congresses of soviets and the local soviets – was based on a draft prepared by an Administrative Commission of the CEC Presidium and Sovnarkom (set up on the latter's initiative), and approved by the Eighth Party Conference on the eve of the Congress of Soviets. See *Vlast' sovetov*, 1919, no. 12, pp. 8–9 and *Vos'maya konferentsiya RKP(b). Protokoly*, Moscow, 1961, pp. 60–2.

34 The illusoriness of any hopes that the Presidium would now act independently of Sovnarkom was pithily demonstrated at the Seventh Congress of Soviets by Avanesov, who had been CEC Secretary up to this time. 'Over the two years of its existence', he said, 'the CEC has brought forward perhaps two, three or four draft decrees of its own. Generally draft decrees are introduced by the people's commissariats, by Sovnarkom or other government agencies. The Presidium will not be adopting any decrees on its own initiative.' *VII syezd sovetov*, p. 235.

35 *Devyatyi syezd RKP(b)*, pp. 41–2. Krestinsky went on to cite an example of the Central Committee's calling the Presidium to order when it had acted outside these parameters. A. S. Kiselev, soon to emerge as one of the leaders of the Workers' Opposition, contested Krestinsky's interpretation of the Congress of Soviets Resolution, charging the Central Committee with frustrating the latter's implementation by its petty interference with the Presidium's activity (*ibid.*, p. 62). This evoked the wrath and sarcasm of Trotsky, who

accused Kiselev of seeking to eliminate party control over the CEC Presidium and other soviet bodies (*ibid.*, p. 75).

36 See Fedorov, p. 94ff.; V. M. Kleandora, *Organizatsiya i formy deyatel'nosti VTsIK (1917–1924gg.)*, Moscow, 1968, pp. 89–90. In 1919–20 the CEC disposed of five such 'agitation and instruction trains' and one 'agitation and instruction boat', which altogether made twenty journeys covering ninety-six gubernias.

37 See *VIII syezd sovetov*, pp. 33–42, 45–9, 54–7, 120–3, 201. It is noteworthy that strong expressions of criticism at the Eighth Congress of Soviets were limited to spokesmen for non-Bolshevik parties. Bolshevik critics, best represented by the 'Workers' Opposition' and 'Democratic Centralists', now voiced their opposition mainly within party forums. There was an amusing incident at the Congress when a provincial delegate attempted to make some clearly unscheduled criticisms of Rykov's report on the establishment of the Gubernia Economic Consultative Boards, and was promptly silenced by the Chairman (*ibid.*, p. 192).

38 Cf. Durdenevsky, 1922, pp. 49–51 and Pietsch, Chapter VIII. One expression of this, which did not begin, however, till 1922, was the inclusion of a minority of non-party delegates in the CEC; these amounted to 2.2 per cent of the membership at the end of 1922, 16.3 per cent in 1923, and 26 per cent in 1924 (Kleandora, p. 21). A similar concern may be seen in the fact that when it was decided in January 1922 to establish an Agricultural Commission 'to unite all forces of the central organs of the Republic on the struggle against the ruin of agriculture', this was attached to the CEC. See *SU* 1922, 11/97.

39 Durdenevsky, 1922, p. 60.

40 *Ibid.*, p. 59.

41 See e.g. *VTsIK VIII: Sten. otchët*, pp. 29–48, 139, 143–4, 155, *III Sessiya Vserossiiskogo Tsentral'nogo Ispolnitel'nogo Komiteta IX sozyva. 12–27 maya 1922.* Byulleten', Moscow, 1922, no. 1, p. 20ff., no. 2, p. 8ff., no. 3, pp. 24–6. Several commissariats gave rather anodyne reports on their activities to CEC sessions in 1921.

42 *SU* 1921, 1/1.

43 There also existed from at least 1920 a Little Presidium (*Malyi Prezidium*), whose membership numbered nine in January 1923. Much of the work seems to have been done by a Secretariat consisting of the Chairman and one or two secretaries. See S. S. Kishkin, 'Tsentral'nye organy RSFSR', *Sovetskoye pravo*, 1923, no. 3, p. 78. The Presidium also made extensive use of standing and *ad hoc* commissions, each chaired by a Presidium member and including officials of central government agencies and other bodies. See Pietsch, p. 131 and Kleandora, pp. 79–87.

44 Pietsch, pp. 128–30; *VTsIK VIII: Sten. otchët*, p. 115. The latter source clearly contains a misprint. It refers to ten meetings of the Full Presidium and nine of the Little Presidium in the six months since the Eighth Congress, but gives the total as 119. Two reports on

the work of the Presidium were given at CEC sessions in 1921. See *VTsIK VIII: Sten. otchët*, pp. 12ff., 115–23. Later the practice was discontinued.

45 *SU* 1921, 1/1.

46 *Sbornik vazhneishikh postanovlenii i rasporyazhenii VTsIK VIII sozyva*, Moscow, 1921, pp. 11–12. In August 1922 the CEC Presidium was empowered to consider and decide on protests against Sovnarkom, STO, and Little Sovnarkom decisions (see Chapter 13).

47 *SU* 1921, 64/476.

48 A somewhat different interpretation is argued in Pietsch, Chapter VIII.

49 Durdenevsky 1922, p. 62. For an outline of other contemporary characterisations of the Presidium–Sovnarkom relationship, see Towster, p. 245.

50 *Pyat' let vlasti Sovetov*, Moscow, 1922, p. 131.

51 There appears to have been no systematic study of the role in government of the executives and parliamentary caucuses of government parties in non-communist systems. For a discussion of the influence on government of parliamentary caucuses in certain Westminster-type systems, see Patrick Weller, *Caucus Minutes 1901–1949. Minutes of the Meetings of the Federal Parliamentary Labor Party. Volume 3: 1932–1949*, Melbourne, 1975, Introduction. There have been periods when the Australian and New Zealand Labour Parties, as represented by their parliamentary caucuses, were evidently more closely involved in government decision-making than was the Central Committee of the Bolshevik Party in the first months of Sovnarkom.

52 *Devyatyi syezd RKP(b)*, p. 32.

53 *Ibid.*, p. 68.

54 The best existing accounts of this transformation are in Schapiro, *The CPSU*, pp. 241–51, and Pietsch, Chapter IX. See also Carr, *The Bolshevik Revolution, 1917–1923*, Vol. 1, Chapter 9, and Robert V. Daniels, 'The Secretariat and the Local Organizations in the Russian Communist Party, 1921–1923', *The American Slavonic and East European Review*, Vol. XVI, 1957, no. 1, pp. 32–49 (cited here-after as Daniels, 1957). For sources of additional data supporting our statements in this section the reader is referred to these authors. At the same time, our discussion here differs from theirs in some significant respects, largely because our central interest is in the effects of these developments on Sovnarkom.

55 *Sed'moi ekstrennyi syezd RKP(b). Mart 1918 goda. Stenografscheskii otchët*, Moscow, 1962, pp. 171–2.

56 See *Vos'moi syezd RKP(b)*, pp. 423–9.

57 See *Protokoly TsK*, pp. 100–1. This body, formed on 10 October, was supposed to take charge during the insurrection, but clearly did not. Six days later a somewhat differently constituted 'Revolutionary Centre' was established, but seems to have had a purely ephemeral and paper existence. See *KPSS v rezolyutsiyakh i resheniyakh syezdov, konferentsii i plenumov TsK*, Vol. 1, Moscow, 1970, p. 518.

58 See *Lenin: khronika*, Vol. 5, p. 94. If this body actually operated, one would have expected to find some reference to Lenin's attending its meetings in this source, which attempts to assemble all available evidence on his day-to-day activities.

59 *Ibid.*, p. 358. The meeting was held on 4 April and discussed the allocation of party cadres, relations with the Ukrainian Rada, and tactics towards the Left SRs.

60 *Ibid.*, Vols. 5 and 6, *passim*.

61 *Vos'moi syezd RKP(b)*, p. 164.

62 Seven Central Committee meetings were held between mid-January and mid-March 1919. See *Lenin: khronika*, Vol. 6, *passim*.

63 See *ibid.*, pp. 284, 319, 328, 577, 588. The name used at this time was simply 'the Bureau'. Trotsky refers in his memoirs to Politburo meetings arranged by Sverdlov in the early Civil War period, and since Sverdlov died before the formal establishment of the Politburo by the Eighth Congress, it is evidently these early meetings he had in mind. See Trotsky, *Moya zhizn'*, Vol. II, p. 84.

64 *Lenin: khronika*, Vol. 6, p. 435, *Sovetskoye gosudarstvo i pravo*, 1977, no. 5, p. 16. It is conceivable that this was a special *ad hoc* body set up to make preparations for the Eighth Party Congress, though the latter source identifies it with the Organisational Bureau formally created by the Congress. An Organisational Bureau operating before the Seventh Congress a year earlier, however, seems to have been such an *ad hoc* body (see *Lenin: khronika*, Vol. 5, p. 277). On the other hand it is possible that *the* Organisational Bureau had an informal pre-history before the decision of 19 January 1919.

65 See *Izvestiya TsK* no. 8, 2 December 1919, no. 16, 28 March 1920, and no. 3(51), March 1923.

66 See *Ibid.*, no. 16, 28 March 1920.

67 *Spravochnik partiinogo rabotnika*, no. 1, Moscow, 1921, p. 114.

68 *Izvestiya TsK*, no. 18, 23 May 1920. The Central Committee met altogether six times, the Politburo forty-eight times, nineteen of them jointly with the Orgburo, while the latter held 110 additional meetings.

69 See *Devyatyi syezd RKP(b)*, p. 38.

70 *Izvestiya TsK*, no. 22, 1920, no. 29, March 1921, and no. 40, March 1922.

71 In proportional terms the overlap in membership between Sovnarkom and the full Central Committee was considerably smaller. In 1919 three of the fifteen full members and one of the eight candidate members of the Central Committee were in Sovnarkom. Subsequently it rose significantly, but in 1922 still amounted to only six of the twenty-seven full members and one of the nineteen candidate members (there were also three Central Committee members holding more junior positions in government bodies).

72 Trotsky refers to this quite frankly. See his *Moya zhizn'*, Vol. II, p. 84.

73 The difficulties encountered by the new-model party officialdom in curbing the arbitrariness of the 'exceptional organs' is well illus-

trated by a Central Committee circular of October 1919 on relations between local Revolutionary Military Councils and party organs (*Izvestiya TsK*, 1919, no. 7). The circular refers to complaints against Revolutionary Military Councils for such high-handed actions as taking over local buildings and personnel and mounting propaganda campaigns without consulting the party committee but, while mildly condemning such 'inconsiderateness', proposes no remedy other than that Communists in the military administration should take more trouble to establish 'correct comradely relations' with the party organs when they move into a new locality. It was not only the state of war that inhibited the power of local party officials over the 'exceptional organs': the Revolutionary Military Councils came under Trotsky, the Chekas under Dzerzhinsky, and the Food Armies under Tsyurupa, and if these powerful leaders chose, as they usually did, to back up their subordinates, they were usually strong enough to frustrate any disciplinary action through party channels.

74 After March 1920 there were three Central Committee secretaries instead of the former one, and these soon adopted the practice of consulting on questions requiring their authorisation but not of sufficient moment to refer to the Orgburo. In time, these consultations evolved into formal meetings, and thus a third collegial body was established under the Central Committee, becoming known as the Secretariat. *See Izvestiya TsK*, no. 31, 20 July 1921.

75 The mechanism whereby the new role of local party bodies resulted in matters reaching the centre via *party* channels, even where the party officials concerned lacked authority over locally deployed officials of central agencies, is clearly illustrated in a letter sent by Lenin to the Party Committee and Revolutionary Military Council in Astrakhan in 1919, when the two were in dispute:

> Conflict with the party committee is impermissible. Take all measures to ensure harmonious mutually-agreed work. All members of the party irrespective of the posts they occupy must join the local party organisation. The party committee should not interfere in the activity of institutions directly subordinate to the centre. It has the right only to present its viewpoint to the Central Committee. All local work is directed by the party centre.

See *Lenin: khronika*, Vol. 6, p. 409. The emergence of the party committee as the control centre for regional and local institutions had reached the point even by late 1920 where a delegate to the Eighth Congress of Soviets could propose without contradiction that 'in the future when the reports of executive committees [of guberniya soviets] are being heard, inclusion of the question of the role of the party organisation in the work of the soviets should be compulsory, *otherwise the reports will be purely formal*' (our emphasis). See *VIII syezd sovetov*, p. 201. This local predominance of the party committee was further entrenched in the next two or three years. See Daniels, 1957.

76 See *Izvestiya TsK*, 1921, no. 28.

77 *Ibid.*
78 *Spravochnik partiinogo rabotnika*, no. 1, pp. 78–9. It is impossible to do justice to the complex politics of provincial appointments here. The failure of similar instructions in 1919 to eliminate conflicts indicates the difficulty of enforcing such arrangements. It is also true that in a conflict between a commissariat and a local party committee the Party Secretariat might often support the former, where the party committee concerned was seen as manifesting 'localism'.
79 See e.g. Lenin, *PSS*, Vol. 52, p. 72. For another example of Lenin's seeking Politburo action on disputed appointments, see *ibid.*, vol. 54, p. 106. The Secretariat and Orgburo took over from *Uchraspred* direct responsibility for an increasing range of appointments. In April–July 1922 they approved 635 appointments at their meetings, of which 167 were to senior government posts. See *Izvestiya TsK*, no. 42, June 1922 and no. 43, July 1922.
80 *Lenin: khronika*, Vol. 7, *passim*.
81 *Ibid.*, pp. 523–4.
82 Lenin, *PSS*, Vols. 51–4, *passim*.
83 *Ibid.*, Vol. 52, p. 125.
84 *Ibid.*, p. 151. In July the Politburo twice considered the targets for the grain tax to be fixed for the Ukraine. *Ibid.*, Vol. 53, pp. 73 and 391.
85 *Ibid.*, Vol. 52, p. 256.
86 *Leninskii sbornik*, xxxvii, pp. 321–2. Alsky was required to furnish fortnightly reports to the Politburo on expenditures from the gold fund.
87 *Ibid.*, p. 322.
88 *Ibid.*, xxviii, p. 418.
89 The author has attempted a characterisation of bureaucratic politics in the USSR in his article, 'Politics in the Mono-organisational Society', in Andrew C. Janos (ed.), *Authoritarian Politics in Communist Europe. Uniformity and Diversity in One-Party States*, Berkeley, Calif., 1976. See also T. H. Rigby, 'Bureaucratic Politics: An Introduction', *Public Administration* (Sydney), Vol. xxxii (1973), no. 1. There is a burgeoning literature on bureaucratic politics in the United States, focused on the work of Graham T. Allison and Morton H. Halperin on foreign policy formation. For a more general discussion, see Francis E. Rourke, *Bureaucracy, Politics and Public Policy*, 2nd ed., Boston, Mass., 1976.
90 Lydia Bach, *Le Droit et les Institutions de la Russie Soviétique*, Paris, 1923, p. 48.

CHAPTER 13: PROPS FOR AN AILING CHAIRMAN

1   The above account of the course and impact of Lenin's illness is based on 'Daty zhizni i deyatel'nosti V. L. Lenina', Lenin, *PSS*, Vol. 44, pp. 660–710 and Vol. 45, pp. 663–718, augmented by information in Fotiyeva, 1967, pp. 172–293; Genkina, 1969, pp. 490–502; Krupskaya,

pp. 459–64 and Valentinov, Chapter II. The last-named author is the source of the reference to Stalin's first concluding that Lenin was *kaput* (p. 37) and of the report of his vainly searching for a document in his drawer on 19 October (p. 62). According to Valentinov's informant, Lenin was very distressed at the document's disappearance, and suspected it was stolen, evidently by Stalin or someone acting on the latter's instructions.

2 Kishkin, p. 86, footnote.

3 See Durdenevsky, 1922, pp. 45–6.

4 See *SU* 1922, 12/117.

5 See Lenin, *PSS*, Vol. 44, pp. 364–6. In this letter, written rather in the style of the anxious master tutoring his journeyman in the mysteries of the craft, Lenin also enjoins Tsyurupa to keep Full Sovnarkom and STO meetings down to one each a week, urges that Kamenev's Supreme Economic Commission should limit its role to securing interdepartmental agreement for draft economic decisions and abolish all its sub-commissions, and that the number of commissions in general should be drastically pruned.

6 The text of Tsyurupa's letter is not available, but it is summarised in *ibid.*, pp. 580–1, note 154.

7 *Ibid.*, pp. 366–7.

8 *Ibid.*, p. 368.

9 The relevant sections of this letter are to be found in *ibid.*, p. 581, note 156.

10 *Ibid.*, note 155. On 22 February, in a letter to Stalin and Kamenev regarding current Sovnarkom business, Lenin had urged that Tsyurupa's proposals be 'thoroughly thought over, checked and doubly weighed up'. See Lenin, *PSS*, Vol. 54, p. 177.

11 See *ibid.*, Vol. 45, p. 671.

12 *SU* 1922, 30/358.

13 It was to consist of a Chairman, two other independent members, and representatives of the Commissariats of Finance, Justice, and Rabkrin. The members were to be appointed by the Full Sovnarkom, which would also designate one of their number to serve as deputy chairman.

14 See V. N. Durdenevsky, 'Polozheniye o Malom SNK', *Sovetskoye pravo*, 1923, no. 1 (cited hereafter as Durdenevsky, 1923), pp. 140–2.

15 For the text of the Statute (*polozheniye*) see *SU* 1922, 75/927.

16 Cf. Durdenevsky, 1923, p. 141.

17 See *SU* 1922, 29/340.

18 See *SU* 1922, 46/579.

19 See *Sovetskoye pravo*, 1922, no. 2, p. 117.

20 See *SU* 1922, 56/709.

21 See *Sovetskoye pravo*, 1922, no. 2, pp. 117–18.

22 See *SU* 1922, 51/649.

23 *Izvestiya*, 29 May 1921. At this time Rykov gave up the Chairmanship of the National Economic Council, but it was specifically stated that he retained voting membership of Sovnarkom.

24 During Lenin's previous absence from work, following his wounding by a would-be assassin on 30 August 1918, Rykov had alternated with Sverdlov in chairing Sovnarkom meetings. See Bonch-Bruyevich, p. 361.
25 See Oppenheim, p. 216.
26 Liberman, p. 66.
27 For Lenin's jocular tribute to the former surgeon of Kaiser Wilhelm who had cured Rykov, see *Odinnadtsatyi syezd RKP(b)*, p. 43.
28 See Liberman, p. 65.
29 The relevant note in the *Collected Works*, 5th edn., reads: 'On December 1, 1921 the Politburo of the CC RKP(b), having heard a report [*soobshcheniye*] of V. I. Lenin on the work of A. D. Tsyurupa, resolved to approve him in the post of Second Deputy Chairman of STO, and on December 5 by decision of the Politburo he was named Vice-Chairman of Sovnarkom' (Lenin, *PSS*, Vol. 44, p. 580, note 153). The hypothesis that Lenin's idea was simply to make Tsyurupa Deputy Chairman of STO is further supported by the terms of his formal motion for the 1 December meeting of the Politburo, which is quoted in a letter he wrote to Tsyurupa on 28 November: 'In addition to Rykov's post as Deputy Chairman of STO (with voting member-ship of Sovnarkom) the post should be instituted of Second Deputy Chairman of STO, with equal powers. Tsyurupa to be appointed, releasing him as People's Commissar of Food Supplies' (Lenin, *PSS*, Vol. 44, p. 253).
30 Lenin was present at the Politburo meeting of 5 December (Lenin, *PSS*, Vol. 44, p. 695). Although, as suggested, he was probably luke-warm about the decision, there is no evidence that he actively opposed it.
31 *Ibid.*, Vol. 44, p. 253.
32 *Ibid.*
33 Liberman, p. 66.
34 Lenin, *PSS*, Vol. 53, p. 309.
35 *Ibid.*, Vol. 44, p. 251.
36 *Ibid.*, Vol. 54, p. 573, note 100. The Sovnarkom decision of 6 Decem-ber implementing this resolution defined the commission's purposes as 'unifying and accelerating work on the systematisation and supple-menting of economic legislation' (*ibid.*).
37 *Ibid.*, Vol. 44, pp. 253–4.
38 See *ibid.*, pp. 364–70.
39 *Ibid.*, p. 370. Lenin pursued the idea of his deputies' drawing on the staff of Rabkrin in exercising their checking and controlling role in a letter to Stalin written on 21 March. He proposed that Rykov and Tsyurupa be allowed to choose, in consultation with Stalin, a few dozen of his best Rabkrin officials, for authoritative investigation of the work of the central government apparatus, reporting both to Stalin and to them. No evidence has been found that this proposal was adopted. One can imagine Stalin receiving it with some scepticism, and perhaps he managed to side-track it. See Lenin, *PSS*, Vol. 45, pp. 55–6.

40 *Ibid.*, Vol. 44, p. 367.
41 *Ibid.*, Vol. 45, pp. 420–6, and p. 534, note 96.
42 See Trotsky Archive, Doc. 744.
43 *Ibid.*, Doc. 749.
44 Lenin, *PSS*, Vol. 45, pp. 180–2.
45 *Ibid.*, pp. 678, 680.

CHAPTER 14: THE LAST MONTHS

1 See Lenin, *PSS*, Vol. 45, p. 57, pp. 510–11, notes 39 and 40.
2 *Odinnadtsatyi syezd RKP(b)*, pp. 43–4.
3 Liberman, p. 66.
4 See pp. 114–15, 202–3.
5 *Odinnadtsatyi syezd RKP(b)*, p. 44.
6 *Ibid.*, pp. 84–5. The Politburo already had a 'budget conference' (*byudzhetnoe soveshchaniye pri Politbyuro*), which had the final word on all departments' financial estimates (see Lenin, *PSS*, Vol. 54, p. 641). Preobrazhensky was allied particularly with Trotsky, whose relations with Rykov were also said to be profoundly antagonistic, a consequence, according to Liberman, of both interdepartmental conflict and the clash of sharply contrary personalities. See Liberman, p. 67. Preobrazhensky was also critical of Stalin's holding two commissariats while simultaneously serving on the Politburo and Orgburo.
7 *Odinnadtsatyi syezd RKP(b)*, p. 162.
8 *Ibid.*, pp. 87–9.
9 *Ibid.*, pp. 144–5. Lenin was no more gentle with Preobrazhensky, whose proposal to form an Ekonomburo he justly berated as unworkable and as perpetuating the very confusion of party and government functions which Preobrazhensky professed to agree should be ended, *Ibid.*, pp. 142–3.
10 *Ibid.*, pp. 430–1.
11 *Ibid.*, pp. 525–6.
12 The Trotsky Archive, Doc. 774, p. 4. This is a Top Secret memorandum addressed by Trotsky to members of the Central Committee and referring to official minutes of the relevant Politburo meetings that had been circulated by Stalin.
13 See Isaac Deutscher, *The Prophet Unarmed. Trotsky: 1921–29*, London, 1970, pp. 38–48.
14 *Odinnatsatyi syezd RKP(b)*, pp. 133–4.
15 *Ibid.*, p. 134.
16 *Ibid.*, p. 430.
17 The Trotsky Archive, Doc. 774.
18 *Ibid.*
19 Deutscher, *The Prophet Unarmed*, pp. 36–7. Deutscher, referring to the Trotsky Archive but without specific citation, states that Lenin had nominated Trotsky as Deputy Chairman on an earlier occasion, namely at a Politburo meeting on 11 April (*ibid.*, p. 35). The present

author has found no reference to this in the Archive, and indeed it is difficult to reconcile it with other facts. It was on 11 April that Lenin circulated his draft Statute on the deputies, which had been some weeks in preparation and which went into great detail about the duties of Rykov and Tsyurupa. It is surely inconceivable that at the same time he would be proposing the addition of a third deputy and thereby making nonsense of the Statute. It is worth noting that the Trotsky Archive contains a copy of the draft Statute (Doc. 744), the text of which is identical with that in Lenin's *PSS*, Vol. 45, pp. 152–9. Moreover, there is no record of Lenin's attending a Politburo meeting on 11 April. Such meetings, which were normally held weekly at that time, are recorded for 6, 13 and 20 April (Lenin, *PSS*, Vol. 45, pp. 672–4). Finally, when Trotsky later had occasion to recount the history of proposals that he be Deputy Chairman, he made no reference to any such proposal before September 1922 (the Trotsky Archive, Doc. 774).

20 The institution of 'Conference of Deputies' had been foreshadowed in the Draft Statute on the Deputies and was already in operation when the deputies were a duumvirate (Lenin, *PSS*, Vol. 54, p. 238). Before his first stroke Lenin had also begun to hold three-man 'conferences' with his deputies to settle important issues (*ibid.*, p. 230). For an example of Lenin calling for a meeting of the *three* deputies in late September to precede a Sovnarkom meeting, see *ibid.*, p. 287.

21 The most valuable source of information on Lenin's activities during this period is his *PSS*, Vols. 45 and 54. Describing the first Sovnarkom meeting after Lenin's return to his office, Fotiyeva stresses the priority he gave to tightening arrangements for preparing business for consideration by Sovnarkom bodies, so as to restore 'order and organisation' to their decision-making. See Fotiyeva, 1967, pp. 224–5.

22 Lenin, *PSS*, Vol. 45, p. 687.

23 *Ibid.*, p. 323.

24 *Ibid.*, pp. 328–9.

25 *Ibid.*, pp. 331–2. See also *ibid.*, p. 588, note 200, and p. 708, entry for 12 December. In this letter Lenin also took issue with Rykov's suggestion that persons wishing to see him should first have to be cleared by one of the deputies or a Central Committee Secretary. In a further note on 16 December he stated that (presumably contrary to what they proposed) Gosplan should be placed under Rykov. See *ibid.*, Vol. 54, p. 327.

26 See Lenin, *PSS*, Vol. 45, pp. 356–62.

27 See his reported remarks to Fotiyeva on 24 January 1923, *ibid.*, p. 476. His stroke on 13 December occurred the day following his conversation on the Georgian affair with Dzerzhinsky, who had investigated the matter on behalf of the Central Committee and supported Stalin. See *ibid.*, p. 708.

28 *Ibid.*, pp. 343–408. These writings, dictated between 23 December 1922 and 2 March 1923, were executed under exceptionally difficult

conditions, which called not only for superhuman will-power to marshal the residue of his physical and mental powers, but also great devotion on the part of his wife and secretaries, who had to contend with the demands of Lenin's doctors and his Politburo colleagues who sought to minimise his activity, while at the same time themselves protecting him from overstrain. Some were published in the following weeks, but the more sensitive writings of this period were merely read to delegates to the twelfth or thirteenth party congresses, and not published in the Soviet Union till after the death of Stalin.

29 See especially Schapiro, Chapter 15; Moshe Lewin, *Lenin's Last Struggle*, London, 1969, and Ulam, Chapter 10.

30 Lenin, *PSS*, Vol. 45, pp. 343–8.

31 *Ibid.*, pp. 386–7.

32 *Ibid.*, pp. 344–5.

33 *Ibid.*, pp. 343, 349.

34 See The Trotsky Archive, Doc. 773, p. 2. Trotsky states here that the proposal was made 'several weeks' after Lenin's return to work (i.e. after 2 October). This suggests November, since it was evidently no longer a live issue by early December, when Lenin was exchanging views with his deputies on the organisation of their work.

35 See Lenin, *PSS*, Vol. 54, pp. 323–9. For a general account of the rapprochement between Lenin and Trotsky and the latter's policies and actions during this period, see Deutscher, *The Prophet Unarmed. Trotsky: 1921–29*, chapter 1. Trotsky claims that he and Lenin had agreed to form a 'bloc against bureaucracy in general and against the Organisational Bureau in particular', and that in pressing him to become deputy Lenin had in mind that he would succeed him as Sovnarkom Chairman. See Trotsky, *Moya Zhizn'*, Vol. II, pp. 216–217.

36 Lenin, *PSS*, Vol. 45, pp. 345–6. By early March Lenin's disgust with Stalin had reached the point where he was threatening to break off all personal relations. See *ibid.*, Vol. 54, pp. 329–30

37 See Schapiro, pp. 267–75, and Daniels 1957, pp. 32–44.

38 This move, however, would have acquired greater significance if Lenin had managed to push through his plans to reorganise Rabkrin at the Twelfth Congress. See his articles, 'How we should Reorganise Rabkrin' and 'Better Less, but Better', *PSS*, Vol. 45, pp. 383–408.

39 The Trotsky Archive, Doc. 775. See also Docs. 773 and 774. As these documents show, the deputies issue was only one aspect of the January 1923 Politburo disputes over the leadership of Sovnarkom. Stalin also proposed a major structural change – merging STO, the 'Board of Deputies' and the Finance Committee. This was his counter-move when Trotsky revived earlier proposals for giving Gosplan executive authority over the economy. Unfortunately for Trotsky, the memoranda in which Lenin now registered his support on this issue were not yet known to the leadership. In fact nothing came of either of these rival proposals for the time being.

40 *Ibid.*, Docs 779 and 799.

41 Schapiro, p. 229.

42 In one of his memoranda he argued that one advantage of his proposals for reorganising the top party organs was that it would give more people 'training in Central Committee work', i.e. top leadership experience. See Lenin, *PSS*, Vol. 45, p. 346.

43 *Dvenadtsatyi syezd RKP(b). 17–25 aprelya 1923 goda. Stenografcheskii otchët*, Moscow, 1968, p. 818.

CHAPTER 15: SOME HISTORICAL REFLECTIONS

1 See John P. Mackintosh, *The British Cabinet*, London, 1962; Hans Daalder, *Cabinet Reform in Britain 1914–1963*, London, 1964; Karl Loewenstein, *British Cabinet Government*, London, 1967; Patrick Gordon-Walker, *The Cabinet*, London, 1970.

2 On British Prime Ministers being overruled by their Cabinet colleagues, see Gordon-Walker, pp. 91–5.

3 Liberman, p. 13.

4 Transfer of such structural devices even between closely similar systems may fail for largely 'cultural' reasons, as a recent attempt to introduce a British-type committee system by the Australian Government illustrates. See R. F. I. Smith, 'Australian cabinet structure and procedures: The Labor government 1972–1975', *Politics*, Vol. xii, 1977, no. 1, pp. 23–38.

5 *Odinnadtsatyi syezd RKP(b)*, p. 84.

6 *Ibid.*, p. 144.

7 *Ibid.*, p. 43.

8 The discussion here of Tsarist institutions has drawn mainly on the following: G. B. Sliozberg, *Dorevolyutsionnyi stroi Rossii*, Paris, 1933, Chapter VI; Anatole Leroy-Beaulieu, *L'Empire des Tsars et les Russes*, Tome ii, *Institutions*, Paris, 1882, Chapter II; N. P. Yeroshkin, *Ocherki istorii gosudarstvennykh uchrezhdenii dorevolyutsionnoi Rossii*, Moscow, 1960; S. V. Yushkov, *Istoriya gosudarstva i prava SSSR, Chast' pervaya*, Moscow, 1950; Hugh Seton-Watson, *The Russian Empire 1801–1917*, Oxford, 1967; Erik Amburger, *Geschichte der Behördenorganisationen Russlands von Peter dem Grossen bis 1917*, Leiden, 1966; N. M. Korkunov, *Russkoe gosudarstvennoe pravo*, Tom ii, *Chast' osobennaya*, St Petersburg, 1905; V. M. Gribovsky, *Gosudarstvennoye ustroistvo i upravleniye rossiiskoi imperii*, Odessa, 1912; N. A. Zakharov, *Sistema russkoi gosudarstvennoi vlasti*, Novocherkassk, 1912; P. A. Zaionchkovsky, *Rossiiskoe samoderzhaviye v kontse XIX stoletiya*, Moscow, 1970, Chapter II; P. A. Zaionchkovsky, *Krizis samoderzhaviya na rubezhe 1870–1880 godov*, Moscow, 1964; George L. Yaney, *The Systematization of Russian Government: Social Evolution in the Domestic Administration of Imperial Russia, 1711–1905*, Urbana, Ill., 1973; Geoffrey A. Hosking, *The Russian Constitutional Experiment: Government and Duma 1907–1914*, Cambridge, 1973; B. E. Nol'de, *Ocherki russkago gosudarstvennogo prava*,

St Petersburg, 1911, Chapter II; and Stephen Sternheimer, *Administration and Political Development: An Enquiry into the Tsarist and Soviet Experience*, Unpublished Ph.D. Dissertation, University of Chicago, 1974, Chapter I.

9 Leroy-Beaulieu, p. 88.

Bibliography of principal sources

A. REPORTS OF CONGRESSES OF SOVIETS

Tretii Vserossiiskii Syezd Sovetov rabochikh, soldatskikh i krestyanskikh deputatov, no place or date.

Stenograficheskii otchët 4-go Chrezvychainogo Syezda Sovetov rabochikh, soldatskikh, krestyanskikh i kazachikh deputatov, Moscow, 1920.

Pyatyi Vserossiiskii Syezd Sovetov rabochikh, krestyanskikh, soldatskikh i kazachikh deputatov. Stenograficheskii otchët, Moscow, 1918.

Shestoi Vserossiiskii Chrezvychainyi Syezd Sovetov rabochikh, krestyanskikh, kazachikh i krasnoarmeiskikh deputatov. Stenograficheskii otchët, Moscow, 1919.

Sed'moi Vserossiiskii Syezd Sovetov rabochikh, krestyanskikh, krasnoarmeiskikh i kazachikh deputatov. Stenograficheskii otchët, Moscow, 1920 (cited as *VII Syezd Sovetov*).

Vos'moi Vserossiiskii Syezd Sovetov rabochikh, krestyanskikh, krasnoarmeiskikh i kazachikh deputatov. Stenograficheskii otchët, Moscow, 1921 (cited as *VIII Syezd Sovetov*).

Devyatyi Vserossiiskii Syezd Sovetov rabochikh, krestyanskikh, krasnoarmeiskikh i kazachikh deputatov. Stenograficheskii otchët, Moscow, 1922.

B. REPORTS OF MEETINGS OF CENTRAL EXECUTIVE COMMITTEE

Protokoly zasedanii Vserossiiskogo Tsentral'nogo Ispolnitel'nogo Komiteta Sovetov rabochikh, soldatskikh, krestyanskikh i kazachikh deputatov, II sozyv, 27 oktyabrya–29 dekabrya 1917, Petrograd, 1918.

Protokoly zasedanii Vserossiiskogo Tsentral'nogo Ispolnitel'nogo Komiteta 4-go sozyva (Stenograficheskii otchët), Moscow, 1920 (cited as *VTsIK IV: Protokoly*).

Pyatyi sozyv Vserossiiskogo Tsentral'nogo Ispolnitel'nogo Komiteta Sovetov rabochikh, krestyanskikh, kazachikh i krasnoarmeiskikh deputatov. Stenograficheskii otchët, Moscow, 1919 (cited as *VTsIK V: Sten. otchët*).

Sessii Vserossiiskogo Tsentral'nogo Ispolnitel'nogo Komiteta VIII Sozyva. Stenograficheskii otchët, Moscow, 1921 (cited as *VTsIK VIII: Sten. otchët*).

I i II Sessii Vserossiiskogo Tsentral'nogo Ispolnitel'nogo Komiteta IX

Sozyva. Stenograficheskii otchët, Moscow, 1923 (cited as *VTsIK IX: I i II sessii*).
III *Sessiya Vserossiiskogo Tsentral'nogo Ispolnitel'nogo Komiteta IX Sozyva. 12–27 maya 1922. Byulleten'*, Moscow, 1922.
IV *Sessiya Vserossiiskogo Tsentral'nogo Ispolnitel'nogo Komiteta IX Sozyva. 23–31 oktyabrya 1922g. Byulleten' (Stenograficheskii otchët)*, Moscow, 1922.

C. REPORTS OF PARTY CONGRESSES AND CONFERENCES
AND CENTRAL COMMITTEE MEETINGS

Shestoi syezd RSDRP (bol'shevikov). Avgust 1917 goda. Protokoly, Moscow, 1958.
Sed'moi ekstrennyi syezd RKP(b). Mart 1918 goda. Stenograficheskii otchët, Moscow, 1962.
Vos'moi syezd RKP(b). Mart 1919 goda. Protokoly, Moscow, 1959 (cited as *Vos'moi syezd RKP(b)*).
Devyatyi syezd RKP(b). Mart–aprel' 1920 goda. Protokoly, Moscow, 1960 (cited as *Devyatyi syezd RKP(b)*).
Desyatyi syezd RKP(b). Mart 1921 goda. Stenograficheskii otchët, Moscow, 1963.
Odinnadtsatyi syezd RKP(b). Mart–aprel' 1922 goda. Stenograficheskii otchët, Moscow, 1961 (cited as *Odinnadtsatyi syezd RKP(b)*).
Dvenadtsatyi syezd RKP(b). 17–25 aprelya 1923 goda. Stenograficheskii otchët, Moscow, 1968.
Vos'maya Konferentsiya RKP(b). Dekabr' 1919 goda. Protokoly, Moscow, 1961.
Devyataya Konferentsiya RKP(b). Sentyabr' 1920 goda. Protokoly, Moscow, 1972.
Protokoly Tsentral'nogo Komiteta RSDRP(b). Avgust 1917–fevral' 1918, Moscow, 1958 (cited as *Protokoly TsK*).

D. BOOKS AND ARTICLES

Akimov, N. N. and Vlasova, M. G., 'V. I. Lenin – predsedatel' soveta rabochei i krestyanskoi oborony', *Voprosy istorii* (1955), no. 1.
Al'bom deyatelei VKP(b), TsK, TsKK and TsRK VKP(b). Moscow, 1927.
Amelin, G. K., *Petrogradskii voyenno-revolyutsionnyi komitet i yego rol' v zakreplenii sotsialisticheskoi revolyutsii (Oktyabr'-dekabr' 1917 goda)*. Moscow, 1963.
Andreyev, A., Pankov, B. and Smirnova, E., *Lenin v Kremle*. Moscow, 1960.
Anikeyev, V. V., *Deyatel'nost' TsK RSDRP(b) – RKP(b) v 1917–1918 godakh. Khronika sobytii*. Moscow, 1974.
Antonova, L. I., 'VTsIK i ego Prezidium v 1917–1922gg.', *Sovetskoye gosudarstvo i pravo* (1967), no. 10.
'Organizatsionnye formy pravotvorcheskoi deyatel'nosti Soveta Narodnykh Komissarov (1917–1922gg.)', *Pravovedeniye* (1968), no. 3.

Anweiler, Oskar, *Die Rätebewegung in Russland 1905–1921.* Leiden, 1958.

Baburin, D. S., 'Narkomprod v pervye gody sovetskoi vlasti', *Istoricheskiye zapiski*, 61 (1957).

Bach, Lydia, *Le Droit et les Institutions de la Russie Soviétique.* Paris, 1923.

Baranchenko, V. Ye., 'Karl Lander', *Voprosy istorii* (1971), no. 1.

Barsukov, M. I., *Velikaya Oktyabr'skaya sotsialisticheskaya revolyutsiya i organizatsiya sovetskogo zdravookhraneniya (oktyabr' 1917g.–iyul' 1918g.).* Moscow, 1951.

Belov, G. A. *et al.* (eds.), *Doneseniya komissarov Petrogradskogo Voyenno-Revolyutsionnogo Komiteta.* Moscow, 1957.

Bogolepov, D., 'Finansovoye stroitel'stvo v pervye gody Oktyabr'skoi revolyutsii', *Proletarskaya revolyutsiya* (1925), no. 4.

Bol'shaya sovetskaya entsiklopediya. 1st edn., 65 vols. Moscow, 1926–1947; 2nd edn., 51 vols. Moscow, 1949–1958; 3rd edn., 26 vols. Moscow, 1970–.

Bol'shevistkiye Voyenno-Revolyutsionnye Komitety. Compiled by G. D. Kostomarov and N. I. Tolokonsky. Moscow, 1958.

Bonch-Bruyevich, V. D., *Izbrannye sochineniya.* 3 vols. Moscow, 1959–63.

Vospominaniya o Lenine. 2nd edn. Moscow, 1969.

Bratus, S. N. and Samoshchenko, I. S. (eds.), *Rol' V. I. Lenina v stanovlenii i razvitii sovetskogo zakonodatel'stva.* Moscow, 1969.

Brodovich, S., 'STO i Ekoso RSFSR', *Vlast' sovetov* (1924), no. 5.

Browder, Robert Paul and Kerensky, Alexander, F., *The Russian Provisional Government 1917. Documents.* Stanford, Calif., 1961.

Bunyan, James and Fisher, H. H., *The Bolshevik Revolution 1917–1918: Documents and Materials.* Stanford, Calif., 1934.

Intervention, Civil War and Communism in Russia. Baltimore, Md., 1936.

Burns, Tom and Stalker, G. M., *The Management of Innovation.* London, 1961.

Calvert, Peter, *A Study of Revolution.* Oxford, 1970.

Carmichael, Joel, *The Russian Revolution 1917.* London, 1955.

Carr, E. H., *The Bolshevik Revolution 1917–1923.* 1st edn., 3 vols. London, 1950–53, repr. 1966.

Chachko, M., *Povest' o narodnom komissare.* Moscow, 1972.

Chamberlin, W. H., *The Russian Revolution 1917–1921.* 2 vols. London, 1935.

Chistyakov, O. I., *Vzaimootnosheniya sovetskikh respublik do obrazovaniya S.S.S.R.* Moscow, 1955.

Stanovleniye rossiiskoi federatsii (1917–1922). Moscow, 1966.

Chistyakov, O. I. and Kukushkin, Yu. S. (eds.), *Istoriya Gosudarstva i Prava SSSR. Chast' II.* Moscow, 1971.

Chugaev, D. A., 'Slom burzhuaznoi gosudarstvennoi mashiny i sozdaniye sovetskogo gosudarstvennogo apparata'. *Vide* Golikov, G. N. *et al.*

Daniels, Robert V., 'The Secretariat and the Local Organisations in the

Russian Communist Party, 1921–1923', *The American Slavonic and East European Review*, XVI (1957), no. 1 (cited as Daniels, 1957).

Red October: The Bolshevik Revolution of 1917. New York, 1967 (cited as Daniels, 1967).

Davitnidze, I. L., *Kollegii ministerstv. Pravovoye polozheniye i organizatsiya raboty.* Moscow, 1972.

Dekrety Sovetskoi vlasti. 8 vols. Moscow, 1957– (cited as *DSV*).

Demidenko, G. G., *Del u revolyutsii nemalo. Ocherk zhizni i deyatel'nosti V. D. Bonch-Bruyevicha.* Moscow, 1976.

Denisov, A. I. (ed.), *Istoriya gosudarstva i prava S.S.S.R. Chast' vtoraya: Istoriya Sovetskogo gosudarstva i prava.* Moscow, 1948.

Deutscher, Isaac, *Stalin: A Political Biography.* London, 1961 (first publ. 1949).

The Prophet Armed. Trotsky: 1879–1921. London, 1970 (first publ. 1954).

The Prophet Unarmed. Trotsky: 1921–1929. London, 1970 (first publ. 1959).

Deyateli Soyuza Sovetskikh Sotsialisticheskikh Respublik i Oktyabr'skoi Revolyutsii (avtobiografii i biografii). Entsiklopedicheskii slovar' russkogo bibliograficheskogo instituta Granat. 7th edn. Vol. 41. Moscow, n.d. Chast' I, chast' II, chast' III.

Directivy KPSS i sovetskogo pravitel'stva po khozyaistvennym voprosam, 1917–1957. Sbornik dokumentov. 4 vols. Moscow, 1957–8.

'Dnevnik zapisi poruchenii Vladimira Ilyicha Lenina', *Istoricheskii arkhiv* (1961), no. 5.

Dorokhova, G. A., *Raboche-krestyanskaya inspektsiya v 1920–1923gg.* Moscow, 1959.

Drabkina, Yelizaveta, 'Zimnii pereval', *Novyi mir* (1968), no. 10.

Drobizhev, V. Z., *Glavnyi shtab sotsialisticheskoi promyshlennosti (Ocherki istorii VSNKh, 1917–1923gg.).* Moscow, 1966.

Drobizheva, L. M., 'Razrabotka i realizatsiya Leninskogo "Nakaza ot STO mestnym sovetskim uchrezhdeniyam"', *Voprosy istorii* (1962), no. 6.

Dunn, John, *Modern Revolutions: An Introduction to the Analysis of a Political Phenomenon.* Cambridge, 1972.

Durdenevsky, V., 'Sovet Narodnykh Komissarov', *Sovetskoye pravo* (1922), no. 1 (cited as Durdenevsky, 1922).

V. N., 'Polozheniye o Malom SNK', *Sovetskoye pravo* (1923), no. 1 (cited as Durdenevsky, 1923).

Dyablo, V., 'Razvitiye Konstitutsii Soyuza S.S.R. v protsesse konstitutsionnoi praktiki (sootnosheniye elementov statiki i dinamiki v sovetskoi soyuznoi konstitutsii)', *Sovetskoye pravo* (1926), no. 3(21).

Fedorov, K. G., *VTsIK v pervye gody sovetskoi vlasti 1917–1920gg.* Moscow, 1957.

Istoriya Sovetskogo gosudarstva i prava. Rostov, 1964.

Fedyukin, S. A., *Sovetskaya vlast' i burzhuaznye spetsialisty.* Moscow, 1965.

Velikii oktyabr' i intelligentsiya. 2nd edn. Moscow, 1972.

Filimonov, V. G., *Obrazovaniye i razvitiye RSFSR.* Moscow, 1963.

Fitzpatrick, Sheila, *The Commissariat of Enlightenment: Soviet Organisation of Education and the Arts under Lunacharsky.* Cambridge, 1970.
Fotiyeva, L. A., *Iz zhizni V. I. Lenina.* Moscow, 1967 (cited as Fotiyeva, 1967).
  V. I. Lenin – rukovoditel' i tovarishch. 2nd edn. Moscow, 1973 (cited as Fotiyeva, 1973).
Gapochko, L. V., 'Istoriki-uchastniki Oktyabr'skoi revolyutsii, Vladimir Ivanovich Nevsky', *Istoriya SSSR* (1967), no. 1.
Genkina, E. B., 'Gosudarstvennaya deyatel'nost' V. I. Lenina v 1921 g.', *Voprosy istorii* (1954), no. 1.
  Lenin – predsedatel' Sovnarkoma i STO. Moscow, 1960 (cited as Genkina, 1960).
  Gosudarstvennaya deyatel'nost' V. I. Lenina 1921–1923gg. Moscow, 1969 (cited as Genkina, 1969).
  'O dokladakh V. I. Lenina v Sovnarkome, Sovete oborony i sovete truda i oborony (1917–1922gg.)', *Istoriya SSSR* (July–Aug. 1973), no. 4 (cited as Genkina, 1973).
Gershberg, S. R., 'V. I. Lenin i sozdaniye VSNKh', *Voprosy istorii* (1958), no. 7.
Getzler, Israel, *Martov: A Political Biography of a Russian Social Democrat.* Cambridge–Melbourne, 1967.
Gimpel'son, Ye. G., *Iz istorii stroitel'stva sovetov (noyabr' 1917g.–iyul' 1918g.).* Moscow, 1958.
Gindin, Ya., *Vospominaniya o Vladimire Ilyiche.* Moscow, 1973.
Gissis, H., 'Outline of the formation of the Soviet Governmental Structure'. Unpublished M.Soc.Sc. Thesis, University of Birmingham, 1971.
Golembo, S. Ya., Yevtikhiyev, I. I., *et al.*, *Ocherki po istorii organov sovetskoi gosudarstvennoi vlasti (materialy k izucheniyu istorii sovetskogo gosudarstva i prava).* Moscow, 1949.
Golikov, G. N. *et al.* (eds.), *Velikaya Oktyabr'skaya sotsialisticheskaya Revolyutsiya: dokumenty i materialy. Oktyabr'skoye vooruzhennoye vosstaniye v Petrograde.* Moscow, 1957.
Gorbunov, N. P., 'Kak sozdavalsya v Oktyabr'skiye dni rabochii apparat Soveta Narodnykh Komissarov', *Pravda*, Nos 6–7, 1927.
  Kak rabotal Vladimir Ilyich. Sbornik statei i vospominanii. Moscow, 1933.
Gorodetsky, Ye. N., *Rozhdeniye Sovetskogo gosudarstva, 1917–1918gg.* Moscow, 1957.
Gorodetsky, Ye. N. *et al.* (eds.), *Stroitel'stvo Sovetskogo gosudarstva.* Moscow, 1972.
Gronsky, Paul P. and Astrov, Nicholas J., *The War and the Russian Government.* New York, 1973 (first publ. 1929).
Gurvich, G. S., *Istoriya Sovetskoi Konstitutsii.* Moscow, 1923.
Ikonnikov, S. N., *Organizatsiya i deyatel'nost' RKI v 1920–1925gg.* Moscow, 1960.
Ionkina, T. D., *Vserossiiskiye syezdy sovetov v pervye gody proletarskoi diktatury.* Moscow, 1974.

Iroshnikov, M. P., 'V. I. Lenin i sozdaniye rabochego apparata Soveta Narodnykh Komissarov (oktyabr' 1917g.–yanvar' 1918g.)', *Sovetskoye gosudarstvo i pravo* (1965), no. 4 (cited as Iroshnikov, 1965).

Sozdaniye sovetskogo tsentral'nogo gosudarstvennogo apparata. Sovet Narodnykh Komissarov i narodnye komissariaty (oktyabr' 1917g.–yanvar' 1918g.). Moscow, Leningrad, 1966 (cited as Iroshnikov, 1966).

'Predsedatel' Soveta Narodnykh Komissarov, V. I. Ul'yanov (Lenin)', *Voprosy istorii* (1970), no. 4 (cited as Iroshnikov, 1970).

'K voprosu o slome burzhuaznoi gosudarstvennoi mashiny v Rossii' (cited as Iroshnikov, 1973). *Vide* Tokarev, Yu. S.

Predsedatel' Soveta Narodnykh Komissarov V. I. Ulyanov (Lenin). Ocherki gosudarstvennoi deyatel'nosti v 1917–1918gg. Leningrad, 1974 (cited as Iroshnikov, 1974).

Istoriya Sovetskoi Konstitutsii (V Dokumentakh) 1917–1956. Moscow, 1957.

Itkina, Anna Markovna, *Revolyutsioner, tribun, diplomat: ocherk zhizni Aleksandry Mikhailovnoi Kollontai.* Moscow, 1964.

Janos, Andrew C. (ed.), *Authoritarian Politics in Communist Europe: Uniformity and Diversity in One-Party States.* Berkeley, Calif., 1976.

Kareva, M., 'Vserossiiskii Tsentral'nyi Ispolnitel'nyi Komitet (1918–1922gg.)', *Bor'ba klassov* (1936), no. 12.

Keep, John L. H., *The Russian Revolution. A Study in Mass Mobilisation.* New York, 1976.

Khesin, S. S. (ed.), *Bor'ba za pobedu i ukrepleniye sovetskoi vlasti 1917–1918. Sbornik statei.* Moscow, 1966.

Kishkin, S. S., 'Tsentral'nye organy RSFSR', *Sovetskoye pravo* (1923), no. 3.

'K istorii organizatsii sovetskogo gosudarstvennogo apparata (1917–1918gg.)', *Istoricheskii arkhiv* (1956), no. 5.

Kleandora, V. M., *Organizatsiya i formy deyatel'nosti VTsIK (1917–1924gg.).* Moscow, 1968.

Klopov, E. V., 'Pervyi den' deyatel'nosti V. I. Lenina na postu Predsedatelya S.N.K.', *Istoriya SSSR* (1961), no. 2 (cited as Klopov, 1961).

Lenin v Smol'nom. Gosudarstvennaya deyatel'nost V. I. Lenina v pervye mesyatsy Sovetskoi vlasti, Oktyabr' 1917–mart 1918g. Moscow, 1965 (cited as Klopov, 1965).

Korenevskaya, Ye. I., *Pervoye sovetskoye pravitel'stvo (pravovye osnovy organizatsii i deyatel'nosti Soveta Narodnykh Komissarov, Soveta Truda i Oborony i Malogo Soveta Narodnykh Komissarov v 1917–1922gg.),* Avtoreferat kandidatskoi dissertatsii. Moscow, 1968 (cited as Korenevskaya, 1968(1)).

'V. I. Lenin i organizatsiya raboty sovetskogo pravitel'stva v 1917–1922gg', *Voyenno-istoricheskii zhurnal* (1968), no. 4 (cited as Korenevskaya, 1968(2)).

'Organizatsionno-pravovye formy deyatel'nosti SNK RSFSR (1917–1922gg.)', *Sovetskoye gosudarstvo i pravo* (1968), no. 7 (cited as Korenevskaya, 1968(3)).

Kositsyn, A. P., *Sotsialisticheskoye gosudarstvo*. Moscow, 1970.
Kotok, V. F. (ed.), *Sovetskoye gosudarstvennoye pravo–bibliografiya 1917–1957*. Moscow, 1958.
Kovalenko, D. A. (ed.), *Sovety v pervyi god proletarskoi revolyutsii (oktyabr' 1917g.–noyabr' 1918g.)*. Moscow, 1967.
KPSS v resolyutsiyakh i resheniyakh syezdov, konferentsii i plenumov TsK. 10 vols. Moscow, 1970–2.
Kramarov, G., *Soldat Revolyutsii: O Sergeye Ivanoviche Guseve*. Moscow, 1964.
Krassin, L., *Leonid Krassin: His Life and Work*. London, 1929.
Krasnikova, A. V. 'Studencheskaya organizatsiya pri Peterburgskom komitete RSDRP(b) i yeyë vklad v sovetskoye gosudarstvennoye stroitel'stvo v pervye posleoktyabrskiye mesyatsy 1917g.'. *Vide* Tokarev, Yu. S.
Kratkaya kharakteristika deyatel'nosti B. SNK, M. SNK, STO i VTsIK. Moscow, 1921.
Kratkaya kharakteristika deyatel'nosti VTsIK i SNK. Moscow, 1921.
Krupskaya, N. K., *Vospominaniya o Lenine*. 2nd edn. Moscow, 1968.
Kukushkin, Yu. S., *V. I. Lenin – predsedatel' Soveta Rabochei i krestyanskoi oborony*. Moscow, 1962.
Sovet oborony (1918–1920). Moscow, 1969.
Kulikova, N. A., 'Deyatel'nost' Soveta Truda i Obonory v period vtoroi mirovoi peredyshki'. *Vide* Ryabtsev, I. G.
Kuznetskaya, L., Mashtakova, K., and Subbotina, Z., *Kabinet i kvartira Vladimira Ilyicha Lenina v Kremle*. Moscow, 1968.
Lane, David, *The Roots of Russian Communism: a Social and Historical Study of Russian Social-Democracy 1898–1907*. Amsterdam, 1969.
Larin, Yu., 'U kolybeli', *Narodnoye khozyaistvo* (1918), no. 11.
Latsis, M., 'Vozniknoveniye Narodnogo Komissariata Vnutrennykh Del', *Proletarskaya revolyutsiya* (1925), no. 2 (cited as Latsis, 1925).
'Tov. Dzerzhinsky v VChK', *Proletarskaya revolyutsiya* (1926), no. 9 (cited as Latsis, 1926).
Leiden, Carl and Schmitt, K. M., *The Politics of Violence: Revolution in the Modern World*. Englewood Cliffs, N.J., 1968.
Lenin, V. I., *Polnoye sobraniye sochinenii*. 5th edn. 55 vols. Moscow, 1958–65 (cited as PSS).
Leninskii sbornik. 38 vols. Moscow, 1924–.
Lepeshkin, A. I., *Sovety–vlast' trudyashchikhsya (1917–1936gg.)*. Moscow, 1966.
Leplevsky, G., *O rabote V. I. Lenina v Sovnarkome v 1921–1922gg*. Moscow, 1971.
Lesnoi, V. M., 'Oktyabr'skaya revolyutsiya i gosudarstvennyi apparat', *Vestnik Moskovskogo universiteta* (1967), no. 3.
Lewin, Moshe, *Lenin's Last Struggle*. London, 1969.
Liberman, Simon, *Building Lenin's Russia*. Chicago, 1945.
Liebman, Marcel, *Leninism Under Lenin*. Transl. Brian Pearce. London, 1975.
Lomov, G., 'V dni buri i natiska', *Proletarskaya revolyutsiya* (1927), no. 10.

Lyubisheva, V. A., 'Vossozdaniye arkhiva predsedatelya sovnarkoma
    V. I. Lenina', *Voprosy istorii* (1969), no. 4.
'Organizatsiya truda v sekretariate V. I. Lenina v SNK'. *Vide* Gorodet-
    sky, E. N. (1972).
Maier, N., 'Sluzhba v komissariate yustitsii i narodnom sude', *Arkhiv
    russkoi revolyutsii*, 8 (1923), Berlin.
Mal'kov, P., *Zapiski komendanta Kremlya*. 3rd edn. Moscow, 1967.
Malyshev, M. O., 'Nekotorye voprosy organizatsii gosudarstvennogo
    apparata v period stanovleniya sovetskoi vlasti', *Uchënye zapiski
    L.G.U. – seriya yuridicheskikh nayk, Vypusk 10*, 'Voprosy gosudarstva
    i prava', ed. G. I. Petrov. Leningrad, 1958.
Meissner, Boris, 'Die Entwicklung der Ministerien in Russland', *Europa-
    Arkhiv* (1948), nos. 2–4.
Meshekhonin, K., 'K vospominaniyam tov. Trotskogo', *Proletarskaya
    revolyutsiya* (1922), no. 10.
Milne, R. S., 'Mechanistic and organic models of public administration in
    developing countries', *Administrative Science Quarterly* (1970), no. 1.
Mints, I. I., *Istoriya Velikogo Oktyabrya*. 3 vols. Moscow, 1967–73.
Moskalev, M. A., *V. I. Lenin v posledniye gody zhizni 1921–1924gg.*
    Moscow, 1956.
Nelidov, A. A., *Istoriya gosudarstvennykh uchrezhdenii SSSR. Chast' I
    (1917–1936)*. Moscow, 1962.
Nesterenko, A. I., *Kak byl obrazovan Narodnyi Komissariat zdravookh-
    raneniya RSFSR. Iz istorii sovetskogo zdravookhraneniya (oktyabr'
    1917–iyul' 1918g.)*. Moscow, 1965.
'Ob E. E. Essene', *Krasnaya letopis'* (1931), no. 3.
*Obrazovaniye i razvitiye organov sotsialisticheskogo kontrolya v SSSR
    (1917–1975). Sbornik dokumentov i materialov.* Moscow, 1975.
Oppenheim, Samuel A., 'Aleksei Ivanovich Rykov (1881–1938): A Political
    Biography'. Ph.D. Thesis, Indiana University, 1972.
Orlov, V. S., 'V. I. Lenin i sozdaniye apparata pervogo v mire raboche-
    krestyanskogo pravitel'stva', *Voprosy istorii* (1963), no. 4.
Parkinson, C. Northcote, *Parkinson's Law or the Pursuit of Progress.*
    London, 1965.
Pestkovsky, S., 'Ob oktyabr'skikh dnyakh v Pitere', *Proletarskaya revolyut-
    siya* (1922), no. 10.
Peters, Ya. Kh., 'Vospominaniya o rabote v VChK v pervyi god
    revolyutsii', *Proletarskaya revolyutsiya* (1924), no. 10.
*Petrogradskii Voyenno-Revolyutsionnyi Komitet. Dokumenty i materialy
    v trëkh tomakh*, ed. D. A. Chugaev *et al.* 3 vols. Moscow, 1966–7.
Pietsch, Walter, *Revolution und Staat. Institutionen als Träger der Macht
    in Sowjetrussland 1917–1922.* Cologne, 1969.
Piontkovsky, S. A., 'Lenin v oktyabr'skiye dni 1917', *Molodaya gvardiya*
    (1923), no. 9–10.
    'Voyenno-revolyutsionnyi komitet v oktyabr'skiye dni', *Proletarskaya
    revolyutsiya* (1927), no. 10 (69).
    'Lenin v Sovnarkome (ot II do III Syezda Sovetov)', *Bor'ba klassov*
    (1934), no. 1.

Podvoisky, N. I., 'Voyennaya organizatsiya TsK RS-DRP(b) i voyenno-revolyutsionnyi Komitet 1917g.', *Krasnaya letopis'* (1923), nos. 6 and 8.

Polyakov, Yu. A., *Perekhod k NEPu i sovetskoye krestyanstvo*. Moscow, 1967.

Polyansky, V., 'Kak nachinal rabotat' Narodnyi Komissariat Prosvesh-cheniya', *Proletarskaya revolyutsiya* (1926), no. 2.

'Porucheniya V. I. Lenina po SNK i STO 1920–1923', *Istoricheskii arkhiv* (1961), no. 5.

Pyat' let vlasti sovetov. Moscow, 1922.

Radkey, Oliver Henry, *The Sickle and the Hammer: The Russian Socialist Revolutionaries in the early months of Soviet Rule*. New York, 1963.

Rakitin, Anton, *V. A. Antonov-Ovseyenko: Dokumental'nyi biograficheskii ocherk*. Leningrad, 1975.

Reed, John, *Ten Days that Shook the World*. London, 1926, new ed., Harmondsworth, 1966.

Remezova, T., 'Pervye shagi organizatsii sovetskogo pravitel'stva v 1917 godu i izmena Zinov'eva i Kameneva', *Istoricheskii zhurnal* (1936), no. 11.

Revolyutsiya i RKP(b) v materialakh i dokumentakh. 7 vols. Moscow, 1925–7.

Rigby, T. H., 'Politics in the Monoorganisational Society'. *Vide* Janos, Andrew C.

    Communist Party Membership in the USSR 1917–1967. Princeton, N.J., 1968 (cited as Rigby, 1968).

    'The Soviet Political Elite 1917–1922', *The British Journal of Political Science* 1, Part IV (1971) (cited as Rigby, 1971).

    'Bureaucratic Politics: An Introduction', *Public Administration* (Sydney), XXXII (1973), no. 1.

Rothstein, A. (ed.), *The Soviet Constitution*. London, 1923.

Rourke, Francis E., *Bureaucracy, Politics and Public Policy*. 2nd edn. Boston, Mass., 1976.

Ryabtsev, I. G. *et al.* (eds.), *O deyatel'nosti V. I. Lenina v 1917–1922 gody: Sbornik statei*. Moscow, 1958.

Savitskaya, R. M., *Ocherk deyatel'nosti V. I. Lenina. Mart–iyul' 1918g.* Moscow, 1969.

Sbornik vazhneishikh postanovlenii i rasporyazhenii VTsIK VIII sozyva. Moscow, 1921.

Schapiro, L. B., *The Communist Party of the Soviet Union*. 1st edn. New York, 1960.

Schapiro, Leonard and Reddaway, Peter (eds.), *Lenin: The Man, the Theorist, the Leader: A Reappraisal*. London, 1967.

Semashko, N. A., *Prozhitoye i perezhitoye. Vospominiya*. Moscow, 1960.

Serebryansky, Z., 'Sabotazh i sozdaniye novogo gosudarstvennogo apparata', *Proletarskaya revolyutsiya* (1926), no. 10.

Shapko, V. M., 'V. I. Lenin i stroitel'stvo Sovetskogo gosudarstva', *Sovetskoye gosudarstvo i pravo* (1977), no. 5.

Shekhvatov, B. M., 'Bor'ba V. I. Lenina za posledovatel'noye osushchest-vleniye printsipa demokraticheskogo tsentralizma v upravlenii narodnym khozyastvom pri perekhode k NEPu', *Vide* Ryabtsev, I. G.

Lenin i Sovetskoye gosudarstvo. Deyatel'nost' V. I. Lenina po sovershen-stvovaniyu gosudarstvennogo upravleniya, 1921–1922. Moscow, 1960.

Shlikhter, A., *Na barrikadakh proletarskoi revolyutsii.* Kiev, 1927.

Shlyapnikov, A., 'K Oktyabryu', *Proletarskaya revolyutsiya* (1922), no. 10.

Skrypnik, Mariya, *Vospominaniya ob Ilyiche (1917–1918).* 3rd edn. Moscow, 1965.

Sliozberg, G. B., *Dorevolyutsionnyi stroi Rossii.* Paris, 1933.

Sobraniye uzakonenii i rasporyazhenii raboche-krestyanskogo pravitel'stva RSFSR, 1917–. Petrograd and Moscow, 1918–22 (cited as *SU*).

Sofinov, P. G., *Ocherki Istorii Vserossiiskoi Chrezvychainoi Komissii (1917–1922gg.).* Moscow, 1960.

Sorenson, Jay B., *The Life and Death of Soviet Trade Unionism 1917–1928.* New York, 1969.

Sovetskaya Istoricheskaya Entsiklopediya. 16 vols. Moscow, 1961–76.

Sovety narodnogo khozyaistva i planovye organy v tsentre i na mestakh (1917–1932). Sbornik dokumentov. Moscow, 1957.

Spravochnik partiinogo rabotnika. No. 1. Moscow, 1921.

Spravochnik tsentral'nykh i mestnykh uchrezhdenii RSFSR, partiinykh organizatsii i professional'nykh soyuzov. 2nd edn. Moscow, 1920.

Stalin, I., 'Oktyabr'skii perevorot', *Pravda*, Nov. 6–7, 1918.

Sochineniya 13 vols. Moscow, 1946–9.

Steinberg, I. N., *In the Workshop of the Revolution.* New York, London, 1953.

Sternheimer, Stephen, 'Administration and Political Development. An Enquiry into the Tsarist and Soviet Experience'. Unpublished Ph.D. thesis, University of Chicago, 1974.

Strizhkov, Yu. K., 'V. I. Lenin – organizator i rukovoditel' bor'by za sozdaniye sovetskogo prodovol'stvennogo apparata (oktyabr' 1917g.–mai 1918g.)'. *Vide* Khesin, S. S.

Stuchka, P., *Ucheniye o gosudarstve i o konstitutsii RSFSR.* 3rd revised edn. Moscow, 1923.

Sukhanov, N. N., *Zapiski o revolyutsii.* 7 vols. Berlin, Petrograd, Moscow, 1922–3.

Sverdlova, K. T., *Yakov Mikhailovich Sverdlov.* Moscow, 1957.

Syezdy Sovetov Soyuza SSR, soyuznykh i avtonomnykh sovetskikh sotsialisticheskikh respublik. Sbornik dokumentov v trekh tomakh 1917–1936gg. 3 vols. Moscow, 1959–60.

Thompson, Victor A., 'Bureaucracy and Innovation', *Administrative Science Quarterly* (1965–6), no. 1.

Tikhonova, Z., *Narodnyi Komissar Zdorov'ya.* Moscow, 1960.

Tishkov, A. V., *Pervyi chekist.* Moscow, 1968.

Tokarev, Yu. S., *Problemy Gosudarstvennogo stroitel'stva v pervye gody sovetskoi vlasti. Sbornik statei.* Leningrad, 1973.

Towster, J., *Political Power in the USSR, 1917–1947.* New York, 1948.

Triumfal'noye shestviye sovetskoi vlasti. Chast' pervaya, ed. by D. A. Chugaev *et al.* Moscow, 1963.

Trotsky, L. D., *Von der Oktober-Revolution bis zum Brester Friedens-vertrag.* Belp-Bern, 1918.

Moya Zhizn': Opyt Avtobiografii. 2 vols. Berlin, 1930.

The History of the Russian Revolution, Vol. III. *The Triumph of the Soviets.* London, 1933.

Trotski, Leon, *Stalin: An Appraisal of the Man and His Influence.* Edited and translated by Charles Malamuth. London, 1947.

Trotsky Archive. Houghton Library, Harvard University.

The Trotsky Papers 1917–1922, ed. and annotated by Jan M. Meijer. 2 vols. The Hague, 1964–71.

Turovtsev, V. I., *Gosudarstvennyi i obshchestvennyi kontrol' v SSSR.* Moscow, 1970.

Turubiner, A. I., *Gosudarstvennyi stroi RSFSR.* Moscow, 1923.

Ulam, Adam B., *Lenin and the Bolsheviks.* London, 1966.

Undrevich, V. and Kareva, M., *Proletarskaya revolyutsiya i gosudarstvennyi apparat.* Moscow, 1935.

Valentinov, Nikolay (N. Volsky), *Encounters with Lenin.* Transl. by Paul Rosta and Brian Pierce. London, 1968.

Van den Berg, Gerard Pieter, 'De Regering van Rusland en de Sovjet-Unie'. Doctor of Laws Thesis, Leiden University, 1977.

Vasil'yev, A. I., 'Vladimir Ivanovich Nevsky', *Voprosy istorii KPSS* (1966), no. 5.

Venediktov, A. V., *Organizatsiya gosudarstvennoi promyshlennosti v SSSR.* Vol. 1. Leningrad, 1957.

Vladimir Ilyich Lenin. Biograficheskaya khronika, 1870–1924. Vols. 5–7. Moscow, 1974–76 (cited as *Lenin: khronika*).

'Vospominaniya ob oktyabr'skom perevorote', *Proletarskaya revolyutsiya* (1922), no. 10.

Vospominaniya o Vladimire Ilyiche Lenine, Vol. 1 edited by N. N. Mor and others, Vol. 2 edited by G. S. Zhuk and others. 2 vols. Moscow, 1957.

Vospominaniya o Vladimire Ilyiche Lenine, edited by G. N. Golikov *et al.* 5 vols. Moscow, 1969–70.

Vysshiye organy gosudarstvennoi vlasti i organy tsentral'nogo upravleniya RSFSR (1917–1967gg.). Spravochnik. Moscow, 1971.

Yaney, George L., *The Systematization of Russian Government. Social Evolution in the Domestic Administration of Imperial Russia, 1711–1905.* Urbana, Ill., Chicago, London, 1973.

Yelizarova, A., 'Stranichka vospominanii o Vladimire Ilyiche v Sovnarkome', *Proletarskaya revolyutsiya* (1929), no. 11.

Yeroshkin, N. P., *Ocherki istorii gosudarstvennykh uchrezhdenii dorevolyutsionnoi Rossii.* Moscow, 1960.

Yoffe, A., 'Pervoye proletarskoye pravitel'stvo', *Kommunisticheskii internatsional* (1919), Cols. 777–782.

Zhurov, Yu. V., 'V. G. Yakovenko', *Istoriya SSSR* (1969), no. 3.

Zubov, N., *F. E. Dzerzhinsky. Biografiya.* Moscow, 1963 (cited as Zubov, 1963).

Pervyi predsedatel' Malogo Sovnarkoma. Moscow, 1975 (cited as Zubov, 1975).

Index

Administrative Commission of CEC Presidium and Sovnarkom, 284 n. 33

administrative conflicts: Bolsheviks vs. Left SRs, 28; central–local in regional economic councils, 264 n. 33; Chusosnabarm vs. revolutionary military councils, 263 n. 17; Gosplan vs. Finance Commissariat, 118; Internal Affairs vs. Justice Commissariat, 81–2; Labour vs. Social Security Commissariat, 134; and labour armies, 90; resolution by Politburo, 117, 186, 212, 230; Revolutionary Military Council vs. commissariats, 85; Trotsky vs. Rykov, 292 n. 6

Agricultural Commission, 285 n. 38

agriculture, *see* peasantry

Algasov, V. A., 28, 243

Alsky, A. O., 140, 187, 289 n. 86

anarchists, 59–60, 280, n. 3, 282 n. 20

Andreyev, A. A., 67, 73, 97, 260 n. 52

Antonov-Ovseyenko, V. A., 3, 18, 60, 130, 145–6, 153, 242–3, 247 n. 10

Arbitration Commission, Supreme, 100

armed forces: demoralisation 1917–18, 29; and Bolshevik takeover, 1; deputies to CEC, 166; and extension of regime's authority, 54; administering supplies for, 85–6. *See also* defence, revolutionary military councils.

Avanesov, V. A., 97, 129, 154, 187, 273 n. 38, 284 n. 34

Avilov, N. P., 3, 126–7, 130, 143, 146, 153, 159, 241, 243

Bach, Lydia, 189

Baltic Fleet: Central Committee of, 130; Commander of, 151

Baltic Germans, 279 n. 13

Bazarov, V. A., 153

Belorussia, 136, 187

boards of people's commissariats, 6, 245–6 n. 11; of P.C. for Agriculture, 27, 138; of P.C. for Finance, 125, 140; of P.C. for Food Supplies, 114, 138; of P.C. for Justice, 106–7; of Committee on Military and Naval Affairs, 42; of P.C. for Railways, 128; of P.C. for Transport, 273 n. 35

Bogdanov, P. A., 137, 146–7, 242–3

Bogolepov, D. P., 36–8, 77, 224, 252 n. 32, 253 n. 48, 260 n. 2

Bolsheviks, *see* Communist Party

Bonch-Bruyevich, M. D., 5

Bonch-Bruyevich, V. D., 3–6, 31, 34, 41, 55–6, 59, 104–5, 131, 137, 224, 245 n. 10, 251 n. 17, 266–7 n. 21

Brest-Litovsk Treaty, 28–30, 38–9, 53–4, 60, 125–6, 130–1, 133, 161, 167, 177

Brilliantov (initials unknown), 259 n. 47

British Cabinet, 223–4, 226, 229

Bronsky, M. G., 242

Bryukhanov, N. P., 88–9, 114, 125, 137, 143, 146, 241, 243

Bubnov, A. S., 15, 125

Bukharin, N. I., 282 n. 20

bureaucracy, Chap. 4; accusations of bureaucratic centralism, 170; in Communist Party, 54–5, 181, 188–9, 228; Lenin on, 11–14,